About the Aut D0086845

Dr Graham Dunkley is Senior Lecturer in Economics in the Faculty of Business, Victoria University of Technology, Melbourne, Australia. He has been a Visiting Fellow at the University of Warwick in the UK and was invited as a Research Fellow by Oetoman University, Japan in 1992. His wide-ranging interests and activities include policy development work with various environmental organisations and also, over many years, with the Australian Labor Party as well as trade unions and the Labor Resource Centre. He has travelled extensively in Europe and Asia, has experience in voluntary project work with Community Aid (Oxfam Australia) and writes for the Australian media. In addition to *The Free Trade Adventure*, he is the author of *The Greening of the Red: Sustainability, Socialism and the Environmental Crisis* (Pluto Press, Australia, 1992).

Other Zed Titles on Trade

With the new Millennium Round of negotiations launched by the World Trade Organization at the end of 1999, trade has moved once again to the top of the world economic agenda. Zed Books has published a small number of titles which are crucial to understanding the issues involved.

Carlos M. Correa, *Intellectual Property Rights, the WTO and Developing Countries: The TRIPS Agreement and Policy Options*

Bhagirath Lal Das, *An Introduction To The WTO Agreements*

Bhagirath Lal Das, *The WTO Agreements: Deficiencies, Imbalances and Required Changes*

Bhagirath Lal Das, *The World Trade Organization: A Guide to the New Framework for International Trade*

Graham Dunkley, *The Free Trade Adventure: The WTO, the Uruguay Round and Globalism: A Critique*

Hans-Peter Martin and Harald Schumann, *The Global Trap: Globalization and the Assault on Prosperity and Democracy*

For full details of this list and Zed's other subject and general catalogues, please write to:
The Marketing Department, Zed Books,
7 Cynthia Street, London N1 9JF, UK
or email Sales@zedbooks.demon.co.uk
Visit our website at: http://www.zedbooks.demon.co.uk

The Free Trade Adventure

The WTO, the Uruguay Round and Globalism—A Critique

Graham Dunkley

Zed Books
LONDON & NEW YORK

For My Mother
Rita Dunkley
With Thanks

The Free Trade Adventure was published in 2000 by
Zed Books Ltd, 7 Cynthia Street, London N1 9JF, UK and
Room 400, 175 Fifth Avenue, New York, NY 10010, USA

Distributed exclusively in the USA by
St Martin's Press, Inc., 175 Fifth Avenue,
New York, NY 10010

First published in 1997 by
Melbourne University Press
PO Box 278, Carlton South, Victoria 3053, Australia

Copyright © Graham Dunkley 1997, 2000
Design and typography © Melbourne University Press 1997

The rights of the authors of this work have been asserted by them
in accordance with the Copyright, Designs and Patents Act, 1988

All rights reserved

A catalogue record for this book
is available from the British Library

Typeset by Syarikat Seng Teik Sdn. Bhd., Malaysia, in 11/13pt Goudy
Additional typesetting by Long House, Cumbria, UK

US CIP has been applied for

ISBN   Hb 1 85649 768 2
          Pb 1 85649 769 0

Contents

List of Tables, Boxes and Figures

Preface

The Uruguay Round was such a huge enterprise and its implications cover such a vast canvas that this book does not attempt to deal in depth with all the topics broached in the negotiations or the possible consequences thereof. Instead it has the more limited objective of introducing the Round, its background, its main outcomes in brief, some of its likely repercussions and a few hidden agendas, all in the hope that a more critical debate and research programme will emerge in the near future. The Round will take as much as a decade to implement fully so the possibility of complete assessment is a long way off. The book is, thus, more of a cautionary tale, explaining the Round, anticipating its directions and warning of unemphasised implications, while throughout touching briefly on Australia's role in the venture and the globalisation process in which the whole story is set.

I have called the book the Free Trade Adventure because the imagery thus conjured up is neutral between the 'miracle' versus 'menace' extremes which pervade the various literatures, and because with the end of the Round the world is indeed embarking upon an adventure of unknown destination. However, this does not mean that my position is neutral. The course and outcomes of the Round have aroused passions throughout the world, both pro and con, yet the latter are virtually totally ignored in the mainstream media and Free Trade literature. If one read just mainstream economic journals one would get the impression that the only possible criticisms of the

Round were those which claim it did not go far enough or left too many loopholes which could be exploited by protectionists. If one also read *The Economist* one would learn that opponents existed, but would be left in no doubt that such people were complete loonies. At one stage when I mentioned such alternative ideas to an Australian trade official I received the puzzled retort that I had been reading a surprising amount of 'fringe literature'.

Reckoning that the Uruguay Round sounded too good to be true, I sought a range of opinion and found many credible criticisms, even if some of the opposition was knee-jerk in nature. Thus, the book seeks to take a critical view of the Round and incorporate both the mainstream and alternative literatures. My views were first floated in some earlier papers (Dunkley 1994a and b), being much corrected and developed since then. One early version, circulated as an ALP Caucus discussion paper by Mr Lindsay Tanner MHR, elicited the response from several Labor ministers of the day that trade liberalisation will surely bring more benefits than costs. In this book I argue that the reverse may be possible. My type of critique is an unconventional one, perhaps being describable as 'green political economy', and which sees the 'non-economic' effects of trade as at least as important as the economic effects, but I draw on experience ranging from my conventional economics lectures to my work with Third World NGOs. My conclusions will not be liked by Free Trade economists and may be ignored, but my reading has uncovered a re-markable amount of questioning levelled against Free Trade theory, even amongst fairly mainstream commentators, let alone amongst alternative social groups. So the notion of free trade is omnipresent throughout the book and I designate it, along with the alternatives of 'Managed Trade', 'Fair Trade' and 'Self-Reliant Trade', in lower case initials for the practice, in upper case for the doctrines and their advocates. Other esoteric terms and concepts are explained in the text and/or glossary, while the style and language are kept as access-ible as possible. Where necessary I use the term 'trade intervention-ism' for the full range of trade-related policies, including industry policy and the like, rather than the traditional 'protectionism' which has now had pejorative connotations bestowed upon it by Free Traders. All dollars are US unless otherwise specified.

I am indebted to a large number of people for ideas, information, discussion and reading of drafts, particularly to Don Feaver, P. J. Gunawardana, John Wiseman, Anand Kulkarni, Dick Copeman and Jay Menon. Additional thanks for these and other services are due to Mr Bob Arnott of DFAT, Lindsay Tanner MHR, Marjorie Griffin Cohen, Tony Webb, Sally Nathan, Bill Cole, John Quiggin, David Spratt, Pat Ranald, Russ Swann, a publisher's reader and various public servants who provided material and periodic telephone interviews. Special thanks are also due to Teresa Pizzinga and Angela Tassone for a marathon typing effort, to Brian Wilder of MUP for his faith in the project, to Victoria University of Technology for study leave during which much of the work was done, to my partner, Jenny Crawford, for many forms of assistance and to my daughter, Kiran, who proved much less disruptive than three-year-olds are reputed to be. Finally, I wish to thank my mother, Rita Dunkley, to whom the book is dedicated, for a lifetime of support and encouragement.

Abbreviations

ABARE	Australian Bureau of Agricultural and Resource Economics
ABS	Australian Bureau of Statistics
AFR	*Australian Financial Review*
AMS	aggregate measurement of support
ANZCERTA	Australia and New Zealand Closer Economic Relations Trade Agreement
APEC	Asia–Pacific Economic Co-operation forum
CFCs	chloro-fluorocarbons
CGE	computable general equilibrium (model)
CUFTA	Canada–US Free Trade Agreement (predecessor of NAFTA)
DFAT	Department of Foreign Affairs and Trade (Australia)
DFI	direct foreign investment
DSB	Dispute Settlement Body (of GATT/WTO)
EOI	export-oriented industrialisation
ETMs	elaborately transformed manufactures
EU	European Union; previous names used where appropriate—EC (European Communities) and EEC (European Economic Community)
FAO	Food and Agricultural Organisation
FOGS	functioning of the GATT system
GATS	General Agreement on Trade in Services
GATT	General Agreement on Tariffs and Trade; GATT47 refers to the original agreement of 1947 and GATT94 refers to all amendments and instruments to 1994; GATT/WTO refers to the trade regulation system as a whole, incorporating both the legal side (GATT and other Uruguay Round agreements) and the organisational side (the WTO), as well as to a continuity of past and present structures.

GDP	gross domestic product
GNP	gross national product
IC	Industry Commission (Australia)—absorbed into the Productivity Commission, 1996
ILO	International Labour Organisation
IMF	International Monetary Fund
IPRs	intellectual property rights
ISI	import-substitution industrialisation
ITO	International Trade Organisation
MFA	multi-fibre arrangements
MFN	most favoured nation
MITI	Ministry of International Trade and Industry (Japan)
NAFTA	North American Free Trade Agreement
NFA	National Food Authority (Australia)—re-named Australia–New Zealand Food Authority (ANFA), 1996
NGOs	non-governmental organisations
NICs	newly industrialising countries
NIDL	new international division of labour
NTBs	non-tariff barriers
OECD	Organisation for Economic Co-operation and Development
RTAs	regional trade agreements
SAPs	structural adjustment programmes (of IMF and World Bank)
SPS	Sanitary and Phytosanitary (Agreement)
TBTs	technical barriers to trade (and Agreement)
TCF	textile, clothing and footwear
TNCs	trans-national companies
TREMs	trade-related environmental measures
TRIMs	trade-related investment measures
TRIPs	trade-related intellectual property rights
UN	United Nations
UNCTAD	United Nations Conference on Trade and Development (representing Third World countries)
USTR	United States Trade Representative (highest US trade official)
VERs	voluntary export restraints
WIPO	World Intellectal Property Organisation
WTO	World Trade Organization

. . . there are some important respects in which those who are not afraid to use tariffs have a broader conception of the national economic life and a truer feeling for the quality of it. Free traders, fortified into presumption by the essential truths—one might say truisms— of their cause, have greatly overvalued the social advantage of mere market cheapness, and have attributed excellences which do not exist to the mere operation of the methods of laissez-faire. The protectionist has often used bad economic arguments, but he has sometimes had a truer sense of the complicated balances and harmonies and qualities of a sound national economic life, and of the wisdom of not unduly sacrificing any part even to the whole. The virtues of variety and universality, the opportunity for the use of every gift and every aptitude, the amenities of life, the old established traditions of a countryside— all those things of which there are many, even in the material life of a country, which money cannot buy, need to be considered. National protection has its idealistic side, too—a side which a well-balanced national economic policy will try to marry with the peace and truth and international fair-dealing of free trade.

If it were true that we should be a little richer, provided that the whole country and all the workers in it were to specialise on half-a-dozen mass-produced products, each individual doing nothing and having no hopes of doing anything except one minute, unskilled, repetitive act all his life long, should we all cry out for the immediate destruction of the endless variety of trades and crafts and employments which stand in the way of the glorious attainment of this maximum degree of specialised cheapness? Of course we should not—and that is enough to prove that the case for free trade, as I began by stating it, has left something out. Our task is to redress the balance of the argument.

J. M. Keynes (1932)

Part One

GATTing a New World Order

Introduction

The greatest agreement in history?

On 15 April 1994 representatives from most major trading nations on Earth gathered in the picturesque Moroccan city of Marrakesh, to sign what GATT Director-General, Peter Sutherland, called 'the greatest trade agreement in history'.[1] This agreement was the Final Act of the 7-year-long Uruguay Round of multilateral trade negotiations, the eighth such round of world-wide talks to be held in the post-war era under the auspices of the General Agreement on Tariffs and Trade, a hitherto obscure international organisation best known for its pun-worthy acronym of GATT. The various elements of the agreement are to be implemented over a 6–10-year period. Many superlatives have been used for the agreement because it seeks the most dramatic step ever collectively taken by the world's leaders towards free trade between nations, and it seeks to do so on more fronts than ever before envisaged. Prognoses regarding its likely impact range from a glorious new dawn of globalism and a massive stimulus for the world economy, to an economic, social and environmental disaster or the creation of a world-dominating bureaucracy which will enable giant TNCs to make the world their oyster.

There can be few doubts about the ambition, breadth and political triumph of the Uruguay Round, but about its virtues, likely accomplishments, future directions and the wisdom upon which it is based there are greater doubts. My assessment of the Round is somewhere between the extremes noted above, but much more critical than mainstream opinion which has dominated in the media to date.

3

The Uruguay Round cannot be assessed separately from the debates about free trade which long preceded it or future trends towards globalisation, of which the Round and the new trading order it seeks to create are an integral part. There is today a powerful world-wide thrust, from many quarters, for full global free trade and wider globalisation, or so-called 'deep integration', of a sort and to a degree never before seen in history. I have termed this the Free Trade Adventure because everyone roughly knows the route but no one can know the ultimate destination, and indeed two partly competing modes of transport are currently in use—regionalism and multilateralism.

The book has two general aims. The first is to provide some background to and a moderately detailed outline of the Uruguay Round and its outcomes. The second is to develop a broad critique of the Round, its general goals of free trade and its anticipated future agenda of globalisation. The critique is a broad one, considering questions arising from the Round itself and how it was conducted, queries surrounding its alleged beneficial outcomes, general problems of Free Trade theory, popular criticism of the Round and free trade overall, problematic aspects of the globalisation agenda and (briefly) some neglected alternatives to the Free Trade Adventure.

The book also contains seven more specific themes upon which some detailed conclusions are drawn. The first of these is that the Uruguay Round has genuinely been a major step towards a new world trading order to which most governments, whether wisely or not, are broadly committed at present, despite scepticism as to this commitment amongst certain commentators, though I am less convinced that there is a widespread desire for full free trade and globalisation in the long term. The second is that the success of the Round, which was by no means assured from the outset, was due to much more complex economic and political factors than the simplistic notion of an anti-protectionist enlightenment so beloved of some Free Traders. In particular I argue that this success was due to the emergence of powerful corporate vested interests in globalisation. The third theme is that, under what I call the 'new model free trade agreement', free trade is a far wider concept than it used to be and is tending to merge with a vision of advanced globalisation. The fourth is that the Uruguay Round and regional trade liberalisation will bring some economic benefits, but that these are probably overstated and the costs underestimated, especially if a wider range of 'non-economic' costs are taken into account than Free Traders usually consider.

The fifth theme is that there is a wider range of possible arguments against free trade than is usually included in the Free Traders' lexicon, especially if 'non-economic' issues are admitted, and consideration of these may dramatically change the conclusions about the virtues or otherwise of free trade. The sixth is that there appears to be a rising international tide of opposition, even resistance, to free trade and willy-nilly deepening integration, for which the Round and the new World Trade Organization (WTO) have become a symbol. Such opinion has been little considered so far in the Free Trade Adventure and must, in my view, be countenanced in future. The final theme is that there are alternatives to free trade and 'deep integration', but that these have been neglected because the predominant world view at present is what I call 'global fatalism'—the notion that deeply integrated globalisation is both highly desirable and inevitable. Conclusions about the virtues of free trade and globalisation are very different if another world view is taken or if development goals other than economic growth are adopted.

More generally, there are three analytical foci of the book: the nature of the Free Trade Adventure, the question of costs versus benefits and the debate about adaptation versus resistance. Free Traders insist that the benefits of trade liberalisation almost invariably outweigh the costs, especially in the longer term, so that all countries should allow global markets to make the requisite structural adjustments. There are many opponents of this view. I argue that, contrary to the Free Traders' insistence, full costs might well outweigh the benefits, so that there is a case both for community control of the structural adjustment process and for a degree of resistance to global change, especially with a view to finding alternative directions of development.

These themes and foci will be discussed conjointly throughout the book, though with Part One centring on the Uruguay Round, the backdrop thereto and the outcomes thereof, and with Part Two concentrating on problems and critiques of the Round in particular and the Free Trade Adventure in general. I will not attempt to cover in detail all issues involved in the Round—such a project would be vast—although Chapter 4 outlines briefly all key elements of the Round and some of the issues flowing therefrom. Instead I will concentrate, by way of critique, on some of the newer or more explosive issues, notably structural change in general, services, intellectual property, the environment, food and other standards and the workings of the new order. Along the way country-specific examples will be used as required, and these will be taken primarily from Australia, Europe, North America and the Third World.

In Part One, the first chapter introduces a number of key concepts and arguments used in the book and the second provides some background to the free trade issue, trade agreements, the rise of multilateralism and GATT itself. Chapter 3 examines the fall of GATT into near-disrepute during the early 1980s, the explosion of protectionism at that time and a little about the Uruguay Round, including why it unexpectedly succeeded. Chapter 4 delineates the outcomes of the Round and Chapter 5 briefly examines the concept of regional trade agreements (RTAs), their relationship to multilateralism and a few examples: ANZCERTA (Australia–New Zealand), APEC, NAFTA and the EU. The resulting picture of the new world trading order is a two-track Free Trade Adventure— a multilateral and a regional track—with some Free Traders, who prefer the former track, ambivalent about the division, and with many critics sceptical about the route itself. The second part of the book examines some of the concerns and criticism, with an outline of the chapters provided in the Introduction to Part Two.

1

The Spirit of the Age?

The Free Trade Adventure and the end of history

On 15 December 1993 the world changed. Maybe not as dramatically as the moment when the Berlin Wall fell, but then unlike that very necessary demolition job, the success of the Uruguay Round was a work of construction . . . It will be seen as a defining moment in modern history.

Put simply, governments came to the conclusion that the notion of a new world order was not merely attractive but absolutely vital; that the reality of the global market . . . required a level of multilateral co-operation never before attempted (Sutherland 1994a: 1).

If founding Director-General of the WTO, Peter Sutherland, is to be believed, the Uruguay Round has a lot to live up to. In the same speech as that quoted above Sutherland attributed to the Round the creation of a universal 'revolutionary framework for economic, legal and political co-operation', firmly linking the Round and its off-spring, the WTO, with the much-heralded process of globalisation or 'deep integration', which he sees as the saviour of the planet. Few governments supported this process more zealously than that of Australia, former Trade Minister Bob McMullan (1995: 9) once singing a veritable paean of praise thereto:

It will not be possible to stop what has become an inexorable movement to an ever more deeply integrated world economy, not least because deeper integration brings tremendous potential economic benefits and broader political and social benefits. It creates ever expanding market opportunities.

So we have it on high authority that the Uruguay Round and its great leap towards global free trade is the harbinger for, and an integral element of, this grand development. In this book I will propose, after a closer look at the issues, a somewhat different picture, as many others are also doing.

The Uruguay Round agreement came at a time of momentous world-wide change—the end of the Cold War, the collapse of the Soviet Union, the political triumph of capitalism, the ascendancy of free market economics, or what in Australia we call Economic Rationalism, and the apparent dissolution of socialist, even social democratic, alternatives. The successful completion of the Round, which for a time seemed in doubt, was a direct result of these developments for in many participating countries there were changes of regime, or even entire ideologies, during the 7-year negotiation period, these often resulting in a strong shift to free trade policies by government. Free Trade is, of course, the logical corollary of Economic Rationalism, being the free market writ global, and so the Free Trade Adventure is an inevitable outcome of the above-mentioned changes in the shape of the world system. Free Trade, it would seem, is the spirit of the age, and is now being echoed in regional free trade experiments everywhere (see Chapter 5) which many hope will one day join together in one big global free trade zone. On that day we may reach what has been called 'the end of history' (Fukuyama 1992).

The new model free trade agreement

Free Trade is not what it used to be. In the nineteenth century the free trade versus protection debate was largely about the odd tariff placed on those few agricultural or manufactured goods which entered world trade. With governments then being predominantly non-interventionist there were few policy measures other than customs duties which impinged upon trade. During the twentieth century, however, especially in the post-war period, there has been an explosion of governmental regulatory activity for a wide range of developmental, structural, redistributive, welfare, environmental and general social purposes, much of it allegedly having direct or indirect effects upon trade. The rise of the interventionist state has also brought a plethora of more direct restrictions on trade and investment ranging from standard tariffs or quotas to a multitude of, often invisible, 'non-tariff barriers' (NTBs), including subsidies and other industry policy systems designed to promote industrial development (see Chapter 3). All such interferences, though legitimate in many people's eyes, lead to what Free Traders call 'non-level playing fields', or very uneven, disrupted avenues of access to national markets, and these are claimed to be the cause of problems ranging from the uncompetitiveness of particular national industries to general inefficiencies and economic stagnation. By the 1980s there was a growing world-wide consensus amongst governments, business and bureaucrats that such measures must be swept away in a thoroughgoing exercise of trade liberalisation.

There are four possible channels for trade liberalisation—unilateral (one country alone removing protective barriers), bilateral (two countries negotiating mutual protection reductions), regional (countries within a region developing liberalisation arrangements) and multilateral (world-wide negotiations for liberalisation and trading rules). During the nineteenth century the first two methods prevailed. Free Traders preferred unconditional unilateral liberalisation by all countries on the grounds of the unnamed doctrine (I call it 'unilateral benefit') that a trade-liberalising country will become more efficient in itself and thus be better off, irrespective of whether or not other countries do likewise. To this day some Free Traders do not like GATT, let alone RTAs, because such bodies and their interminable trade negotiations allegedly take time and resources, while always risking political compromise. They simply want 'pure' unilateral liberalisation by all countries. However, the world has impure habits and over time trade politics became a chaotic mix of regionalism, bilateralism and even 'aggressive unilateralism' through which some countries (mainly the USA) have sought to impose purity upon others (see Chapter 3). Moreover, most governments have preferred to negotiate bilaterally because they, along with domestic interest groups, often suspected that protectionist countries were snatching an unfair advantage, at least in relation to particular industries. In order to avoid such 'unfair' trade, a concept which Free Traders generally reject,[1] governments and international bodies have evolved regional and multilateral mechanisms for negotiating reciprocal liberalisation processes in a manner which ensures that no one gets offended or interest groups get suspicious. In the absence of 'pure' unilateralism Free Traders have adopted multilateralism as their next preference, and so GATT was born of this logic.

In the meantime economists were endlessly debating free trade versus protection. From the mid-nineteenth to the mid-twentieth century the view held sway that despite the undoubted virtues of free trade, there were a number of circumstances in which protection was economically justified, notably in cases where a country had market power, where there were 'externalities' or 'market failures' and where 'infant industries' needed help (see Chapter 6). During the 1950s and 1960s Free Traders challenged these presuppositions —monopoly-rectifying tariffs risked retaliation; infant industry protection was unnecessary; market failures were best dealt with domestically. During the 1970s and 1980s the 'Public Choice' school of economics argued that market failures were largely self-rectifying and that 'government failure', including the lobbying and corruption (or so-called 'capture') allegedly associated with the scramble for protection, outweighed the costs of any externalities (Bhagwati 1989 and see Chapter 3).

By the start of the Uruguay Round there had emerged what I call a 'new model free trade agreement' which, in theory at least, sought no less than to take a bulldozer to the 'playing fields'. All forms of protection—tariffs, subsidies, NTBs, everything—should be reduced and ultimately eliminated; all protection cuts should be made permanent, or 'bound'; safeguards and exceptions should be subject to strict rules and kept limited; technical standards should be harmonised; trade liberalisation should be extended to services; intellectual property rights (IPRs) should be protected; capital flows and direct foreign investment (DFI) should be liberalised or at least 'trade-related investment measures' (TRIMs) reduced; dispute-settlement procedures should be systematised and buttressed with meaningful sanctions. The new model was gradually incorporated into the EU and formed the basis of North American (CUFTA/NAFTA) and Australia–New Zealand (ANZCERTA) agreements, ultimately providing a framework for the Uruguay Round.

In 500 pages of text and 26 000 pages of country-by-country commitment schedules, the Uruguay Round proposes to, over the course of a decade, reduce all tariff levels by at least a third, completely eliminate tariffs in many sectors, bring agriculture fully into GATT, abolish some NTBs, tighten up on a wide range of rules, restrict government subsidies, lay the basis for harmonising technical standards, create an unprecedented new pair of agreements covering services and intellectual property, begin an assault on investment controls and strengthen the disciplinary processes of the multilateral system. GATT now has teeth in the form of new rules and enforcement procedures, although we are yet to find how sharp they are. In many of the above-mentioned areas the degree of liberalisation in the Round was moderate, or what I call 'soft-edged', compared with the 'harder-edged' versions in many RTAs which go much further towards full trade and investment de-regulation. So the GATT/WTO system is one of reciprocally-negotiated multilateral rules rather than simply a *laissez-faire*, unilaterally deregulated one as Free Traders originally preferred. Such a system is the most liberalised that can be attained for now because, in my view, although most present-day governments are committed to multilateral liberalisation they want to retain some policy-making autonomy, and thus their actual policies are ambivalent, at times bordering on the hypocritical.

On the other hand, the more ambitious Free Traders want to press ahead with continued liberalisation of trade and investment until, early in the new millennium, all developed world economies are 'deeply integrated', or integrally linked at all levels, as opposed to the 'shallow', arm's-length integration of today (Lawrence and Litan 1990; Bergsten 1996). The rationale often used for the rush to liberalisation is a so-called 'bicycle theory' which holds that this process must be pedalled to the end of the road or else the rider will fall off, particularly as the great villains of the story, the protectionists of the world, may re-group and organise against further liberalisation. The ultimate vision of 'deep integration' is that of a global economy in which business firms may freely enter all 'markets' (i.e. nations) of the world at will, and where the Earth is spanned by computerised transactions networks in which governments intervene only to reinforce the system. Free Traders say they do not want to remove every bump in the playing fields and that they accept some residual national policy-making space of the sort which state and local governments retain within nations. But they do want to remove all impediments to trade and investment, to harmonise product standards, to make tax policies non-discriminatory and so forth. The result would be to leave nations with some autonomy but certainly with much less than they have at present. In my view this vision needs to be challenged.

Trade theory and protectionist plots

Free Trade theory is beguilingly simple and attractive. For over two centuries mainstream economists have largely agreed that any nation can benefit economically by specialising and trading in production of goods or services for which it has 'comparative advantage'; that is, the least cost in terms of other production forgone. Every country, whether large or small, rich or poor, populous or sparse, has comparative advantage in something so can obtain 'gains from trade', though not necessarily all to the same extent or in the same way. Trade is a mutual exchange, not a battle with national winners and losers. Trade leads to structural rationalisation which in turn leads to a more efficient resource allocation and to 'static gains' (a one-off increase in income level), while the longer-term stimuli of trade lead to so-called 'dynamic gains' from induced technological improvements and the like. A nation's 'welfare' (i.e. consumption and income) can thus be maximised simply by governments refraining from intervening in international trade between private enterprises.

As will be outlined in Chapter 6, there are a number of assumptions and corollaries underlying this theory which complicate the story and which some critics think undermine its validity. The key implication of the doctrine, however, is that trade will require a restructuring of the economy from which some people and industries lose, though the nett gains are said to be almost always positive. So although the gainers could compensate the losers and the whole economy remain better off for trade, there is a temptation for potential losers to rebel and urge protection. In the demonology of GATT no beast looms larger or more sinister than that of protectionism, and none have articulated this near-paranoia better than Peter Sutherland. During 1993 when the Uruguay Round looked in trouble, Sutherland called on governments to 'face down vested interests and to place political leadership before expediency', warning that 'once parochial priorities begin to pull at the sleeve of global integration, a downward spiral of deepening isolationism is set in motion', with dire consequences for investment and growth.[2]

However, I will argue throughout the book that this is an unduly simplistic, inaccurate view of people's motives for opposing free trade, even though vested interests in protection can obviously arise. As noted above, most Free Traders have always accepted a few arguments for moderate trade restrictions, although they do not like permanent, high levels of protection, and there also are other, more radical, economic arguments against full free trade (see Chapter 6). In addition, there have always been a range of what economists like to call 'non-economic' objections to free trade, which today seldom rate more than a paragraph or two in economic textbooks, although some 'non-economic' *benefits* are claimed for free trade (see Chapter 6). Traditionally the non-economic arguments against free trade have involved 'security arguments'—defence, food self-reliance and the like—but are now extended to what I call 'community–sovereignty' arguments—preservation of the environment, culture, community, sovereignty rights and so forth (see Chapter 6). Although I consider many *economic* arguments against Free Trade theory to be at least partly valid, I primarily argue against the totality of that doctrine on the *non-economic* grounds that free trade, and trade *per se*, can have a wider range of adverse community–sovereignty or other non-economic impacts than economists usually consider.

This is an unorthodox position to take in the field of economics, but not unknown amongst economists, its most notable exponent being none other than one of the greatest, J. M. Keynes, as beautifully exemplified in the quotation at the head of this book (p. xv). Occasionally Free Trade economists betray a sneaking sympathy with the non-economic goal of self-reliance (see Chapter 12) or drop some hint of deeper meanings than can be found in economic textbooks. For instance, former head of the OECD Economics Department, David Henderson, once revealed that 'the case for free trade is largely economic', and French Economic Rationalist, Henri Lepage, has ruminated that protectionist ideas contain an (unacceptable) 'holistic philosophy which presupposes that collective wholes have a personal existence'.[3] The unstated implications are that a 'non-economic', more socially, culturally or even spiritually oriented world view will result in different conclusions about free trade, which many think are valid even if those particular writers do not. The great dissenting historian, Karl Polanyi (1944: ch. 13), saw nineteenth-century protectionism as a broad, principled movement in many respects, and I argue that this remains the case.

By-and-large Free Traders are unmoved, however, believing for the most part that non-economic issues are either trivial or else adjustable domestically without the need for trade intervention. The current *enfant terrible* of international economics and mild dissenter, US Keynesian-oriented economist Paul Krugman (1995), largely agrees, suggesting that traditional Free Trade theory is *almost* watertight. Indeed, I accept that some specialisation, whether by individuals, nations or any units between, can be economically more beneficial than 'autarchy' (though see Chapters 6 and 12). However, theory and practice can diverge. Krugman (1995: 31) says that the economics profession has a 'dirty little secret'—that the costs of protection, or the benefits of trade liberalisation, are real but *very* small. Estimates of likely economic benefits from the Uruguay Round are indeed rather paltry, the more bullish figures relying on a rather speculative concept of 'dynamic gains' (see Chapter 7). One Australian study (EPAC 1995) claims that the benefits of our current trade liberalisation programme will be a hefty 15 per cent of GDP, but we will have to wait a quarter of a century to fully gain them! A 1993 survey of Australian economics professors found most believing that, in theory, trade liberalisation would increase 'welfare', but less than half believing that in practice protection should be greatly reduced by 2000.[4]

It is a central contention of this book that if the 'static' gains from trade liberalisation are small and the 'dynamic' gains speculative, then total economic gains may well be outweighed by 'non-economic' or other costs, the nett outcome depending critically upon the society's long-term goals, which I believe have not been adequately debated in Australia as yet. Free Trade will have massive impacts reaching well beyond the economic sphere, but economists seldom broach the implications of this. Some foretaste of the possible effects of the Free Trade Adventure can be gleaned from the experience of a 20-year-long experiment with trade liberalisation and economic de-regulation through IMF/World Bank structural adjustment programmes (SAPs), and this seems at best ambiguous, some say disastrous, especially when a range of non-economic criteria are used (see Chapter 12). At the end of the day, Free Trade theory is saying that unimpeded trading across 'level playing fields' can increase most people's consumption a bit and perhaps add some extra long-term economic growth. However, there are at least three increasingly accepted heresies which challenge this theory and these will be touched upon throughout the book. First, it may be domestic productivity rather than trade which drives economic growth and development. Second, domestically-generated growth and development via so-called 'cumulative advantage' may lead to trade rather than the reverse. Third, growth and higher consumption may, for 'non-economic' reasons, be now less desirable than in the past to many people and societies, in which case Free Trade theory loses much of its point. These propositions give rise to the startling possibility that the dire struggle for national competitiveness and the urge to increase trade, with which governments are currently obsessed, might largely be misplaced zeal.

GATT, globalism and the end of history

Some years ago a US state official, Francis Fukuyama (1992), startled the world's academic establishments by declaring that history had come to an end. By this he meant, not that events have stopped, but that human society has now identified its final 'ideal' form. Plenty of theorists have postulated such an ending to history, notably Hegel and Marx, but whereas Marx prophesied culmination in the abolition of private property and the establishment of co-operative communism, Fukuyama sees the final form as 'liberal democracy' or what many might call 'global capitalism'. The hallmarks of Fukuyama's end of history include democracy, private enterprise, free markets, consumerism, the ascendancy of science and technology, global free trade and strong international institutions, or what is now being called 'globalisation'; the ideals have now been agreed upon, only full construction and dissemination remaining to be accomplished. Clearly the new GATT/WTO system is destined to play a key role in Fukuyama's 'end of history'.

The phenomenon of globalisation is rapidly becoming one of the most discussed topics in contemporary scholarship with definitions or descriptions thereof including: the intensification of worldwide inter-relations; increasing international inter-dependency; the inter-penetration of socio-cultural systems; the contraction of social time and space; the relativisation of values; the universalisation of modernity; or, more prosaically, the emergence of global 'wholes' as key units of analysis. I define it simply as a process in which the foci of forces affecting people's lives, both formally and informally, shift from the local and national to the trans-national. This process is complex, uneven, cross-cutting, will probably never be complete and may in time be reversible, at least at certain points, if so desired by sufficient numbers of people. Some claim that globalisation is occurring at all levels of society, but the areas most commonly discussed are the so-called 'global economy', 'global society', 'global politics' and 'global culture'. Some see incipient globalisation as dating back to the Renaissance, while others see it as relatively recent. Some see economic globalisation as beginning in the nineteenth century with current developments being a return to 'the norm', while others see it as beginning in earnest during the 1970s with earlier precedents being minor curtain-raisers.

The spectrum of attitudes to globalisation ranges from what I call 'global fatalism'—the view that it is both inevitable and desirable—to 'autonomism'—the view that it is neither necessary nor very desirable. 'Global fatalists', particularly found amongst governments, trade administrators, big business and Economic Rationalist economists, tend to see globalisation as 'unstoppable' and promising glorious opportunities. 'Autonomists', found amongst some left theorists, NGOs, social activists and, arguably, much of the general public, tend to be suspicious of at least the 'global economy' and elements of the 'global culture', whose chief agent is the large 'transnational company' (TNC), seeing potential threats to communities, cultures or national sovereignty. Autonomists thus prefer the maximisation of national autonomy in most spheres.

However, in most accounts the issues are more complex than this. Some see globalisation as allowing differentiation to prevail over homogenisation, ideological diversity to combat narrow nationalisms, broad outlooks to supersede particularism or alternative models to rival Euro-American forms of modernisation. According to some theorists, much will depend on whether the globalisation process becomes 'hegemonic' (dominated by one power or perspective—most likely that of the USA), or differentiated. A variety of theorists and activists now advocate the latter but fear the former unless a 'global civil society' can be constructed to promote common interests, critical views or alternative values, and to protect the environment.[5]

My position is on the 'autonomistic' side of the spectrum, though by no means at the extreme end, and I concur with many of the above-mentioned concerns. In Chapters 11 and 12, I will propose some elements of an alternative world order which incorporates a few global institutions, but I will also argue throughout the book that, under the 'new model free trade agreement' the Free Trade Adventure is in danger of taking the 'hegemonic' form of economic globalisation.

Free Trade and globalisation are two sides of a coin and the former must be judged in part by the effects of the latter. Extreme Free Traders want liberalisation of everything, including audiovisuals and all cultural services, for instance, but in Chapter 9 I will note some potentially catastrophic effects of this. I will use the term 'global' for those highly integrative processes which I consider predominantly undesirable, and 'international' for looser communicative processes which I consider preferable and necessary.

The current free trade debate has been virtually totally dominated by an 'elite consensus', i.e. amongst governments, business, bureaucrats and Free Trade economists, that there is no alternative to free trade-led globalisation. This is not a conspiracy in any simplistic sense, but an emergent world view as reflected in current policy-making orthodoxy. Even some conventional theorists speak of what mainstream US economist, John Williamson, has termed the 'Washington consensus', i.e. a general agreement amongst Washington-based bodies on free market, free trade policies, especially as implemented by the IMF and World Bank (see Krugman 1995 and Chapter 12). In the case of the Free Trade Adventure we could speak of a 'Geneva consensus', and the Uruguay Round was cast in this mould. Likewise, there has emerged in Australia a 'Canberra consensus', with which I will take issue, that we must turn away from the so-called 'Australian settlement' based on Federation-era notions of protectionism, public welfare institutions, inward-looking self-reliance and so forth, seeking instead a new era of GATT-fearing trade liberalisation, private sector-led growth and Asia-focused globalism.[6]

In many eras throughout history people have thought their society an ideal state, some cultures still believing in an ultimate return to a golden age modelled on the past, and I certainly do not believe we have reached the end of history. Western societies remain too inequitable and environmentally unsustainable for that (see Dunkley 1992; Cruttwell 1995), as even Fukuyama obliquely concedes. In Chapter 12, I sketch out three alternatives to the Free Trade doctrine—Managed Trade, or new forms of discretionary policy processes; Fair Trade, or new rules to avoid inequitable aspects of global markets; and Self-Reliant Trade, or options for more trade-reducing, sovereignty-preserving trade and economic systems. I also briefly propose an alternative world trading order to that of the 'Geneva consensus', based on alternative trade strategies, development models and social goals or values, there being links between these three dimensions which have not been adequately recognised in the Free Trade Adventure debate.

2

How We Got GATT

A mildly heretical history of trade agreements

When proclaiming the virtues of trade, economists like to point out that inter-community trading dates back to prehistoric times and that human nature has, as Adam Smith put it, a 'propensity to truck, barter, and exchange one thing for another' (Smith 1776: 17). This is doubtless historically true, the earliest known trade dating back to the Stone Age. But pre-industrial trade was based on a variety of rationales ranging from utilitarian requirements to ritual exchange and social status, often using reciprocity rather than measured payment. Some believe that economic development led to trade rather than the reverse, and dependence on long-distance trading sometimes left societies vulnerable during times of instability. A few societies consciously endeavoured to ensure that trade and other foreign contacts did not fundamentally change their own culture or values.[1] Moreover, early trade was often political, imperialist, unequal, designed to 'open up' the markets of reluctant trading partners and sometimes involved dubious commodities such as arms, slaves or opium.

For most of human history trade has been no more than an adjunct to community-centred activities and in most societies was but a small proportion of the economy until the twentieth century. Only with the Industrial Revolution and incipient internationalisation did trade and other international transactions come to dominate whole societies. The world trade ratio (proportion of world production traded across national borders) actually fell dramatically during the first half of this century, but has increased from about 7 per cent in 1950 and 15 per cent in the mid-1970s to around 22 per cent today (WTO 1995b: 17), and is 30–50 per cent for some industrial countries. Australia was slower to raise its trade ratio, which hovered around 13 per cent for much of the post-war period, until recent years whence deliberate policies to raise the traded portion of our GDP and integrate into the global economy have brought the figure close to 20 per cent. The exceptions are the USA and Japan with ratios of about 10 per cent and 13 per cent respectively, this being apparently because large size confers upon an economy greater possibility for diversity and self-reliance. It is common to claim that rising trade ratios indicate the naturalness of trade and globalisation (e.g. WTO 1995b), but another interpretation is that this depends on the nature of consumption, it being widely noted that luxury goods, elaborately transformed manufactures (ETMs) and high-tech products are more traded than the norm. Sophisticated, consumerist societies trade more than those with modest needs.

Trade issues have been debated since the start of European expansionism, and since Adam Smith (1776) unrestricted cross-border trade has been widely regarded by economists as the natural, and certainly preferable, order of things. However, the great economic historian, Karl Polanyi (1944: 139ff.), has suggested that the 'free' market in general, and free trade in particular, did not evolve naturally but had to be forcibly introduced by government, often against the wishes of the people. Polanyi saw the most natural human order as a small-scale local economy based on community networks and reciprocity, a state which he would like to see restored eventually. In a different vein US international economist, Gerald Meier, has suggested that '. . . trade liberalisation has to be deliberately pursued and enforced; free trade is not a natural state of affairs . . .', while rather more militantly, the Indian-born Neo-classical development economist, Deepak Lal, has said that if free trade does not come naturally '. . . a courageous, ruthless and perhaps undemocratic government is required to ride roughshod over . . . special interest groups' which stand in the way of the glorious goal.[2]

Many modern Free Trade theorists tend to believe that free trade could be the natural order of things if only sectional interests were tamed and the public were given adequate information about its virtues. However, I suggest below and in later chapters that this is simplistic because the trade question has always been subject to a wide range of views and because the virtues of free trade are always likely to be contested, especially in an imperfect world where governments and people attach greater importance to security, self-reliance or other 'non-economic' values than to the abstract prospect of economic gains from trade (see Lake 1988: 9).

Trade treaties for everyone

One of the earliest known trade treaties was that between Egypt and Babylon around 2500 BC, while trade regulation for protective and revenue purposes dates back even further, trade intervention having been the norm for most of human history. The first great flurry of trade liberalisation, akin to that which we have seen in recent years, occurred during the middle part of the nineteenth century, culminating in the Anglo-French trade liberalisation agreement of 1860. This agreement introduced the most favoured nation (MFN) principle, which the WTO (1995b: 21) claims led to a spate of parallel bilateral agreements throughout Europe, triggering off a great age of trade and prosperity. The claim is probably overstated. Although the contemporary free market ideology did lead to market-driven trading, freely-convertible currencies and a *laissez-faire* approach by most governments to trade balances and macro-economics, Europe of the day was no more than a patchy free trade area and even this did not last for long.

The motives of governments in their Free Trade zeal varied and often were less idealistic than Free Traders impute to them. Many early trade agreements contained hidden political agendas such as the desire of France to isolate Austria, and were to some extent a response to pressure from emergent exporting interests, such an example being the 1820 petition to the British Government from merchants calling for the abolition of all import duties. It is often claimed that the 1846 abolition of British Corn Laws (agricultural protection) was designed to boost manufacturers' profits by cutting food prices and wages and to discipline workers through international competition (Polanyi 1944: 138; Hudson 1992; Kapstein 1996). However, a number of factors were increasingly favouring trade and the liberalisation thereof, including difficulties with the proliferating maze of trade regulations as economies became more complex, problems in enforcing protection and combating smuggling, growing inter-dependence between economies, a range of technological improvements which made long-distance trade more feasible and the spread of Free Trade doctrine and cosmopolitan ideas.

The period from the late nineteenth century to the early 1920s saw a revival of protectionism, which many economists attribute to the re-assertion of self-seeking domestic interests, but the motives of protectionists varied. Some believed that protection would enable their nations to catch up with Britain; some believed that the trade explosion was responsible for economic instability and depressions such as that of the 1890s; some wanted free trade confined to their empires, for patently political and imperial reasons; some, particularly in the USA, believed in the non-economic ideals of isolationism, or, after World War I, in defence-related autarchy; above all, many sought relief from the social ravages of the Industrial Revolution, the wrenching structural changes and the proliferating 'non-economic' costs attributed, rightly or wrongly, to free trade (Polanyi 1944: ch. 11). There also emerged in nineteenth-century Britain the concept of a 'moral economy', since popularised by social historian E. P. Thompson, which entailed a demand amongst common people for protection against the undue exportation of staple food or other resources from a district or country, an injustice which is often illustrated by reference to the continuing export of potatoes from Ireland during the Great Famine. Economists frequently claim that reinvigorated protection hindered development, but this is questionable, as protection clearly did not much delay German or US development any more than did free trade save Britain from economic decline.

Of course, Free Trade ideals did not disappear. The post-World War I period saw the earliest proposal, associated with US administrator Cordell Hull, for an international trade organisation and the proposition by Hull and Woodrow Wilson that trade led to peace. This period also saw the revival of trade treaties and several efforts at trade liberalisation negotiations (Wilcox 1949). However, such efforts collapsed at the onset of the Depression and at the world-wide return to protectionism with a vengeance, the latter beginning in the USA with the infamous Smoot–Hawley tariff increases passed by a Republican-dominated US Congress in 1930. This measure was the stuff of legends.

Free Traders still believe that it was forced upon Congressmen by panicky, parochial protectionist interests, that it led to a disastrous world tariff war which prolonged the Depression and that common sense later prevailed when Roosevelt returned to freer trade. The WTO (1995b: 22) claims that the Smoot–Hawley tariff converted a recession into Depression, while some US right wingers, including former President Ronald Reagan, believe it *caused* the slump.

Needless to say this 'legend of the Thirties', as I call it, is over-simplified. Certainly there was sectional pressure on Congress, as a much quoted study by the economist E. E. Schattschneider has shown, most labour and small manufacturing interests supporting the Smoot–Hawley Bill. But other factors were at work, including the idealistic isolationism of President Hoover and many Republican Congress-members. As regards the stemming of the protectionist tide by Roosevelt and the subsequent re-orientation to freer trade, revisionist US historians Ferguson and Rogers (1986) have shown that this derived more from political alignments than economic purity, particularly with the rise of powerfully organised export interests. That period saw the emergence, possibly for the first time, of an organised export coalition which brought together capital-intensive TNCs and international financial companies, including, General Electric, IBM, Pam Am, Standard Oil, Bank of America, Goldman Sachs and so forth. Such companies, which exported extensively but did not employ much labour, agreed to support Roosevelt's expansionist, pro-labour New Deal and to finance the Democratic Party in return for free trade policies. Other factors in this turn-around included the rise of free trade-oriented agrarian Southerners in the Democratic Party, the influence of Hull, who had become Roosevelt's Secretary of State, and the absorption of formerly protectionist trade union leaders into the Roosevelt Administration, many of whom swapped their protectionism for New Deal labour and social programmes (Kindleberger 1987; Vernon and Spar 1989: ch. 3). So the politics of the trade issue were complex, with a jumble of interests and motives involved, as opposed to the simplistic 'protectionist plot' view taken by many Free Trade iconoclasts.

In most other countries the free trade vs. protection debates of the 1930s likewise ranged around a variety of issues rather than pure sectional interests. In Britain Labour supported free trade to get cheap food for the workers while the Tories advocated support for key industries and Empire preferences (i.e. liberalised trade within the British Empire). In some countries, including Australia, labour governments and union movements followed the views of J. M. Keynes and sundry left intellectuals who were advocating protection for supposedly employment-generation reasons. So there were cross-cutting patterns of both the principles and interests involved in the debate, and more recently some economists have questioned whether or not the 'tariff war' of the 1930s was as damaging as Free Traders claim (see p. 117 below).

Legends persist, however, and the 'Legend of the Thirties' led to a formal consensus amongst wartime governments that post-war recovery must be based on freer trade and stronger multilateral trading rules, though caveats such as 'infant industries', 'temporary protection' and 'priority for employment over import liberalisation' were often slipped into government statements. In time this consensus led to GATT, but there were also underlying divisions of opinion in the debate about the post-war order, particularly that between Free Traders and Keynesians or proto-Managed Traders, an intellectual battle which engulfed the diplomatic world during and after the war and has continued, to some extent, ever since.

The Keynesian view began with the great man himself but was widely espoused at the time by many public servants, economists and governments, including those of Britain and Australia which were both active in international forums. This view advocated a planned domestic interventionist macro policy for full employment, a flexible international trading system which allowed some protectionist safeguards and an international monetary system with a bias towards growth and employment generation, in contrast to the old Gold Standard which had a contractionary bias because governments were required to reduce demand in the event of a balance of payments deficit. Australia's Labor Post-War Reconstruction Minister, John Dedman, at one stage emphasised the crucial links between industry protection policy, employment and welfare, urging that trade policy be centred around the positive aim of full employment rather than the 'negative idea of merely reducing trade barriers' (Crawford 1968: 55). So in the eyes of some, trade liberalisation was a means to a macro-economic end, not a goal in itself. By contrast, the Free Trade view, while not totally *laissez-faire* or anti-Keynesian, passionately proclaimed that Free Trade principles should predominate world-wide, should be enshrined in a new system of multilateral trade rules and should be administered by an international body, as Hull had long advocated.

The US leadership has always been torn between inward- and outward-looking forces, these being roughly in balance between the 1880s and the 1930s (Lake 1988). During the war US leaders were divided between Keynesians and globally inclined Free Traders until the death of Roosevelt and the succession of Truman in mid-1945, whence the former were purged. The USA finished the war with a staggering economic dominance of the world, accounting for almost two-thirds of the world's manufacturing production and for a third of the world's total output and trade. The post-war US leadership sought advantage from this dominance by, for instance, insisting that the British end their imperial preference system (some say because the USA wanted access to the vast Empire markets), by seeking to displace British predominance in Middle Eastern oil-rich countries, by providing aid programmes with many free trade, anti-communist, anti-Soviet strings attached and generally by pressing Free Trade views in international forums. Officially the USA nobly wanted to make the post-war order safe for peaceful co-operation, democracy, high employment and even a modest social 'safety net', along with liberal trading rules. In practice post-Roosevelt leaders sought actively to oppose collective welfarism, nationalisation of industry, general government intervention, protectionist industry policy, attempts by Third World countries to promote commodity price stabilisation schemes and so forth. A key US trade administrator of the day, Clair Wilcox, has said that US post-war trade policy was based on two principles: one being that the volume of trade should be big because 'big imports mean big exports', the other being that trade should be undertaken by private enterprises because these are efficient, competitive and non-discriminatory.[3]

This US political and economic dominance critically shaped the institutions of the post-war world. At the now-famous 1944 Bretton Woods conference, which proposed a trio of international bodies to administer finance, development and trade, Keynes advocated a world trading currency, strict controls on private capital flows and a tax mechanism for redistributing exchange from surplus to deficit countries, all designed for a world system biased towards growth, stability, employment expansion and development. But this and other such schemes were scuttled by a US leadership scornful of both their interventionist and autonomy-reducing aspects, although capital and exchange rate controls survived until the 1970s, three relatively non-interventionist bodies—the International Monetary Fund (IMF), the World Bank and the International Trade Organisation (ITO)—being mooted instead. Of these, the first two were quickly established, nominally under the auspices of the UN, in practice largely autonomously from the outset, and the USA as their major donor has strongly influenced their policies ever since.

The third of the triplets, the proposed ITO, faced a more difficult birth as different countries had differing views of its intended nature and role. The USA wanted extensive trade liberalisation, de-regulation of controls on private investment and an economically weighted voting system which would have given the USA a fifth of the votes in the ITO. Facing a hostile majority of UN members and strong resistance from South American delegations, however, the USA eventually dropped these demands and sought alliances with more amenable First World countries. At a meeting of such countries on 30 October 1947 attendees agreed to a package of tariff reductions and approved a 'general agreement on tariffs and trade' (GATT) which was to be incorporated into the ITO. The Havana Charter, as the 1948 ITO formation document became known, provided for: tariff reductions; restrictions on 'invisible tariffs' (now known as NTBs); limitations on domestic taxes and regulations which affected trade; restrictions on international monopolistic private business practices; the commercialisation of public enterprises; general liberalisation of private investment flows; the establishment of, but restraints on, international commodity agreements; the facilitation of government policies for economic stability and full employment; fair labour standards at work; and general

assistance for developing countries. The ITO was to have a bureaucracy, a disputes settlement mechanism enforceable through the
UN-affiliated International Court of Justice and was to be located
within the Economic and Social Council of the UN.[4]

The ITO proposal was something of a hotchpotch due to the
competing ideological forces behind it, as outlined above. It was
much broader than GATT, at once more trade liberalising (e.g.
covering business practices, investment and public enterprise which
GATT did not) and more socially based (e.g. covering employment
issues and being linked to the UN). Yet there was plenty in the ITO
draft to which various interests could object. Many poorer countries
felt it would do little to help them. Some British and Australian
politicians, including R. G. Menzies, thought it would jeopardise
the Empire and ensconce US dominance. Many political and business groups in the USA and elsewhere, including the Australian
Chambers of Manufactures, feared that it would reduce national
sovereignty (Crawford 1968: ch. 3). US investors, who had requested an investment clause in the ITO, were grumpy because the
final provisions (Article 12) only called for new investment opportunities, allowing host countries to set terms for foreign investment
and to guard against political influence by investors (McCulloch
1990; Dryden 1995: 28).

A few countries, including Australia, ratified the ITO, but in
the USA there was so much opposition that Truman never submitted it to Congress, thus causing other nations to lose interest and
leaving the orphaned GATT as the world's only multilateral trade
agreement. The GATT came into force on 1 January 1948, not as an
organisation but as an interim agreement amongst twenty-three
'contracting parties' (i.e. countries) with its Geneva-based staff technically leased from the UN body set up to administer the defunct
ITO. So GATT's beginnings were less than auspicious, its members
accounting for two-thirds of world trade compared with 90 per cent
for the fifty-four nations which had initially signed the Havana
Charter. In time there emerged a distinction between the socially
oriented UN system, based on 'one nation/one vote', and the more
economically focused Bretton Woods institutions (the IMF and
World Bank) with voting based on financial contributions. GATT
fell between the two camps, having both an economic focus and the

'one nation/one vote' principle, since the US proposal for money-based voting in the ITO was scotched (see above). The new WTO retains this ambivalence and in Chapter 12 I will propose that it be shifted closer to the UN system, in the spirit of the ITO, with the UN and Bretton Woods systems preferably being merged.

The GATTing of wisdom

The underlying theory and structure of GATT appear to reflect the view that, as I indicated above, free trade is not a natural state of society but has to be constructed and enforced. From the outset the key roles of GATT have been to provide a set of rules and processes for trade liberalisation, as well as a mechanism for implementing them, after a fashion. GATT has often denied that it is a free trade organisation as such, for indeed it has never sought complete free trade, even in the Uruguay Round, though it seeks a world free trade order as its ultimate goal. Rather, it is primarily concerned to create a fair, open, non-discriminatory, multilateral, rules-based trading system, much of its work focusing on the nitty-gritty detail of trade relations.[5] GATT remains the key agreement underlying multilateral trade rules. The central principles of GATT are as follows.

1 Liberalisation or 'market access'—this is the goal of gradually reducing most forms of protection and fixing or 'binding' (see Glossary) these reduced levels. GATT47 proscribed quantitative restrictions on imports and a 1955 amendment (Article XV1:4) also outlawed export subsidies, but gradual tariff reductions have become GATT's trade mark.

2 Reciprocity—the basic negotiation process used by GATT entailing each country making successive tariff reduction offers until a schedule of mutually agreed reductions is reached, a mechanism which some Free Trade critics of GATT say is flawed because it ignores the 'unilateral benefit' concept (see Chapter 1 and Glossary).

3 Non-discrimination—this concept, implying equality between GATT members, takes three forms: first, GATT rules apply equally to imports and exports; second, trade concessions granted

to any country must be extended equally to all other GATT members—the 'most favoured nation' (MFN) principle (see Glossary); third, no tariff, tax or other measure should discriminate between domestic and foreign suppliers—the 'National Treatment' principle (see Glossary).

4 Transparency—this principle states that any form of protection a signatory chooses to use within the framework of GATT's rules should be clearly and fairly stated, should be consistent and ideally should take the form of visible tariffs.

In practice GATT94 is a flexible document with a range of what Free Traders, prior to the Uruguay Round, saw as over-generous loopholes, the plugging of which was a key aim of the Round, though many of these are still applicable to varying extents. These include:

- Article VI, which allows 'anti-dumping duties' and 'countervailing duties' to be levied when a country considers itself disadvantaged by subsidies or other 'unfair' price-reducing practices used in another country (tightened by the Round).

- The concept of 'safeguards' (Article XIX), which allows a signatory to temporarily suspend tariff concessions when a sudden 'surge' of imports threatens 'serious injury' to domestic producers, or to apply temporary import quotas when a serious balance of payments deficit threatens its foreign currency reserves (tightened by the Round).

- Article IV, which allows signatories to set minimum screen-time quotas for 'cinematographic films of national origin', provided that the quota allocation is non-discriminatory and subject to negotiation for 'limitation, liberalisation or elimination' (still applicable).

- Article XXIV, which exempts signatories from MFN obligations if they wish to enter a free trade area or customs union (minimally amended by the Round—see Chapter 5).

- Exemptions, or so-called 'special and differential measures', for 'under-developed' countries (Article XVII) through which signatories with 'low standards of living in the early stages of development' may be exempt from some GATT requirements or be granted preferential treatment (still applicable).

- Article XXXV, which exempts a GATT member from making concessions to another member if the former had never negotiated with the latter or did not consent to its admission. This clause was used a lot in the early years of GATT (Croome 1995: 103), though less so now, and has been enshrined in Article XIII of the new *WTO Agreement.*

- A so-called 'grandfather' clause which allowed founding GATT members to retain pre-existing legislation inconsistently with the National Treatment provisions of GATT, a practice which later extended to the 'protocols of accession' for new members. 'Grandfathering' was largely abolished by the Round.[6]

- Articles XX and XXI, which allow exemptions on grounds such as public morals, 'human, animal or plant health', conservation of 'exhaustible natural resources', preservation of cultural 'treasures', national security and so forth (still applicable).

- Article XXV, which allows the GATT/WTO Council to grant general waivers for purposes not covered elsewhere. This provision was tightened by the Round (see Chapter 11) and existing waivers are to be terminated within two years unless an extension is granted under the new rules.[7]

In time these loopholes have proved quite elastic but their existence indicates clearly that the founding signatories of GATT wanted plenty of let-outs and spheres of autonomy. It is also important to understand what GATT is not. It is not a body which can set standards, direct government policy, make rules about investment flows or supervise the business activities of private companies, although the proposed ITO (see above) was to have some of these functions. Even top officials can at times misunderstand GATT. A former Australian ambassador to GATT (Oxley 1990: 194) has said, for instance, that free trade laws are the international equivalent of domestic competition laws, but this is certainly not the case. GATT affects only what governments can do to would-be-traders, not what private firms can do to each other or to the public. In short, GATT is only a maker of, largely voluntary, trade rules and a restricted range of rules at that.

The organisation that wasn't

For a body which was an agreement rather than a formal organisation (see above) GATT gradually became rather organisation-like,
with a Geneva-based staff (currently 420 people) to fulfil its many
research, monitoring and negotiation roles. When the GATT
Secretariat became the WTO on 1 January 1995 it had 128
members, though not all had fulfilled the Uruguay Round obligations required to join the WTO automatically. By mid-1996 the
WTO had 123 members and 37 observers. Once the original 128
plus some 20 new applicants (including China and Russia) are
confirmed, the WTO will have about 150 members, which is fewer
than the UN but is almost three-quarters of the world's 207 nations
and it will cover virtually all significant trading countries.[8]

GATT (and now the WTO) is headed by a Director-General,
the best-known incumbents in recent times being Swiss diplomat,
Arthur Dunkel, who presided over most of the Uruguay Round,
and his interim replacement, Irish and EU official Peter Sutherland,
who presided over the culmination of the Uruguay Round and the
formation of the WTO. The current Director-General is Italian
businessman and former politician, Renato Ruggiero. The decision-
making structures of GATT94 were modified by the Round (see
Chapter 11), but the 'one member/one vote' system has been
retained. Thus, the GATT/WTO system is nominally democratic,
although in reality many smaller countries cannot always afford to
send delegates to the main bodies, let alone to all the associated
committees which are appointed from time to time, and some
commentators claim that traditionally GATT decisions have informally required the agreement of the USA, the EC and Japan (GAO
1994: 27).

Over the years GATT became the world's main avenue for
the resolution of trade disputes. Settlement procedures begin with
GATT-mediated negotiations and 'Green Room' talks in the
Director-General's chamber of that name, resorting if necessary to a
three-member disputes panel. GATT's original rules were unclear
about the exact status of panel reports but the practice evolved that
there had to be unanimity in the GATT Council before a report

could be accepted or sanctions authorised against a country found to be in breach of trade rules. This meant, in effect, that a country subject to complaint could veto any action against itself, as a result of which only one such action (the Netherlands against the USA) was ever attempted. This rather weak sanctioning capacity of GATT was addressed in the Uruguay Round (see Chapter 11).

The ultimate function of GATT is to reduce trade barriers, which it has sought to do through periodic rounds of multilateral trade negotiations, although unilateral and bilateral liberalisation is also encouraged. GATT has traditionally advocated the multilateral approach as the most beneficial for smaller countries, and as the most likely to curtail protectionism, even though some Free Traders prefer unilateralism (see Chapter 1). The early GATT Rounds involved only 20–30 countries but resulted in substantial tariff cuts. The Kennedy Round (1964–67), involving 62 countries and a tariff-cutting target of 50 per cent, saw some further cuts and an anti-dumping agreement. The most ambitious, the Tokyo Round (1973–79) involving 102 countries, cut average tariffs by a third across thousands of items, produced some industry-specific agreements (dairy, meat and civil aircraft) and concluded some new (non-compulsory) codes on matters such as NTBs, subsidies, countervailing measures, anti-dumping practices, government procurement, technical standards and trade procedures.

By the end of the Tokyo Round average world tariff levels had been reduced from about 40 per cent when GATT was formed to under 5 per cent, with tariff duties eliminated entirely from some industries. Hundreds of trade disputes had been resolved in the direction of liberalisation under GATT's auspices. Between 1950 and 1990 world trade grew at an average annual rate of 6 per cent compared with 4 per cent for world output, a result for which GATT claims a good part of the credit, though not all observers accept this claim. This record suggests that GATT has been highly successful, but progress has been slow, leading many cynics unkindly to call GATT a 'toothless old hag' and claim that its initials really mean 'general agreement for talk and talk'. However, the greatest concern of GATT and its Free Trade supporters has been that as tariffs came down via the GATT rounds, these were quickly replaced by the supposedly much more insidious NTBs, which thus became the main target of the Uruguay Round.

Conclusion

Free Trade may not be what its champions claim—a universally good idea. Some free trade-sympathising economists have conceded that the Free Trade concept does not come naturally, although most think this is due only to the machinations of protectionist vested interests. However, the notion of vested interests can cut both ways. There are now plenty of vested interests, politically apparent since at least the 1930s, in exports, foreign investment and the opening of other countries' markets thereto. Such interests are only morally superior to protectionism if we discount a range of arguably legitimate national concerns of the sort that I will note in other chapters. The defeat of the proposed ITO, the evolution of GATT and the US-sponsored post-war Free Trade thrust all demonstrate a complex overlapping of a wide variety of interests and national concerns which cannot be overlooked in assessing today's passion for the Free Trade Adventure.

3

The Fall and Rise of GATT

Background of the Uruguay Round

During the 1980s negotiations over reform of GATT played a central role in, and became a symbol of, the Free Trade Adventure. At the start of the decade GATT was widely seen as failing, or even dead, its rules apparently being regularly flouted with impugnity and protectionism clearly being on the increase. Yet by the early 1990s the successful completion of the Uruguay Round was being hailed as the harbinger of a liberalising, integrating world order in which, for the first time in history, some proclaimed, most nations adhered to the same ideology, i.e. democratic capitalism and free markets (e.g. Fukuyama 1992). In this chapter I will briefly examine a few of the factors involved in the fall and rise of GATT, particularly the resurgence of protectionism, some economic forces for global change and the complex mélange of political–ideological factors which came to the rescue of GATT and ensured the success of the Uruguay Round. The causes of the fall and rise of GATT defy glib generalisations, but I suggest that two factors were of critical importance—the worldwide political shift to Economic Rationalism during the 1980s, culminating in the 'Geneva consensus' (see Chapter 1), and the emergence during the 1970s and 1980s of organised corporate groupings with vested interests in global economic expansion.

The fall of the house of GATT

It did not take long for GATT's rules to be bent. In 1951 a Cold War-minded US Congress voted to withhold trade concessions from

Soviet-bloc countries and the USA was granted a waiver by GATT to discriminate against Czechoslovakia. Japan was kept out of GATT until 1955 and even then some European countries were granted waivers, under Article XXXV (see p. 30 above), to continue discrimination against Japanese exports. In the same year the USA was granted a waiver to introduce export subsidies in agriculture, one of the near-taboo items in GATT, and others followed suit, which allowed bindings and other disciplines to dissolve and effectively, though not officially, caused agriculture to slip out of the GATT orbit. Between 1952 and 1960 Australia enjoyed a waiver to use licensed quotas across almost the entire range of its imports, on the grounds of a balance of payments safeguard, and this appears to have helped economic development (see Dunkley 1995).

In a sense GATT became the victim of its own success for as tariffs came down other barriers went up, though according to Free Traders this was due to protectionist backsliding at the behest of pressure-group politics, not to deficiencies in the Free Trade doctrine. The catalogue of alleged protectionist sins included: excessive use of GATT's emergency safeguard provisions (see p. 29 above); use of anti-dumping and countervailing duties for selective long-term protection rather than just a short-term safeguard as GATT intended, especially by the USA, Canada and Australia in industries under strong competitive pressure; the continuing use of quotas and other measures officially restricted or outlawed by GATT; the development of an array of subsidies, such as direct payments, credits, interest rate concessions, tax rebates and the like for both export and domestic industries, all of which could cause unlevel playing fields; the emergence of 'trade-related investment measures' (TRIMs) which placed conditions on foreign investors and thus supposedly adversely affected trade; the widespread use of 'counter-trade' or international barter systems; and the invention of innumerable 'grey-area' measures or 'non-tariff barriers' (NTBs)—see below.

The number of possible NTBs is almost infinite but several major categories are notable. The first, and most abhorred by Free Traders, includes so-called 'orderly marketing arrangements' and 'voluntary export restraints'—VERs (see Glossary), the best-known example being that of the 1974 'multi-fibre arrangements' (MFA) under which the USA and the EC forced Third World countries to limit textile exports and the growth thereof to target annual rates. Over time GATT was induced to accept the deal, which has been likened to keeping a brothel in a cathedral (Waldman 1986: ch. 9), such arrangements thence being extended to many other products under hundreds of bilateral and multilateral agreements. The second category of NTBs involves misuse of customs procedures for protectionist purposes, such as the way the French once directed all Japanese electronic imports through a single small port, or the one-time practice by Japanese customs authorities of processing their own airlines' freight more quickly than that of other national carriers.

A third category of NTBs entails distortion of administrative practices and technical standards for protectionist purposes, of which the Japanese produced many amusing examples. At one time foreign baseball bats would only be admitted if tested and certified in Japan, but could not be admitted without a test certificate; a brand of imported potato crisps was re-classified as confectionery, which attracted higher duties; some drugs could only be admitted if accompanied by health certificates for all company executives; foreign products were virtually disbarred from endorsement by the two main Japanese domestic standard-setting bodies. The South Koreans frequently threaten purchasers of foreign cars with a tax audit (Thurow 1996: 202). The fourth category is 'misuse' of government authority for protection through public enterprises, co-operative marketing boards, government procurement contracts and networking with industry to boost competitiveness or promote exports, which is known in Japan as *Keiretsu* (see below). A final category of NTBs entails use of subsidies, both domestic and export-oriented, both overt and covert, examples of covert measures including local content requirements, interest rate relief, tax concessions, export credits and the like.[1]

For Free Traders the protectionist problem was even more fundamental than the above list because such measures were often built into the very structure of industry and governmental policy-making for a wide range of economic, social and developmental purposes, this generally being referred to as commercial or industry policy. The case most cited is that of Japan where government procurement operated through over 140 agencies and sub-agencies, each maintaining special (sometimes corrupt) relationships with supplying companies, and where private corporate systems, called *Keiretsu*, bound a chain of companies together in a way which excluded foreign competition. Some 150 *Keiretsu* groups are thought to control 40 per cent of Japan's economy and up to 80 per cent of its trade. The structure as a whole is linked through the Ministry of International Trade and Industry (MITI) into a systematic industry policy and economic planning process, which some see as the key to the Japanese 'miracle'. Throughout the 1980s the USA put massive pressure on Japan to open up its system and in 1982 the EC complained to GATT that the entire Japanese system was one big protection racket.[2]

However, in the EC itself many member countries had, throughout the post-war period, built up extensive industry policy systems using a wide variety of subsidies, NTBs and government-industry planning systems. It has even been suggested that many European companies had *Keiretsu*-type systems, albeit not as tight as those of Japan (Miyashita and Russell 1994). The goal of European policy was, quite openly, to make EC industry more competitive with that of the USA and Japan. During the 1980s France pressed the EC, with only limited success, to adopt a Europe-wide industry policy of this sort (Pearce and Sutton 1985). Australia has largely eschewed industry policy systems and most NTBs, though with a modestly increased usage under the Labor Government. In the mid-1980s 84 per cent of our protection consisted of tariffs, 13.5 per cent import restrictions, 2 per cent subsidies and 1 per cent export incentives, our main 'offence' being persistently high tariffs and periodic use of quotas, notably in the vehicle and textile, clothing and footwear (TCF) industries, as well as a few export promotion programmes.[3]

Likewise, the USA has not formally used industry policies and some commentators claim that it is the odd country out in not having home-grown *Keiretsu*-type corporate systems, although there have been plenty of advocates within the US for such systems and even for a MITI-type planning structure. Nevertheless the Department of Commerce and the US Trade Representative (USTR) have often favoured activist industry policy and some protection, while many government departments maintain close links with industry through military procurement and twenty or so official agencies. This has resulted in a number of 'strategic' defence and high-tech sectors being heavily subsidised. As a consequence of the Smoot–Hawley episode and the 'Legend of the Thirties' (see Chapter 2), Congress divested itself of power over industry-specific tariff decisions, in part to protect itself from pressure, with these functions being redistributed to the President or other government bodies. President Carter later devolved some of his trade policy powers to these other bodies and Reagan set up an extensive series of consultative groups designed to articulate the interests of industrialists and traders. By the time the recessionary and balance of payments crises of the 1980s hit there was a surge of protectionist tariffs, quotas and subsidies, many of which are still in place, the motives being a mix of sectional pressure and general economic panic (Vernon and Spar 1989: ch. 3; Destler 1992; Oppenheim 1992).

The revival of protectionism alongside free trade preachments, especially in the USA, seems remarkably hypocritical, but the idea of a world-wide hypocrisy plague is simplistic. The persistence of industry protection systems throughout the world suggests that such systems play a legitimate role in stabilisation or in minimising social adjustment costs. Factors which various writers have identified as enhancing protectionist pressure include: unemployment and recessions of the 1970s and early 1980s which led to demands for job security; increasing imports from the Third World (see Chapter 8); changing international comparative advantage; the rise of pro-protectionist schools of economic thought (see Chapter 6); large size and high concentration of industries, which strengthen protectionist demands; the level of unionisation in, and labour intensity of, vulnerable industries; the tendency for industries to become identified with particular districts; concerns about the impact of structural change on income distribution and social welfare (Grilli 1991). So the basis for protectionist demands and the degree of justification thereof is very broad, can be subject to interminable debate and varies over time.

However, there can be no doubt that the rising protectionism of the 1970s and 1980s had considerable economic impact and undermined GATT. It has been estimated that by the end of the 1980s 25–35 per cent of world trade was in some degree affected by NTBs, industry policies and so forth, with NTBs applying to 30 per cent of all manufactured trade, 50 per cent in agricultural, 65 per cent in iron and steel and 67 per cent in clothing. The use of NTBs was thought to raise effective protection from the formal level of about 10 per cent for most OECD countries to several times that figure—some say to 70 per cent for Japan. One study estimated that the total abolition of Japan's NTBs would have raised that country's imports by 7 per cent and manufactured imports by 27 per cent, although this would have constituted only 0.75 per cent of GDP, and would nowhere near account for the US trade deficit with Japan as many US commentators claimed (Christelow in King 1990: 52–4). Some sceptics suggested that GATT's coverage had shrunk from the 50 per cent of world trade claimed by GATT in the early 1980s to around a bare 7 per cent by late in the decade. In short, GATT had clearly had a serious fall and was looking rather like a doughnut under gun fire.[4]

GATT is dead!

Free Traders have variously attributed the fall of GATT to the politics of protectionism, government interventionism, discrimination against Japan, bilateralism, the emergence of regional trading blocs, double standards by the USA, the politicisation of GATT, the concessional admission of unenthusiastic Third World countries, the general flouting of GATT rules by most countries and the so-called 'diminished giant' syndrome, whereby a weakened USA no longer has the will or power to lead the world towards free trade. For these sorts of reasons Managed Traders have been particularly unkind to GATT, Clyde Prestowitz (1991) and his colleagues once referring to the Uruguay Round negotiations as 'the last gasp of GATTism', while Thurow (1992) declared that, owing to the rise of competing super-powers (the USA, the EU and Japan), GATT was for all intents and purposes dead. As it turned out this was the last word in false prophecy.[5]

Some commentators saw the greatest threat to GATT as coming from the purported protector of free trade, the USA itself, in the form of so-called 'aggressive unilateralism', or what I call 'economic gunboat diplomacy'. This policy began with provisions in the 1962 Trade Expansion Act which allowed the President to retaliate against foreign practices deemed discriminatory against US exports, these later being strengthened by provisions in other Acts known as Section 301, Super 301 and Special 301 (see Glossary), which are still in place. These devices enable the USTR to investigate and seek redress for corporate complaints about another country's 'acts, policies or practices', including export targeting, industry policies, *Keiretsu* systems, lack of IPRs and general barriers to US products. The rationale for economic gunboat diplomacy is that US exports are more damaged by foreign protectionism than the reverse.

Major 'gunboat' targets during the 1980s included Brazil for import licensing, protection of the local computer industry and lack of IPRs, Japan for protection of her satellite, super-computer and forest products industries and India for foreign investment controls, protection of the insurance industry and lack of IPRs. The USTR has, under Super 301, established a 'Priority Watch List' of major offenders and a lesser 'Watch List' of more minor miscreants, the latter list including Australia for our high tariffs, restrictions on DFI, TV local content rules and weak IPRs, although recent reports have cleared us somewhat on certain of these 'charges' (USTR 1993 and 1994). Almost a quarter of GATT member countries have been on these lists in recent times. To date only a few retaliatory trade sanctions have been used, notably against the EC over issues ranging from aircraft subsidies to the latter's ban on meat with growth hormones, and against Brazil for lack of IPRs. However, a number of countries have succumbed to US demands under Section 301 duress. This policy has widespread support in the USA on the grounds of alleged deficiencies in GATT or the supposed need to open up foreign markets. However, a wide range of critics regard the Section 301 system as unjustifiable because its definition of 'unreasonable' actions by other countries is broad and vague, because it places arbitrary power in the hands of the USTR, because its main thrust is clearly outside the spirit of GATT and because it is a severe imposition upon the sovereignty of other nations. Most Free Traders oppose it for these sorts of reasons.[6]

In sum, by the mid-1980s GATT's various alleged sins of omission and commission included accusations that its exemptions and safeguards loopholes, notably the anti-dumping and countervailing duties codes, were too loose and much abused, that subsidies and

NTBs merely replaced tariffs and quotas in national trade policy systems, that industry assistance measures, taxes and general administrative practices were creating 'unlevel' playing fields, often in the guise of formal industry policy, and that new permutations of unilateralism, bilateralism and regionalism were displacing multilateralism. Due to a loose waiver system agriculture had slipped out of GATT, while GATT itself had sanctioned the MFA, which enabled textiles to also evade the net. Dispute panel decisions were difficult to enforce, and although most countries complied voluntarily, they often did so only in part or after long delays, the USA being as much an offender as anyone else, despite its loud complaints about rule-breaches. In short, most countries were regularly bending GATT rules with impugnity. It was to these problems that the Uruguay Round was directed.

Long live GATT

GATT's comeback was one of the most spectacular since Lazarus. Free Traders tend to explain the 'miracle' in terms of supposedly inexorable international trends and rising economic rationality, while many have adopted the influential 'Public Choice' theory of trade politics. The latter theory argues that governments are like entrepreneurs in maximising votes by responding to interests in their electorates, but that sectional interests have more to gain from protectionism than the general public has to lose so the former can be more effective, although this tendency can be countered by better public information and more resolute pro-liberalisation activity on the part of governments. Accordingly, Public Choice theory suggests that the recent free trade revival has come about because governments are now resisting sectional pressure, urged along by Free Trade advocates and GATT leaders, and because people have become more economically rational so are now aware that free trade is, on balance, in their own best interests. In my view, however, this theory can be questioned on a number of grounds.

First, it draws the lines of interest group politics too tightly. Some domestic industry leaders favour rather than oppose liberalisation, despite possible threats from imports, on grounds such as the need for competition or future export opportunities. On the other hand, non-threatened industries and workers may oppose liberalisation for fear that their turn will come eventually, while many people may think like workers rather than consumers, worrying more about insecurity than relishing the prospect of the slightly lower prices which might result from enhanced import competition. Second, the virtues of free trade, both perceived and real, may not be as clear-cut as Public Choice theory assumes. In most countries opinion polls show the public to be sceptical of, or outright opposed to, liberalisation (see Introduction to Part Two), often because people take a wider, non-economic view of the issues, so that much social opposition may be based on principle rather than sectional interest. Third, many scholars have found that trade policy-making is shaped by a much wider range of factors than Public Choice theory recognises, including political traditions, conflicts between executive and legislature, tensions between large and small businesses or between exporting and domestic sectors, perceptions of national strategic interests, public opinion, general ideological trends and so on.[7]

A fourth reason for questioning the Public Choice view of trade politics is that externally oriented interests may not be as hapless in the face of domestically focused groups as the theory claims. Export-oriented sectors with comparative advantage tend to accrue great economic and political power over time and are likely to be strongly favoured by government when balance of trade problems loom. During the 1970s and 1980s such interests became well organised and very powerful in the politics of many Western countries (see below). In the USA the conversion of the Democratic Party leadership to Free Trade views during the 1980s, as in the 1930s (see Chapter 2), appears to have been due more to the internal influence of globally focused business interests than to Free Trade principles, and Congress members with strong business backing voted heavily for NAFTA.[8]

Finally, Public Choice theory has not proved effective at predicting which sectors will obtain protection (Quiggin 1996: 139ff.), probably because the above-mentioned factors make the picture a complex one. In short, it may be that the recent ascendancy of Free Trade ideology and the revival of GATT has been due more to a political victory of exporting interests over other social groups than to a flash of global rationality. However, the factors involved in this process are numerous and complex, these including, in addition to those discussed above, the conversion of most Western governments and public service elites to Economic Rationalism, albeit incompletely, the ostensibly accelerating globalisation of the world economy and the alleged, if disputed, need for concomitant economic deregulation. Globalisation and de-regulation contain their own self-reinforcing logic which I call a 'vicious circle of globalisation'. According to Free Traders the floating of exchange rates world-wide has rendered trade barriers less effective because the exclusion of imports tends to raise the exchange rate which then counteracts the protective measure, and thus trade should be liberalised. Freer trade then requires sectoral restructuring, which will be accomplished more efficiently if capital can readily move across borders, and hence capital flows should be de-regulated. Finally, all of this is done more efficiently if labour is flexible and mobile, so labour markets should be de-regulated (which some think should be done first). These presumptions can be challenged and the sequence has been questioned, but by the mid-1980s most governments were adopting this all-round de-regulatory agenda, to which a reformed GATT was central. Some economists believe that trade liberalisation, with its accompanying structural adjustment implications, can be accomplished more easily at a time of growth and rising economic optimism when job opportunities are expanding, and such conditions prevailed in many countries during the later 1980s as the Uruguay Round got under way.

During the 1970s and 1980s another crucial liberalisation-enhancing set of developments was occurring in the business sectors of many OECD countries as the political–economic balance began shifting from domestic industries to externally-oriented export sectors, as the global reach of TNCs expanded and as a so-called 'third sector' of corporate interests emerged. The latter sector consists of high technology firms which are not necessarily large, but which are characterised by economies of scale and scope, research intensity, high inputs of intellectual property, intense global oligopolistic competition and heavy reliance on access to expanding export markets, either directly or through 'alliances' with firms in recipient countries. This sector strongly backed the US Section 301 system, heavily lobbied for the inclusion of IPRs in the Uruguay Round and generally supported the revival of GATT (Milner 1988 and in Bhagwati 1990). In many countries exporters have become the main pressure group for free trade, regularly advocating the opening of domestic markets in exchange for 'market access' in other countries (Krugman 1991: 102). So by the mid-1980s and the commencement of the Uruguay Round there had emerged, in many countries and world-wide, a well-organised new business grouping with strong vested interests in 'opening up' national markets, promoting liberalisation in general and ensuring the success of the Round.

Under a combination of commercial pressure from outward-looking business sectors and ideological pressure from Economic Rationalists, governments of various debtor countries, including the USA and Australia, decided to take a punt on an export-oriented strategy targetted at rectifying their burgeoning trade deficits. Some economists believe that protection can only influence the volume and composition of trade, not the balance thereof, which is determined ultimately by national savings and investment (e.g. Destler 1992: ch. 9), but this is disputed (e.g. Thurow 1996: 208–10) and in any case it could mean that trade liberalisation was not very helpful either. Nonetheless, in Australia the former Labor Government chose an outward-looking strategy in the hope that this would bring a shift towards manufactured exports, especially into the booming markets of Asia. This strategy included substantial tariff reductions, a mildly interventionist industry policy (see Chapter 12), greater economic orientation to Asia and strong backing for the Uruguay Round with a pledge to raise tariff bindings from 25 per cent to 97 per cent. Also as part of this strategy, Australia founded the so-called Cairns Group of primary exporting countries to oppose EC, US and Japanese agricultural protection, and this group argued throughout the Uruguay Round for far-reaching liberalisation in agriculture. The Labor Government of the day was able to convert much of the, hitherto protectionist, trade union movement to this strategy, while the Australian business community, though divided as elsewhere (see above), also drifted towards free trade, thus ensuring a widespread pro-GATT consensus in Australia. Hence, Australia's policy strategy of the 1980s, even if centred largely around national interests in a period of economic crisis, favoured the revival of GATT.[9]

In short, by the second half of the 1980s there had emerged a mighty array of pro-GATT forces both within many influential countries and internationally. These forces were not without opposition and the simplistic view that an irresistibly rational economic enlightenment had arrived cannot be sustained, but certainly Economic Rationalist, Free Trade views had become predominant amongst economists, economic policy-making bureaucrats and corporate boardrooms in most Western countries. The 'Geneva consensus' had been born, and in 1989 the Jamaican Ambassador to GATT was thus able to declare that the Uruguay Round was 'doomed to succeed' (Oxley 1990: 57).

To Punta del'Este and back

The tangled web of Uruguay Round negotiations took almost eight years to complete. In fact the first efforts to kick-start a new round occurred at the 1981 G7 summit and a subsequent 1982 Ministerial Meeting of GATT members, the latter adopting an in-principle moratorium on further protection increases, proposing a so-called 'standstill and rollback' of protection and beginning a discussion programme which ultimately led to the Uruguay Round. There followed a steady stream of quiet diplomacy by GATT leaders and supporters, a variety of reports on how to revive GATT, notably the Leutwiler Report (1987), some intense lobbying by newly militant TNCs, especially by information companies and 'third sector' industries (see above), while many governments launched a range of domestic consultations and debates about the issues involved. Among governments, the main protagonist of a new round was the USA whose trade officials arranged regular meetings of ministers from twenty-five sympathetic countries between 1983 and the start of the Uruguay Round (Croome 1995: 17). In the early stages the EC, preoccupied with its own integration process, was uninterested in a new round, while Japan was content with bilateral negotiations (Croome 1995: 10–11).

A 1985 preparatory meeting, initiated by USTR, Clayton Yeutter, and a subsequent 1986 Ministerial Meeting at the Uruguayan resort of Punta del'Este finally decided on a new round, whose overall goal was to 'halt and reverse protectionism and to remove distortions to trade'. Thereafter the talks proceeded at GATT headquarters in Geneva with fits and starts, with several false finishes and with a stalled period in the early 1990s when the EC and the USA could not agree on agricultural issues. At times negotiations were heated and tempers frayed. On one occasion a burly Peter Sutherland in frustration pinned Japan's chief negotiator to a wall demanding the prime minister's phone number, and he often contacted national leaders to pressure them into a completion of the Round, including a direct phone call to President Bill Clinton at one point.[10]

Over the years of negotiation various, often overlapping, coalitions of countries emerged, some on specific issues, some on general strategies, some for agenda setting and some for issue-blocking purposes. During the course of the Round separate bilateral side-agreements were made, some countries undertook unilateral protection cuts, new members joined GATT, governments rose and fell, while entire ideologies and outlooks changed. Two of the key coalitions were the Australian-led Cairns Group (see above), which lobbied for complete trade liberalisation in agriculture, and a bloc of many Third World countries, led by India and Brazil, which for a time resisted inclusion in the Round of new issues such as services, investment and IPRs, until the USA threatened to call off the entire exercise if these were not included (Dryden 1995: 334). Cutting across these coalitions was the de la Paix Group, so called because it customarily met at the de la Paix Hotel in Geneva, which comprised fourteen smaller First and Third World countries, including Australia, who believed that their interests were better served by multilateralism than by a superpower-dominated trading system. The aim of the group was to ensure that the Round was completed successfully in the face of the USA–EC rivalry which regularly threatened to sink the negotiations.

Motives of the Round's participants varied. Some were said to be interested in just a single issue, e.g. Argentina in agriculture. Others, such as Mexico, had joined GATT recently because a new Free Trade-oriented government sought to bind domestic policy in the face of protectionist opposition. Countries like Australia wanted to strengthen multilateral rules in favour of medium-sized and smaller members, while the EC and Japan, who were actually less than ecstatic about free trade, were anxious to head off US economic gunboat diplomacy, especially by dissolving GATT and forming a new organisation (see Chapter 11). The USA wanted a second string to its Section 301 bow and has amply demonstrated since the end of the Round that it has no intention of sinking its gunboats (see Chapter 11). Many small-country members at the Round were inactive, and only joined GATT to gain a few MFN benefits, because of Cold War era inducements by the USA or through compulsion under IMF/World Bank loan conditionalities. For much of the Round the USA and the EC held their own mini-round and their mutual intransigence, especially over agriculture and specifically a long-running dispute over oil seeds, stalled the Uruguay Round for some time. Completion of the Round was in the end facilitated by the so-called Blair House (Washington) accords under which the EC conceded greater protection cuts in agriculture and the USA agreed not to push for elimination of EC domestic film and television quotas. Also, a July 1993 G7 Summit agreed on a programme of tariff cuts to be incorporated into the Uruguay Round and urged that the negotiations be completed soon.[11]

The Round was finalised on 15 December 1993 and signed in the Moroccan city of Marrakesh on 15 April 1994. About 125 countries had participated at least nominally in the Round, some 110 actively doing so and signing the Final Act at Marrakesh, though not all immediately signing the *WTO Agreement* itself. The 128 nations which were GATT members at the end of the Round were given two years to ratify the agreement. In fact most ratified it during 1994 with little domestic debate, though some countries, notably Japan and South Korea, said they would refuse to do so if the USA withheld ratification, and there was militant resistance in India. In the USA a post-election 'lame-duck' Congress ratified with an opt-out proviso (see Chapter 11). In Australia, one of the few countries in the world where the executive (Cabinet) may alone ratify external treaties (Sylvan in Alston and Chiam 1995: 113), the agreement was approved and seven pieces of enabling legislation were passed in late 1994 with virtually no public debate. The WTO came into existence on 1 January 1995 and co-existed with GATT for a year, whence the latter, as an organisation, passed into history. GATT is dead, long live the WTO!![12]

Conclusion

The fall and rise of GATT has been one of the surprising developments in a decade of historic surprises. The fall of GATT, culminating during the recessed early 1980s, was partly due to its own success at reducing world-wide tariff levels when most nations still wanted to be protectionist, for reasons which Free Traders attribute to greedy vested interests but which should be seen as multi-causal and at least partly justified. The revival of GATT was due variously to globalising economic forces, the emergence of organised corporate vested interests in global 'market access', the widespread conversion of many governments to Economic Rationalism, the adoption of 'outward-looking' development strategies by many countries, including Australia, and pressure on Third World countries by First World institutions to de-regulate their economies and join GATT. These factors resulted in a 'Geneva consensus' that GATT needed reviving and the world needed a Free Trade Adventure.

The negotiation of the Uruguay Round was a complex affair in which a mélange of cross-cutting interests, coalitions and hidden agendas shaped the outcome, and which was dominated by the three Great Powers of the era, particularly the USA. A former Australian Ambassador to GATT has said that the Round 'belonged' to former USTR, Clayton Yeutter, and that its proceedings were driven by the USA with its crusading Free Trade fervour (Oxley 1990: ch. 5). So the Round was apparently successful and GATT lives on, reincarnated as the WTO, but not everyone is content with the outcome, as Part Two will indicate.

4

Towards a GATT-fearing World

The results of the Uruguay Round

The Final Act of the Uruguay Round is said to consist of 28 agreements, over 400 pages of script and 26 000 pages of appended schedules detailing just who has agreed to what, although it is actually a rather messy conglomeration of 19 agreements, 8 'understandings', 24 ministerial decisions and 3 declarations. The core document of the Final Act is the *Agreement Establishing the World Trade Organization* (hereinafter, *WTO Agreement*) and its three key annexes containing the crucial decisions of the Round.[1] In general the Final Act is written in reasonably accessible and sensible, though often rather inelegant, language. The Uruguay Round discussions employed 15 negotiating categories, each with its own working group, but to keep matters manageable I will summarise the outcome under eight headings: (a) tariffs and related matters; (b) NTBs and loopholes; (c) technical aspects of trade; (d) trade-related investment measures (TRIMs); (e) trade-related intellectual property rights (TRIPs); (f) the General Agreement on Trade in Services (GATS); (g) the plurilateral agreements; (h) the functioning of the GATT system (FOGS).

THE URUGUAY ROUND IN BRIEF

a Tariffs and other protection reductions
  • Textiles, clothing and agriculture integrated fully into GATT.

49

- Textile and clothing tariffs cut by 22 per cent; other market access concessions.
- Agriculture quotas to be 'tariffed', tariffs then to be cut by 36 per cent (24 per cent for developing countries), market access restrictions reduced, a minimum market access of 5 per cent required; export subsidies and domestic assistance to be cut.
- Industrial tariffs of OECD countries to be cut by 38 per cent to an average of 3.9 per cent; 43 per cent of all imports to be admitted duty free; most tariff levels to be bound; some reductions in tariff 'escalation'; free trade in 11 key sectors within a decade.

b **NTBs and loopholes**
- VERs and certain other NTBs eliminated.
- Subsidies: export or local content assistance outlawed ('red light'); subsidies which significantly affect another country restricted and actionable ('yellow light'); research, environmental or other generally applicable subsidies permitted for five years ('green light').
- Anti-dumping and countervailing duties: more restrictive rules for application and investigation.
- Safeguards: conditions restricted but still permissible via temporary tariffs.

c **Technical matters**
- Customs valuation, inspection and licensing procedures to be streamlined; rules of origin to be harmonised.
- Technical barriers (specifications, standards, labelling etc.) to be harmonised internationally, made transparent, based on 'scientific' principles and minimally trade restrictive.
- Sanitary and Phytosanitary (food, human, plant and animal) standards to entail similar principles.
- Standards to be set by three international advisory bodies.

d **Trade-related investment measures (TRIMs)**
- Restrictions on foreign investors such as local input quotas, limitations on imported components, trade balancing

measures etc. outlawed and actionable through the WTO.

e **Trade-related intellectual property rights (TRIPs)**
  • Establishes unprecedented global rules for all key IPRs; developing countries have 10 years' grace.
  • Protection periods are: copyright, databases and computer programs (50 years); trade marks (7 years); industrial designs (10 years); patents (20 years) and trade secrets (indefinite).
  • TRIPs disputes are subject to WTO disputes-settlement procedures, including possible retaliation.

f **Services**
  • An unprecedented new agreement (GATS) covers all commercial services for the first time in history.
  • All basic GATT principles apply to all services and to four modes of provision, but in several different ways: transparency and progressive liberalisation apply to all members; MFN applies on a 'negative list' basis; 'National Treatment' and 'market access' apply on a 'positive list' basis (see Glossary).
  • In scheduled sectors, government regulatory capacity, including the right to limit foreign investment, is curtailed.
  • Special agreements and continuing negotiations for finance, telecommunications, maritime transport and aviation.

g **Plurilateral agreements**
  • Extensions of Tokyo Round agreements on bovine meat, dairy, civil aircraft and government procurement.
  • Government procurement agreement now covers more sectors and public entities than before and enhances rights of foreign tenderers.
  • These agreements are signed voluntarily but binding on signatories.

h **Functioning of the GATT system (FOGS)**
  • New system a 'three-legged stool'—the WTO as seat, with GATT, GATS and TRIPs as legs.

- WTO replaces GATT Secretariat and has comparable legal status to UN.
- GATT remains as an agreement covering goods and providing key trade principles.
- All WTO members must accept all Final Act agreements of Uruguay Round except plurilateral agreements.
- Voting procedures rationalised: general decisions, simple majority; waivers and interpretations, 3/4 majority; amendments, 2/3 majority or unanimity to change voting rules.
- Disputes panel reports adopted and implemented automatically unless there is unanimity against doing so.
- Cross-retaliation allowable for rule-breaches.

The generally stated, though not unanimously espoused, goals of the Round were: to halt and 'roll back' the rising tide of protectionism by absorbtion of agriculture and textiles more fully into the GATT orbit, by negotiating a new round of tariff reductions, by eliminating or restricting selected NTBs and by increasing the levels of most bindings; to make GATT rules more effective through closing or tightening various loopholes; to make the GATT system more universal, in contradistinction to the Tokyo Round system of voluntary codes; to include investment, services and intellectual property in GATT, thereby applying multilateral trade rules to almost all trading activity; to devise a more formal structure and effective dispute-handling system for GATT; and generally to increase world-wide 'market access' (see Glossary) through reductions in all forms of protection and through commitments by all participating countries to eliminating at least some access restrictions. In short, the central aim was to re-construct GATT along the lines of the new model free trade agreement (see Chapter 1) and to lay the foundations for continuing and accelerating long-term liberalisation. By and large these goals were achieved, though with some qualifications which will be noted below or in later chapters. The following account of the Round's achievements is largely confined to description, with more extensive analysis of some areas in Part Two.

(a) Ta ta to tariffs (almost)

The most comprehensive, complex and contentious area of the Round involved the coverage and level of general protection, particularly tariffs, resulting in three main outcomes—the phasing out of the MFA, or the 'brothel in the cathedral' system (see p. 36 above), the fuller integration of textiles and clothing into GATT, the complete coverage of agriculture by GATT and the general reduction of all goods' tariffs by an average of a third. Most parts of the Round are to be implemented over a 6–10-year period.

Under the *Agreement on Textiles and Clothing* the MFA quota system, which limited world exports of these products (see previous chapter), is to be phased out over a ten-year period from 1 January 1995 in three roughly equal stages, and non-MFA protection gradually eliminated. Market access into restrictive countries is to be gradually increased through measures such as the raising of import growth ceilings in each phase, the abolition of various NTBs, a doubling of duty-free admissions, tariff reductions of 22 per cent by industrial countries and increased tariff bindings, though some transitional safeguards are to be allowed. A Textile Monitoring Board will oversee the integration, handle disputes arising therefrom and register all members' protective practices and transitional safeguards. Some commentators and Third World countries are concerned that the transitional safeguards may be abused, that the ability of countries to select the sequence of items liberalised will slow the process, that the inclusion of traditionally low-protection items such as belts and umbrellas in the new definition of textiles will enable importers to fudge protection reduction targets and that overall protection levels are to remain high (see Table 4.1). On the other hand, the *Agreement* will clearly integrate textiles and clothing into GATT, thus subjecting the sector to all future multilateral trade liberalisation negotiations (Cline 1995: 4–5; UNCTAD 1994b: ch. 5).

Negotiations on agriculture were among the most contentious of the Round, the final *Agreement on Agriculture* seeking reforms for a 'fair and market-oriented agricultural trading system', but with special consideration for poorer countries and for non-trade concerns such as food security, environmental protection or schemes for diversification from narcotic crops and the like. The key aims of the Agreement were to greatly reduce subsidies or other domestic support schemes which encourage over-production and limit market access; to convert most forms of residual protection to bound tariffs (so-called 'tariffication'); to harmonise world food and agricultural standards under a separate sanitary and phytosanitary agreement (see Section c below); and generally to establish quantitative rules where agricultural disciplines had become weak under the old GATT.

The core of the *Agreement on Agriculture* is in three parts— increases in market access, reduction in export subsidies and limitation of domestic support systems—and is to be phased in over six years (from 1995) for developed countries and ten years for developing countries, with least developed countries exempted from these requirements. The market access provisions require the elimination of all NTBs (including VERs, the Japanese ban on rice imports etc.) and their conversion to tariffs, with tariff rates thence to be reduced by an average of 36 per cent from 1986 levels and by a minimum of 15 per cent for each tariff item (24 per cent and 10 per cent respectively for developing countries) and bound at those levels. All countries are to eventually allow imports a minimum market share of 5 per cent, with Japan's minimum market access for rice to rise from 0 to 8 per cent and South Korea's to 4 per cent. A complex but modest safeguards clause is provided by Article 5 whereby additional duties (up to a maximum of one-third) may be applied when the import share of a product reaches a trigger level or when import prices fall below a trigger level. Agricultural export subsidies are to be cut from their 1986–90 levels, over a 6-year period, by 36 per cent in value terms (24 per cent for developing countries) and 21 per cent in quantity terms (14 per cent for developing countries), then bound at that level. Some areas will have larger cuts, e.g. 88 per cent for US rice subsidies.

In the case of domestic agricultural subsidies and income support schemes, or so-called 'amber box' measures, Article 6 of the *Agreement on Agriculture* establishes the concept of an Aggregate Measurement of Support (AMS), which is the current budgetary expenditure on these items. Over the implementation period all member countries (except the 'least developed') are to reduce their

AMS from the average 1986–88 level by 20 per cent (13 per cent for developing countries), with some credit for AMS reductions made since 1986. Each government may decide which measures within the AMS total are to be reduced, but the reduced AMS total may not be increased again after the implementation period. The *Agreement* rather generously excludes from the AMS, and thus from reduction obligations, various so-called 'green-box' (non-countervailable) and 'blue-box' (countervailable) measures including: assistance which is less than 5 per cent of the value of production (10 per cent for developing countries), payments for limiting output, income support unrelated to production, drought or other emergency relief, regional development programmes, infrastructure support, research, disease control, extension and advisory services, environmental programmes, food security policies and so forth (Article 6 and Annex 2). These are exempt on the grounds that they are not particularly trade-distorting so long as they do not entail price supports to farmers and are paid for by governments, not consumers. A Committee on Agriculture is to administer the implementation process.

Most commentators believe that the *Agreement on Agriculture* will succeed in liberalising farm trade and particularly benefit Third World countries, even if modestly so. On the other hand, many Free Traders and Third World interests fear that Western countries will manage to retain existing protection levels via loopholes such as: the discretion governments have in selecting components of the AMS to be reduced; the exemptions allowed; manipulation of the way they propose to convert quotas and NTBs to tariffs, or so-called 'dirty tariffication' (see Glossary); the base period chosen (1986–88) whence prices were low so that tariff equivalents will be high; the arbitrary setting of high binding levels which give room for 'tariff-creep'. However, the agreement ensures that agricultural trade is now subject to rules and to inclusion in future WTO rounds.

Tariff reductions in all other industrial sectors are detailed in the 26 000 pages of annexes of the Final Act, and member countries are to make their agreed tariff reductions in five equal annual instalments as of 1 January 1995, from 1986 base rates. The industrial countries agreed to tariff reductions averaging 38 per cent across all product categories, thus reducing average duties from 6.3 per cent

Table 4.1: Tariff reductions of developed countries by industrial product group (excluding petroleum)

Product Category	Import Value US$b	Average Tariff*			Duty-Free†	
		Pre-	Post-	Reduction	Pre-	Post-
All industrial products (excluding petroleum)	736.9	6.3	3.9	38	20	43
Textiles and clothing	66.4	15.5	12.1	22	2	4
Metals	69.4	3.7	1.5	59	36	70
Mineral products, precious stones and metals	72.9	2.3	1.1	52	59	81
Electric machinery	86.0	6.6	3.5	47	5	30
Leather, rubber, footwear & travel goods	31.7	8.9	7.3	18	16	19
Wood, pulp, paper & furniture	40.6	3.5	1.1	69	50	84
Fish & fish products	18.5	6.1	4.5	26	21	24
Non-electric machinery	118.1	4.8	2.0	58	11	48
Chemicals & photographic supplies	61.0	6.7	3.9	42	14	34
Transport equipment	96.3	7.5	5.8	23	16	21
Manufactured articles n.e.s.	76.1	5.5	2.4	56	15	49

Notes: * Average tariff is the standard *ad valorem* rate, i.e. the tariff duty in that industry as a percentage of import value; the reduction is the percentage by which these tariff rates were reduced by the Round.

† Duty-Free refers to the percentage of imports admitted without tariffs pre- and post-Uruguay.

Source: *News of the Uruguay Round*, GATT, Geneva, April 1994, from Tables 5 and 6

before the Round to 3.9 per cent. The proportion of imports admitted duty free is to rise from 20 to 43 per cent, though with considerable variation across product categories (see Table 4.1). Many Third World countries also agreed to reduce tariff levels, but to a lesser extent. Tariff bindings were massively increased, so that only in parts of Africa and Asia will there be much less than 100 per cent binding, either in terms of tariff lines bound or the share of imports under bound rates. Some reduction in tariff escalation was also agreed to, this being the practice of placing higher duties on more processed products, a system which many Third World nations and resource-producing countries like Australia see as a bar to their industrial development.

Although the Uruguay Round was not a full-blown free trade agreement, by early next century tariffs in most industries other than agriculture will be minimal and will probably be unable to offer any meaningful protection against imports. In some sectors tariffs will actually be a thing of the past, the world's major trading countries having agreed to eliminate, over a 10-year period, all tariffs in the following sectors: steel, pharmaceuticals, construction, medical and farm equipment, furniture, wood, toys, paper, beer and spirits, along with low, harmonised tariffs in the chemical industry. Further, with near-universal binding, these levels cannot be readily raised again. As a result of the Uruguay Round and contemporaneous bilateral negotiations with twenty-five countries, Australia will soon have duty-free market access for half our exports and secure binding for 86 per cent, while most of our exports will face tariff rates of only about 2 per cent. Our coal exports are likely to be greatly boosted, by up to A$1b per annum, through reduced domestic production subsidies in the EU and elsewhere (DFAT 1994b). By early next century we will be living in a minimal tariff world, some implications of which will be discussed in Chapter 8.

(b) Away with all loopholes

The framers of the Uruguay Round were anxious to ensure that such substantial tariff cuts were not circumvented, as in the past, via NTBs or misused safeguard measures. A series of agreements and understandings was therefore aimed at outlawing many NTBs, notably VERs and some subsidies, while tightening loopholes such as anti-dumping or countervailing duties and safeguard clauses.

The Agreement on Subsidies and Countervailing Measures

Subsidies had always been a problem for GATT, there being two broad types—export subsidies, which directly affect trade, and general domestic subsidies, which may or may not affect trade depending on how they are targeted. GATT94 had no more than cautioned against subsidies, while later amendments discouraged price-reducing measures or those which might give a country more than an 'equitable share' of agricultural exports (Croome 1995: 70ff.). The Tokyo Round subsidies code outlawed non-agricultural export subsidies and disciplined domestic subsidies, but this was only signed by twenty-seven GATT members and did not apply to developing countries. Domestic subsidies were, in principle, notifiable and actionable, but at no stage had 'subsidy' been defined and in practice disputes over such matters were rare.

The Uruguay Round *Subsidies Agreement*, covering all non-agricultural sectors, begins by rather awkwardly defining a subsidy as an actual or potential transfer of goods, services or funds (including grants, loans, equity infusions etc.) to an industry by a government, public body or commissioned private organisation involving foregone revenue, and in a way that confers a benefit. Income or price support schemes and government purchases are also defined as subsidies, but general infrastructure expenditures are not. Both industry-specific export subsidies and trade-affecting domestic subsidies are covered by the Agreement, while general tax measures are not. Third World and 'transitional' (ex-Soviet bloc) countries are covered but are given a more lenient subsidy-reduction programme and timetable. At first US negotiators had pushed for the outlawing of all types of subsidies, both the export and domestic varieties, on the grounds that the USA made less use of subsidies than other countries, and had argued for a very broad definition. However, the EU, the Nordic nations, Canada, India and other subsidy-using nations argued for a narrow definition, pressing strongly for plenty of permissible categories, and during the Round the USA itself swung to at least some permissibility after certain high technology and joint government-business projects were adopted by the Clinton Administration (GAO 1994: 55–6; Croome 1995: 200ff.; Cline 1995: 8–9).

The final version of the *Agreement* adopted what has been called a 'traffic lights' system involving three categories of subsidies and remedies. The first category, prohibited or 'red light' subsidies, covers any which specifically seek to enhance exports or which are contingent upon the use of local content in preference to imports, and these must be phased out within three years from 1 January 1995 (eight years for 'developing countries', with the 'least developed' exempted). Examples specified include all direct export subsidies, direct or indirect tax concessions for exporters, transport or freight charge concessions, export credit guarantees, export insurance programmes, currency retention schemes and so forth. The second category, 'actionable' or 'yellow light' subsidies, includes any measure which 'injures' another country's exports or prejudices another country's interests. Subsidies whose value is more than 5 per cent of the recipient firm's sales, assistance for firms or industries to cover operating losses and write-offs of government debt are specified as prejudicial to other countries (Article 6.1 and Annex IV), although this provision does not apply to the civil aircraft industry and is to be reviewed with a view to abolition after five years (Article 31). Sector-specific assistance, such as Australia's current bounty on computer production, will probably remain GATT-legal but actionable, as was the case under the old GATT94. Complainant countries may raise 'yellow light' measures with the subsidising country and after sixty days of unsuccessful negotiation take the matter to the WTO's Dispute Settlement Body. If a disputes panel finds against the subsidy the complainant may take counter-measures, probably in the form of reduced tariff concessions or countervailing duties (Article 7).

The third category—unrestricted, or 'green light' subsidies— is 'non-actionable', which means that these measures cannot be challenged through the WTO disputes panel. This category includes four classes of measures—general subsidies which are not specific to an industry, such as general tax concessions; assistance for private contract-based research up to 75 per cent of research costs and 50 per cent of 'pre-competitive development' costs; assistance to disadvantaged regions where criteria such as per capita income (at least 15 per cent below the territory average) or unemployment (at least 10 per cent above the territory average) clearly indicate disadvantage; and assistance to adapt plant and equipment to new environment requirements, up to 20 per cent of the cost, so long as this does not confer any manufacturing cost savings. However, non-actionable subsidies must be reported to the WTO prior to implementation and may be subject to challenge by other countries where 'serious adverse trade effects' have allegedly resulted. Research subsidies are to be reviewed after nineteen months and all 'green light' measures after five years, possibly with these becoming actionable ('yellow light') unless otherwise negotiated.[2]

The *Agreement on Subsidies and Countervailing Measures* also seeks to tighten up on the use of potentially protectionist countervailing measures, traditionally used as a 'defence' against other countries' subsidies, by providing clear guidelines for investigations, specific formulae for the calculation of countervailing duties, a time limit of eighteen months for investigations and a 5-year maximum for duties. A committee has been created to administer subsidies and countervailing measures, along with a Permanent Group of Experts appointed by the committee to advise dispute panels. The final agreement was a compromise between countries which wished to minimise the world-wide plethora of subsidies and those wishing to retain the right of subsidisation. Only time will tell how the *Subsidies Agreement* may be implemented and interpreted by national authorities and WTO panels, but it would seem to have made some inroads into the flexibility of governments to use a key traditional form of industry policy.

Anti-dumping

Anti-dumping measures, another alleged surreptitious channel for protectionism, are dealt with in the *Agreement on Implementation of Article VI of the General Agreement on Tariffs and Trade 1994 (Anti-Dumping Agreement)*. Article VI of GATT rather vaguely defined dumping as occurring when export prices are less than 'the comparable price in the ordinary course of trade' and permitted duties equivalent to this 'dumping margin', but did not detail how anti-dumping investigations were to be conducted. This led to messy, inconsistent usage of anti-dumping provisions, although the Tokyo Round tightened the rules a little. Some economists query the rationality of dumping, and thus the validity of anti-dumping, on grounds that a firm cannot export below cost indefinitely. Most agree, however, that dumping is unfair and disruptive where it constitutes price discrimination, where it takes the form of 'predatory pricing' to gain a foothold in a market, where intermittent dumping of surpluses de-stabilises other countries' markets or where certain 'non-economic' effects occur. On the other hand, the concern is that anti-dumping remedies may be exploited for protectionist purposes, especially where tests for 'injury' from dumping are lax, or may be used to harass importers. Trade economists tend to assume that those countries which heavily use anti-dumping measures, notably the USA, Australia, Canada and the EU, are indeed being protectionist (see Trebilcock and Howse 1995: ch. 5). However, research on Australian anti-dumping processes by Melbourne economists Feaver and Wilson suggests that, although these do not conform well to GATT requirements, they are not particularly protectionist and at one point in the process may even be slightly disadvantageous to domestic applicants.[3]

The Uruguay Round *Anti-Dumping Agreement* seeks to tighten rules for investigations, to make the criteria for determining injury more transparent and to formalise procedures for determining and imposing duties. Investigations of 'injury' must be fair, cover a wide range of criteria and consider other factors which might be causing the injury. Applications for investigation must be very detailed, while complainant firms should represent more than half the output of the domestic industry and not less than a quarter, meaning that there must be a substantial industry-wide consensus for an investigation to be undertaken. An investigation should not proceed if the dumping margin is less than 2 per cent of the export price or if the volume of the allegedly dumped goods is less than 3 per cent of imports. The agreement also requires that 'all interested parties', including consumer organisations, have the opportunity to make submissions to an investigation (Article 6.2), which is the first time such a provision has been included in the GATT system, although consumer groups suspect that the terms would be laid down by the investigating body (Evans 1994: 74).

Anti-dumping duties are to follow a formula which some think may favour potential dumpers more than in the past by, for instance, requiring that start-up costs be allowed for and that weighted average costs of various exporters be considered (Article 2). The duties are not to exceed the dumping margin and should be less if that would suffice to remove the injury to a domestic industry. An anti-dumping investigation must take no longer than eighteen months and duties must be terminated after five years unless a review deems them to be still required, though provisional duties or bonds are allowed. It will be some time yet before the effects of these changes become clear, but some commentators believe that they will make it more difficult for local producers to resist dumping, especially as paperwork requirements have been increased (e.g. Webb 1994), while many Free Traders fear that the computational systems prescribed by the new agreement, many deriving from US and EU law, remain lax and will continue to foster protectionism.[4]

Safeguards and NTBs

Safeguards are one of the more controversial components of GATT. Article XIX of GATT94 allows members to use temporary protection where 'unforseen developments' or prior trade concessions threaten domestic industries or result in proven injury thereto, while Articles XII and XVIII(B) permit similar safeguards for balance of payments purposes. The rationale of these provisions is said to be for allowance of a breathing space while industries adapt or scale down in the face of import competition from countries with comparative advantage in the product concerned. Unlike anti-dumping and countervailing duties, safeguards are not meant to compensate for trade distortions or market failures, which has led some Free Traders to deem them 'ordinary protection' or even 'legalised backsliding' (Finger 1995), although most economists regard them as a tolerable minor escape clause and as a pragmatic price for negotiating trade agreements. Indeed safeguards remain integral even to new model free trade agreements and are included in most RTAs. GATT's own view of safeguards clauses is that these serve to direct protectionist temptations into disciplined, limited channels.

In the event, however, Article XIX appears to have proved too constraining, particularly in its consultation requirements, its allowance of compensation claims by affected countries and its insistence that safeguards be applied in a non-discriminatory (MFN) manner. It is generally believed that governments have avoided Article XIX because of possible compensation costs and because the MFN requirements meant that all exporting countries would be affected by an action even if one single country was the source of the import 'surges' concerned. Instead many countries have resorted to the less detectable but more damaging expedients of anti-dumping measures, VERs and all manner of other NTBs.[5]

The Uruguay Round *Agreement on Safeguards* was therefore designed as a curious sort of trade-off in which the safeguards clause was loosened a little, i.e. to encourage slightly *more* short-term protectionism, in exchange for clamping down on NTBs, the hope being that WTO members will henceforth switch to well-behaved safeguards. The *Agreement* calls for the phasing-out of all VERs within four years, though each member may 'grandfather' (retain) one for an extra year, and it bans any new VERs, orderly marketing arrangements or other similar measures (Article 11). Comparable private sector deals and *Keiretsu*-type arrangements are not affected, although these are *not* to be *encouraged* by governments (Article 11.3) as has happened in many countries (see Chapter 3). New rules are laid down for the formulation of safeguards. A public enquiry must be held into whether or not an industry is being seriously 'injured' by an import surge, procedures must be transparent, other possible causes of injury must be examined and a wide range of 'injury' criteria must be considered, although less thoroughly investigated provisional measures are permitted for up to 200 days (Article 6).

The types of safeguard measures which may be taken are not specified but quotas and temporary tariffs are implied. These measures are normally to be operational for up to four years, with a maximum of eight (ten for developing countries), they are to be relaxed over time if possible and they are not to be re-applied for at least two years after expiry. The compensation deterrence problem (see above) has been alleviated by not allowing affected countries to seek compensation for three years after initiation of the safeguards (Article 8.3), and although any quotas used should not be selective between countries, temporary departure from this rule is allowed when imports from a particular country have 'increased in disproportionate percentage'. There is a fear in Third World circles that the new safeguards system might result in the re-introduction of VERs through the back door (UNCTAD 1994b: ch. 2), although this seems unlikely, and safeguard measures may not be used against imports from developing countries where these constitute less than

3 per cent of total imports per country or 9 per cent collectively (Article 9). The *Agreement* is to be administered by a WTO Committee on Safeguards and member countries must notify the Committee of all laws, regulations and administrative procedures relating to safeguard measures, failing which other countries may do so, which could be called a 'dob-in' clause (Article 12:6).

The other area of safeguards, those relating to measures taken for balance of payments reasons under Article XII of GATT94, are now covered by the Uruguay Round's *Understanding on the Balance-of-Payments Provisions of the General Agreement on Tariffs and Trade 1994*. Measures may be taken to rectify a balance of payments deficit so long as these are generalised, not directed against particular imports, and do not exceed what is required to reverse the imbalance. The preferred forms of protection are 'price-based measures' such as import surcharges, import deposit requirements and temporary increases in tariffs, including bound tariffs if required, but quantitative restrictions are to be avoided unless it can be shown that price-based measures are inadequate. No time limit is imposed but it can be assumed that, as under GATT94 Article XII, the emergency measures are only to be used while the imbalance lasts and measures must be reported to the WTO. Such safeguards are now seldom used by OECD countries because they are thought unnecessary with floating exchange rates (safeguards are for *payments* imbalances not *trade* deficits), but they are still commonly used by Third World countries (under Article XVIIIB of GATT94).

In conclusion, the Uruguay Round has generally tightened up the various loopholes and escape hatches of the old GATT, but not to the complete satisfaction of Free Traders who believe that anti-dumping and safeguard provisions could continue to be misused. On the other hand, many trade interventionists fear that the 'loopholes', which they tend to see as legitimate flexibility clauses, may have been tightened too much, especially in the case of subsidies where the possibility of activist industry policy may have been greatly impaired. In my view this section of the Final Act has struck a sensible balance between liberalisation, rationalisation and maintenance of legitimate escape clauses, which most governments clearly want retained, although I concur that the *Subsidies Agreement* will probably limit industry policy options and should be reviewed at some future date.

(c) Down with technical barriers

A major new impetus of the Uruguay Round was the international harmonisation of various practices and technical matters relating to trade. This was promoted on the grounds that differences in such practices between countries can cause unlevel playing fields, impede trade, or even be used for surreptitious protectionism. Some of the new agreements, notably those on customs valuation, pre-shipment inspection and import-licensing procedures, are aimed at improved efficiency or stemming corruption and are not controversial. The *Agreement on Rules of Origin* relates to the proportion of a product which is required to be produced in, say, Australia to be deemed Australian and thus not subject to duty. The issue relates mainly to preferential systems, such as regional trade agreements (RTAs), but as tight rules of origin can be protectionist the agreement seeks to harmonise rules and procedures. Article 9 proposes that the country of origin be deemed to be either that whence the good was wholly obtained or that where 'the last substantial transformation has been carried out', which would allow a product labelled 'Made in Australia' to consist predominantly of imported, possibly lower quality, inputs, and which critics fear could adversely affect our consumption or export standards (Webb 1994). Discussions on the issue are continuing and product classifications are being reviewed.

A more controversial measure, the *Agreement on Technical Barriers to Trade* (*TBT Agreement*), seeks to harmonise internationally a wide range of technical regulations such as product standards, packaging provisions, marking or labelling requirements, assessment procedures and so forth, 'on as wide a basis as possible' for all industrial and agricultural products. The formulation of technical regulations must minimise 'unnecessary obstacles to international trade', must be based on the 'best available' scientific and technical information and should be no stricter than is necessary to ensure adequate standards (Articles 2–5). National governments must ensure that sub-central governments and non-government bodies comply with these rules, must maintain a central 'enquiry point' for standardised regulations, should conduct regular 'conformity assessment procedures' and should join appropriate international standardising bodies.

Product requirements are to be specified 'in terms of performance rather than design or descriptive characteristics' (Article 2.2–8), which some critics fear may prevent action against environmentally damaging production processes, and the agreement as a whole applies to products, processes and production methods (Annex 1:1). Each country may set its own standards for the 'protection of human, animal or plant life or health, or the environment', for the prevention of 'deceptive practices' or for security purposes (Preamble), so long as these do not constitute 'arbitrary or unjustifiable discrimination between countries'. A country's risk assessment procedures must be 'scientific' and other countries' differing standards must be accepted where these meet domestic requirements adequately, a concept known as 'equivalence'—Article 2.2–7 (see Chapter 10).

Closely linked to the *TBT Agreement* is the *Agreement on the Application of Sanitary and Phytosanitary Measures (SPS Agreement)*, which covers matters such as human, plant and animal health, quarantine measures and food standards, including pesticide residue levels and so forth. Its theory and provisions are similar to those of the *TBT Agreement*, encouraging WTO members gradually to harmonise all standards and requiring that these not discriminate between countries or be applied in a way which unduly impedes trade (Article 4). Countries can only maintain standards above the harmonised international norm if there is adequate 'scientific justification' (Article 3), although it is permissible to adopt a 'provisional' standard until full scientific information can be obtained (Article 5.7). For purposes of the *TBT* and *SPS Agreements* WTO standards are to be set mainly by three hitherto rather obscure international bodies, the Codex Alimentarius Commission (Codex) for food standards, the International Office of Epizootics for animal health and the Secretariat of the International Plant Protection Convention for plant matters, which are to become key multilateral standard-setting and advisory bodies.

In sum, this group of agreements in the Uruguay Round Final Act constitutes a probably unprecedented attempt to develop harmonised global technical standards for purposes of reducing alleged impediments to trade. Officially the agreements allow for national flexibility and do not seek rigid uniformity, but some commentators fear that the standards harmonisation process could spark a 'race to the bottom' in a competitive globalising world (see Chapter 10).

(d) TRIMmed at the edges

One brief, innocuous-sounding component of the Final Act, the *Agreement on Trade-Related Investment Measures* (TRIMs), has stirred up a storm of controversy, at least in Third World and NGO circles. Although the ill-fated ITO was to cover investment matters (see Chapter 2), GATT has never done so directly. Investment has always been a sensitive issue, with Free Traders and TNC interests regularly pressing for reduced national controls, but with most Third World countries, NGOs, left-wing activists and so forth favouring, often passionately, the control of DFI for a variety of social and national sovereignty reasons. It has been suggested that the inclusion of investment in the Round was in response to international pressure for rules on private property rights (UNCTAD 1994b: 4).

The USA, home to a vast array of TNCs, initially sought to include in the Uruguay Round measures which would greatly liberalise national controls on DFI, but this was implacably opposed by many Third World delegations, notably India and Mexico. However, a curious convergence occurred as liberalising regimes came to power in some Third World countries during the Round, while in the USA itself a surge of DFI led to a few new restrictions and moves by Congress for extensive controls. Some countries (the EC, Argentina, Singapore and many other Third World members) wanted to focus only on effects, not the measures themselves, and to rely on existing GATT provisions, notably Article XXIII which has occasionally been used to disallow certain TRIMs, while others, notably the USA and Switzerland, wanted most trade-distorting TRIMs outlawed. The eventual compromise was that only measures affecting trade would be included as GATT was primarily a trade agreement.

There are two types of TRIMs: 'positive' (e.g. tax concessions to attract DFI) and 'negative' (requirements placed on DFI), although many are a bit of both; that is, 'carrots' for DFI plus 'sticks' for performance requirements. The latter include requirements that TNC investors use a quota of local inputs, limit the use of imported components, match foreign exchange usage to the volume of exchange generated, use a quota of local equity, adopt local labour hiring targets, employ a quota of local managers, conduct a quota of R and D locally, generate a quota of exports and so forth. Many OECD nations and most Third World countries have used TRIMs extensively for a variety of foreign exchange, industry policy and developmental purposes, and their use of these measures appears to have risen, along with other NTBs, as tariffs were reduced under GATT. The concern of Free Traders is that TRIMs may distort trade and investment flows, thus adversely affecting the global strategies of TNCs, although many Third World countries and NGOs see this as a perfectly legitimate and desirable goal.

The final *TRIMs Agreement* was a rather mild compromise, prohibiting only those goods-related TRIMs deemed inconsistent with GATT94 Articles III (National Treatment) and XI (elimination of quantitative restrictions on imports). An appended 'illustrative list' prohibits local content requirements, export linkages, trade or foreign exchange balancing measures and limitations on imported inputs, although it has been suggested that export performance requirements, which are commonly used by Third World countries, may still be permissible (UNCTAD 1994b: 143). All such TRIMs are to be reported to the proposed Council for Trade in Goods, and are to be phased out within two years (five and seven for developing and least developed countries respectively).

Some claim that the agreement is biased towards TNCs insofar as 'positive' TRIMs, which are used by many OECD countries and favoured by TNCs, are not covered by the TRIMs agreement and are covered only in a limited way by the *Subsidies Agreement*, while many negative TRIMs, which are particularly used in the Third World and not favoured by TNCs, have been demolished (e.g. Evans 1994: 34ff.). This may prove true in practice, but in principle the *TRIMs Agreement* is primarily aimed at eliminating compulsory TRIMs which provide a trading advantage to the implementing country in breach of GATT's National Treatment rules, although developing countries may obtain some temporary exemptions. Nonetheless, mild though the *TRIMs Agreement* might be, many believe it to be the thin end of a wedge presaging an impetus for greater investment liberalisation (see Chapter 11).[6] Further, the agreement could rule out policy options such as controlled, conditional strategic alliances between government and TNCs for investment and job-creation purposes, a concept which is advocated even by some mainstream economists (e.g. Dore 1993).

(e) TRIPping the information revolution

Perhaps the most contentious and anomalous component of the Uruguay Round, the *Agreement on Trade-Related Intellectual Property Rights* (TRIPs) introduces IPRs into GATT for the first time, although the issue of counterfeiting was raised by the USA and the EC during the Tokyo Round. The inclusion of IPRs in a trade liberalisation agreement is anomalous because it adds rather than removes a form of protection, but these have become integral to the new model free trade agreement. Some commentators believe that the *TRIPs Agreement* was unnecessary as most of its functions have, for up to a century, been fulfilled by a series of international conventions such as the Paris Convention for patents, trade marks and designs, the Rome Convention for recording and broadcasting, the Berne Convention for copyright and the UN-based World Intellectual Property Organisation (WIPO) which administers these conventions and generally promotes IPRs.

The 32-page *TRIPs Agreement* states its purpose to be the creation of a '. . . multilateral framework of principles, rules and disciplines dealing with trade in counterfeit goods' and the reduction of 'tensions' through a multilateral disputes resolution procedure. It decrees that IPRs are private rights (Preamble) which are to be effectively and adequately protected by member countries on the basis of National Treatment and MFN, so long as these rights are not abused or used as a restraint on trade (Article 8).

The forms of IPRs protected by the agreement are copyright (including databases), computer programs (which are treated as literary works), trade marks, geographical indications (especially for wines, e.g. Burgundy etc.), industrial designs, patents, 'undisclosed information' (or trade secrets) and lay-out designs of integrated circuits. Copyright protection is generally to be for fifty years, trade mark protection for seven years and indefinitely renewable, industrial design protection for a minimum of ten years and integrated circuit design protection for ten to fifteen years. Trade secrets, apparently to be indefinitely protected from unfair disclosure, are a controversial addition to IPR conventions and their protection was strongly advocated by US technology companies wanting coverage for non-patentable research processes or for information submitted to government testing authorities.

Patents are to be for the generous period of twenty years, which is longer than currently offered by most countries, and cover virtually all inventions of both a product and process nature, the two being conjoined at the behest of pharmaceutical companies to combat the widespread practice of using process-only patenting to make cheap drugs (see Chapter 9). Governments may exclude certain products or processes from patentability for moral, health or environmental reasons so long as this is not done just because the commercial exploitation of the product or process is prohibited by its own laws; for example, an Islamic country may not prohibit an alcohol patent (Evans, 1994: 41). In other words, the exclusion must be for general reasons, not just for reasons of a country's own culture and identity. Diagnostic, therapeutic and surgical methods can also be excluded from patentability, as can natural plant and animal breeding, but most forms of biotechnology, awkwardly described in the agreement as 'micro-organisms (and) non-biological and microbiological processes' must be patentable. Although plant patenting, a heated issue in the Third World, is not required as such, plant varieties must be protected either by patenting or some *sui generis* (locally devised) system of similar effect. The inclusion of biotechnology and plant varieties had been strongly pressed for by pharmaceutical and agro-chemical TNCs, their endeavours being rewarded by Article 70.8 which requires the immediate registration of their patent applications pending the commencement of patenting.

TRIPs are to be administered by a Council for Trade-Related Aspects of Intellectual Property Rights and this body must be notified of all national TRIPs legislation. Trade mark counterfeiting or commercial copyright piracy must be made a criminal offence and national laws must provide for the seizure of goods made by, and equipment used for, production which infringes the *TRIPs Agree-*

ment (Article 61). Disputes are to be handled through the WTO disputes-settlement process, which includes the possibility of retaliatory action for breaches of the agreement. Least developed countries are to be given ten years grace before they need to implement the agreement, developing and transitional countries four years and all others just one year. Concerns about the *TRIPs Agreement* which are held by many commentators and social movements in the Third World and which have led to riots in parts of India, are complex and will be further discussed in Chapter 9.

(f) The getting of GATS

The greatest revolution of the Uruguay Round was the extension of GATT to services through the *General Agreement on Trade in Services* (GATS), a step which had been proposed by some business think-tanks and trade officials since the 1970s, pushed by the USA since the early 1980s, strenuously opposed by some Third World countries and finally adopted in a weak, compromise form (Drake and Nicolaidis 1992). GATS is a three-tiered agreement incorporating general rules, annexes on specific sectors and schedules of liberalisation commitments by member countries.

The rules section involves basic GATT principles of MFN, National Treatment, market access, transparency, safeguards, progressive liberalisation, integration of developing countries and dispute-settlement procedures, as well as some GATS-specific obligations and disciplines. The latter include rather mild provisions for restrictions on monopolies and uniform trade practices, non-discriminatory recognition of foreign professional qualifications, reduction of distortionary subsidies and commitments to negotiations for further liberalisation. However, some of these rules are applied in differing ways and certain disciplines are applicable only to services specifically scheduled for liberalisation (see Chapter 9).

The annexes section covers air transport, maritime transport, finance and telecommunications, mainly laying down general rules for liberalisation, although the annex on telecommunications contains the important provision (paragraph 5c) that overseas suppliers must have full access to a member country's telecommunications and information networks, with a few exceptions allowed. The schedules section lists those sectors which each country has agreed to liberalise, following many years of reciprocity-based bargaining, a process which is continuing in the four above-mentioned sectors.

GATS is to be administered by a Council for Trade in Services which must be notified annually of changes in relevant national laws and which deals with members' complaints about other members' regulations (under Article III.5, or what I call the 'dob-in' clause). Disputes are to be handled under general WTO mechanisms (see Chapter 11) but each country is also required to set up special tribunals to which aggrieved service suppliers may promptly appeal against any of a nation's legislative or administrative measures deemed to be impeding market access (Article V1.2). Being the first world-wide agreement in history to seek the liberalisation of services, trade and investment, GATS is a highly controversial document for reasons which will be discussed in Chapter 9.

(g) Of procurement and other matters

The Final Act included, in a separate annex, modified versions of four agreements first negotiated during the Tokyo Round, and these so-called 'plurilateral' agreements are the only component of the Uruguay Round which are voluntary; that is, the treaties are voluntarily entered but their provisions are binding for all signatories. The bovine meat, dairy and civil aircraft agreements were barely changed from the Tokyo Round, although the civil aircraft sector, a hot potato between the EU and the USA who agreed in 1992 on subsidy limits, is to be covered by most provisions of the Uruguay Round *Subsidies Agreement*.

Potentially the most far-reaching of these plurilateral treaties was the *Agreement on Government Procurement*. GATT47 did not require National Treatment obligations to apply to government procurement practices and so most member governments had established extensive domestic preferences in their purchasing policies. Free Trade purists consider this to be disguised protectionism, and with the rapid growth of public sectors the market has grown to hundreds of billions of dollars. The Tokyo Round code was thought to cover no more than about 10 per cent of public sector procurement in the few signatory countries, especially as sub-national governments and the military were excluded. The loudest grumbles were coming from the USA which claimed that it had opened up its procurement policies much more than other signatories, at one stage the EU and the USA having $15–20m of trade sanctions against each other. The chief target of US companies has been the $15b EC public telecommunications sector which is subject to extensive intra-Europe procurement regulations.

The final agreement greatly extended the Tokyo Round code to a wider range of government sectors, including services and construction, as well as to sub-central governments and public utilities, though on a reciprocal, not MFN, basis in order to prevent 'free riding'. There are new rules for government contracting, there are to be limits on 'offset' systems (which require foreign bidders to guarantee local content, local research etc.), there must be an appeal procedure against government procurement decisions and there is to be a code of legal rights for any foreign firms wishing to tender for government contracts. One paradoxical clause provides for compensation should privatisation of an entity deprive a private contractor of certain benefits. The agreement was signed by most of the original nineteen Tokyo Round signatories plus five newcomers, but Australia has not yet acceded. The WTO hopes to extend the agreement to all members, though the issue is a contentious one for the many countries in which domestic procurement preferences are a popular, and arguably legitimate, form of assistance for local industry.

(h) Lifting the FOGS

The shape of the new GATT was negotiated under the amusingly acronymed heading 'The Functioning of the GATT System' (FOGS). Concerns about the way the FOGS had evolved included: the uncertain legal status of GATT; fragmentation under the Tokyo Round system of voluntary codes; the ease with which waivers were obtainable; the ability of accused countries to veto panel decisions; the limitation of retaliation to the product category in dispute; and the generally slow-moving nature of GATT processes. These perceived deficiencies were addressed and largely rectified by the Uruguay Round. The nature of the new system was also in dispute, the EU and Canada pressing for a new body, akin to the original

ITO, which would limit the USA's use of economic gunboat diplomacy under Section 301 (Chapter 3), while the USA favoured a 'GATT II' or 'GATT Plus' model which would streamline GATT but leave Section 301 intact. The USA finally accepted the new body with the proviso that TRIPs and stronger discipline measures be included in its armoury (GAO 1994: ch. 3; Raghavan 1993).

The new FOGS can be characterised as what I call a 'three-legged stool' with very uneven legs. The seat of the stool is the WTO as enshrined in the *Agreement Establishing the World Trade Organization* (*WTO Agreement*), the core agreement of the Uruguay Round. The three legs represent the supposed key activities of world trade, i.e. goods (covered by both GATT94 and the Uruguay Round agreements), services (covered by GATS) and knowledge or IPRs (covered by the *TRIPs Agreement*). I suggest the legs are uneven because GATT itself, despite now being deemed a mere leg of the stool and technically only an annex of the *WTO Agreement*, remains a key document in international trade law and the repository of the system's basic principles. GATS is new, experimental and strictly sectoral, while the *TRIPs Agreement* covers only a small aspect of world trade, is controversial and arguably increases rather than reduces protection, so these are only minor legs. The WTO is to have a 'legal personality' equivalent to that of the UN, the IMF or the World Bank and to work more closely with the latter two bodies. Members are to accord the WTO the legal status necessary to fulfil its functions and grant its personnel the same privileges and immunities as those of the UN (Article VIII).

The preamble to the *WTO Agreement* opens by declaring, in language which will not win its drafters the Nobel literature prize, that the purpose of relations between WTO members entails:

> raising standards of living, ensuring full employment and a large and steadily growing volume of real income and effective demand, and expanding the production of and trade in goods and services, while allowing for the optimal rise of the world's resources in accordance with the objective of sustainable development, seeking both to protect the environment and to enhance the means for doing so in a manner consistent with their respective needs and concerns at different levels of economic development.

Later paragraphs indicate that it is to be the WTO's job to 'develop an integrated, more viable and durable multilateral trading system' in order to seek the above-quoted goals. Article 5 suggests that the WTO 'may' seek co-operative arrangements with 'non-governmental organisations', although no NGO sectors are specified and one Third World commentator has surmised that TNCs are more likely to be consulted than public interest groups (Raghavan 1990). Two innocent-sounding, but potentially far-reaching, clauses at the end of the agreement decree that the Final Act takes precedence over any other multilateral trade agreement and that 'each member shall ensure the conformity of its laws, regulations and administrative procedures' with all Uruguay Round agreements.[7]

WTO membership requires adherence to all Final Act agreements except the non-compulsory plurilateral group (Section g above) and submission of market access schedules for all goods and services. Upon fulfilling this requirement all 128 members of the old GATT automatically accede to the WTO, but new applicants require acceptance by two-thirds of the WTO membership, while aggrieved members may withdraw, upon six months notice. The extent to which GATT/WTO provisions prevail within a member country varies with domestic legal practices. The current EU practice is that GATT and other international agreements are 'self-executing' upon ratification and take precedence over national laws, whereas in the USA such agreements are not applicable until incorporated in enabling legislation and GATT is not deemed a full treaty (GAO 1994: 34).

Australian practice is similar to that of the USA, with GATT rules being used as a guide for legislation and a reference point for judicial deliberations rather than being incorporated in law as such, and with ratification by the Governor-in-Council (cabinet) alone once enabling legislation has been passed by both houses of parliament. A 1990 Federal Court decision held that national law overrides GATT provisions, although a 1995 High Court decision suggested that there was a legitimate expectation that treaties will be acted upon once ratified. Many Australian commentators are critical of executive-only ratification and some argue for Parliamentary approval before treaties are signed, a step which, at the time of writing, the Federal Government was proposing.[8] Some observers see treaties as a threat to national sovereignty, although, curiously, a few right-wing commentators are more worried about human rights or environmental treaties than the Uruguay Round,[9] the latter having, in my view, far more profound implications for sovereignty (see Chapter 11).

Conclusion

The Final Act of the Uruguay Round has laid the basis for a new world order which Free Traders like to characterise as an open, rules-based liberal trading system, albeit one which still falls short of complete free trade. The Round has cut tariffs, brought most economic activities into the WTO's multilateral orbit, tightened loopholes and formalised much of the old GATT's procedures. Many Free Traders forecast that anti-dumping provisions, safeguards and TBTs will continue to be exploited by protectionists in the post-Uruguay world and former Australian Ambassador to GATT, Alan Oxley, says the system is still like a Swiss cheese.[10] On the other hand, many trade interventionists, including myself, believe that the Round, whatever its sundry benefits, may already have gone too far towards a de-regulated order with too few questions asked, and may be the thin edge of an even more de-regulatory wedge. The WTO seems designed to match the market-opening, privatising, globalising trends of today's private enterprise-dominated world and it now has teeth with which to clinch its mission. If so, then it faces a controversial future.

5

There Goes the Neighbourhood!

The regional Free Trade Adventure

A new type of merger mania has hit the planet—the mania of regionalism. For most of GATT's lifetime regional trade agreements (RTAs) were rare and survival amongst those few even rarer, but GATT47 did allow for such a venture. In recent years there has been an explosion of RTA proposals, and the Free Trade Adventure is advancing more quickly regionally than globally. Of the several possible channels for liberalisation and integration noted in Chapter 1, unilateralism, bilateralism, regionalism and multilateralism, Free Traders like regionalism the least because RTAs have traditionally been preference-based, thus contravening the MFN principle, and in theory such systems may actually *reduce* economic welfare. Believers in the 'bicycle theory' (see Glossary and Chapter 1) heaved a sigh of relief when the Uruguay Round was safely signed because they feared a 'degeneration' of the world into inward-looking trade blocs, although a more ideologically sound form of 'open regionalism' has now been devised. In this chapter I will examine some of these concepts, a few examples of RTAs, and suggest some reasons different from those of the Free Traders as to why RTAs might not be a good idea.

Keeping it in the family

Of the seven possible 'steps' on the ladder of integration (see Box 5.1), most RTAs have attempted only the lower rungs although in

---

Box 5.1: The ladder of integration

1 Low level economic co-operation, e.g. co-ordination of technical standards, establishment of basic communications etc.

2 Preferential trading arrangements—partial liberalisation of trade between a, usually limited, group of countries who thus offer trade preferences to each other.

3 Free trade area—the elimination of trade (and perhaps other) barriers between a group of countries, but each maintaining existing barriers with other countries.

4 Customs union—a free trade area with the additional step of all members establishing common barriers (i.e. uniform customs duties etc.) against other countries.

5 Common market—the elimination of all barriers to the free flow of goods, services and resources (labour and capital) between the member countries; may or may not have common external tariffs.

6 Economic union—a common market with the additional step of unifying most economic policies, tax levels, legal systems, social policies, environmental and other technical standards and so forth, probably including the adoption of a common currency; often referred to as 'deep integration'.

7 Political union—an economically and politically integrated nation, usually as a federation, with varying degrees of integration possible.

---

the past some regions such as the German, American and Australian states, have taken all steps to become a united (usually federated) nation. Many early post-war RTAs failed or stagnated due to factors such as unequal benefits, mutual suspicions, political conflicts, diverging development goals, similarity rather than complementarity of each country's economies or because extra-bloc links became more significant than intra-bloc trade. However, the 1980s resurrection of regional-mania has been due variously to the perceived success of the EU, the conversion of the USA to regionalism from its earlier hostility and generally to a reductionist version of the Free Trade Adventure. Motives for seeking, and perceived benefits from, RTAs include the efficiencies and gains from trade hypothesised by Free Trade theory, economies of scale, opportunities for 'regional-scale infant industries', improved security and bargaining power for small countries, control of migration flows, political stability and so forth. Other, arguably more questionable, motives include the fear of being 'left out' of RTAs, or the 'domino effect' of regionalisation, and the desire of some governments to use external agreements for 'locking in' domestic liberalisation policies (see below).

Between 1947 and 1994 about a hundred RTAs were registered with GATT under Article XXIV and eleven under the 1970 Enabling Clause for Third World countries, forty of these in the 1990s alone, although this number includes extensions of or accessions to the EU and a variety of minor preferential arrangements. About eighty of these remain operative. Most RTAs take the first four forms in Box 5.1, especially free trade areas, a range of examples being listed in Box 5.2. Until the mid-1980s RTAs tended to cover only a limited range of issues, but thereafter many have been influenced by the US-inspired new model free trade agreement, extending their scope to investment, services, IPRs and so forth (WTO 1995a). Members must notify the WTO of any new or amended agreements into which they enter and in the past a 'working party' has scrutinised all proposals, although RTAs have seldom been formally approved by GATT. In February 1996 a single Committee on Regional Trade Agreements was established for this purpose, and RTAs are supposed to report regularly to this body. Today all WTO members belong to at least one RTA.[1]

Article XXIV of GATT94 exempts from MFN requirements any countries wishing to enter RTAs so long as these take the form of free trade areas or customs unions, cover 'substantially all trade in products' and do not increase barriers against non-participants. In practice few RTAs have conformed to even these limited guidelines and the Tokyo Round 'Enabling Clause' exempted developing countries from the requirements. Former GATT Director-General and drafter of the original Article XXIV, Oliver Long, has said that

Box 5.2: Examples of regional trade arrangements

Name or Countries	Date of Commencement or Proposal	Details
European Union (EU)	1957 and extended thereafter; monetary and political union agreed to in 1992 Maastricht Treaty	Economic union and proposed political federation—Austria, Belgium, Denmark, Finland, France, Germany, Greece, Ireland, Italy, Luxembourg, Netherlands, Portugal, Spain, Sweden, UK.
Central European Free Trade Agreement (CEFTA)	1993	Free trade area—Hungary, Poland, Czech Republic and Slovakia.
North American Free Trade Agreement (NAFTA)	1992	Free trade area—USA, Canada and Mexico, to be extended to Chile.
ASEAN Free Trade (AFTA)	Association of South East Asian Nations (ASEAN) 1967; AFTA 1992	Co-operation from 1967; Preferential trading arrangement from 1977; Proposed free trade area over 15 years from 1993, excluding agriculture and services— Brunei, Indonesia, Malaysia, The Philippines, Singapore, Thailand and Vietnam.
Asia–Pacific Economic Co-operation forum (APEC)	Proposed 1989, Secretariat 1992, Detailed goals, 1994 Scheduled completion, 2020	Proposed free trade area for goods and investment— AFTA, Australia, Canada, Chile, China, Hong Kong, Japan, Korea, Mexico, New Zealand, Papua New Guinea, Taiwan and USA.
Australia and New Zealand Closer Economic Relations Trade Agreement (ANZCERTA)	1983, with subsequent addenda	Common market—Australia and New Zealand.
Southern Cone Common Market (MERCOSUR)	1991, operational from 1995	Customs union—Argentina, Brazil, Paraguay and Uruguay.
Caribbean Community and Common Market (CARICOM)	1973, replacing 1966 predecessor	Common market—covering most Caribbean states.
Common Market for Eastern and Southern Africa (COMESA)	1996; supersedes earlier RTAs; to be implemented over ten years	Customs Union and partial common market; free movement of persons and

Name or Countries	Date of Commencement or Porposal	Details
		businesses—Angola, Burundi, Comoros, Eritrea, Ethiopia, Kenya, Lesotho, Malawi, Mauritius, Rwanda, Sudan, Swaziland, Tanzania, Uganda, Zaire, Zambia, Zimbabwe.
South Asian Association for Regional Co-operation —Preferential Trade Arrangement (SAPTA)	1993	Preferential trade arrangement—Bhutan, India, Maldives, Nepal, Pakistan and Sri Lanka.

Sources: WTO (1995a); Husted and Melvin (1995): 268–9; Ruggiero (1995): 13

the founders of GATT did not have in mind an RTA of the dimensions of the EU (Snape et al. 1993: 104), and it has even been suggested that the original EEC may have been GATT-illegal but that GATT 'blinked', which set a precedent for being soft on other RTA proposals (Hoekman 1995a: 52). Some commentators believe that RTAs have seldom been adequately investigated by GATT and only six of sixty-four RTA investigatory working parties have ever reached a consensus that the proposal in question was GATT-compatible, although no RTAs have been rejected (WTO 1995a: 3). A minor Uruguay Round agreement on RTA matters, the *Understanding on Article XXIV*, did little more than rationalise compensation calculations, give the WTO the job of estimating effects of RTAs and fill in a few gaps, such as specifying a period of ten years for full implementation of an RTA. The *Understanding* also urged that RTAs '. . . to the greatest possible extent avoid creating adverse effects on the trade of other members'.

Free Traders' concerns with RTAs stem from the latters' preferential nature and from the fact that whilst intra-bloc liberalisation might create new trade, some trade is also diverted from previous trading partners. In addition, various inefficiencies may arise, especially in the case of free trade areas which require rules of origin and other administrative devices to prevent imports sneaking in through the member country with the lowest barriers against non-bloc trade. The nett welfare effect of an RTA will depend on the balance between its trade 'creating' and 'diverting' effects, which in turn depends on a complex of factors such as: the comparative advantages involved; the initial levels of MFN tariffs in each member country; whether or not the bloc arrangements result in higher trade barriers against non-bloc countries; the openness of the bloc to new members; and the extent to which the bloc generates demand for imports from non-bloc countries.

Many Free Traders fear the proliferation of inward-looking, trade diverting, regional blocs and some commentators (e.g. Thurow 1992) have forecast a 'tri-polar' world of tight-knit regions (Europe, North America and North East Asia), one study suggesting that this could cost the world $600b in lost income (Stoeckel et al. 1990). However, evidence on the matter is mixed. Many studies during the 1980s suggested that world trade was indeed becoming more intra-regional, but recent work by Australian trade economist Kym Anderson (1993), which allows for changing regional trade shares, indicates that, overall, intra-regional trade has not changed much in the post-war period, increasing in Europe, the Americas and Africa but declining in Asia and the Middle East. In the early 1990s about half of all world trade was intra-regional compared with one third in 1948 and 39 per cent in 1928, while the proportion was about 70 per cent for Europe, 50 per cent for Asia, 30 per cent for North America and only 20 per cent for Latin America (WTO 1995b: Chart 1.5, p. 11). Intra-European trade has been a stable proportion of total trade since 1890, the main effect of the EU apparently being trade creating, except for agriculture (Sapir 1993). North American free trade under CUFTA/NAFTA has been minimally trade-diverting, except in cars, textiles and a few niches (Wilkinson in Panic 1995).

However, the picture is becoming increasingly complex as RTAs proliferate, change their goals, produce overlapping blocs and take on a so-called 'hub and spoke' pattern with one major country (notably the USA) at the centre of several blocs. An emerging view is that RTAs can increase world income and abet multilateralism so long as they remain open to new members, avoid raising external trade barriers, enhance intra-bloc growth through scale economics, stimulate competition, reduce transport costs, avoid protectionist rules of origin or anti-dumping regimes and generally force recalcitrant interventionist members to liberalise more rapidly than they otherwise would.[2] The WTO (1995a: 3) has decided that the co-existence of GATT and RTAs is 'at least satisfactory, if not broadly positive', albeit requiring continual efforts to maintain compatibility. WTO leaders have thus resigned themselves to the inevitability of more RTAs and have decided that these can complement multilateral free trade goals through so-called 'open regionalism' so long as they provide a first step to liberalisation for member countries, seek to be GATT-consistent, endeavour to enhance the trade-creating factors outlined above and gradually extend MFN to non-members (Sapir 1993). However, some Free Traders, especially 'bicycle theorists', believe that RTAs eventually reach what could be called a 'critical point', usually after Step 4 or 5 (Box 5.1), from which stage further progress allegedly requires 'deeper integration' at the domestic policy-making level lest imbalances and anti-liberal interests induce some backsliding (Lawrence and Litan 1990).

Other commentators have different qualms, particularly the concern that RTAs between countries of widely varying per capita income and development levels may lock the poorer members into their less advanced economic structures. Free Trade economists reject this concern, citing evidence that RTAs, so long as they are extensively liberalising, can greatly raise the income levels of smaller and less developed members relative to the more advanced partners (Anderson 1993). However, critics are also concerned that the most powerful member of an RTA may come to dominate a region economically, politically and culturally as capital and other forces expand freely into the smaller RTA member countries, a concern which is already being widely expressed in Canada and Mexico regarding NAFTA. For this reason some commentators think small nations are better off in a multilateral system like GATT.[3] Such concerns, with which I concur, will be examined briefly in the following outline of several RTAs and will be expanded upon in later chapters.

The kiwi lies down with the kangaroo

Few Australians realise that their country shares with its neighbour across the Tasman one of the world's most advanced RTAs. Like most new model free trade agreements ANZCERTA extends well beyond goods trade to services, investment, harmonisation of standards and even the (relatively) free movement of labour, thus now bordering on being a fully fledged common market (Step 5 in Box 5.1). This cross-Tasman integration process, beginning modestly in the 1960s, was motivated primarily by a mutual belief in the need for structural adjustment and a common fear of being 'left out' in a regionalising world.

The objects of ANZCERTA are modestly stated to be closer economic relations through the elimination of trade barriers and the promotion of fair competition, the treaty employing a 'negative list' approach to liberalisation (see Glossary). Most tariffs were eliminated within five years and most NTBs by mid-1995, including any internal taxes, industry policies, export subsidies or government purchasing practices which discriminated against goods from the other member country. Under amendments of 1988 and later years all tariffs and quantitative restrictions were ended by 1 July 1990, anti-dumping duties were effectively eliminated and business laws were harmonised, while most customs, quarantine, food and other technical standards are being standardised. Free trade in services was added to ANZCERTA in 1989, though with exemptions for broadcasting, postal services, shipping, telecommunications, health, third party insurance and airport management.

ANZCERTA is officially open to new members, the two governments generally seeking GATT-consistency in policy-making. External trade barriers have been lowered unilaterally by both countries, although they do not have common tariff walls as yet, which thus requires discriminatory rules of origin, 50 per cent Australian or New Zealand content being required at present for products to be duty free within ANZCERTA. Most of these features are very ideologically sound from a Free Trade point of view, and former Australian ambassador to GATT, Alan Oxley (1994: 8), has described ANZCERTA as 'probably the cleanest free trade agreement ever negotiated'.[4]

The main effects of ANZCERTA have been greatly increased trade and investment between the two countries and accelerated domestic structural change, especially in manufacturing, as both countries previously had some of the highest tariff barriers in the world. Many companies have shifted investment sites, often setting up plants in both countries, and there has been a marked increase in intra-industry trade, which is usually a sign that the manufacturing sector has become more sophisticated and the economy more industrialised, although this can also be an indicator of trade diversion from other countries.

Overall, the impact has been much greater on New Zealand, for whom Australia is a much larger trading partner than the reverse. A 1989 study by the Australian Bureau of Industry Economics estimated that ANZCERTA would, over time, boost Australia's annual national income by just 0.3 per cent and New Zealand's by 4.5 per cent, so the latter stood to gain much more than Australia, but the study warned that New Zealand's adjustment costs could be high. A more recent study by the same body suggests that total benefits from ANZCERTA have, in the event, been positive but minuscule, Australia gaining a 0.01 per cent rise in GDP and a 0.52 per cent increase in exports while New Zealand's gains have been 0.02 per cent and 1.21 per cent respectively. For both countries total imports have outgrown exports as a result of ANZCERTA, while Australia has lost its earlier trade surplus with New Zealand. The small size of these overall benefits, despite the considerable increase in trans-Tasman trade, is probably explainable by the low starting base of mutual trade, and some commentators think that longer-term 'dynamic' gains (see Chapter 7 on this concept) will be much greater.[5]

Non-economic costs have been given little consideration, generally being thought minimal because of the similar cultural backgrounds of the partners, yet some concerns have arisen in New Zealand about issues such as Australian economic and cultural imperialism, dominance of Australian TV programmes (although in 1996 the Federal Court ruled that New Zealand material be deemed Australian content), brain drain and so forth, with some Australian whinges about Kiwi dole bludgers.[6] Integration of the two economies has now become so close that many Free Traders claim the two countries have reached the 'critical point' (see above), so consolidation of benefits or further progress will require 'deep integration' (Step 6 in Box 5.1), including complete harmonisation of economic policies, common external tariffs and perhaps monetary union.

Others, however, believe that further integration will involve such curtailment of sovereignty that neither country has the desire for such a step, a view with which I agree, and I suggest that there needs to be more public information and debate about the possible long-term effects of ANZCERTA.

Living in a Pacific Basin

Of all the major established or proposed RTAs APEC (see Box 5.2) is arguably the most tenuous, even improbable. The idea of APEC had its origins in discussions of the 1960s and 1970s about the concept of integrated 'Pacific Basin' development or a 'Pacific Rim strategy', its first institutional structures dating from 1967 and its first ministerial meetings from 1989, the key formative summit being that held in Bogor, Indonesia, on 15 November 1994. APEC now has a Singapore-based secretariat and a number of working groups are continuing to develop its structure.

The prime impetus for APEC has come from Australia under the former Hawke/Keating governments, the main motives having been a jumble of factors, including: our new-found export-orientation of the 1980s (see Chapter 3); our growing trade with the Asian region, which now takes some 70 per cent of our exports; concern about our declining share of Asian trade as intra-regional trade rose in East and South East Asia; a view that RTAs can depress the prices of non-bloc commodity exports; a general fear of 'trade diversion' (see above) which was thought likely to reduce our trade and economic growth rates if we were to be left out of the big RTAs; a widespread belief in the so-called North East Asia Ascendancy and the accompanying prospect for an export bonanza in Asia; the earlier desire for a fallback should the Uruguay Round fail; and perhaps a stratagem to use such international agreements for 'locking-in' internal and external de-regulatory policies. Other APEC members share at least some of these motives, although rationales for, and enthusiasm about, the project vary considerably. In particular the USA has nursed a desire to lead the 'Pacific Community' as well as, like Australia, wanting to tap some trade from the much-vaunted Asian dynamism.

APEC leaders have to date sought advice primarily from just the bureaucracy, business and Free Trade academics, two bodies established by APEC being particularly influential. The first, the Pacific Business Forum, consisting of two business delegates from each country, has argued that Asian 'economic dynamism' is driven by the private sector and has recommended an anti-interventionist policy of business-oriented liberalisation. The second body, the so-called Eminent Persons Group (EPG), consisting of a delegate from each country and chaired by US Free Trade economist Fred Bergsten, has recommended 'open regionalism' (see above), policy harmonisation and complete liberalisation of trade and investment, but has sensibly rejected what it called the 'over-institutionalisation and over-bureaucratisation' of the EU model.[7]

The model adopted by APEC leaders at Bogor is officially described as free and open regionalism based on 'the three pillars of sustainable growth, equitable development and national stability'. The main features of the model include: GATT-consistent rules; relatively easy access for new members; a moratorium on protection increases; elimination of goods tariffs by 2010 for industrial members and 2020 for less developed members; complete de-regulation of investment flows by the same dates; a voluntary dispute resolution process; negotiations for standards harmonisation in selected policy areas—initially electrical and rubber products, plastics and food labelling; and general co-operation to improve data flows, trade processes, market access for business and so forth. To date the APEC model does not cover services, IPRs, common external tariffs, safeguards or such like, so it does not conform fully to the new model free trade agreement. The APEC structure includes key committees for trade and investment matters, economic policies and administration, as well as working groups on issues such as energy, resources, science and technology, telecommunications, transport, tourism and human resources.[8]

Outside the elite consensus of bureaucratic and academic enthusiasts, APEC-scepticism abounds, not the least reason being that the region is extremely culturally diverse, encompassing four continents, innumerable islands, three sub-regional RTAs (ANZCERTA, AFTA and NAFTA—Box 5.2) and a complex criss-crossing of intra-regional relations. Other reasons for scepticism include: a less than total commitment by Asian countries as intra-Asian economic and political relations strengthen, and the preference among some for a purely Asian regional body; general doubts in Asia about the virtues of free trade, and a desire by Japan and South Korea to exclude agriculture from liberalisation commitments; a less that total commitment by the USA whose key interests are in South America, whose main Asian focus is Japan and whose officials doubt APEC's liberalisation prospects, an ambivalence which has been criticised by the previous Australian Labor Government;[9] trepidation in the US business community about the prospect of free trade with Japan via APEC, and a converse fear by Asian countries that the USA will use political clout to get a leg into Japanese markets ahead of everyone else;[10] a general rising tide of desire, both world-wide and particularly in Asia, to protect at least a degree of economic, political and cultural sovereignty; and the long-term nature of the key free trade targets— most Bogor signatories will be retired or dead by the due dates. A contentious issue already emerging is the tendency for some members to declare certain sectors as 'sensitive' (i.e. to retain protection), notably rice in Japan and Korea, cars and textiles in Australia. At present the Australian Government is under hefty pressure to retain vehicle tariffs, which Free Traders want eliminated, in the face of mounting imports from Asia where vehicles are still protected by licensing, quotas and tariffs of up to 200 per cent. Industry interests and Managed Traders believe that trade intervention is giving Asian NICs cumulative advantage (see Chapter 6) and entrenched export platforms well ahead of the free trade target dates. Indonesia, for instance, has a 10–20-year plan to develop its own car industry and is determined to maintain 'infant industry' protection for that purpose, beyond the 2020 deadline if necessary. Japan is threatening an appeal to the WTO against Indonesia's policy.[11]

Many commentators have been unkind to APEC and Australia's role in it, US Asia scholar, Chalmers Johnson, describing it as a 'political gimmick' and a 'pipe dream' into which the USA has been 'suckered' by an Australia too weak deal with Japan and China. US Managed Trader, Lester Thurow (1996: 120ff.), believes that

APEC could become an inward-looking bloc, but will be destabilised by 'great power' tensions between the USA, Japan and China, and that it lacks 'non-economic' goals which can transcend the present narrow economic agendas. Australian economist, Helen Hughes, has characterised Keatingesque economic preachments to Asian countries by a crisis-ridden Australia as the 'joke of Asia', warning that APEC could increase our defence insecurity and jeopardise our cultural identity while being decidedly tenuous as many Asian nations increase their independence of outlook.[12] Econometric models tend to show that all members would gain economically from APEC although Australia's manufacturing sector could be adversely affected (see Chapter 8).

Many NGOs, using less economically focused criteria, have expressed qualms about the possible social and environmental effects of APEC, especially as it will be the first RTA in history to combine a number of First and Third World countries. Some groups even question the basic development model underlying Asian 'dynamism'.[13] Critics also claim that APEC negotiations have, to date, been excessively secretive and business-dominated, a view echoed even by the present Australian Foreign Minister, Alexander Downer, who has said that the project requires community acceptance.[14] I concur with such criticisms and suggest that the APEC concept does not at present enjoy remotely near enough community support in member countries to be sustainable.

The very model of a modern RTA

The North American free trade movement began as a series of unilateral and bilateral liberalisation measures by and between the USA, Canada and Mexico during the 1980s, culminating first with the 1989 Canada–USA Free Trade Agreement (CUFTA) and in 1992 with the NAFTA (see Box 5.2). Implemented from 1 January 1994, NAFTA is said to be the most comprehensive free trade treaty ever signed, the key example of a new model free trade agreement, the first ever to involve a First and a Third World country, the largest free trade zone (360 million people) and the largest contiguous economy on Earth (a GNP of $6 trillion). The CUFTA/NAFTA model became, at the behest of US negotiators, a crucial template for the Uruguay Round.[15]

The rationales for NAFTA have been many and varied. It is said that the USA had two major motives, one being to help 'lock in' Mexican liberalising reforms and the other being to promote growth and industrialisation south of the border so as to stem the flow of illegal immigrants from Mexico. There has also been powerful business pressure for 'market access' into Latin America, as well as a wider US agenda to lead the 'Western Hemisphere'.[16] Canada's official motives were to gain guaranteed access to the US market and, as with Australia, to avoid being 'left out' of RTAs in an era when development imperatives supposedly required an outward orientation, especially should the USA make a separate deal with Mexico. The Canadian position illustrates the self-generating nature of a free trade push and the 'vicious circle of globalisation' (see Chapter 3). Mexico's motives were riddled with turgid domestic and global politics. After its debt crisis of the early 1980s the Mexican Government was heavily pressured by the USA, the IMF and the World Bank into structural adjustment, financial liberalisation, privatisation and increased market access for foreign traders and investors, as well as into joining GATT. Domestically, successive governments became more free market-oriented to accommodate this pressure, dismantling the country's traditional nationalistic policies in the process, while at the same time becoming more politically repressive to control the extensive social dissent which the whole process engendered. Conservative regimes then sought, through their obligations under NAFTA, to 'lock-in' these 'reforms' in the face of continued political opposition to them, as regularly requested by US businesses wanting increased market access and enhanced security for their investment plans.

NAFTA seeks almost complete free trade and investment through the phasing out of all industrial and agricultural tariffs, over 10 to 15 years, as well as the elimination of most import quotas and agricultural export subsidies. In principle, general subsidies are also to be abolished eventually, although the details are still being negotiated. It is expected that by 1999, 70 per cent of US goods will be entering Mexico duty free and 90 per cent of Mexican manufactures will enter the USA without tariffs, though with a few GATT-type safeguards allowed. NAFTA's provisions for investment liberalis-ation, the most comprehensive outside the EU, entail the following five forms of protection for intra-NAFTA investors to which even governments and public enterprises are bound: National Treatment and MFN along the same lines as for trade agreements, including a clause preventing upper limits on shareholding by foreign investors; elimination of all TRIMs; freedom of transfer for most types of funds—profits, dividends, capital gains, royalties, proceeds of liqui-dation and so forth—from one NAFTA country to another; limi-tations on governments' powers of expropriation or nationalisation of foreign assets—expropriation must be for a 'public' purpose, be non-discriminatory, be in accordance with international law, be subject to full compensation and even some forms of taxation may be deemed expropriation; mechanisms for dispute settlement which allow an aggrieved investor to use NAFTA processes (see below) or to seek financial compensation through binding international arbi-tration, thus enabling an investor to avoid the host country's legal system.

However, many exceptions to these investment provisions have been allowed, at the insistence of the various parties, especially for Mexico which has already greatly watered down traditional constitutional provisions which once banned or restricted foreign ownership in some sectors. Both Canada and Mexico have reserved the right to screen foreign acquisition or merger proposals above a certain threshold, while the USA has obtained a number of invest-ment restriction rights, especially in high technology sectors, on national security grounds. Nevertheless, NAFTA seeks to liberalise investment so extensively that some left and NGO commentators suggest it is an agreement for free investment rather than free trade, while even one US government authority (GAO 1993: 19) has said the key US goal was to reduce Mexican investment controls and 'lock in' legal protection for investors.

NAFTA also has a more comprehensive services agreement than all other RTAs except the EU, its main features including: 'negative listing'; National Treatment; right of investment and establishment (i.e. for providers to set up shop); right to cross-border service sales; market access for service professionals, including abolition of citizenship requirements upon professional practice;

transparency of government regulations; and extensive harmonisation of professional services standards. NAFTA contains liberalising sectoral agreements for finance, telecommunications, land,
transport and government service procurement, the main goal, often
unashamedly stated by business interests and trade negotiators,
being the elimination of Mexico's extensive regulations in these
areas. A number of sectors have been exempted either generally (e.g.
civil aviation, shipping and basic telecommunications) or country-
specifically (e.g. Canadian cultural 'industries' and oil or gas drilling,
and some Mexican transportation sectors). Overall, most services
will eventually be subject to bound de-regulation and, due to 'negative listing', all new service industries will be fully subject to the
agreement.

Other provisions of NAFTA include: extensive IPRs; harmonisation of technical and other standards; a government procurement code which greatly reduces domestic preference schemes;
separate sectoral agreements for motor vehicles and textiles involving special liberalisation timetables; a ban on most export restrictions, even to the extent that the USA can demand access to
Canadian water and energy resources. Many commentators fear that
the public sectors of NAFTA members will be undermined by provisions for the commercialisation of government entities (ch. 15,
Article 1502: 3b of NAFTA), by requirements that new government
programmes have the consent of all three countries and by private-
sector compensation clauses—see below (Cohen 1994).

NAFTA is the first RTA to include environmental clauses,
appended at the insistence of President Clinton in response to strong
environmentalist lobbying, the main provisions being: the harmonisation of health, safety and environmental laws, officially to
the 'highest common denominator'; the right to ban imports not
conforming to environmental standards; the right of sub-national
governments to have higher standards; priority to some international environmental agreements over NAFTA; and a variety of
associated environmental improvement programmes. NAFTA does
not allow free cross-border migration or provide labour standards,
and although a subsequent agreement sponsored by the Clinton
Administration established a Trinational Commission to enforce
labour rights and related standards, many are sceptical about how
effective implementation is likely to be (see Chapter 8).

Enforcement and dispute-settlement mechanisms under NAFTA are comprehensive and controversial, involving a Trilateral Trade Commission, disputes panels and provisions for private arbitration on a wide range of commercial and investment matters. The most controversial aspect of the system is the provision for extensive retaliation and compensation applications by companies claiming to have been injured by governmental breaches of the agreement (see Chapter 11 for examples). However, the USA has strongly asserted that domestic law overrides NAFTA and that Section 301 (see Chapter 3) applies within NAFTA, threats already having been made against Canada (Sinclair in Grinspun and Cameron 1993).

Reactions to NAFTA have ranged across the spectrum from glee amongst business interests at their increased market access in the partner countries, to strong opposition amongst some labour, consumer, environmental and social groups. Most Free Traders are pleased with NAFTA's liberalisation and passable compatibility with GATT, but at the same time are irked by the agreement's extensive exemptions, continued protectionist elements, the special treatment for the vehicle, textile and energy sectors and so forth. Of particular concern to many Free Traders are the tight rules of origin provisions which require 60 per cent of value added or 50 per cent of nett cost to be produced in NAFTA countries before an item qualifies for NAFTA preferences. This was aimed against an earlier Canadian practice of allowing Japanese car re-exports to the USA with only a small Canadian content, and at the danger of Asian countries using Mexico as an export 'platform' into the USA. For Free Traders this provision renders NAFTA less open and 'deep integrationist' than they would like to see. Most economic modelling suggests that NAFTA will benefit Mexico significantly but the others minimally (see Chapter 7).

However, critics see NAFTA as the leading edge of a new world order which is privatising and de-regulating economies, massively shifting power to the corporate sector, dismantling welfare states and undermining democracy. Some of these claims may be over-stated, but as I will argue in later chapters, they are not without some validity, which is why I refer to NAFTA as a 'hard-edged' free trade agreement compared with the softer edges of the Uruguay Round. The most powerful passions have been aroused in Canada where CUFTA/NAFTA is seen by many as entailing a wide range of economic and non-economic costs. In fact NAFTA has become so contentious that President Clinton was initially advised to abandon it (Dryden, 1995: 381) and public opinion remains sceptical (see Introduction to Part Two). Lack of full community acceptance remains the Achilles' heel of NAFTA, as with many other grandiose integration schemes.[17]

The disunited union

The mother of all RTAs is the EU. Established in 1957 and gradually extended in both membership (see Box 5.2) and degree of integration, the EU is today an economic union (Step 6, Box 5.1) and proposed political federation (Step 7). The initial post-war motive for its formation was the most noble desire to avoid further fratricidal conflict, but over time the standard Free Trade arguments of allocative efficiency, market access and gains from trade have been the chief rationale of its proponents, including the notion that internal competition will generate more growth and external competitiveness. During the 1980s some economists claimed that the EC had reached the 'critical point' (see above), so that the union had to choose between partially integrated stagnation or 'deep integration', the latter option being chosen in 1992 with the Maastricht Treaty. Most economists claim that unification has brought considerable economic benefits (see Chapter 7). There is dispute about whether or not the EU has been on balance trade-creating or trade-diverting, but it has been suggested that countries such as Austria and Sweden were forced into the Union by a drift of capital to EU members as deregulation has proceeded.

Today the EU boasts almost completely free internal trade and resource flows, formally impeded only by a few remaining administrative, technical, tax and general NTB measures, though more informally hampered by residual barriers of language, culture and national jealousies. Most law-making (some estimate as much as 80 per cent) and much administration now emanates centrally, particularly from the non-elected European Commission based in Brussels, rather than from individual national capitals. The Council of Ministers, the executive body representing each member country, uses a roughly population-weighted decision-making system but the precise number of bottoms on seats is in some dispute (Hama 1996: 90). The directly elected European Parliament, the most democratic component of the EU, is weak. The EU structure contains a variety of social, cultural and regional organisations, a provision requiring members to improve the environment and a 'social clause' (Article 117) guaranteeing, in general terms, a range of social, labour, welfare and equal opportunity rights. The 'social clause' is designed to harmonise labour standards, but it is a rather weak provision with Britain currently creating disharmony by opting out of its requirements and attracting capital through 'social dumping'; that is, offering lower wages and conditions as a 'carrot' (Hama 1996: 54ff.; Brenchley 1996).

Despite its apparent success, however, the EU has more than its share of major problems. Many matters, particularly foreign policy, internal security and so forth, are still made nationally which continues to impede unity and has, for instance, bedevilled the EU's peace-making role in the former Yugoslavia. Many countries, including the evangelically unionist German government, have been tardy in adopting Commission directives and although stragglers may be taken to the European Court, cases may involve delays of up to five years.[18] Members' budgets and economic policies remain sufficiently uncoordinated that Union-level policy-making is unstable. An element of *leger de main* in statistical and policy terms was required on the part of some countries in order to meet the stringent criteria for joining the single currency by 1999. The politics of exchange rate setting has been extremely de-stabilising. Although in theory the proposed common currency would solve this problem, it would not eliminate concern about German monetary dominance and member states fear the loss of financial autonomy. In fact, at least one prominent economist, as well as the powerful head of the German central bank, Hans Tietmeyer, have suggested that the single currency is more a political symbol than an economic or technical necessity.[19] Power struggles within the EU system are under way, particularly with the European Parliament demanding more influence, while a German constitutional court has ruled that, although the Maastricht Treaty is legal, national parliaments must retain adequate administrative powers (Hama 1996: 45–6). Many sub-national governments are demanding relaxation of central constraints and Maastricht-induced budgetary limits.

In spite of lingering disunity, the high degree of proposed structural unification is eliciting concerns about loss of members' national sovereignty, domination by Germany and France, remote control from Brussels and so forth. Europe's now largely open borders are giving rise to problems of mobile drugs, terrorism and crime, Dutch attempts to introduce a liberal narcotics policy having been undermined by this mobility, for instance.[20] Restive regionalism and even militant separatism is growing and this is widely thought to be at least in part a reaction to over-centralisation.[21] Overall, there is widespread community disillusionment with the Union, a popular view abounds that its strictures are causing economic and social problems, many prominent supporters of unification are changing their minds, public opinion is increasingly ambivalent about union (see Introduction to Part Two), there is now a strong Euro-sceptic movement in most member countries and an anti-EU political party is being formed.[22] In short, despite its supposed economic rationality the costs of European unification are now appearing, particularly in areas of social, cultural and sovereignty sensitivity which are affected by the 'deep integration' so favoured by many Free Trade economists. It is likely that the EU project has more to do with the narrow priorities of economists and the empire-building fantasies of politicians than the real aspirations of people. This clearly gives rise to serious queries about the virtues of the regional Free Trade Adventure.

Regionalism versus multilateralism

Proposals for the further development of RTAs abound, including grandiose schemes to extend the EU to Eastern Europe, to link the EU with AFTA and the Middle East, to join the EU and NAFTA and to expand NAFTA into one vast 'Western Hemisphere' free trade zone entitled the Americas Free Trade Area (another AFTA). Yet despite this proliferating ardour for RTAs, the current debate about the virtues of regionalism is at best inconclusive, many Free Traders and free trade critics opposing the concept for the varying reasons discussed above. Some small countries believe they can do better with multilateral collective bargaining than in an RTA which risks being dominated by the largest member. Others prefer to seek a regional economy, or what many African governments call 'collective self-reliance'. Some business people relish the idea of worldwide market-opening through multilateralism while others find the GATT/WTO system remote and bureaucratic, preferring more accessible regional-level systems.

Prognoses for the future of regionalism vs. multilateralism are equally unclear. Some still think that a retreat into closed blocs is possible while others believe that the notion of 'open regionalism' is now well established (see above). Some observers see RTAs as a stepping stone to multilateralism and global free trade, while others hypothesise a permanent two-tier system and a few suspect that the USA is playing RTAs off against GATT for its own benefit. The emergence of new growth areas such as Hong Kong–Southern China or the Singapore–Johore–Bantan Triangle might create hybrid units and in time give a new meaning to the concept of regionalism.[23] Many commentators believe that TNCs, and even finance, remain home-oriented or regional rather than truly global (see UNCTAD 1994a: 146ff.), which could ensure a long life expectancy for RTAs.

A popular view amongst some Free Traders at present is that, as RTAs tend to be more liberalising than GATT, presumably because of proximity and established trust, regionalism may lead the way to 'deeper integration' through mergers of RTAs (e.g. Lawrence and Litan 1990). However, many others are sceptical surmising, for instance, that the steps involved are too politically difficult, that regional economies may take on divergent characteristics and that RTAs may contain at least four self-limiting mechanisms. The first is that as new members accede to an RTA, the preferences enjoyed by existing members are eroded, thus creating an incentive to limit membership. Second, as many RTAs are strongly emphasising investment liberalisation, this may create a vested interest against trade liberalisation amongst mobile firms once they establish costly plants and marketing systems in other member countries. Third, governments and officials often suffer from 'negotiation exhaustion' which could cause long delays in the further steps, if not indefinite postponement. Fourth, closer integration may generate a backlash against erosion of national sovereignty, as I suggested above is already happening.[24]

I share many of these doubts about the likely benefits and viability of regionalism, which suggests a preference for, or at least some grounds in favour of, multilateralism, although in Chapter 12 I will propose a greatly modified version thereof. However, in addition I suggest other concerns with regionalism which are also applicable to multilateral liberalisation, most of which have been touched upon above. In particular, the present-day RTA movement appears conducive to domination by one country, is highly focused on investment liberalisation even though that issue is still hotly debated, is excessively influenced by business interests and is strongly driven by a technological, de-regulatory, privatisationist ideology from which there is increasing dissent in most countries. Also, most RTAs appear to lack convincing support within their own communities. This suggests a need to question more extensively the Free Trade Adventure in general, its regional dimension in particular and its 'deep integrationist' implications.

Conclusion

The proliferation of RTAs and proposed extensions thereto have become both an integral part of, and perhaps a distraction from, the wider Free Trade Adventure. Some Free Traders fear that regionalism is antithetical to the multilateral movement for global free trade, while others see the two as compatible provided the RTA models adopted are open, pro-liberalisation and integrationist. One Free Trade view holds that all integration projects reach a 'critical point' in the process which requires a progression to 'deep integration' if full and efficient liberalisation is to be achieved, and at present most countries are more likely to take such a step regionally rather than multilaterally. A common inference from this is that regionalism must be tolerated as a 'stepping stone' towards multilateral globalisation, but there remain plenty of sceptics both as to the feasibility of the stepping stone theory and as to the desirability of the 'deep integrationist' project *per se*. In my view there are many grounds for the latter form of scepticism which are now becoming apparent in various RTA experiments, some of which will be further touched on in Part Two.

Part
Two

*Problems and Critiques
of the Uruguay Round's
New World Order*

Introduction

Putting the fear of GATT into them

George Orwell once wittily observed that when he became a police officer in colonial Burma, for the first time in his life he was important enough to be hated. During the Uruguay Round negotiations GATT too achieved such a status, having hitherto been generally seen as an innocuous, ineffective, distant international bureaucracy. From the late 1980s the Uruguay Round proposals, particularly in their near-final Dunkel Draft form, evoked a small tide of opposition around the world amongst unions, farmers' groups, environmental movements and a wide variety of NGOs, while in 1990 a Korean farmer tried to commit suicide outside GATT's Geneva headquarters (Dryden 1995: 367).

The anti-GATT movement was symbolically launched during December 1990 with a 30 000-strong demonstration in Brussels, at what was meant to be the final meeting to conclude the Uruguay Round, the protesters being assorted individuals and members of the above-mentioned sorts of groups from many countries.[1] Representatives of various NGOs attended the Uruguay Round signatory meeting in Marrakesh and presented alternative public briefings but they were only admitted to the meeting as 'press', Denmark being the sole country which had NGO representation on its delegation (Bach 1994). At the 1992 Rio Earth Summit NGOs signed an alternative 'treaty' on trade matters, various world-wide NGO coalitions regularly meeting since then to formulate a critique of the Uruguay Round and alternatives thereto.[2] In North America opposition to GATT and NAFTA has been merged, especially in Canada where the Action Canada Network, along with other groups and coalitions, has been active since the signing of CUFTA. In the USA two groups in particular, 'The Alliance for Responsible Trade' and 'The Citizen's Trade Campaign', are active in resistance to GATT and NAFTA, while the 'Mexican Action Network on Free Trade' has brought together many anti-NAFTA NGOs in Mexico.[3] There are equivalent groups in Europe and some Third World countries. The most intense anti-GATT campaign has been in India where innumerable farmers' groups, trade unions and NGOs have persistently lobbied against the Uruguay Round provisions, particularly TRIPs and GATS, have held demonstrations of up to a million people and have called strikes of up to fifteen million workers. In addition, NGOs have criticised the elitism and secrecy of the Uruguay Round negotiations, while in New Zealand Maoris have also declared that the *TRIPs Agreement* violates their rights, and claim exemption from WTO obligations.[4]

The views of such groups about the Uruguay Round and free trade are many and varied, but include concerns that: the new tariff regime will continue selective protection for the First World while opening up the Second and Third Worlds to Western TNCs; proposed agricultural 'reforms' may provide a few export opportunities for the Third World but will increase food import-dependency for many countries; the new subsidies, anti-dumping and TRIMs provisions will greatly reduce the capacity of governments to use constructive industry policies; industry restructuring will adversely affect women and many weaker social groups, thus greatly exacerbating existing inequities; TRIPs will greatly advantage First World TNCs and enable them to unfairly exploit the resources and traditional knowledge base of Third World societies; GATS will facilitate the flooding of Third World countries with Western-style commercial services; harmonisation provisions will reduce labour, environmental and human rights standards to a world-wide lowest common denominator; the new WTO system will be secretive, undemocratic, bureaucratic, pro-Western and dominated by people with a narrow economic perspective. More generally, it is feared that free trade and investment will promote a materialistic style of development, enable TNCs to dominate the world, accelerate privatisation and 'marketisation', emaciate national governments, destroy communities, preclude alternative development options, facilitate the monopoly of a particular world view and inundate traditional societies with the hedonistic culture of the West.

Free Trade economists have largely ignored the anti-GATT movement, while the mainstream press has painted such groups as rather silly, sometimes paranoid, dupes of vested interests and has characterised their concerns as, at best, ill-informed knee-jerk reactions, at worst, conspiratorial delusions.[5] Clearly some vested interests are involved in the anti-free trade movement and certain of its claims are arguably poorly documented over-reactions, but in my view the stronger accusations are unfair for, as I will argue in Part Two, the above-mentioned concerns have at least some validity. Many of these anti-free trade coalitions are very broadly based, including churches, humanitarian organisations and a variety of credible social action movements all clearly expressing genuine concerns rather than narrow economic interests.

Such groups may reflect rather than influence public opinion, which throughout the world has always tended to reject trade liberalisation, and appears recently to have been displaying scepticism about economic integration projects. For instance, most US opinion polls, dating back to the 1950s, have found majorities opposed to import liberalisation, sometimes very strongly so, with employment being the main concern (Destler 1992: 180–1). Likewise regarding NAFTA, US polls have consistently shown public opinion to be as much as two to one against the project and one analysis of the Congressional vote on NAFTA has found pressure from business in favour of NAFTA to have been much more apparent than the influence of any other discernible interest groups, although 'rust belt' members were strongly anti-NAFTA (Mishel and Teixeira 1993). Canadian polls have found a mere 4 per cent favouring CUFTA, the rest wanting revision or abandonment of the deal, while the 1993 national election saw the Conservative Party, which negotiated CUFTA and NAFTA, reduced to just two seats in parliament.[6] In Mexico, polls and other expressions of public opinion are ambivalent about NAFTA, many people hoping for economic improvements but others fearing various non-economic consequences, even near-annexation by the USA (Browne 1994: 68–9). Certainly opinion polls can be fickle, contradictory and susceptible to influence by the way the question is phrased, but one Australian poll has found most people favouring protection for the car industry *despite* the poll containing a leading question which warned of possible price increases (see Chapter 8, p. 161).

The EU has done systematic polling, using consistent questions, for up to twenty years on some issues, and the results indicate considerable ambivalence about the integration project.[7] In most EU member countries majorities of about 70–80 per cent think that general unification is a good thing, but there are considerably smaller and generally declining majorities who feel that membership of the EU is good for their country, the figure for Germany having slipped to 53 per cent by 1993 and that for Britain to 43 per cent. In most member countries only a third or so would 'feel very sorry' if the EU were scrapped, most of the remainder suggesting they would feel indifferent and a quarter of Britons would feel relieved. In most countries support for the single market (Maastricht Treaty), a common currency and political federation is weaker than that for the spirit of unification in general, and many, including Germany, have majorities opposed to these initiatives. Only 40 per cent of European citizens feel well informed about EU affairs and a meagre 26 per cent feel that they have any input into EU decision-making, the latter figure being as low as 15 per cent in France. All this suggests that support declines the more integrated the proposed structure becomes. Within less than a year of voting for entry into the EU by majorities of around two-thirds, support in Austria and Sweden had shrunk to about a third as the realities of rule from Brussels and the stringent requirements for monetary union (see Chapter 5) hit home.[8] It would seem that, world-wide, community support for the Free Trade Adventure is ambivalent and limited, which in my view constitutes grounds for, if not opposition to free trade and 'deep integration *per se*', then at least considerable caution.

Part One of the book has outlined the Uruguay Round, its outcomes, the explosion of regionalism and some aspects of debate about the Free Trade Adventure. I have suggested that the Round is likely to prove a watershed in the globalisation process, that present-day governments, via the 'Geneva consensus', are committed to this process, but that there remains some ambivalence and the desire for a degree of continued autonomy. Part Two will provide more detail on the emerging new global order and indicate some problems or critiques thereof. I cover two major themes. The first relates to the question of costs versus benefits. The orthodox view, as noted in Chapter 1, is that the benefits of free trade almost invariably outweigh the costs, whereas I will argue that, when non-economic issues are factored in, the reverse may be true. The second theme relates to the question of adaptation versus resistance. In general there are three possible responses to the Free Trade Adventure—accept its goals and allow the market to make the requisite structural adjustments; accept its goals but governments intervene to smooth the adjustments and cushion the blows; or reject the goals, resist adjustment and seek alternatives to free trade. I argue that intervention is certainly required and that there are grounds for selective resistance in a search for alternatives, not only to free trade but also to the economic and human development models it usually entails.

Chapter 6 introduces the critique by outlining Free Trade theory and the main arguments against free trade which have been formulated over the years. To these I have added some 'non-economic' cases which are not normally emphasised in the literature. Chapter 7 critically examines the claim that there will be a universal economic bonanza to be had from the Uruguay Round, concluding that its likely benefits have probably been over-stated and its possible costs underestimated or even ignored. Chapter 8 continues that analysis at a more micro level by examining some structural and non-economic implications of the Round. Chapter 9 examines the two key Uruguay Round additions to the GATT/WTO system—the GATS and TRIPs agreements—and their likely implications, especially as regards possible 'non-economic' costs. Chapter 10 critically analyses two particularly sensitive, largely non-economic, issues which have arisen in the contemporary free trade debate—the environment and the Round's proposal to seek harmonisation of technical and food standards—arguing that trade liberalisation could have adverse effects. Chapter 11 outlines the likely workings of the new GATT/WTO system and its expected future globalisation agenda, which includes the 'hot potato' of investment liberalisation. I conclude that potentially epoch-making events are unfolding, but that their possible costs have not been remotely near adequately assessed. Chapter 12 briefly enumerates some possible alternatives to Free Trade theory, which I designate as Managed Trade, Fair Trade and Self-Reliant Trade, though I use these terms in ways which may differ from the usual meaning. I propose that whilst a system of multilateral trade rules is desirable in the long-run, a very different, looser, more democratic, more UN-centred world order is required from that which is now evolving under the 'Geneva consensus'.

6

Doctrine and Heresy

Two centuries of the free trade debate

The Uruguay Round did not aim at full free trade but its champions have urged that the next Round seek near-complete free trade and economic globalisation (Sutherland 1994b), betraying not the slightest doubt about the virtues of these aims or the doctrines underlying them. In this chapter I will outline various sets of arguments which are often levelled against the Free Trade doctrine, the assumptions upon which it rests and even the goals which it pursues, especially as Peter Sutherland once proclaimed that 'GATT equals growth'[1] despite the frequent questioning of economic growth today. Two questions are asked in the free trade debate—is some trade better than less trade or no trade, and if so should trade be unrestrained?—Free Traders answering both in the affirmative. The latter question is the more debated and will be the focus of this chapter, though the former will be touched upon in later chapters. The debate has traditionally been couched in terms of free trade vs. protection, the latter term implying a limited, negative concept of propping up ailing industries with tariffs, whereas in fact a range of policies, both protective and encouraging of new activities, can be used constructively to plan and develop a society, including tariffs, quotas, subsidies, industry policy and government–industry co-operation. I therefore prefer the term 'trade intervention' which I will use in this and later chapters, although other terms will be used where appropriate.

Trade intervention is just one of many possible policy measures which entail government intervention in market processes, others including domestic economic and social regulation of various sorts. Free Traders always stress that both economic and 'non-economic' problems should be dealt with through domestic rather than trade policies wherever possible, although in my view the two arenas are now so closely inter-connected that both types of policy must often be used together. By and large both the domestic and international arenas are governed by the same general economic principles and so the 200-year debate over intervention versus non-intervention applies to both. Most economists accept the legitimacy of some intervention in both arenas, particularly in response to various 'market failures', but debate over the degree thereof is heated. The traditional debates covered in this chapter conventionally only apply to goods, not to services, investment or IPRs, and in Chapter 9 I will question the simplistic extension of trade theory to services. The conclusion of this chapter is that, whilst traditional Free Trade theory is not in total disarray as some claim, there remain sufficient problems to warrant a questioning of the Free Trade Adventure and its alleged virtues.

Invisible hand and visible doctrine

From about 1500 to 1800, when European trading power was in the ascendant, trade policy-making was dominated by a doctrine known as 'mercantilism', an early trade interventionist stream of thought to which detractors have attributed many furphies, such as the view that a nett inflow of 'specie' (precious metals) was required for economic progress or that one nation's trading advantage had to be at the expense of another's. Revisionist scholars have found that mercantilist doctrine actually encompassed a wide range of perspectives and insights, including early analyses of development economics, environmental and resource problems, demand theory, increasing returns, 'cumulative advantage' (see below) and even some macroeconomic theories which anticipated Keynes,[2] but the reign of mercantilism was brought to an end by Adam Smith's 'invisible hand' revolution. Smith's (1776) doctrine was based on the premises that the wealth of nations is derived from specialisation, that specialisation is limited by the extent of the market and that this limit can be removed by abolishing the governmental interference with trade and private business which prevailed under mercantilism.

Smith's work began the evolution of modern Free Trade theory, of which there are two elements. The first is the doctrine of 'mutual gains from trade' which asserts that nations can gain economically by specialising in production, then trading the surplus produce. The second element, originally expounded by British political economist and stockbroker, David Ricardo, suggested that specialisation and trade were based on 'comparative advantage', or relative costs, rather than primarily on physical advantage (resources) or 'absolute advantage' (production costs) as had earlier been thought. In Ricardo's famous illustration, Britain had a comparative advantage in cloth and Portugal in wine because the former had to forgo less wine to produce its cloth than the latter had to, and vice versa. Thus, so long as there was a difference between countries in tastes, technologies or resource bases, mutually beneficial trade would tend to occur spontaneously via the 'invisible hand' of the market. Normally every country could expect to have a comparative advantage in something as it was unlikely that any two economies would find themselves with identical comparative costs.

The twin doctrines of gains from trade and comparative advantage still constitute the core of Free Trade theory, along with the following key corollaries:

1 Trade can increase the efficiency of resource allocation, and economic stimuli flowing therefrom can provide an 'engine for growth'.

2 Any country can obtain what I call a 'unilateral benefit' (see Glossary) through increased efficiency just by cutting its own protection, though the benefits will be enhanced if other countries do the same.

3 Trade will require some 'structural adjustment' of an economy as resources shift to sectors with greatest comparative advantage.

4 Trade will create winners and (temporary) losers, but if the former 'bribe' or compensate the latter so as to facilitate their adjustment, everyone will be economically better off.

5 Conversely, renewed protectionism in one country would render most of its own citizens, and most of those in other countries, worse off, so this would normally only be demanded by those sectional interests who might gain from protectionist measures.

6 In occasional circumstances an entire country might obtain nett benefits from protection, but this is likely to be at the expense of other countries and such protection is called a 'beggar-thy-neighbour' policy.

7 Trade will bring closer, beneficial links between nations, resulting in what Adam Smith called 'cosmopolitanism' (now globalisation), and nineteenth century Free Trader, Richard Cobden, once declared that free trade would end 'the antagonism of race and creed and language . . . uniting us in the bonds of eternal peace' (Capie 1983: 20).

However, classical Free Trade doctrine, as well as the more 'scientific' neo-classical theory (see Glossary) which later absorbed it, rested in its ideal form on a number of crucial but questionable assumptions, notably that: there is perfect competition between firms; buyers have perfect information about market conditions; labour and capital are perfectly mobile within a country but do not routinely move internationally; production processes embody fixed technologies and exhibit constant 'returns to scale' (as opposed to 'increasing returns'—see Glossary); there is no significant or long-term unemployment of factors (labour or capital); international trade is voluntarily entered into; a country's gains from trade will accrue to nationals who spend locally; each country's external trade is always in balance; market prices will accurately reflect relative real costs; inflation and other internal monetary factors will not affect trade; goods are traded but not services; there are no 'externalities' (see Glossary). Many of these assumptions are still used both in theory and in modelling (see next chapter), but most are regularly breached in practice, as economics textbooks are beginning to acknowledge (e.g. Todaro 1994: ch. 12). Neo-classical theory also introduced the key concept of 'optimality', or the state of maximum efficiency in which no one can be made better off without making someone else worse off, a state which Free Traders believe can best be achieved, under the above assumptions, by world-wide free trade.

Only a few major ideas were added to the Free Trade doctrine during the twentieth century, the most important being the proposition, advanced by Swedish economists Hecksher and Ohlin, that a nation's comparative advantage is shaped by its resource base so that capital-scarce developing countries, for instance, would best specialise in labour-intensive products. A corollary of this model, the so-called 'factor price equalisation' theorem, holds that free trade would, through competitive pressure, gradually raise the price (i.e. income) of the intensively used factor until all factor prices (wages, profits, interest etc.) were equalised world-wide and factor movements would cease. An extension of this corollary, the Stopler–Samuelson theorem, suggests that the incomes of scarce factors, labour in rich countries and capital in poor countries, would be adversely affected by trade, so these groups may be expected to resist free trade. Some believe that this prognosis is now coming to fruition through competitive globalisation (see Chapter 8, pp. 161ff.).

A doctrine made for heretics?

Free Traders stand by their doctrine, its corollaries and assumptions, arguing that even if these seem unrealistic they are at least workable approximations of reality whose validity is confirmed by experience and empirical evidence (Dillon et al. 1990). Others are not so convinced and opponents have variously attacked the theory, assumptions, corollaries, practices or goals of the doctrine. Free Traders have acknowledged only a few arguments for divergence from free trade, though most have accepted some pragmatic cases such as temporary relief from imports, revenue raising, retaliation or defence, and domestic subsidies are the preferred form of rectification, these being deemed more efficient than tariffs or other types of border protection. Arguments against free trade are multifarious and overlapping, some embracing the goal of growth, others qualifying it, but for convenience I will examine them under three headings—orthodox, radical and non-economic.

Orthodox arguments

These are cases within the framework of traditional Free Trade theory which are accepted by most orthodox Free Traders as valid departures from pure free trade; that is, where trade intervention would leave a country economically better off than under free trade.

1 Optimum tariff argument Some strict Free Traders accept as the only valid argument for protection the cases where a country has a large enough share of an import or export market to affect the world price; for example, where US demand raises import prices to its own disadvantage or Australian supply of wool reduces prices to our own disadvantage. In such cases a tariff (or export tax) may be 'optimal' (i.e. increase economic benefits) if it reduces import prices (or raises export prices) by more than it increases costs, although other countries may be slightly worse off. Despite this form of protection being theoretically acceptable and economically feasible (see Quiggin 1993: 66), many economists believe that it is politically limited in practice and does not justify very high tariffs (Krugman and Obstfeld 1994: 232).

2 Infant industry argument First argued by US statesman, Alexander Hamilton, in 1791 and later by German economist, Fredrick List, this case suggests that industries with potential comparative advantage may need some initial protection to obtain internal and external economies of scale, to overcome competition from established imports or to 'appropriate' the full benefits of their pioneering efforts. List argued only for temporary protection until all countries had attained comparable industrial development, after which there should be global free trade. Ever since Mill (1848: 283), most economists have accepted some form of this argument, though many Free Traders remain sceptical on the grounds that excessive protection may damage a new industry's competitiveness, that an industry with true comparative advantage should be able to stand on its own feet from the outset, that subsidies may be more effective than tariffs to ensure the infant will 'grow up' (Corden 1974: ch. 9) and that interventionist policy-making may be 'captured' by protectionist interests (Bhagwati 1989). Many economists see the infant industry issue mainly as a 'market failure' problem (see Glossary)— for example, the capital market allocating inadequate resources to high-risk sectors—which is best rectified by domestic reforms or subsidies. Yet despite the acceptability of such selective subsidies the Uruguay Round has restricted their use (see Chapter 4).

3 Second best argument This concept suggests that where domestic market failures, be they labour practices, private monopolies or the like, are distorting trade, removal of one such failure alone may be less beneficial than not removing any, and hence certain domestic or trade interventionist policies could increase welfare while such market failures persist, though the 'first best' policy is to remove all 'distortions'. For example, a tariff or subsidy may be used to help a labour-intensive industry even if the real 'culprit' is thought to be excessive wages. The 'first best', or 'optimum', policy would be to 'reform' the labour market, but if this is not politically possible, trade intervention may be the 'second best' optimum policy. If market failures are frequent and intractable then permanent trade intervention systems may be justified, although Free Traders are reluctant to concede this. Yet complete free trade would presumably deprive governments of such options, despite their general acceptability to most economists.

4 Externalities argument It is widely acknowledged by economists that intervention in the market is warranted where externalities (see Glossary) exist, the main debate being about what problems constitute legitimate externalities and how they should be handled. In the case of trade-related externalities, most Free Traders argue that these should be treated directly at source (e.g. a domestic tax on the sources of cross-border pollution, or research and training subsidies for 'infant industries') rather than through trade restriction. However, strict Free Traders believe that in practice it can be difficult to identify externalities and prescribe appropriate remedies, so that policies directed at such problems may be subject to political manipulation and should be used sparingly.

In sum, orthodox Free Traders accept only the four above-mentioned arguments for trade intervention, all of which entail, in one form or another, the concept of market failure (see Glossary). Even then many strict Free Traders are sceptical about each argument in theory, practice or both, and two major qualifications are usually raised. The first is that many factors other than just trade are at work and market failures are usually domestic in origin, so domestic measures should be used before resorting to trade intervention because these can get closer to the source of the problem. Although I do not object to the appropriate use of domestic policies, in a globalising world the source of market failures is likely to be increasingly supranational; for example, large TNCs may be monopolistic in a number of countries and cannot be regulated by any one host government, or may use questionable practices which the home government will not regulate. In such cases a mix of internal, external and international co-operative policies may be required. The second qualification, that intervention, even for externality reasons, should be minimised because of likely political misuse, is a rather negative view which overlooks the manifold costs of economic growth and is unhelpful for dealing with non-economic issues (see below) which by their nature require political judgments to be made.

Radical arguments

Some arguments go much further in challenging the basic principles or assumptions of Free Trade theory and these are not generally accepted by Free Traders. A number of mainstream economists admit that free trade is the optimal policy only when the key assumptions, as outlined above, hold good (e.g. Corden 1974: 8; Panic 1988: ch. 17), though there is disagreement about the extent to which the failure of assumptions would undermine traditional theory, one mild critic, Paul Krugman (1987), having observed that, due mainly to market imperfections, the case for free trade is now more in doubt than at any time since Ricardo. The following arguments suggest the need for at least some trade (and other) intervention, without necessarily completely undermining Free Trade theory as a whole.

5 **Historical arguments** These seek to make empirical generalisations about trade issues from historical evidence. Opponents of free trade are fond of pointing out that most countries industrialised under a tariff regime and that even Britain, in its more mercantilist days, obtained an initial boost from protective devices such as the Navigation Acts (which required exporters to use British ships), restrictions on textile imports, assisted immigration for skilled artisans and export bans on textile technology (e.g. Hudson 1992: chs 5 and 6). Even Adam Smith (1776: 485) supported the Navigation Acts and Mill (1848: 282) thought that these Acts had been crucial in establishing British maritime supremacy. This implies a case for at least infant industry protection and suggests that countries might

only adopt free trade when their industries are established or when it otherwise suits them to do so.

Free Traders often reply that development probably occurred despite protection rather than because of it, one study suggesting that nineteenth century tariffs were not particularly protective and that in many countries development preceded the protectionist era of the late nineteenth century (Capie 1983). Others, however, have offered apparently contrary examples—Portugal's cloth industry (used in Ricardo's model to illustrate comparative disadvantage) was devastated by a 1703 free trade treaty and the skilled workers emigrated rather than turn to wine-making or agriculture as the Ricardian model would have predicted (Hudson 1992: 127ff.); many European countries began their industrial development when British exports ceased during the Napoleonic Wars, then regressed when these exports resumed (Hudson 1992: 109); European countries derived much of their early growth impetus from domestic rather than external sources, so that trade may be more a 'handmaiden' for growth than an 'engine' as the classical Free Traders surmised; certain liberalising countries did not gain much from free trade; some studies suggest reverse causality—domestic growth leads to trade.[3] Such evidence is sketchy but it suggests that free trade might not be optimal and that trading might not be as crucial for development as Free Traders claim.

6 Circumstances and imperfections arguments Free Traders have always been adamant that, except for cases of 'optimum tariffs' and certain externalities (nos 1 and 4 above), protection cannot increase a nation's income or employment, though jobs can be redistributed. Others disagree and have identified circumstances, especially where imperfections are present, in which trade intervention, perhaps combined with some domestic intervention, could boost a country's income and/or employment, at least in the short term. These include: where the elasticity of demand for a country's exports and the elasticity of supply of its imports are low, but its elasticity of demand for imports is high (Robinson 1960); where a country has downwardly inflexible wages, capital-intensive exports and incomplete specialisation;[4] where there is uncertainty about markets, prices or terms of trade so that intervention might act as an insurance policy;[5] where uncertainty is combined with various production and consumption rigidities (Cheng 1987); where a small country faces increasing returns but declining export prices in world markets;[6] where wages are rigid, mark-up pricing is used by companies and trade intervention would enable the government to boost demand without worsening the trade balance (the Cambridge Economic Policy Group—see Dunkley 1995); where there is equilibrium unemployment and sectoral wage differentials so that labour markets do not adjust smoothly and certain new industries may be discouraged.[7]

Free Traders usually reply that such circumstances are exceptions rather than the rule, that trade intervention is 'second best', may be at the expense of other countries (beggar-thy-neighbour) or may risk retaliation, and that the imperfections are best countered by domestic policies such as labour market de-regulation and insurance or equities markets. These responses are valid to some extent but are over-simplified, as ironing out imperfections may not always be possible or socially desirable. Many Keynesian economists claim that classical Free Trade theory, which assumed full employment (see above), is undermined, or even 'reduced to wreckage' as Joan Robinson (1960: 205) once put it, by persistent unemployment, especially when combined with labour immobility, 'sticky' (downwardly inflexible) wages and so forth.

During the Great Depression Keynes left Free Traders aghast when he decreed that trade intervention, via tariffs or exchange rate devaluation, could increase production, employment and welfare, contrary to what the textbooks then said and mostly still say. Keynes' reasoning was that a temporary respite from imports could create jobs, increase income, raise demand and bolster the profit expectations of entrepreneurs, thereby generating multiplier effects in the direction of full employment and stimulating activity in a way which could not occur in a recessed economy. This mechanism need not be a 'beggar-thy-neighbour' one if it boosts demand for imports. Keynes broadly accepted Free Trade theory in principle, worried about beggar-thy-neighbour effects and opposed long-term high protection levels, but, along with Kaldor and others, he held that the trade intervention option should be a permanent part of any macro stabilisation policy arsenal.[8]

Free Traders still believe in the 'legend of the Thirties' (see Chapter 2), that the protectionist explosion of the 1930s caused or exacerbated the Depression, but Kaldor (1964) has argued that it was the Depression which caused the trade slump, not the reverse, and that British protectionist policies of the era greatly stimulated economic development. Recent econometric evidence seems to support this view, suggesting that tariffs and exchange rate devaluation (some say primarily the latter) were crucial recovery factors in Britain and other countries, that British GNP was 2.3 per cent higher in 1938 than it would have been without the 1932 tariff increase and that Irish employment grew substantially during the 1930s in response to extensive protection. In addition, a series of strategic bilateral trade agreements enabled Britain to boost exports and avoid retaliation by other countries.[9] A leading expert on the Depression era, Charles Kindleberger (1987: 124), believes that protectionism has been overrated as a cause of the Depression and iconoclastic US economist, Paul Krugman (1991: 103), says that the alleged connection between the two is nonsense.

Some contemporary economists think that trade multipliers might not be large enough for protection to boost the economy in the way Keynes and Kaldor surmised, but British modellers Ford and Sen (1985) have argued that a combination of expansionary policies and protection can increase employment and income without beggar-thy-neighbour effects so long as all countries use phased, co-ordinated protection measures rather than willy-nilly retaliation. Many Keynesians, notably Kaldor, have argued that Free Traders overlook the adverse impacts that trade liberalisation could have on a country's external balance, and US macro-economist John M. Culbertson has claimed that Free Trade theory does not hold in a world of trade imbalances where some countries are forced to regularly adjust their domestic policies for balance of payments purposes.[10]

In sum, it is argued by various economists that there are circumstances where trade intervention can benefit a country without necessarily being at the expense of other nations, particularly so in the face of unemployment or other market imperfections which may not be as readily removable by domestic measures as Free Traders believe. This suggests the need for at least some continued trade intervention.

7   Absolute advantage argument   Critics of free trade have particularly savaged the classical assumption of capital (and labour) immobility which Ricardo (1817: 155) posited on the subjective premise that a businessman has a 'natural disinclination . . . to quit the country of his birth'. Even in Ricardo's day both factors moved to some extent, labour emigration often being forced by the effects of free trade (Hudson 1992: 130–1), and the more so in our electronic age, although long-term investment (DFI) is less mobile than speculative finance. Free Traders claim that modern trade theory does allow for capital mobility (Dillon et al. 1990: 35), seeing investment as a substitute for trade and subject to the same economic laws. However, some economists argue that capital mobility has shifted the basis of trade from comparative to absolute advantage because TNCs can now readily identify, and move to, the lowest absolute cost locations. Some mainstream economists have acknowledged this in the instance of labour mobility (e.g. Krugman and Obstfeld 1994: 182–3) but are silent on the capital mobility case. This gives rise to the possibility of 'exploited labour' or other social problems as governments compete to attract DFI, a possibility which some economics textbooks now accept (e.g. Todaro 1994: ch. 12), and so suggests the need for some capital controls or TRIMs.[11]

8   Terms of trade argument   During the 1950s several economists, including UNCTAD founder Raoul Prebisch and West Indian Nobel Laureate Sir Arthur Lewis, uncovered what many still think is a major flaw in Free Trade theory. Classical trade theory ignored 'income elasticities' (i.e. the responsiveness of demand to a rise in consumers' incomes) and potential trade asymmetries, but Prebisch and others suggested that a country facing low income elasticity for its exports and high domestic elasticity for imports could suffer declining terms of trade (export prices relative to import prices) and a perpetual balance of trade deficit. These theorists argued that this was the case for Third World countries whose demand for manufactured imports outgrew First World demand for primary products, and they proposed an interventionist 'import substitution industrialisation' (ISI) strategy which became widely used, though is now being abandoned (see Chapter 12). Some mainstream economists accept this argument (e.g. Sloman 1991: 868;

Todaro 1994: ch. 12), but Free Traders have generally rejected it on the grounds that other factors such as relative growth rates or First World protectionism could explain the terms of trade problem, and that the declining terms of trade trend is not clear. Nonetheless, many Third World commentators and NGOs still argue that the problem persists, at least for some Third World products and regions, especially Africa,[12] and that interventionist development models may be an answer (see Chapter 12). If so, the current thrust towards global free trade and the restriction of policy instruments such as subsidies and TRIMs could make some rectification options difficult for poor countries.

9 Unequal exchange arguments Writers from various disciplines have for some time argued that in a world of uneven development free trade, or even trade *per se*, may be inherently unequalising, this being for a range of reasons, including: the terms of trade argument (no. 8 above); wage–price spirals in industrial countries which inflate import prices for poor countries; inherent economic disadvantages of labour-intensive industries; unfairly low wages in poor countries; differential wages or labour inputs between exports and imports; differences in technological levels between rich and poor countries which may be perpetuated and amplified by trade; and the adverse 'backwash effects' of trade on traditional industries, which were first analysed by Swedish Nobel laureate Gunnar Myrdal. Most mainstream textbooks acknowledge at least some of these arguments (e.g. Todaro 1994: 426ff.), while a few orthodox theorists (e.g. Samuelson 1969) have accepted that the gains from trade can be unevenly spread and that some countries can actually lose. Free Traders tend to argue that the 'first best' solution to such problems is trade liberalisation combined with specialised development assistance, in effect winners 'bribing' losers into restructuring, but others have argued that such assistance measures do not always work and that continued trade interventionism may be necessary (e.g. Streeten 1982).

Another set of unequal exchange arguments centres around the notion that, as a result of factors such as increasing returns, economies of scale in production (see Glossary), cumulative advantage (see below), 'first mover' benefits and so forth, free trade might lock countries into an existing industry pattern, to their long-term disadvantage. One exponent of this view is the otherwise highly orthodox French economist, Nobel laureate Maurice Allais, who has gone as far as to oppose the free trade provisions of the EU (Ormerod 1994: 8), while others include such luminaries as Paul Krugman and Nobel laureates Robert Solow and Robert Lucas. Lucas has argued that by ignoring concepts such as economies of scale, increasing returns to capital, 'learning-by-doing' (see Glossary) and unequal access to technology, neo-classical economic theory has overlooked the possibility of capital and trade flows favouring industrially developed countries, a popular solution being to enhance 'human development'.[13]

A particularly heretical challenge to orthodox trade theory, and to neo-classical economic theory in general, comes from the so-called neo-Ricardian and post-Keynesian schools of thought, especially the work of Italian-British economist Piero Sraffa. These schools argue that the key concept of 'marginal productivity', which supposedly drives markets, may be tautological (e.g. the value of capital is measured in terms of its own returns), so that it might be 'administered' profits, wages or other factor incomes, as shaped by the distribution of power, which drive relative prices rather than the reverse as orthodoxy assumes. This startling critique opens up the possibility that, for instance, institutions are more important than markets in economic processes, that trade is based on bargaining power rather than fair exchange, that comparative advantage is created rather than natural (see argument no. 11 below) or that non-economic goals are feasible and can be achieved with appropriate domestic and trade intervention (see Edwards 1985: esp. ch. 4).

10 Exploited labour argument   No protectionist argument, irritates Free Traders more than the so-called 'cheap labour' argument, that First World industries need protection against 'unfair' competition from products made by 'cheap' or 'pauper' labour; that is, by low-wage Third World workers who can exist on a 'bowl of rice a day'. The Free Traders' retort is that low wages will normally reflect genuine comparative advantage based on low productivity and that, in any case, cheap products benefit consumers of the importing country, so that 'gains from trade' theory still applies.

The first of these replies is not unreasonable. In theory a labour-intensive production process employing many low-wage, low-skill workers could have unit costs the same as or higher than an equivalent capital-intensive one using a few highly paid workers, depending on relative comparative advantage. However, in an era of mobile capital and technology transfers, TNCs in many Third World countries might employ inappropriate capital-intensive Western technology but pay labour-intensive wage levels and use many exploitative techniques, so that workers would be paid much less than is justified by productivity, thus resulting in what I have called 'unit cost gaps' (see Glossary). Joan Robinson (1960: 193) has pointed out that this would represent 'cheap labour' even in a First World country and could confer on exporting nations a capacity to unfairly undersell others in a wide range of products, despite the Free Traders' theorem that every country can be competitive in something. This might better be called 'exploited labour' or 'social dumping' and in my view it clearly warrants some form of selective intervention. However, I accept the Free Traders' argument to some extent and suggest that such intervention must be confined to cases where below-productivity wages or labour rights violations are prevalent, not where fair labour-intensive wages are being paid. Attempts should also be made to eliminate the exploitation, but this could take time, and the question of inappropriate technologies should also be addressed (see Chapter 12).

In relation to the Free Traders' second reply, that cheap-labour goods nonetheless benefit the importing country, one recent textbook has declared that: 'Commerce is not a game; it is a business . . . (and) can be ruthless'. The inference is that competitive firms will always pursue minimum costs and consumers deserve access to the full range of available, low-priced goods or services irrespective of how they were produced (Husted and Melvin 1995: 202–3). However, this excessively pragmatic view ignores the possible social costs of losing an industry to exploitation-based imports and overlooks the fact that some consumers are willing to avoid such products. In short, the problem of 'exploited labour' may be the grounds for an interventionist 'Fair Trade' policy (see Chapter 12).

11 Cumulative advantage argument From the outset, Free Trade theory has tended to assume that comparative advantage was a largely static, God-given characteristic of nations, even though Mill (1848: 283–4) recognised that it may derive from 'acquired skill and experience' when one society begins an industry sooner than another.

More recently various writers, mainly in the industrial economics and economic history fields, have argued that comparative advantage is 'cumulative', being based on historical development processes, acquired skills, cultivated industry patterns or 'first mover' benefits, so it can change over time, can be shaped by governments or industry leaders and can decay through neglect. Free Traders now tend to accept that comparative advantage is dynamic, but nonetheless argue that governmental attempts to 'pick winners' can be wasteful and that the process of change should be left to the market (Dillon et al. 1990: 37–8; Krugman 1994, ch. 9). However, one group of cumulative advantage theorists have suggested that, in the case of Britain for instance, leaving industry development to the market has been the problem not the solution and that greater intervention is required.[14] If this concept is valid then many forms of domestic and trade intervention are likely to be justifiable.

12 Strategic trade arguments The starting-point for this set of arguments is the ostensible inability of traditional trade theory, based on the premises of small competitive firms, fixed technologies and other standard assumptions (see above), to explain phenomena such as intra-industry trade (see Glossary), the apparent self-generation of comparative advantage by countries like Japan or South Korea, the rise of TNCs which both invest and trade in a huge number of countries or a range of other corporate behavioural traits. Free Traders tend to claim that orthodox theory can be adapted to explain these phenomena (Dillon et al. 1990), but not all agree, there being a number of alternative explanations, which for convenience I will note under two headings—'new international economic theory' and 'strategic management'.

New international economic theory focuses on 'real world' factors such as imperfect competition, economies of scale and scope, market failures, externalities, informational and transactions costs, learning curve effects, or 'learning-by-doing' (see Glossary on these) and the increasingly apparent reality that large firms can influence the structure and processes of markets to their own strategic advantage in ways which conventional trade theory allegedly ignores. This suggests a number of circumstances in which some mix of domestic and trade intervention might, at least theoretically, be economically justified, four in particular being commonly cited: 1 where protection facilitates the establishment of local firms and enables them to reap economies of scale, learning-by-doing benefits and so forth— effectively an up-dated infant industry case; 2 where protection and/or domestic assistance enables national firms to become established in domestic and international markets through reputation, servicing, networking with related firms and so forth; 3 where government assistance (mainly domestic) enables certain industries to obtain 'external economies' or 'positive externalities' (see Glossary) through research, 'linkages' to other sectors, high 'value added' and so forth; 4 where 'rent snatching' is possible, i.e. where tax or assistance policies shift revenue from the home to the host country, thus resulting in a growth 'bonus' for the latter.

'Strategic' policy-making uses one or more of these circumstances to render a firm or industry, and thus the country as a whole, better off economically (higher real income) than it would otherwise have been. Policies adopted could include traditional protection, tax-subsidy systems, industry policy, 'networking' between firms or even strategic alliances with TNCs (see Chapter 12). Free Traders remain sceptical about the whole concept, claiming that it requires strict assumptions to be successful, that it may involve beggar-thy-neighbour effects, that it risks retaliation or escalating 'competitive' protectionism, that it is primarily suited to large countries and that governments are not good at 'picking winners' (i.e. identifying the above-mentioned circumstances which might 'pay-off' in higher growth). Even some 'new international' theorists share such qualms and do not advocate much intervention, but there are many who support strategic trade and domestic policies targetted to growth-oriented goals. In addition, as I will note below and in Chapter 12, it is possible to formulate alternative, partly 'non-economic' goals for strategic policy-making, in which case the Free Traders' concerns are less relevant.[15]

'Strategic management' schools begin from both the above-mentioned 'real world' factors and corporate managerial considerations, the best-known approach being that of US competitiveness theorist Michael Porter (1990). Porter's model regards a nation's competitive advantage as deriving from a 'diamond' of four elements —factor conditions, corporate strategy, demand conditions and industry linkages, the most competitive countries being those whose 'diamonds' produce well-established, innovative firms, including adaptation to a disadvantage (e.g. a dry country producing innovative irrigation systems), a notion very different from conventional comparative advantage. The model sees economic history as passing through four periods, i.e. factor-, investment-, innovation- and wealth-driven phases, of which only the first resembles the world described by traditional economic and trade theory, the second being based on corporate expansion, the third on rivalry for innovation and the last being a phase of stagnation. Extensive public intervention is relevant only to the second phase, thereafter the government's role being to support innovation and avoid the dreaded fourth phase.

Porter's approach has been used by both pro- and anti-interventionists to back their cases, but on balance the model would seem, in my view, to suggest at least a secondary role for government and an active role in some areas such as environmental regulation which can, Porter argues, stimulate productivity- and competitiveness-enhancing innovations beyond what the market alone might have induced.[16] Critics of Porter question the usefulness of his 'diamond', its narrow focus (e.g. its exclusion of labour, social forces etc.), its relevance to resource-exporting industrial countries like Australia or Canada, its extreme emphasis on innovation and its neglect of wider arguments for an active government role.[17]

A more interventionist 'strategic management' model is that proposed by Harvard business scholars, David Yoffie and associates (1993), which sees five bases for competitive advantage—country advantages, industry structure, corporate attributes, government policy and managerial inertia—and which identifies four market situations—comparative advantage, oligopolistic competition, regulated competition and political competition. In only the first of these four market situations does the traditional Free Trade model hold, with government intervention of various sorts playing at least some role in the other three.

There are no generally accepted conclusions from this debate, 'strategic management' theorists tending to favour at least some domestic and trade interventionism while 'new international' economists mostly opt for the 'safety' of relatively free trade. Indicative of this ambivalence is the position of Paul Krugman, a pioneer of the new international economic theory, who acknowledges many of the 'real world' problems of pure free trade theory but who is sceptical about the practicality of intervention where precise measurement is often not possible and where subjective political judgments, interest group pressures or policy uncertainties abound. He points out that the present obsession with competitiveness and relative national productivity levels is misplaced because these are largely irrelevant to comparative advantage, other than special cases of the sort discussed above. Krugman calls himself a 'cautious activist', advocating 'a limited government industry policy' for industries characterised by increasing returns or other clear-cut externalities, but he favours 'carefully targeted subsidies' rather than tariffs or import quotas.[18]

The various 'radical' arguments discussed above call into question many aspects of Free Trade theory, without necessarily completely undermining its validity, and thus indicate the need for at least a degree of active government intervention in markets, both domestically through measures such as industry policy and subsidies and externally through continued trade intervention to at least a moderate degree. Yet, as noted above and in Chapter 4, the Uruguay Round and some RTAs appear to restrict the use of such policies, and many advocates of full free trade, or 'deep integration', regularly argue against such measures. However, it remains to be seen whether or not the WTO's new world order will constrain such options.

Non-economic arguments

Virtually all trade theory is formulated in economic terms, with 'welfare' gains from trade usually gauged by the higher consumption and real income which is said to result from trade, and which may lead to accelerated economic growth. Needless to say, however, other criteria for trade decision-making are possible, which I will categorise as 'socio-economic' and 'non-economic'. Socio-economic issues relate to social consequences of trade-induced economic change, such as the need for workers to shift or re-train, for capital to re-tool or re-locate and so forth, and these can be quantified to some extent but evaluation may be subjective and require political judgments. These will be touched on in the next two chapters. Non-economic issues are political, social, cultural and other such matters which require consideration separately from, perhaps in contradistinction to, economic factors and which cannot normally be quantified. Mainstream economists do not entirely ignore non-economic issues, and indeed often claim that there are non-economic *benefits* from free trade (see next chapter) along with a few potential costs, but such issues tend to be allocated a low priority. There are four main ways in which Free Traders treat non-economic factors. The first is an almost Social Darwinian assertion that some things must be sacrificed in the interests of progress. Another is to compart-mentalise societal and cultural institutions, arguing that economic progress does not significantly affect them. A third treatment is to argue that economists are not qualified to say much about the non-economic costs of trade but that these are probably rather small and are likely to be outweighed by the economic and non-economic benefits of maximising trade and growth. The fourth possible treatment is to regard the adoption of non-economic goals as the legitimate, if sometimes misguided, prerogative of governments, and thence to seek implementation methods which might minimise the economic costs of such policies. The standard conclusion from this approach is that, in general, non-economic goals can most efficiently be achieved through domestic measures such as market reform or subsidies, with trade continuing to be conducted at world market prices even if at a reduced volume, although the result is seen as 'second best' to free trade.[19]

However, the range of non-economic goals considered by mainstream economists is a very narrow one, usually being confined to situations involving sectoral production limits, regional employment retention and the like, whereas many non-economic goals clearly negate unrestrained trade or the expansion thereof. Goals of this sort might include military and food security, protection of national sovereignty, the fostering of a traditional or non-materialistic way of life and political-economic self-reliance (see Chapter 12). In the case of self-reliance, economists concede that trade intervention, preferably in the form of tariffs, is the optimal policy where the reduction of imports is required (Bhagwati and Srinivasan 1969).

Non-economic goals entail what Keynes called 'the wisdom of not unduly sacrificing any part even to the whole' (see quotation

p. xv). There is good reason to believe that today the importance of non-economic issues is increasing throughout the world, though more amongst the public rather than amongst governments or economists, with goals such as globalisation, 'deep integration' and even economic growth coming under challenge. In my view many people tend to trade off economic and non-economic values in search of a satisfactory lifestyle rather than maximum material gains, in which case conventional indicators such as GDP growth, whether via trade or domestic sources, do not reflect true welfare. J. S. Mill (1848: 114) once queried the growth assumption, writing: 'I know not why it should be a matter of congratulation that persons who are already richer than anyone needs to be, should have doubled their means of consuming things'. Daly and Cobb's alternative environmentally based indicator suggests that US welfare peaked in the mid-1970s and is now declining; US 'happiness' polls peaked as far back as 1957; a mid-1970s Norwegian poll found three-quarters of respondents thought their living standard was *too high*.[20] If the assumption of material 'welfare' maximisation is dropped, then a wide range of conventional economic propositions, including free trade itself, are called into question. The following is a brief list of possible non-economic arguments against free trade which might arise when non-economic perspectives and goals are considered. Numbers 13 to 16, which I will call 'security' arguments, have regularly been noted in economics textbooks, but numbers 17 to 20, which I will call 'community–sovereignty' arguments, are less familiar. Most of these will also be touched on in later chapters.

13 Defence argument   One of the oldest non-economic arguments for protection asserts the desirability of self-reliance in defence-related needs and it is generally accepted by Free Traders, Adam Smith (1776: 487) once declaring that defence was more important than opulence. There are sceptics, however. Mill (1848: 282) thought it unlikely that any nation would be attacked by all other countries at once, such that all supplies would be cut off. Many contemporary economists prefer a limited defence subsidy, pointing out that almost all US industries, including lacemakers and candlemakers, have at some time claimed defence-relevance in an effort to obtain tariff protection (Husted and Melvin 1995: 207).

14 Food security argument   The logic of Free Trade theory, in the context of market-led, technologically determined economic growth, is that some nations are likely to develop a comparative *disadvantage* in agriculture, energy or other basic industries, and thus free trade would lead to heavy import dependence for fundamental needs. This has happened in a number of European, Asian and African countries and arguably can have various adverse implications for security and standards. Free Traders largely reject this argument, although some concede the need for a degree of food security (e.g. Oppenheim 1992: 123) and GATT makes some allowances for this. However, many countries remain genuinely concerned about the issue and the Uruguay Round liberalisation process is likely to exacerbate the problem for some (see Chapter 8).

15 Environmental argument Free Traders accept trade intervention for 'externalities' (argument 4, above), but only in regard to a limited range of cross-border environmental problems and they claim that rectification can mainly be done domestically. However, some economists (e.g. Daly and Goodland 1993) and many environmentalists argue that the domestic and trade-related environmental problems are integrally linked, so that extensive domestic and trade intervention are necessary (see Chapter 10).

16 Industry balance argument Free Trade theorists argue that unrestrained international exchange maximises efficiency and growth no matter what industries are the basis of a country's comparative advantage and every country will find something to export. Although this seems logical in theory, many critics claim that it is not always applicable in practice for a range of economic and non-economic reasons. Too *much* reliance on agriculture may lead to low living standards, dependence on commodity exports and instability, but too *little* reliance may mean food insecurity, excessive use of machine-chemical agriculture and a divorce of people from nature, Keynes (1932) having once surmised that a well-rounded society needs contact with changing seasons and closeness to the soil. Too *little* manufacturing may lead to dependence on imports for basic requirements, but too *much* may lead to excessive urbanisation and pollution. Too *little* reliance on the services sector may deprive industry and the community of basic services, but too *much* reliance may hamper growth or lead to a balance of trade deficit as some critics of 'post-industrialism' argue (see Chapter 8). A goal of 'industry balance' might therefore require a national product mix quite different from that shaped by global markets, thus resulting in the desirability of domestic and trade intervention for what Keynes (see quotation p. xv) called a 'well-balanced national economic policy'.

17 Culture preservation argument Trade can, broadly speaking, affect culture in two ways—through direct displacement of cultural items or through inducement of wider cultural change. The first might involve imports such as books, comics, magazines, films, television programmes and the like, or export demand for a society's artefacts. Most countries reserve the right to control imports or exports of such items as required, some restrictions of this sort being allowed by GATT and NAFTA, but Free Traders are sceptical about such measures (see Chapter 9). As regards forces for wider cultural change, anthropologists say that almost any outside influence engenders some impacts for the importing society and all should be prepared to accept a certain degree of change, although some societies have endeavoured to minimise such impacts and there are people in most countries who would like to see these restrained. Free Traders argue that there is a variety of non-trade policies which can be used for cultural purposes, but in my view many of these are now inadequate in the face of globalisation, especially given the massive world-wide changes which globalisers wish to encourage, and given that many industries and services come with hidden 'cultural baggage' (see Chapter 9).

18 Community maintenance argument It is a serious blind spot in Free Trade theory, and neo-classical economics generally, that 'resources' are seen as perfectly, or at least highly, malleable and that people are not deemed as living in communities or other social arrangements which they choose for conviviality. It is tacitly assumed that people can move relatively costlessly to locations required by the market or that capital can shift to new sites without changing living arrangements to anyone's disliking. Free trade has little room for the 'spirit of place'. The idea of people being socially or sentimentally attached to a locality may be considered irrationally romantic and tends to be ignored by mainstream economists today, although both Smith (1776: 477) and Ricardo (1817: 155) believed that such sentiments applied at the national level. Ricardo claimed that most businessmen would forgo opportunities for higher profits overseas and admitted that he would be sorry to see such national sentiments weakened, though he did not apply this insight to domestic communities. Keynes spoke of the need to maintain 'the old established traditions of a countryside' (see quotation p. xv), while many 'non-economists' go even further, seeing community as a repository of culture, values, stability or the like, and the break-down thereof as a leading cause of social dislocation, crime and so forth.

The most common community-based opponents of free trade are rural towns or districts centred around single industries which may be affected by trade-induced structural change, a process which even some mainstream economists admit can lead to a cumulative decline, first postulated by Myrdal, as people and services leave a region (e.g. Krugman and Obstfeld 1994: 182–7). Free Traders usually see such concerns as special pleading which could be allevi-ated by compensation out of the gains from trade, but such compen-sation is seldom assured and is usually designed to assist adjustment, not save the community. Free Traders greatly underestimate the value that people attach to traditional community and the extent to which community structures are being adversely affected by capital mobility, globalisation and trade in sensitive services (see Chapter 9). If community maintenance is to be a policy-making consider-ation, which I argue it should be, then non-trade support measures are certainly required, as Free Traders point out, but trade-restricting policies may also be needed where it is global forces which are in-ducing the undesirable changes (see Daly and Cobb 1989: ch. 11).

19 Subsidiarity argument   Formally, Free Trade theory pays little or no heed to levels or location of decision-making, the result being that some Free Traders can advocate 'deep integration' of the world economy without considering the wisdom or desirability of having decisions made in far-distant administrative centres or boardrooms. However, some economists and other commentators suggest that there may need to be a trade-off between economies of scale, with their centralising tendencies, and the desirability of diversity with its de-centralist implications (Cooper 1994).

Not surprisingly, this issue is being considered in the world's most advanced RTA, the EU, where reference is often made to the so-called 'subsidiarity principle', which states that decisions should be made at the lowest level (i.e. closest to the citizenry) consistent with efficiency and accountability. This concept, with its origins in the post-Reformation Christian churches, has now been incorporated in the EU Charter of Local Self-Government and the Maastricht Treaty, often being employed to support various regional schemes, de-centralisation measures and programmes to involve interest groups in decision-making (Horsman and Marshall 1994: part 3, ch. 4; UNCTAD 1994a: 315; Hama 1996). However, there is no consensus as to what it ultimately means for the integration project, some seeing it as a hypocritical sop to regional interests (Hama 1996: 73), while others argue that such a principle militates against free trade-driven integration or globally constraining trade rules in favour of government de-centralisation and perhaps even smaller nation states. Certainly opinion poll evidence from the EU (Introduction to Part Two) seems to suggest that many Europeans now see decision-making as being too far-removed from their spheres of existence. Although the 'subsidiarity principle' is usually only applied to a polity, it could equivalently be used in relation to corporate decision-making. To the extent that free trade, 'deep integrating' regionalism and globalism foster large administrative units or allow business decisions by TNCs to be shifted 'offshore', then the virtues of these processes are called into question.

20 Sovereignty argument Sovereignty questions, involving the right of a nation to decision-making autonomy, have not usually been considered by trade theory because its early exponents did not envisage 'deep integration', because international transactions have usually been seen merely as arm's length commercial deals rather than as matters of power relations and because many economists now think that national economic sovereignty needs to be curbed in the interests of global economic stabilisation, although some economists claim that sovereignty is only re-located as a result of integration, not diminished (Jovanović 1992, p. 10ff.). However, under the 'new model free trade agreement' global trading rules and deepening integration clearly are undermining national sovereignty and are designed to do so (see Hirst and Thompson 1996, ch. 7). This trend of sovereignty diminution will be enhanced by the Uruguay Round's services liberalisation, standards harmonisation and TRIMs provisions, by current proposals for investment de-regulation and by the concept of 'locking-in' which is now commonly invoked in free trade politics. Few commentators claim that national sovereignty should be totally unfettered but, equally, many now believe that the Free Trade Adventure is creating excessive fetters, an issue which is coming to the fore in the EU and increasingly world-wide (see Chapter 11).

This list by no means exhausts the possible non-economic arguments against full free trade, others including concern that trade may harden materialistic values, bring undesirable ways of life and worsen the already grotesquely unequal distribution of world income and wealth—the world's 358 billionaires are said to possess as much wealth as the poorest 45 per cent of the human race.[21] The security arguments (nos 13 to 15), which are at least in part accepted by some Free Traders, may be rectifiable by minor forms of domestic assistance, as Free Traders assert, but the more complex, inter-connected community–sovereignty arguments (nos 16 to 20) are likely to require a wide range of policy interventions, both trade and domestic, both economic and social, as will be touched on in later chapters.

Conclusion

The theory behind the Free Trade Adventure in general, and the Uruguay Round in particular, derives directly from the basic free trade principles of Smith and Ricardo which Free Traders believe remain at least workably adequate despite all the changes of the last two centuries. In this chapter I have examined twenty possible theoretical arguments against complete free trade, and to some extent against trade itself, the latter being further discussed in Chapter 12. Free Traders tend to accept, if sometimes hesitantly, the orthodox arguments (nos 1 to 4) and some economists accept a selection of the radical and non-economic arguments, while social activists and NGOs accept a wide range thereof.

Some claim that recent theoretical developments have left the Free Trade idea in tatters. The foregoing survey suggests that this is an unwarranted inference, especially as few advocates of the 'strategic trade' argument claim this, but it does suggest that there are many grounds, beyond those normally accepted by orthodox theorists, for modifying Free Trade conclusions. In my view the free trade debate remains, and probably will ever remain, unresolved. Thus, whether Free Traders like it or not, there will always be sufficient grounds for doubt about their doctrine to ensure that trade interventionism has extensive support, especially when non-economic arguments are adequately considered. If so, then there is good reason to seriously question the Free Trade Adventure, which arguably is being imposed upon the world by what British Japan-expert and Free Trade critic, Ronald Dore (1993: 152), has described as 'the almost total control that free trade dogma has over the whole world's ideological airspace'.

7

The Best Thing since Sliced Bread?

Benefits and hidden costs of the Uruguay Round

If the proclamations of GATT admirers are anything to go by then the Uruguay Round was indeed a miracle of our time. Around the world the press declared that the agreement would pull the global economy out of recession. GATT Director-General, Peter Sutherland, opined that it could bring peace and prosperity to the world and he eagerly, though highly improbably, attributed the 9 per cent growth in world trade for 1994, which was the highest annual figure since 1976, to confidence engendered by the Uruguay Round. Sutherland also insisted that there would be no losers from the Uruguay Round, only winners![1] The Round brought to the fore a new generation of computer modellers whose work has suggested that there could be world-wide income gains of many billions, up to about 1 per cent of world GDP, although I will argue in this chapter that interpretation of such results requires considerable qualification and that many likely costs have been overlooked.

The politics of estimating benefits

During the early 1990s, when the Uruguay Round was on the verge of collapse, GATT leaders urged persistence, citing computer model projections for world-wide income gains from the Round of some $500b, more than double the estimates of other groups, while the USA proclaimed that the Round would be worth $6 trillion over fifteen years (Raghavan 1990: 4). The Australian Government was claiming, on the basis of OECD and IC studies, a GDP boost for Australia of A$2.5 to 3.7b, though some trade officials privately thought that A$1b was more likely.[2] At one stage the OECD Secretary General, Jean Claude-Paye, dismissed such figures as a 'pretty theoretical exercise', but Peter Sutherland stood by them manfully and once testily asked a sceptic 'don't you believe in free trade?' (Raghavan 1990: 3–4).

Curiously, for all the passion with which most mainstream economists defend Free Trade theory, many studies of its likely benefits in practice are surprisingly modest, one estimate suggesting that liberalisation under the earlier GATT rounds was probably worth 1 per cent of GDP for the USA, 2 per cent for Europe and a few per cent for Canada and Australia.[3] One of the early computerised models estimated that elimination of all post–Tokyo Round tariffs would raise world income by a minuscule 0.01 per cent and employment by 0.26 per cent (Deardorff and Stern 1983). This is what Krugman (1995) claims to be economists' 'dirty little secret' (see p. 14 above). Trade liberalisation does, of course, increase export opportunities, as Australian government departments are fond of pointing out (e.g. DFAT 1994a–d), sometimes in unexpected ways. It is surmised, for instance, that Australian wool exports to Mexico could benefit from NAFTA through a stimulus to the Mexican textile industry. By the same token, liberalisation also means higher imports and the nett effects are seldom clear in advance, so must be gauged by aggregate 'econometric models' (see Glossary).

The latest version of such models, known unglamorously as the computable general equilibrium (CGE) model, is based on all known linkages in an economy and is designed to test the effect of any one change upon the rest of the system. Most models measure 'static gains', or short-term benefits arising from the more efficient use of resources which trade liberalisation is thought to bring, with two variants respectively assuming perfect and imperfect competition (see Glossary). A few models measure 'dynamic gains', or the longer-term benefits which arise when the static gains are re-invested and technological innovations follow. Models used to assess the Uruguay Round varied both in these respects and with respect to other assumptions such as how the Round would be implemented, how fully NTBs would be removed and the base year employed for the computations. Interpreting the modelling results thus presents traps for the unwary and manifold opportunities for misuse.

Lies, damned lies and models

By the conclusion of the Uruguay Round GATT's official models (GATT 1994) had produced estimates of post-Uruguay world GDP increases ranging from $109b to $510b, the lower estimates being based on perfectly competitive models and the higher figures, which GATT favours, being based on imperfect competition assumptions. Estimates by other modellers ranged from $139b to $274b (USITC 1994: 1–12). The two most quoted studies, one done jointly by the OECD and the World Bank (Goldin et al. 1993), the most authoritative and widely quoted at present (see Table 7.1), and the other by Canadian economists (Nguyen et al. 1993), arrived at almost identical figures for world benefits—$213b and $212b respectively, though using differing assumptions and base years. These projected benefits are likely to be distributed rather unequally, Goldin et al. even projecting losses for certain countries and regions. The EU, the USA and Japan are likely to reap most of the benefits because of the considerable protection cuts these countries are supposed to make in their inefficient agricultural sectors, although the gains do not translate into large national benefits for these countries because their agricultural sectors are so small relative to GDP. Most models show only very small gains from liberalisation of manufacturing because tariffs in this sector are already quite low. The forecast by Goldin et al. of a minuscule 0.1 per cent GDP gain for Australia and New Zealand is well below the 0.7 to 1.6 per cent of GDP variously projected by other studies,[4] and the IC's estimate for Australia of a A$4.4b gain in GDP from the Round is reduced to A$1.2b when gauged by national income, the IC's preferred 'welfare' measure,[5] all of which demonstrates how sensitive modelling results are to the assumptions and indicators used.

These sorts of estimates have been poorly explained by their authors and have been widely misinterpreted by journalists, who often incorrectly depict them as sums available on an annual basis, beginning immediately. In fact the Uruguay Round is to be phased in over six to ten years, although OECD modeller, Ian Goldin, has

Table 7.1: Changes in real income from trade liberalisation

	Partial Liberalisation	Full Free Trade
	%	%
Low Income Asia	0.6	1.3
China	2.5	4.5
India	0.5	1.8
Upper Income Asia	2.6	8.2
Indonesia	−0.7	−2.6
Other Africa	−0.2	−0.9
Nigeria	−0.4	−1.8
South Africa	0.6	0.1
Maghreb	−0.5	−2.3
Mediterranean	−0.4	−2.4
Gulf Region	0.5	−1.0
Other Latin America	0.6	1.3
Brazil	0.3	0.4
Mexico	0.0	−0.4
United States	0.2	0.3
Canada	0.2	0.0
Australia/New Zealand	0.1	1.0
Japan	0.9	2.7
European Community	1.4	2.8
European Free Trade Area	1.4	3.0
European Economies in Transition	0.1	−0.1
Former Soviet Union	0.1	0.9

Notes: The figures represent per cent changes in real income. This is measured as the change in welfare in the year 2002 divided by the value of GDP in the year 2002 in the base simulation.
Column 1 is based on measures similar to those finally adopted by the Uruguay Round.
Column 2 is based on elimination of all tariffs, quotas and some NTBs.

Source: Goldin et al. (1993): Table 3.5, p. 95

explained (Raghavan 1990) that the benefits are modelled as accruing in a one-off GDP increase at some future date. In general 'static' gains from trade bring a one-off rise in real income due to a 'better' allocation of resources, or a lift of the GDP growth graph without an increase of slope, while 'dynamic' gains are claimed to be an acceleration of growth, or a further upward shift of the graph with perhaps an increased slope (see McKibbin and Salvatore 1995). Uruguay Round forecasts suggest that by 2005 (the end of the Round implementation period) the annual world income will be 0.2 to 1.3 per cent higher than it would otherwise have been. A figure in the upper range could be said to be 'non-trivial', but a figure in the lower range would, as US modeller Alan Deardorff has said, 'hardly be noticed', or, as Thurow has said, would be within rounding error.[6] Subsequent studies have tended to scale the estimates down further still, though mainly due to growing pessimism about how fully countries will implement the Round in practice, Nguyen et al. having, just a year after the end of the Round, reduced their forecast for total gains from $212b to $70b, or 0.4 per cent of world GDP. Some modellers now suggest that the Round will have no impact at all if countries 'cheat' through 'dirty tariffication' or the like.[7]

Free Traders claim that, for several reasons, these results underestimate the possible benefits of the Uruguay Round and of trade liberalisation in general. First, all the above-mentioned studies cover only the goods areas of the Uruguay Round, not services, TRIPs and the like, so that allowing for these would increase the benefit estimates. One US government study[8] estimated services and TRIPs to be worth $11b each, but most economists regard these areas as too speculative to bother modelling, so this claim is unproven at present. Second, the Uruguay Round's liberalisation efforts were rather limited and greater degrees of liberalisation may bring proportionately greater benefits. This argument is feasible but also unproven. Goldin et al. have modelled a full free trade option and found that it would little more than double the Uruguay Round benefit estimates, from $213b to $450b, the latter being 1.5 per cent of world GDP, while some countries would incur reduced gains or even magnified losses (see Table 7.1).[9]

A third reason claimed for greater benefits is the possibility of longer-term 'dynamic' gains from trade, of which two types have been identified, these being what US trade economist, Robert Baldwin, calls the medium-term and long-term 'growth bonuses'. Medium-term 'bonuses' derive from the higher savings and investment or greater returns on capital which are expected to arise from trade liberalisation. Long-term 'bonuses' derive from a combination of further specialisation, 'human capital' accumulation (education, skill enhancement etc.) and technological innovation, all of which can theoretically induce continuing growth. Baldwin estimates dynamic gains from European unification to be double the static gains and US studies put dynamic gains from the Uruguay Round at two or three times the static gains.[10] An Australian study (McKibbin and Salvatore 1995) using dynamic assumptions such as induced capital flows and productivity increases projected permanent world benefits from the Uruguay Round of around $200b, although this is only in the upper range of estimates by static models. One study of Australia's unilateral tariff reform programme (EPAC 1995) has forecast dynamic gains of up to ten times earlier projected static gains, totalling 15 per cent of GDP. But these benefits will take thirty years to accrue (1990 to 2020), arguably a speculatively long time, they depend 'to an unknown extent' on accompanying microeconomic reform and even then they represent only 0.5 per cent per annum, a lower figure than some of the more bullish estimates of static gains from the Uruguay Round. A more critical assessment by Quiggin (1996, ch. 10 and 210–11) suggests that Australia has gained little growth from tariff reductions, that micro-economic reform is likely to be worth less than a tenth of the 5.5 per cent of GDP originally expected and he is sceptical about the concept of 'dynamic gains'. Neither the theoretical basis nor the empirical estimates of dynamic gains are universally accepted by economists at present, and the real value of the hypothesised gains depends on how society assesses the worth of the innovations concerned (see below). Overall, it may be that the models have underestimated the benefits of trade liberalisation, but overestimation is also possible for reasons which will be examined below.

Attempts to model the effects of RTAs involve similar problems. Estimates of static gains from European unification range from 2.5 to 6.5 per cent spread over a number of years, and perhaps twice that when dynamic gains are included. Baldwin has surmised that this might permanently increase the EU growth rate by 0.2 to 0.9 percentage points, although others have suggested that such gains are likely to be very unevenly distributed, with almost no benefits for the more industrialised members.[11] As noted in Chapter 5, ANZCERTA is projected to bring a small gain for Australia, with larger gains (and costs) for New Zealand. Early studies of the APEC proposals forecast income gains ranging from 1.1 per cent for the USA to 9.8 per cent for China, with 3.4 per cent for Australia, 8–9 per cent for New Zealand, Malaysia, Singapore and the Philippines and 1.8 per cent for APEC as a whole (Murtough 1994b). On the other hand, another study using the IC's Salter Model, has found that Australia's real national income could *decline* by 0.7 per cent as a result of declining terms of trade unless other APEC members removed certain protective barriers.[12] Some of the most detailed modelling available relates to NAFTA, with a confusing range of results (summarised in Table 7.2) which mostly suggest very small gains for the USA, larger gains for Mexico and a mixed picture for Canada. In all, the real value of such projected benefits seems questionable, except perhaps for Mexico, some of the gains forecast being virtually negligible or even negative, as will be further discussed below.[13] Likely income gains from NAFTA for the average US worker have been estimated at 0.01 to 0.03 cents per hour (USITC 1993: 2.3)!

The sorts of models discussed above are complex, sophisticated and technically brilliant, but even some of their exponents admit to certain limitations. Global models often consist mainly of a 'world sector' tacked on to an existing national model, with information about 'elasticities' (responsiveness of various elements of an economy to changes, e.g. demand to prices rises etc.) being sketchy for many countries or even assumed constant between countries to save calculation time. Some modellers thus concede that global models are less reliable the more countries that are included and the longer the time-span modelled. Both national and global model results depend heavily upon the elasticities adopted, of which there are millions for a complex economy, the underlying economic relationships assumed and the data used. Data for OECD countries are now fairly reliable, but less so for many Third World nations. It has recently been suggested, for instance, that China's much-reported

Table 7.2: Modelling results for NAFTA

(Projected percentage increases)

Country	Real GDP	Nett Welfare	Employment	Real Wages	Nett Trade
USA	0.02–0.5	0.3	0–2.5	0.1–0.3	0.17
Canada	0.1–0.4	0.7	0–7.3	0–0.5	10.0
Mexico	–0.4–3.4	5.0	0.1–6.6	0.7–16.2	–0.6

Notes: The figures in columns 1, 3 and 4 are based on the results of 12 leading models (all but one a CGE model) surveyed by the US International Trade Commission and the ranges noted here cover the dispersion of their various findings. Some higher results have been found, such as an 11.4 per cent real GDP increase for Mexico and a similar figure for Canada, but these are regarded as unreliably exceptional. Column 2 is based on national income in a separate study and is not comparable with column 1. The figures mostly represent one-off percentage gains to GDP over an unspecified period.

Sources: Columns 1, 3 and 4 are from *Economy-Wide Modelling of the Economic Effects of a FTA with Mexico and a NAFTA with Canada and Mexico*, USITC, 2508 Washington DC, May 1992 and USITC (1993): ch. 2. Columns 2 and 5 are from a study by Drusilla Brown, summarised by L. Waverman, *The World Economy*, 15/1, January 1992: Table 4.

super-growth of 10 per cent plus per annum since the early 1980s has been massively overstated due to a variety of measurement problems, difficulties establishing measurable prices, unwarranted extrapolation from high growth areas, the shifting of barter transactions into the measured monetary economy and plain fibbing by growth-obsessed authorities. It is said that the real figure is more like 1–5 per cent per annum, but the bullish forecasts for China in the models discussed above may reflect the overstated data.[14] The models probably also overstate the likely gains from trade liberalisation for those Third World countries where some of the trade will simply displace hitherto unmeasured subsistence production.

The underlying theory implicit in most such models derives largely from neo-classical economic principles (see Chapter 6), entailing assumptions which can be subjected to the following criticisms.

1   Many models assume perfectly competitive markets and high elasticities, i.e. smooth, virtually instantaneous adjustment by factors of production (labour, capital etc.) to price or other changes, and their projections imply that the greater the elasticity, or 'flexibility', of an economy, the greater the benefits which result from trade

liberalisation. However, some economists believe that most econ-omies are becoming relatively inelastic and it is unlikely that all sectors will be made equally elastic through 'micro-economic reform', so that such models probably overestimate the feasibility of, and likely benefits from, trade liberalisation.

2   As noted above, those models which assume imperfect competi-tion and economies of scale project greater benefits from trade liber-alisation than do those assuming perfectly competitive markets, but many modellers believe that the perfect competition assumption is the more accurate for the world as a whole because internationalised markets tend to be more competitive than domestic-oriented sectors, particularly in the agriculture and resource sectors from which most of the Uruguay Round gains are expected to derive. So the lower-bound benefit estimates may be the more accurate and these often project quite minor gains. Furthermore, some critics suggest that those models positing economies of scale might in any case be over-estimating benefits, for several reasons. In monopolistic or oligo-polistic sectors the assumed increasing returns could be counteracted by allocative inefficiencies; mark-up pricing could be used to avoid passing the benefits on to consumers; the extra import competition might be countered by reduced domestic competition as local firms collapse; and the results of such models are highly sensitive to the pricing methods assumed. When such factors are considered, the benefits are often no greater than for constant-return models.[15]

3   The standard models assume full employment for all factors of production, which implies that workers displaced by imports will quickly find new jobs at similar wage rates and capital will find new investment outlets with similar returns. Under this assumption there are few adjustment costs and no reduction of aggregate demand. If, as many economists believe, this is an unrealistic assumption (see Koechlin and Larudee 1992), then such models will understate the costs of trade liberalisation and overestimate its benefits.

4   Neo-classical models tend to assume that income is distributed through the market and is affected by trade only through income shifts between factors of production (land, labour and capital). How-ever, some economists, including Keynesians, believe that income and wealth distribution is also determined by social institutions and that trade liberalisation may increase unemployment, worsen

inequalities, cut savings and thus reduce growth. If this is true then the conventional models would overestimate the benefits of trade liberalisation.

5   CGE models usually ignore the question of trade balance, assuming that the exchange rate will always adjust as required to retain full employment. But Keynesian critics believe that the exchange rate may not always adjust adequately, so that trade balance would have to be achieved through a downward adjustment of employment and income, or what some Australian modellers have irritably called a 'perverse Keynesian response' (Toohey 1994: 173), thus possibly negating at least some of the initial benefits from trade liberalisation.

6   Most models assume that long-term investment does not easily cross national boundaries in response to trade liberalisation, but evidence now suggests that firms can readily shift investment, especially within RTAs, and business surveys in Canada have found, for instance, that a large portion of major firms are planning such shifts (Campbell 1993)—also see Chapter 8. Thus, conventional models may be greatly underestimating the costs to some countries of free trade agreements which include investment liberalisation.

If these criticisms are valid then many of the commonly used models may entail an in-built bias towards free trade. British modeller, Paul Ormerod (1994), suggests that such a bias occurs because of various mechanistic assumptions which so many models employ, such as competitive general equilibrium, individualism, rational behaviour and the general virtues ascribed to free markets. The Australian Keynesian economist, John Quiggin, has explained that modelling systems incorporate, along with a formal component containing the basic equations and data, an informal component which contains the underlying theory and philosophy, and which often guides or even overrules the formal component. In the case of the Industry Commission's ORANI model, which has been used to formulate Australia's current policies, the informal component contains the presumptions that corporate monopolies do not adversely affect the economy but labour 'monopolies' do, that complete free trade is the optimum trade policy and that private sector activity is inherently more efficient than public equivalents, all of which leads the IC to be an invariable advocate of free trade and privatisation. Other critics point to outdated data, dubious assumptions and questionable inferences employed in ORANI, including an alleged massive overestimate of the price elasticity of demand for Australian commodity exports which thus overrates the benefits of tariff and wage cuts. However, defenders of ORANI reply that the key data and relationships are updated regularly, that precise elasticity estimates do not much affect results, especially in CGE models, and that real world inelasticities or imperfections are allowed for as much as practicable.[16] However, the issues are complex and there arguably should be more public scrutiny of such models now that they are regularly used for policy assessment and government decision-making.

In conclusion, it can be said that currently used models have forecast small to medium economic benefits from the Uruguay Round and other trade liberalisation options, some practitioners even claiming that these estimates are conservative, but there is a possibility that these models overestimate the benefits and underestimate potential costs.

How much does free trade cost?

According to conventional Free Trade theory protection entails a range of costs such as less product availability, more expensive consumer goods, higher input prices for producers and so forth, with partially offsetting benefits to protected producers and to government revenue (in the case of tariffs). Trade liberalisation will reverse these balances, normally resulting in positive nett benefits overall, as measured by accelerated income growth, these being the greater the closer a liberalising country comes to full free trade. In addition, Free Traders suggest that there may be a range of socio-economic and non-economic *benefits* from trade and other forms of liberalisation such as: easier movement of goods, services and people; greater variety of goods and services; better quality of goods and services through competition and access to the 'world's best'; wider ranges of choice; reduced inflation due to enhanced competition; access to new knowledge and ideas; advancement opportunities for people; less political corruption or other costs which may arise from lobbying for protection, import licences and the like; and broader social outlooks and cosmopolitanism.

No doubt such benefits of trade liberalisation are real, albeit somewhat materialistic, but the more fundamental question is whether there are hidden costs of various sorts. Most economists suggest that the costs of protection are small where those protection levels are low, as in many OECD countries now, but higher where trade barriers are significant. Some estimates put the cost of US protection around the start of the Uruguay Round at a minuscule 0.26 per cent of GNP, and up to 10 per cent for a few high-protection countries, but generally less than 5 per cent (Krugman and Obstfeld 1994: 229; Krugman 1995: 31–2). Where such costs are small, the corresponding benefits of liberalisation are also small, as borne out by some of the studies cited above, so much so that Krugman (1991: 104ff.; 1995: 33) suggests the case for free trade entails a 'leap of faith' and is largely political or symbolic. If this is true then unexpected economic costs, such as adverse terms of trade effects, may readily convert these anticipated gains to losses. US modellers, Deardorff and Stern (1983), for instance, found that 20 out of the 34 countries they modelled would suffer small overall 'welfare' losses from the complete elimination of tariffs. Australia's elder statesman of trade theory, Max Corden (1996) has estimated that, on balance, free trade would raise Australia's GDP by 2 per cent or so, which he admits is small but he claims it would still build a lot of schools and hospitals. However, given that Australian tax revenue is now less than a third of GDP, the public benefit would be limited and could be outweighed by the sorts of costs noted below and in the next chapter. Quiggin (1996, ch. 10) denies that Australia's post-war protection has been a brake on growth as the 'Canberra consensus' proclaims, 'costing' only 0.2 per cent of GDP or 1–2 per cent if the variance of tariff levels is allowed for.

Peter Sutherland's rhetorical claim that there will be no losers from the Uruguay Round is belied by results from Goldin et al. who identified five countries or regions which could suffer real income losses from the Round and eight which could lose from full free trade (see Table 7.1). Such losses would derive mainly from adverse changes in the terms of trade, because most world market prices will rise after trade liberalisation and a few will fall. The countries most likely to lose, such as Indonesia and some African nations (Table 7.1), will be those heavily dependent on food imports whose export prices fall or whose import prices rise substantially. In particular, the prices of wheat, coarse grains and dairy products are expected to rise while those for coffee, cocoa and rice are expected to fall (Goldin et al. 1993: Table 3.4, p. 94). Thus, even though many Second and Third World countries are expected to benefit from the liberalisation of agriculture, textiles and light manufacturing, most export growth will accrue to the Asian NICs while a 1.3 per cent *fall* has been projected for the exports of the African, Caribbean and Pacific countries. Even the World Bank, the IMF and the UN's Food and Agricultural Organisation (FAO) are expecting widespread Third World losses and are therefore considering compensatory finance for the 'victims' of Uruguay.[17]

Other hidden costs of the Uruguay Round for Third World countries could include: erosion of their existing preference systems as falling general tariff levels dilute the value of existing concessions; increased compliance costs such as tougher inspections, new information requirements, trips to Geneva and so forth; higher patent administration and royalty payments under the TRIPs Agreement (see Chapter 9); possible dangerous reductions in world food stocks, already at an unprecedently low 47 days' supply, as First World surpluses decline and are only slowly replaced by Third World production; and a wide range of socio-economic adjustment costs (see Chapter 8). Economic legend has it that poor countries will gain through trade-induced 'trickle-down' from the rich, but modelling by Goldin et al. (1993: 86) suggests that the Third World will gain little from OECD countries' post-Uruguay growth.

Further possible sources of economic costs from trade liberalisation, not normally recognised by Free Traders, include factors of the sort discussed in the previous chapter such as unequal exchange or loss of opportunities to use 'strategic trade' policies for 'cumulative advantage'. A final economic cost of liberalisation worth noting is the loss of tariff revenue by governments, a cost which Free Traders regard, not unreasonably, as small and likely to be greatly outweighed by gains from trade, but one which is not trivial. Australian budget losses are running at about A$3.5b per annum at present, or some 3 per cent of Commonwealth revenues, and this figure will increase with the Uruguay Round tariff cuts. Equivalent losses in the USA are over $20b, which is a lower proportion of the federal budget than Australia's figure but it has become a political issue in that country. I agree with Free Traders that this should not be a basis for opposing liberalisation in OECD countries, but it may be a bigger issue in the Third World where governments often rely heavily on easily collectible border duties for their key working revenues.

Some factors which I have referred to as 'socio-economic' costs often receive minimal attention from Free Traders and are seldom included in econometric models of the sort discussed above. These consist primarily of income loss and social disruption for workers or capital-owners arising from general structural change, as well as the direct costs of re-training, re-location and so forth. Models which do consider such costs identify much smaller gains from trade liberalisation. Stanford (1993: Table 3) has identified likely losses in employment, investment and wages for Canada and the USA as capital migrates to Mexico under NAFTA, with GDP gains of 13.1 per cent for Mexico, but a minuscule 0.04 per cent for the USA and a substantial loss of 1.47 per cent for Canada. 'Capital flight' from the USA to Mexico could be as much as $53b, thus reducing US employment by up to half a million, whereas the mainstream models predict small employment gains.[18]

Free Traders often illustrate the alleged costs of protection by painting assistance measures as an implicit indirect tax, US studies suggesting, for instance, that textile and clothing protection via the MFA costs the US consumer $17.6b per annum. This type of calculation often leads economists to avow that it would be cheaper to pension off all the workers in a protected industry and close it down. However, an alternative study of the US textile and clothing industry by Managed Traders, Scott and Lee (1991), has found that because conventional studies assume perfect competition they overlook the fact that some of the alleged costs of protection are simply oligopolistic retail mark-ups. These authors found that trade intervention can provide market security and the 'breathing space' required to raise productivity, which could then reduce protection costs from the alleged $17.6b to just $3.65b. Scott and Lee also found that conventional models underestimate the costs of past trade liberalisation because many displaced workers have taken very long periods to find new jobs and many have had to take pay cuts. The authors estimate the cost of eliminating MFA protection for

US textiles at \$852b, far higher than conventional studies have suggested. The same authors reached similar conclusions for the US steel industry, although they argued that tariffs or quotas would have been more efficient than the VERs used until recently.[19] Free Traders always claim that 'winners' can compensate 'losers' through assistance programmes, but the problem with this proposition is that compensation does not proceed automatically, may be inadequate, can be resisted by the gainers and is even more difficult to implement internationally than domestically, while nett gains might not even eventuate. Moreover, most econometric models treat compensation as a lump sum, but if it is not delivered in this way then the cost of programme administration will reduce the actual gains from trade liberalisation (Quiggin 1996: 45). In any case Free Traders also tend to favour public-sector budget cuts, of which redistributive measures are frequently a victim. GATT has never proposed a formal compensation system of this sort, although the WTO is now calling on the IMF and World Bank to help the, according to Peter Sutherland, non-existent losers. Some economists also point out that trade in OECD countries is increasingly *intra-industry* (see Glossary), which means that liberalisation will entail lower socio-economic costs than traditional *inter-industry* trade because displaced workers will often be able to remain in the same industry and use their accustomed skills. Although the latest empirical evidence suggests that this trend is indeed occurring,[20] there are likely to be at least some residual re-training or re-location requirements, and the intra-industry trend is much less applicable in Third World countries. It could also be argued that the world-wide shipping of only marginally differing products, merely to please whimsical, advertising-induced consumer tastes, is inefficient in the extreme.

Even if the economic and non-economic benefits of trade liberalisation measurably outweigh economic and socio-economic costs, then consideration of non-economic costs might still swing the balance against liberalisation, especially if the perceived cost–benefit gap is already small. Such costs would be of the sort briefly examined in the previous chapter—what I have called security and community–sovereignty costs—involving what I term a 'linear fallacy' (see next chapter). These costs are, of course, less easy to perceive, analyse or act upon than economic and socio-economic costs, often being intertwined with other issues, and may only be evident in the longer term, but they are real none the less. The possibility of non-economic costs particularly places a question mark against the notion of dynamic gains from trade, discussed above, because the true social value of innovation and new technologies is difficult to assess, because these today are arguably often of a trivial consumerist nature, because demand may be reaching saturation point in some sectors and because the long-term benefits of technology may be diminishing.[21] It is said, for instance, that perhaps one half of all large-scale computer systems are failures, while US computer entrepreneur, Charles Wang, has admitted that his company has sold unsuitable systems and that a third of the $1 trillion business has now spent on information technology may have been wasted. Yet the services involved in installing such systems will already have been counted as additions to the GDP, most services being measured by their input value. There is also evidence that the competitive pressure to innovate has, through defective software and the like, accelerated the rate of industrial accidents.[22]

The fine print in some economics textbooks hints that an equitable distribution of income is required for the gains from trade to be fully reaped, otherwise the rich may obtain less satisfaction from their trade-induced profit or salary boosts than the plebs obtain from their protection-enhanced wages, although this point is usually treated as a minor one.[23] The distributive impacts of trade liberalisation are difficult to assess but some anecdotal evidence suggests that global competition is inducing massive executive pay rises, packages of over A$1m per annum being not unusual. In response to Australian concerns about this, one business consultant has proclaimed '. . . that a tradition of egalitarianism and views of fairness are not what is needed today'.[24] If so, free trade and globalisation may bring considerable long-run costs in terms of equity or even cultural traditions, and there is some evidence that trade-induced structural change can adversely affect income distribution.[25]

Conclusion

Studies of the likely economic gains from the Uruguay Round have produced a confusing array of forecasts, generally ranging from 0.2 to 1.3 per cent of world GDP, with most estimates now gravitating

towards the lower end of the range. If the effects of other Round outcomes such as services liberalisation were included, along with
longer-term 'dynamic' gains and certain non-economic benefits, the
perceived gains would probably be greater, although these are difficult to measure and would likely bring attendant non-economic
costs, while the concept of dynamic gains is speculative. Similar
debates surround estimates of benefits from RTAs, although larger
gains are forecast for less developed countries within a liberalising
area than for industrialised countries. Overall, it would seem that the
likely economic benefits from the Uruguay Round, and perhaps even
from full free trade, are rather modest and could easily be outweighed
by various socio-economic and non-economic costs which are not
measured by econometric models. Some examples of such costs will
be further touched on in forthcoming chapters.

8

Structural Change for Whom?

Structural impacts of the Uruguay Round and beyond

The Uruguay Round has elicited some spectacular forecasts ranging from a glorious new dynamic global economy to a catastrophic collapse of First World employment. The reality is likely to be between such extremes, but Peter Sutherland (1994b: 4) has warned that '. . . global market development implies also global economic restructuring. The importance of that process cannot be exaggerated. The Uruguay Round results alone will cause restructuring at a quickened pace in the industrialised world in particular'. A critical corollary of Free Trade theory is that a shift from protection to relatively free trade will accelerate the rise of industries with comparative advantage and the decline of those so lacking, thereby changing the structure of the liberalising economy. The gains from liberalisation derive from the efficiency-enhancing process of structural change itself, which is said to be ultimately driven by consumers, in search of the lowest available prices, choosing freely between domestic products and imports. This process is essentially economic, but there is inevitably a wide range of consequential non-economic changes to communities, regions, industries, sectoral mixes, social structures, income and wealth distributions, settlement patterns, cultural traits and ways of life in general. Trade is by no means the only force behind such changes, technological development being another, but trade is usually closely linked to the other forces. It is an unwritten 'social contract' of free trade that society must accept some structural change, and now perhaps even be open to perpetual 'global motion', in return for 'welfare' (income) gains. There must be short-term pain for long-term gain. This chapter examines possible structural impacts of the Uruguay Round and some RTAs, suggesting that many likely costs have been overlooked in the Free Traders' arguments for liberalisation and globalism, that the market alone is unlikely to make the required adaptations and that some resistance to change may be justified.

Structural change for everyone

The main elements of the Uruguay Round which are likely to bring structural change include agricultural reform, industrial tariff reduction, abolition of the MFA and VERs, restriction of subsidies and NTBs, the tightening of anti-dumping rules and services liberalisation, though most modellers think the bulk of the welfare gains will come from agricultural reform and abolition of the MFA. The main structural changes being forecast are shifts of First World sectoral output from agricultural and light industrial sectors to more sophisticated manufacturing and services, with shifts to light manufacturing, especially textiles and clothing, in the Second and Third Worlds. Export structures would broadly reflect these changes, although most countries are projected to obtain increased exports in most product categories due to an anticipated 20 per cent rise in world trade volumes, including increases of 2 per cent in agriculture, 5 per cent in services, 6 per cent in textiles and 7.2 per cent in other areas, mainly manufacturing (Nguyen et al. 1993: Table 6). Countries like USA, Australia, New Zealand and Canada, with large 'industrial' agricultural sectors, are forecast to increase agricultural output and exports, but *not* employment.

The most dramatic effects are likely to be on employment with large relative shifts out of agriculture in most parts of the world and out of light manufacturing in the First World (Table 8.1). Most OECD countries except Australia and New Zealand are expected to experience declines in agriculture from 20 to 40 per cent, with services and most industrial sectors increasing somewhat. The small percentage increases in service employment will translate into large absolute numbers, and this sector will be the predominant source of new First World jobs. Some commentators have played down the

Table 8.1: Structural effects of the Uruguay Round

Projected percentage changes in sectoral employment*

	Agriculture and Food	Fabricated Goods, Textiles Chemicals etc.	Mining and Resources	Light Industries, Clothing, Furniture etc.	Forestry and Fishing	Capital Goods, Vehicles etc.	High Tech Manufacturers	Intermediate Manufacturers, Electrical Equipment etc.	Services
Middle Income Agricultural Exporters†	-5.1	1.1	-4.3	44.3	1.9	-9.4	-6.7	-5.8	1.4
East Asian NICs	-27.3	25.8	-7.2	104.5	-5.4	-24.1	-18.5	-18.2	†1.2
Former Soviet Bloc	0.9	-0.3	-1.0	3.4	-0.1	-1.5	-0.8	-0.1	0.1
Scandinavia and Austria	-29.0	2.4	5.0	-18.4	4.0	5.2	10.6	4.2	3.7
USA	-21.3	-11.6	3.8	-22.6	-6.4	9.0	8.6	6.0	4.2
Canada	-23.0	-12.1	1.2	-13.2	0.0	7.1	6.6	6.7	5.6
EU	-32.3	3.0	7.6	-17.4	3.7	7.4	10.7	5.2	4.3
Japan	-40.5	6.3	5.9	10.9	-0.4	7.0	7.9	5.5	6.5
Australia and New Zealand	2.1	-1.7	-0.7	-32.6	1.2	-7.1	-7.7	-7.1	0.3
Rest of the World	3.7	-1.3	1.6	-10.5	-0.1	-4.9	5.9	-7.0	0.3

Notes: * Based on early projections of a comprehensive liberalising outcome, the Final Act being less liberalising than assumed here.
† Includes Brazil, Argentina, Indonesia, Thailand, Malaysia and Philippines.

Source: T. Nguyen et al., 'The Value of a Uruguay Road Success', *The World Economy*, 14, 1991: Table 4, p. 369

likely aggregate effects of the Round, Deardorff (1994) suggesting that only 1 per cent of the world's work-force will be required to change jobs, or about 0.2 per cent per annum when spread over the 5–10-year implementation period. Nevertheless, this means that up to seven million workers world-wide could be affected, possibly up to 30 million people when their families are included, and the figures are much higher for some countries—4.1 per cent of the work-force in Japan and 12.3 per cent in Hong Kong, for instance.

Possible effects on unemployment have not been calculated by the orthodox modelling groups as CGE models are not designed to do so, but the issue has been hotly debated in the context of NAFTA. The sorts of mainstream models discussed in Chapter 7 tend to forecast structural changes similar to those stemming from the Uruguay Round, but Stanford's (1993: Table 4) alternative model, which considers capital outflows to Mexico, forecasts small aggregate employment losses of up to 0.28 per cent in all three countries, including Mexico, due to the inability of industry to absorb all agricultural labour likely to be displaced. Other Canadian trade union and NGO economists have pointed out that, largely due to US TNCs moving branch plants out of Canada under CUFTA, manufacturing employment has fallen by a staggering 20 per cent or so with a number of sectors losing up to 35 per cent, much more than could be accounted for by the recession and which even the OECD has said is without precedent in the post-war era (CLC 1993; Anderson 1993).

Projections for structural changes in Australia are less dramatic but nonetheless significant. Early IC forecasts of Uruguay Round impacts found a likely shift from manufacturing industry (1.6 per cent output loss) to the other sectors whose output gains would be 4.28 per cent for agriculture, 0.47 per cent for services and 0.27 per cent for resources, with even larger increases in the exports of each sector. Projections for the combined effects of the Uruguay Round and APEC forecast larger gains still, but with a 2.16 per cent loss in manufacturing output (Dee and Welsh 1994; BIE 1995: 63ff.). However, as noted in Table 8.1, Nguyen et al. forecast substantial employment losses from the Uruguay Round for Australia and New Zealand in all manufacturing sectors and even the resources sector, with (small) gains only in agriculture and services. Work with the ORANI model shows similar sectoral shifts and nett employment gains of up to 1 per cent or so, the larger gains deriving from projections based on increasing returns assumptions—see Chapter 7 (Abayasiri-Silva and Horridge 1996: Table 6).

Modelling by ABARE indicates output and export gains for Australia from both the Uruguay Round and APEC but large *losses* in manufacturing, the most dramatic figure being a projected 42 per cent drop in general manufacturing under APEC (Table 8.2), even though national income would increase due to allocative efficiencies (Murtough 1994a and b; BIE 1995: 61ff.). Such results, which must be regarded as tentative, suggest that Australia would be slightly richer for trade liberalisation, but could be left with a depleted manufacturing sector, while being in some danger of higher unemployment and an exacerbated trade deficit, although the phasing-in of the Uruguay Round and APEC will allow some space for adjustment.

Table 8.2: **Structural impacts on Australia of the Uruguay Round and APEC**

Sector	Uruguay Round		APEC	
	Output Per cent Change	Exports US$	Output Per cent Change	Exports US$
Agriculture	3.5	529	6.0	1 450
Forestry and Fishing	−1.2	4	8.4	226
Minerals and Energy	16.3	3 049	38.3	7 407
Processed Food	3.5	633	0.4	198
Resource-based Manufactures	−7.6	−2 111	−21.4	−6 473
Other Manufactures	−16.1	−9 331	−42.1	−27 295
Services	1.2	−1 707	4.0	4 864
Real Income	1.3		3.4	

Source: Murtough et al. (1994a): Tables 6–9

There, but for dirty tariffication, go I

The stauncher Free Traders tend to play down concerns about structural adjustment on the grounds that there will be a nett increase in jobs and income, that winners can compensate losers out of the higher income via government programmes and that market processes will make the necessary adjustments, especially where liberalisation is phased in and intra-industry trade reduces adjustment costs (see Chapter 7). However, there is reason to doubt these grounds. As regards the first assumption, the previous chapter and the foregoing section of this chapter suggest that the modelling and other evidence is, at best, ambivalent about the prospects for substantial income boosts or large employment increases from the Uruguay Round and RTAs.

With regard to the compensation assumption, even if there *are* winners, adequate recompense relies on discretionary government programmes which are often *ad hoc* and inadequate. Most OECD countries spend less than 2 per cent of GDP on labour market programmes and Third World countries almost nothing, while in the USA the Reagan Administration slashed adjustment assistance to little more than tokenism (Destler 1992: 152–3), with further welfare cuts under way at present. Australia has spent 1.5 per cent of GDP in recent years but this is now being slashed by more than a quarter under the Liberal Government. It has been estimated that it would cost $238b to re-train all workers currently unemployed in OECD countries, or $49b in the USA alone compared with the $10b spent on US programmes at the moment, and such funding increments are simply not forthcoming (Kapstein 1996: 27). Yet even present spending levels are begrudged, the Australian Industry Commission having some years ago recommended against special structural adjustment assistance lest these provide a disincentive for adjustment (IC 1991, 2–6). A (tenured) Canberra bureaucrat once advised that displaced workers would have to 'make a sub-optimal re-location decision'.[1] Some Free Trade sympathisers admit that governments seldom do enough to ameliorate adjustment costs, and fear that this leads workers to resist trade liberalisation (e.g. Kapstein 1996).

As regards the third assumption, there are grounds for doubting the capacity of the market to make the necessary adjustments, as will be considered more closely in Chapter 12. For one thing, labour markets world-wide are in no state to take more structural shocks, and for another, the assumption overlooks many socio-economic costs of adjustment, a few examples of which will be discussed below. During earlier GATT rounds US studies by leading trade economist Robert Baldwin and others showed that the benefits of trade liberalisation can be outweighed by adjustment costs in certain industries, especially once unemployment duration is over the twenty-four weeks mark, and that, though transitory, such costs should be considered in trade policy-making.[2] US structural adjustment of the 1980s did result in nett employment creation, but *half* the new jobs were at pay rates below the poverty line and entailed an average wage reduction of 10–15 per cent, while *half* the displaced workers were unemployed for more than six months (Browne 1994: 4–5), so the socio-economic costs had almost certainly increased (also see Chapter 7). Studies of large-scale retrenchments in Australia indicate that *half* the workers laid-off remain unemployed after three years (Quiggin 1996: 135)!

Since the earlier GATT rounds, world-wide labour market conditions have greatly deteriorated, particularly in OECD countries. Unemployment rates are now chronically near 10 per cent in many countries, including Australia, and much more if estimates of 'hidden unemployment' (i.e. 'involuntary part-time' work and 'discouraged workers') are included, Australia's figure having reached a staggering 19 per cent in recent years. Much unemployment is now 'structural' (i.e. the skills of the unemployed do not match available jobs) rather than 'cyclical' (due to weak demand) and so will not go away with economic recovery, as even the Australian Industry Commission (IC 1991–92: 7) admits, although it blames 'inflexible' workers for the problem. The structural form of unemployment is said to be 7–10 per cent of the work-force in many European countries, and some commentators have identified a world-wide epidemic of 'downsizing', especially due to information technologies, which is now affecting all sectors, including services, and is occurring *despite* an economic recovery supposedly being under way.[3] The duration of unemployment and the numbers of the long-term unemployed have worsened in most OECD countries, about 60 per cent of Australia's jobless being unemployed for six months or more and a third for a year or more.

In most countries youth and regional unemployment rates are even higher than the above-mentioned averages, joblessness among Australian 15–19 year olds being 28 per cent (early 1996), for instance, and up to 50 per cent in some regions. The Australian situation will be exacerbated by certain recent Uruguay Round-related decisions, such as the removal of tax advantages for fruit juices with at least 25 per cent Australian content, and a similar change in the tobacco industry which is expected to increase the Mareeba-Dimbulah unemployment rate from 20 per cent to 45 per cent, thus requiring a A$35m structural adjustment package.[4] The severe impact of structural change on regional economies has been widely documented for many countries, and regions often miss out on their fair share of nationally aggregated compensation packages.[5] Such structural adjustment problems are probably fueling the social discontent and right-wing politics which are burgeoning in many parts of Australia.

Some Free Traders have claimed that trade liberalisation will help women, especially in the Third World, by creating new 'modern' jobs in the export sector. Others are not so convinced because a disproportionate number of such jobs go to men, while those which do go to women are often insecure, low skilled and subject to exploitation compared with traditional agricultural and handicraft-based self-employment, or other domestically oriented activities which could be created.[6] In OECD countries women's jobs are particularly vulnerable to structural change, Canadian research, for instance, finding that women have been badly affected by CUFTA and NAFTA because, while they hold 45 per cent of all jobs and 30 per cent of manufacturing employment, they hold up to 80 per cent of the vulnerable jobs in some sectors, including the services sector which is supposed to be a good potential source of jobs for women, and there are few signs of high-tech sectors making up the job losses. Further, women tend to have more difficulty finding new jobs than do men and often their new work is at lower pay rates. Some commentators claim that NAFTA has already resulted in the extensive destruction of women's jobs, especially in labour-intensive sectors (USA) and agriculture (Mexico). Until the mid-1980s Australian women lost jobs faster due to restructuring than did men, and although this was reversed thereafter, many women's jobs are part-time and insecure, while the most vulnerable groups are migrants of both sexes.[7]

Current UN projections suggest that by 2000 women will constitute at least half the work-force in most countries, up from a third in 1990, but at present three-quarters of all women workers are in ill-paid, insecure jobs of the sort which are growing rapidly in numbers, and their average wage is two-thirds that of men. At the current rate it will take 475 years for women to reach parity with men in terms of employment and advancement opportunities.[8] A distinction is often drawn between *opportunity* and *empowerment*. The emerging 'global factory' is posited substantially on female labour and the wage-easing effects of a complementary, largely female informal sector, so there will be job opportunities but little empowerment in terms of time, resources, advancement options or influence. As a result, women are frequently forced into onerous triple roles in formal, informal and home working, a trend which some find increasing even in the First World. Many women are, thus, showing signs of resistance to globalisation and structural change, seeking instead traditional or alternative economic roles (see Ward 1990).

The standard Free Trade argument as to the overall effects of trade liberalisation is that increased competition will induce greater technical efficiency within firms and better allocative efficiency between sectors, with much of the adjustment being of the less onerous intra-industry form. However, some critics of this view think that the operative factors are market shares, scale economies and the like rather than efficiency, with import growth being liable, in industries where economies of scale are important, to squeeze local firms into smaller niches and lower product volumes, thus raising unit costs and potentially causing entire industries to collapse. Some Australian economists fear that removal of the remaining, now rather low, tariff margins will barely improve efficiency but may be the last straw for some industries. Econometric models which assume constant rather than increasing returns would not pick up this possibility. Melbourne-based modeller, Peter Brain, once estimated that

Australia could lose 1.6 jobs for every job created through trade liberalisation, and this figure may be even worse, at least in the short term, if widespread 'industry collapse' were to occur.[9]

Most econometric models deal only with sectoral output shares and assume full employment, so cannot forecast whether or not overall unemployment might increase with trade liberalisation. Present trends are not promising, with many OECD countries experiencing 'jobless growth' (rising GDP but stagnant employment levels) and the ILO is forecasting a deterioration or no improvement in unemployment for the majority of these. Almost all OECD countries require incremental growth rates of two to three percentage points by the turn of the century just to get unemployment down to 5 per cent, which is well above the growth-boost of one percentage point or less which is expected to result from the Uruguay Round—see previous chapter (UNDP 1993: 35ff.; ILO, 1995: 160).

Of course, Free Traders believe labour market flexibility and deregulation can ensure that trade liberalisation is accompanied by adequate job re-generation, but critics have raised at least two sets of objections to this claim. First, most OECD countries have now greatly reduced real wages, and have increased labour market flexibility to some extent, without much apparent benefit to employment. In fact some argue that de-regulation and greater flexibility of work practices has resulted in less employment security, harsher workplace relations and a range of disadvantages for weaker groups, including women (ILO 1995). Second, some commentators suggest that rising trade ratios and globalisation have *adversely* affected employment through economic, financial and exchange rate instability, Third World competition (see below) and loss of national macroeconomic policy-making autonomy, all of which render budgetary expansion difficult for any one country and thus impart a deflationary bias to the global system (see Banuri and Schor 1992; Hutton 1994 and 1996; ILO 1995: parts 4 and 5). If this is so, then a policy of macro expansion, wage stabilisation and perhaps job subsidies may be more effective than labour market flexibility *per se*.

In sum, there is good reason to believe that the economies and labour markets of many countries are not in a good state to absorb structural change or generate new jobs at present, while socio-economic costs may be growing, which is in part why there is widespread resistance to protection cuts. A 1991 Australian opinion poll, for instance, found that 71 per cent of respondents opposed tariff reductions, 76 per cent amongst blue collar workers, and a 1995 survey of motorists found that 72 per cent support motor vehicle protection *even* if this means more expensive cars and less variety.[10] Some authorities now admit that the restructuring process is likely to be long and hard, will probably encounter resistance and may need a help along from government (e.g. ILO 1995: 40–1). As noted in earlier chapters, many countries may be spared major structural adjustment traumas due to dilution of the Uruguay Round resolutions through 'dirty tariffication' and the like, but the WTO, along with many Free Traders, wants to keep up, even accelerate, the current pace of trade liberalisation.

Our brand-new international division of labour

There are at least two conflicting sets of views about how structural change under free trade is likely to proceed. Free Traders' prognosis is that OECD countries will restructure 'up-market' to so-called high-tech, high-skill, knowledge-intensive industries and services which provide 'good', well-paid jobs, thus vacating medium-skill rungs for NICs, and so on down the ladder. Another set of views, sometimes called the 'new international division of labour' (NIDL) perspective and widely advocated by many left-wing writers, trade unions, NGOs, Fair Traders and the like, sees restructuring as driven by the desire of TNCs to create a minimum-cost global production system based on 'absolute advantage' (argument no. 7, Chapter 7), with TNCs and some skilled classes the only beneficiaries.

The grimmest prophet of such views was Anglo-French business tycoon Sir James Goldsmith (1994), a former member of the European Parliament, who argued that in the foreseeable future GATT-induced global trade liberalisation will bring an extra 4000 million people from the Second and Third Worlds into the global labour market, most of these being newly displaced from farms into urban slums and being paid at wage levels which are determined by exploitation not by bargained social contracts. This is likely to place unprecedented downward pressure on First World wage levels, but with Third World workers gaining little themselves due to domestic or TNC repression and exploitation, and Western unemployment will soar because of imports, capital exports or 'runaway industries'. Sir James advocates a backdown from global free trade in favour of free capital flows and inward-looking RTAs. Such dramatic claims would seem to be overstated, but many Managed Traders and Fair Traders argue likewise (e.g. Nader et al. 1993) except that they are inclined to see capital mobility and RTAs as co-culprits.

I will refer to these views as the 'Third World competition' argument, of which there are investment-related and trade-related elements. As regards investment-related elements, Third World countries, which now often have better skills, greater political stability and a more pro-TNC stance than in the past, have become major targets for First World DFI, and this allegedly diverts jobs to the lower-cost, 'exploitative' countries. Free Traders reply that capital flows are usually connected with trade and are based on comparative advantage so should be liberalised, and that investment diversion to the Third World is insignificant. However, whilst this was true in the past and may still be so for some capital-exporting countries (ILO 1995: 54), the picture is changing rapidly, especially if, as some claim (e.g. Thurow 1996: 115), anything can now be produced and sold anywhere. Third World countries (or the dozen richest) now receive almost half the world's DFI flows, employment in foreign affiliates of many TNCs has been growing faster than at home and increasing numbers of First World firms are shifting 'offshore' (UNCTAD 1994a: ch. 2). In recent years German companies exported enough capital to have otherwise created 315 000 jobs at home (Sussens-Messerer and Smit 1996); even Britain is now attracting EU and other global DFI through low wages and welfare dilution (Brenchley 1996); corporate re-locations from the USA and Canada to Mexico under NAFTA are said to be increasing (IPS 1996). On balance, therefore, it is probable that investment diversion from First to Second and Third World countries will accelerate in future, though more slowly than Goldsmith implied, and there is still plenty of Third World resistance to full absorption into the global economy.

As regards trade-related elements of the Third World competition argument, Free Traders have several answers which downplay employment diversion: low wages reflect low productivity, not exploitation; competition from low-wage countries is insignificant for most OECD economies; First World countries need only improve their productivity to keep ahead; exploitation is limited in time because improved productivity will gradually raise wage rates and reduce income inequalities; technological development is reducing the advantage of low-wage production; and any adverse employment effects of imports will be countered by rising exports. However, many advocates of the 'Third World competition' thesis are now arguing what I have called an 'exploited labour' case, not the fallacious 'cheap labour' concept (argument no. 10, Chapter 6). This case suggests that a combination of TNC cost-reduction strategies, mobile capital and technologies, limitations on labour rights and general political repression can result in *both* low wages *and* high productivity for at least some sectors of Third World countries, thus ensuring persistent 'unit cost gaps' (see Glossary) between First and Third world economies, in which eventuality the above-mentioned arguments of Free Traders may not generally hold (see Mead 1990).

Evidence on this issue comes from NAFTA experience where Mexican productivity is 80 to 100 per cent of that in many equivalent US industries, but wages are only about a tenth of US levels and have actually been declining since the late 1960s. Thus, whereas Mexican labour could not compete with high-productivity/high-skill US labour around 1980, it can now do so more than adequately thanks to the ease with which TNCs can transfer technology, the use of de-regulation by governments to encourage unit cost gaps and the widespread abuse of labour rights in order to limit pressure for improvements in wages and conditions (Mead 1990; Stanford et al. 1993: 14). Such abuses by both Mexican and US companies have been well documented by labour groups, including actions such as sackings for union activities, suppression of trade unions, use of 'tame' unions, the flouting of health and safety standards, exploitation of women and children and imprisonment, torture or murder of political activists.[11] The Mexican case illustrates the fact that where repression is strong 'exploited labour' may persist for a long time, contrary to the Free Traders' claim that market forces will soon eradicate it.

Unit cost gaps between countries derive from many factors including wages, working hours, conditions, welfare levels, tax rates, environmental policies and so forth, all of which can reflect legitimate differences in political–social preferences, but which are vulnerable to global pressure. Unit cost gaps can also exist between First World countries. For instance, Canadian unit labour costs are 40 per cent higher than those of the US and 154 per cent higher when welfare costs are considered because US social spending relative to GDP is now about the same as that of Brazil or South Korea, though still a bit higher than that of Mexico. Such cost gaps place huge competitive pressure on firms from countries with high labour and welfare standards. Surveys have found 60–70 per cent of Canadian firms admitting they have plans for shifting to the USA or Mexico because of cost advantages, most acknowledging that Canada's economy would suffer as a result.[12] US surveys have found up to 40 per cent of corporate executives making similar confessions or pledging to use NAFTA as a lever for holding wages down, one suggesting that US wages must come closer to those of Brazil or Korea before the US can be adequately competitive (Browne 1994: 74–8). Even in Britain, low wages and welfare costs are playing a role in attracting DFI from other EU countries and Asia (Brenchley 1996).

Some commentators extend the Third World competition argument to the welfare state and other national institutions such as industrial relations systems, suggesting that the pressures of globalisation may force countries with high levels of welfare and other government expenditures to either reduce these or shift their funding onto consumers in order to reduce taxes, ease business costs and enhance the country's competitiveness. Others suggest a counter-trend in which public spending rises with globalisation, particularly where industry assistance, education and so forth may enhance competitiveness or where higher welfare is required to meet adjustment costs. But there is mounting research and anecdotal evidence for the welfare-reduction thesis, notably in Canada where welfare spending and programme coverage have been scaled down to US levels under CUFTA/NAFTA.[13] In practice it is difficult to distinguish between the effects of globalisation and anti-welfarist ideological trends, but it is likely that there will be downward pressure on taxation and welfare in future as the pressures of globalisation grow, with cost considerations becoming more important (Jovanović 1992: 11; Thurow 1996: 130–1) irrespective of how well such institutions serve 'non-economic' needs. Many economists still believe that there is a trade-off between social equity and the sort of 'efficiency' which global competitiveness and 'deep integration' are meant to bring (e.g. Hama 1996: ch. 4).

Mainstream economists are also debating the 'Third World competition' argument, early contributors concluding that rising Third World industrial exports could, at least for a transitional period, increase unemployment and reduce wages in OECD countries, a factor which some say is already easing wage pressure and inflation in the West.[14] Recent debate has mainly centred around the details and possible causes of an apparent 'hollowing out' or unequalising of labour incomes in some First World countries as salaries of highly skilled workers rise relative to wages of the low skilled. Some Western neo-classical economists, such as Bhagwati, have attributed this trend mainly to technological change and inflexible wages, while others, notably British economist and former World Bank adviser Adrian Wood, have attributed it substantially to import pressure from low-education, low-wage labour in industrialising Third World countries, as was earlier predicted by the 'factor price equalisation theorem' (see Chapter 6). Based on sophisticated but controversial data and statistical techniques, Wood's work dramatically suggests that Third World import competition and related technological innovation has reduced the manufacturing sectors of First World countries by about five percentage points and the demand for unskilled labour in manufacturing and services by about 20 per cent, which is ten times the impact identified by previous studies. The debate is still in flux, with many economists, even the World Bank, accepting that Third World competition can constrain Western wages, at least for a time, although technology, immigration and competition from *other* OECD countries are also seen as possible culprits, with technology the most favoured contender.[15]

A few Western economists favour interim trade intervention to combat Third World competition (e.g. Gray 1985), but most advocate freer markets to facilitate adjustment and even Wood eschews protection in favour of training, public-sector employment and income redistribution in order to encourage up-market restructuring. The widespread nomination of technology as a culprit is interesting, given that Western economists have long denied its guilt in causing unemployment or other adverse structural changes, although few advocate controlling technology. Most prefer labour market de-regulation, re-training or the like and think that technology-induced income increases can create plenty of new jobs. However, it is quite possible for *both* imports *and* technology to play a linked role in reducing First World wages, Wood arguing, for instance, that trade influences the pace and direction of 'defensive' technological change, so together they can affect labour even if import volumes are small.

There may even be a case, albeit heretical, for constraining *both* technology and imports on a range of economic structural and 'non-economic' grounds. Technology would seem to be having a more adverse impact than in the past due variously to the extension of computerisation to services and almost everything (Rifkin 1995; Maiden 1996), to possible demand saturation in some sectors (see ILO 1995: 167), to the fading desirability of economic growth amongst many people and to escalating social or environmental costs of many technologies (see Dunkley 1992). Reasons to con-strain imports would include the socio-economic costs of structural change discussed above and doubts about the benefits of such change. Various research and anecdotal evidence suggests that a good deal of the new employment resulting from First World restructuring consists of low-quality, low-paid 'Macdonaldised' service-sector jobs (Rifkin 1995); that the much vaunted high-tech/high-pay jobs are mainly confined to limited sectors in 'global cities' (Sassen 1991); that globalisation is increasing inequality and poverty even in First World countries (Sassen 1991; Hutton 1994; Keegan 1996); that on current Canadian experience at least, there are few signs of an emerging 'knowledge sector' which many see as the saviour of the West (Campbell 1993: 5); and that even the job potential of the service sector may be shrinking in OECD countries due to a combination of 'Third World competition', outward invest-ment flows and computerisation (Rifkin 1995; Sussens-Messerer and Smit 1996).

Furthermore, some deny that Third World workers will benefit as much from their new-found trade or investment competitiveness as Free Traders claim, due to socio-economic costs, the likely trans-

fer of inappropriate high technology, the 'industrialisation' of agriculture and dislocation of farming (Goldsmith 1994; Korten 1995),
some fifteen million small Mexican farm families being expected to
be displaced under NAFTA, for instance (Barry 1995: 194; IPS
1996). In short, although trade theoretically benefits both partners,
in practice structural change can have adverse effects from which
both can suffer in their own ways.

Thus spake the market

In Free Trade theory the golden rule of structural adjustment is 'thou
shalt accept the judgment of the market', even if some countries
have to 'miss out' on some industries, and Free Traders get impatient
with countries which want their own steel, computer or other high
'value added' sectors at all costs. It is doubtless true that many
governments have squandered resources on unwarranted national
ego projects (dams, airlines, giant steelworks and the like) and most
are probably now over-computerising. The notion of seeking high
value added sectors (e.g. aluminium processing and products rather
than just mining), so fashionable in Australia, may be limited
because not all countries can be high on the value added chain for
any one product, and various Australian studies have questioned the
viability of extensive processing here (Lloyd in Hamilton 1991).

Nevertheless, Managed Traders and other critics see as a cost of
free trade and market-led structural adjustment the possible loss of
'strategic trade' options (see Chapter 6) and the foregoing of control
over long-term development (e.g. Hamilton 1991: 281). Kaldor
always argued, for instance, that manufacturing can induce faster
growth than other sectors because of high multipliers and 'linkages',
while Keynes (1932) once specified the car, steel and farm sectors as
worthy of long-term protection for various economic, social and
community maintenance reasons. Machine tools, computers and
high technology have been claimed as crucial for competitiveness
and long-term industrial growth, while some think services are too
dependent upon manufacturing to be an autonomous growth sector
and that excessive investment in some global services may be detrimental to the latter.[16] It has been claimed that in New Zealand a
combination of macro-economic contraction and unilateral trade

liberalisation were responsible for negative economic and employment growth between 1985 and 1992 (Kelsey 1995: esp. ch. 14).

Consideration of non-economic factors such as 'industry balance', environment, community-sovereignty or other long-term concerns poses even more doubts about the virtues of market-led structural adjustment. On the evidence of Tables 8.1 and 8.2 (above) a post-Uruguay Australia may become a nation of 'factory farms', mines and tourist destinations, with only scattered 'niche' manufacturing, but this might not be the sort of society Australians want and such sectors do not create many jobs. Some of the more profound concerns about structural change are illustrated by the case of agriculture. Free Traders regard the agricultural sector as the most 'distorted' in the world and passionately advocate its 'reform'. There is doubtless much validity in the claim. Among the distortions caused by the $400b plus which OECD countries annually provide in agricultural support are the following: over-production due to subsidies; over-pricing due to price supports; flooding of world markets due to export promotion policies; inefficiencies due to huge administrative schemes; inflation of land prices; and redistribution of income mainly to large-scale farmers. In many Third World countries farmers are under-paid as a subsidy to urban industrial development, thus resulting in disincentives and inequities. Reforms proposed by the Uruguay Round stand to eliminate some of these distortions and, barring 'dirty tariffication', would be worth $190b in additional world income, with full free trade worth $430b, Australian farm income being projected to rise by A$900m.[17]

However, in the short term declining agricultural protection might simply shift more people on to social welfare benefits, thus saving little (Hama 1996: 79), while in the longer term causing adverse structural changes. One such change is a likely reduction in the food self-sufficiency ratios of many countries. The Uruguay Round is projected to substantially reduce this ratio for China, Sub-Saharan Africa, Japan and the Middle East, to less than 50 per cent in the latter two cases (Goldin et al. 1993: Figures 2.1 and 2.2, pp. 57–8). Most OECD countries are projected to become more self-sufficient in food crops and livestock but to experience large reductions in agricultural employment (Table 8.1), which even now constitutes only 2–5 per cent of the total work-force. This implies a shift to larger scale 'industrial' agriculture and perhaps substantial rural de-population, so that many countries face becoming the first societies in history to have scarcely anyone living and working on the land. In 1993 the US statistical bureau ceased counting farm-dwellers in the population census because barely 2 per cent of the US work-force is now employed in agriculture, with 32 per cent of farm managers and 86 per cent of labourers no longer living on the land they work. Even Australian agriculture, which is expected to benefit export-wise from the Uruguay Round, may suffer a similar fate because 60 per cent of farms do not currently cover costs, although many small, traditional farmers are efficient and do not carry debt. In New Zealand trade liberalisation and domestic de-regulation appear to have greatly increased large-scale agribusiness and foreign ownership thereof.[18]

Such structural changes are likely to present some major potential problems. On the one hand food-import dependence can destroy the national agricultural base, reduce food variety, help to create a junk food culture and submit national food supply to the wiles of advertisers and global food TNCs. On the other hand 'industrial' farms and 'agribusiness' can increase the use of chemicals, accelerate tree-cutting, reduce governmental and farmer control over farming policies, undermine rural farmer-managed co-operatives, reduce diversity of crop species, discourage experimentation with alternative sustainable methods, increase the use of inappropriate technologies, cause rural inequality, eliminate family farms and destroy traditional rural communities. By contrast, there is some evidence that small farms are more efficient and environmentally sound than large-scale agribusiness but cannot compete with TNC networks.[19]

Free Traders see as the epitome of protectionist evil those demands by farmers' groups in France, Japan and elsewhere for special assistance on the grounds of maintaining traditional community and culture. But although such demands are in one sense self-interested, the grounds are not necessarily invalid. Anecdotal evidence suggests that community life, amenities and population levels are preserved much better in areas where there are small farms than where agribusiness dominates, which has been confirmed by an early post-war US study of Californian communities, by a Canadian study of foreign agribusiness penetration and by recent New Zealand experience.[20] Other more subjective arguments for preserving the rural sector include: the tradition in Japan and Korea that rice should be grown within the country or even in one's own district;[21] the notion, advocated by Keynes (1932) as well as by some contemporary environmentalists, that a society in which a number of people maintain contact with the soil will be better balanced and more ecologically aware than a society where people are alienated from the land; the belief that rural people embody traditional culture and national spirit, recently propounded by the Australian Catholic Bishops as a rationale for assisting rural industries.[22] Furthermore, market-driven structural change tends to accelerate urbanisation, Free Traders assuming that people will learn to love city life, but the latter presumption is questionable. Most First World countries are now experiencing some de-urbanisation, a 1993 British survey finding that four million people intended to leave cities for rural areas and a staggering thirteen million wanted to do so but were unable to.[23]

Free Traders respond that such quaint values would be costly to maintain and should only be supported through the welfare system, not by protection, although they also tend to advocate smaller welfare states. However, many environmentalists, alternative farmers and NGO groups are now advocating new approaches which would reduce the $400b per annum currently spent worldwide on agricultural protection and re-direct much of it away from policies which encourage inefficiencies, surpluses, food dumping and environmental damage. Proposed alternative uses of the funds include promotion of organic agriculture and organic food consumption, development of more appropriate technologies, support for food self-sufficiency in the Third World and the requirement that farm income support be subject to the use of sustainable methods, while in many countries farmer–consumer links through 'community-supported agriculture' schemes are becoming popular.[24] European opinion polls suggest that the public would endorse agricultural subsidies aimed at policies of this sort, by remarkable majorities of up to 80 per cent depending on how the polling question is phrased (Lang 1993: 39), while a few Free Traders accept the notion of some agricultural protection on non-economic grounds (e.g. Oppenheim 1992: 123).

Free Traders often argue that elimination of farm subsidies would help the environment because small, allegedly inefficient farms cause most pollution. But this is true only to the extent that many subsidy programmes specifically target machine–chemical inputs (Pearce and Warford 1993: 319–20) so re-direction of assistance to organic inputs may be more effective than elimination. Relative to 'industrial' agriculture organic farming is environmentally superior, reduces input costs, generates more employment and reinforces community structures, but has similar per acre productivity so will not cause starvation as some ill-informed critics claim (see Dunkley 1992: 89ff.). But the Uruguay Round *Agreement on Agriculture* could make such policies difficult as it appears to outlaw discrimination between industries or products on the basis of production methods (see Chapter 10) and NAFTA specifically seeks to increase the scale of agricultural production, which may lead to more machine–chemical methods (Ritchie 1992: 225).

Structural change in agriculture entails a good example of what I call the 'linear fallacy', or the notion that successive technological changes bring proportionate and continuing economic and social benefits. To the contrary, many critics now argue that machine–chemical technology may be reducing soil productivity through adverse ecological impacts but disguising this trend with artificial fertilisers (see Dunkley 1992: 26–8). Trade-induced specialisation exacerbates this trend by narrowing the traditional range of foods produced, by inducing a need for artificial (often imported) inputs and by generating dependency on mono-crops, as has happened with the widespread addiction to bread or other Western-style foods in some Third World countries. One UN scientist, Dr George Tzotzos, has said that agricultural free trade will soon make it impossible for any nation to insulate itself from genetically engineered crops, yet in time many may wish to do so, there already being evidence of potentially dangerous cross-breeding with weed species in a way which biotechnologists said would not happen.[25] It could also be argued that the linear fallacy applies in the fishing industry where ultra-modern, computerised technology enables a decreasing number of fishermen to catch increasing numbers of fish from more and more ecological niches, but results in massive fish stock depletion, ecological damage and destruction of traditional fishing communities. As an alternative many Third World countries are finding that the maintenance of labour-intensive fleets and more traditional methods might be ecologically and socially optimal, as a result of which there is increasing resistance to industrialisation and globalisation of the fishing industry.[26] Yet free trade will, in all likelihood, exacerbate the latter trends through pressure for cost-cutting from ever fiercer global competition.

As Free Traders regularly point out (e.g. Dillon et al., 1990: 43), structural change is influenced by a range of domestic and international factors besides trade, including technologies, demand patterns, economies of scale and scope, relative sectoral growth rates, labour market trends, macro-economic variables, commodity prices and exchange rates. However, trade and globalisation can also influence these factors, in turn being influenced by them, and the various economic, socio-economic and non-economic costs of structural change are real nevertheless. The question therefore arises of whether to fully accept market-led change via trade liberalisation, as Free Traders urge, whether to embrace liberalisation but with governments assisting in adaptation and socio-economic cost reduction as many economists advocate (e.g. Kapstein 1996) or whether to selectively resist liberalisation and change, a view which is emerging in many quarters as noted briefly throughout this chapter. As US social commentator, Edward Luttwak (quoted in Maiden 1996), has heretically advised: 'A society that is rich in GNP and poor in tranquility ought to be thinking of ways to impede change, to secure and stabilise, not ways to increase change for the sake of efficiency'. In Chapter 12 I will argue that there is certainly a case for adaptation policies and probably a case for selective resistance to change, along with planning for alternatives.

Conclusion

We have the word of Peter Sutherland that the Uruguay Round will bring extensive structural change to most countries involved, though almost certainly to a lesser extent than the more dramatic claims suggest, especially owing to the phasing-in of changes and to the likely intra-industry nature of some adjustments. Econometric modelling indicates that the main structural effects are likely to be accelerated industrialisation of Third World countries and, for the First World, a shift to higher technology manufacturing or services, along with less employment, lower unskilled wages and perhaps the near-elimination of agricultural work-forces. For Australia the combined effects of the Uruguay Round and APEC are likely to see considerable shrinkage of our already small manufacturing sector (currently about 15 per cent of GDP) and a shift of resources to agriculture, mining and services. Likely nett employment effects are unclear from modelling but for many countries these do not look promising. Yet, owing to existing high unemployment and a long-term trend of 'jobless growth', the labour markets of most countries are in no state to absorb more workers displaced by restructuring. So the socio-economic costs of trade liberalisation could be marked and non-economic costs considerable, thus giving rise to a strong case for assisted adaptation and perhaps some grounds for resistance.

9

At Whose Service?

Services and intellectual property in the Uruguay Round

The greatest revolution of the Uruguay Round was the incorporation of services and intellectual property into the GATT system through the GATS and TRIPs agreements (see Chapter 4). During the 1980s these sectors became part of the new model free trade agreement, particularly as advocated by the USA, both being included in agreements such as the 1985 USA–Israel agreement and CUFTA/NAFTA. However, both sectors contain a host of socially sensitive matters and their respective agreements are controversial, for reasons examined in this chapter, and may entail many hidden costs. One commentator asserts that the former Labor Government 'sold out' Australia in signing the *TRIPs Agreement* (Braithwaite 1995: 116). I conclude that the two agreements may need to be rethought and that full free trade in services should be avoided, perhaps resisted.

The rise and rise of services

Services were long regarded as amorphous, unproductive by-products of, and inputs into, the industrial system whose value was not fully included in the GDP of many countries (e.g. the former Soviet Union) or in the trade statistics of most countries until the 1970s. Measurement had once been difficult because many services—energy, design, research, accounting and so forth—were intermediate sectors 'invisibly' embodied in final goods, but as statistics were improved it appeared that Western countries had become 'post-industrial', or predominantly service-producing societies. In Australia, for instance, by the 1990s services accounted for 76 per cent of GDP, 78 per cent of employment and 20 per cent of exports, the largest sectors being finance, property, business services, retailing and community services. The most common explanation for the growth of the service sector relates to the displacement of workers from agriculture and manufacturing industries by technology and rising productivity, along with the tendency of people to spend their consequent income increments on services.

By the early 1980s, as the Uruguay Round was being contemplated, Free Traders reached a consensus that, theoretically, trade in services was subject to the same 'laws' of comparative advantage and gains from trade as that for goods, despite a few differences, but it was noted that all countries greatly restricted services trade through a wide range of domestic and external regulations. Newly consolidated statistical data were also showing that services accounted for a fifth of world trade and half of all DFI flows, the most traded sectors being tourism and transport. By the mid-1990s the value of world services trade was $1100b per annum, of which the USA had a huge 17 per cent share, France 8.7 per cent and most countries less than 2 per cent (Australia 1.3 per cent), although the EU members collectively accounted for about 40 per cent (WTO 1995b: 14). Most service firms had begun as adjuncts to manufacturers and had globalised along with their 'hosts', but during the 1980s many of these had 'splintered' so as to themselves become global TNCs, most notably accounting, advertising and business consultant companies.[1]

Pressure for service trade liberalisation came from three key sources. The first was Free Trade economists who argued that liberalisation would be just as efficiency-inducing as for goods, especially as services were allegedly becoming amenable to 'packaging', privatisation and user-pays market disciplines. The second source was large corporate service interests, led by American Express, who for many years lobbied the Reagan Administration, other governments and GATT for global services de-regulation (Drake and Nicolaidis 1992; Underhill 1993; Dunkley 1994a). The third source of pressure was governments of countries with substantial service export sectors, initially the USA in particular with its chronic trade deficit, but the

EU, Japan and Canada joined the fray when they finally calculated that a services agreement would suit them (Kakabadse 1987: 56; Underhill 1993: 129).

At first many countries, especially from the predominantly service-importing Third World, resisted inclusion of services in the Uruguay Round and much negotiation time was spent just compiling statistics, identifying impediments to trade and discussing particular sectors. Some countries were deterred by aggressive emphasis on 'market access' and service privatisation by the US government and negotiators, the US ambassador to India once sternly lecturing his hosts on the 'need' to privatise industry (Dunkley 1993: 5). The final consensus on GATS was limited to the extension of GATT-type rules to services and the liberalisation of selected sectors, with many details postponed to later negotiations (Croome 1995: 122ff.). Some Third World governments ultimately agreed to GATS when new statistics revealed that their countries seemed to be developing a comparative advantage in certain services, Korea, Taiwan, Mexico, Thailand, India and Egypt, for instance, each now accounting for 1–2 per cent of world services trade, which is more than the shares of some industrial countries (WTO 1995b: 14). By contrast, US enthusiasm for wholesale services liberalisation waned as it became apparent that some American service sectors were losing comparative advantage, so many US concessions were finally offered only on a reciprocal basis.

The guts of GATS

As briefly outlined in Chapter 4, GATS provides multilateral trading rules for services, particularly with a view to reducing those impediments to trade which stem from regulation of services by government and non-governmental authorities. The preamble to GATS does recognise the right of members to continue regulating services in a GATS-consistent manner and to introduce new regulations where required, although a reassuring phrase 'Recognising the sovereignty of national economic space' used in earlier drafts was omitted from the Final Act. Traditional definitions of services pictured these as 'invisible', non-storable exchanges of activities requiring the simultaneous presence of buyer and seller, although economists now point out that many services involve equipment or infrastructure (transport, energy), some do not require proximity (accounting) and some can be delivered long distance by post or electronically (television, information, education), so that the picture is changing. There is no specific definition of services in GATS, but traded services are usually classified into four modes of delivery:[2]

1 **Cross-border supply:** where a service provider sends requisite items to, say Australia, without either buyer or seller moving; for example, international mail order, short-wave or satellite broadcasting, designs sent by post etc. This type of supply is seldom regulated, although some controls are possible.

2 **Consumption abroad:** where Australians move overseas to obtain the service directly from a foreign provider; for example, tourism, specialist medical services etc. This mode can be regulated through visa restrictions and certain controls on providers such as the delightful Balinese rule that buildings be no taller than a coconut tree.

3 **Commercial presence:** where the provider establishes a physical presence in Australia, whether through a subsidiary, an agency or a franchise, and supplies directly to Australian consumers; for example, business services, law firms, retailers, McDonald's and the like. This mode is often regulated by a variety of restrictions on what foreign providers can do, on the degree of foreign ownership allowed and so forth, and hence the liberalisation thereof, known as the 'right of establishment', effectively introduces investment de-regulation into the GATT system.

4 **Presence of natural persons:** where the provider or an employee spends short periods of time in Australia supplying the service; for example, architects or engineers on a particular project, business consultants, academics on short-term contracts, visiting ballet companies and so forth. This mode is subject to some regulation, usually by immigration restrictions for non-citizens or limitations on what they can do.

GATS is a three-tiered agreement covering all four modes of service delivery and extending the GATT principles to all service sectors except government services and procurement, but with the principles applied in several different ways. First, the principles of transparency and progressive liberalisation apply to all WTO members and all delivery modes. Second, MFN applies on a 'negative list' basis (see Glossary) to all members except where exemptions, which have a 10-year time limit, are specifically listed by the member country. Exceptions listed by various countries include preferential systems, such as internal EU processes, international cargo-sharing arrangements or airport landing rights, and reciprocal requirements whereby a country, mostly the USA, will only grant market access concessions to countries which do likewise. Australia has listed film co-productions (preferential) and stock exchange services (reciprocal), as well as reserving the right to take action against other countries restricting market access for Australian audiovisual services, somewhat incongruously, given our own restrictions in this sector.[3]

Third, the National Treatment and market access principles are applied on a 'positive list' basis, meaning that a country is only committed to liberalising any sectors, with regard to any delivery mode, which it formally schedules for that purpose and even then it can list caveats in the schedule. In sectors so scheduled a country is required under Article XVI to eliminate (unless a caveat to the contrary is listed) the following market access regulations: numerical and value quotas on foreign suppliers; limitations on numbers of foreign services personnel allowed entry; restrictions on the type of corporate or joint venture structure which foreign suppliers may use; limitations on the proportion or volume of foreign shareholding in local service firms, this effectively introducing investment liberalisation into the GATT system for the first time, although members may still schedule general DFI controls as Australia has done. In all scheduled sectors foreign service suppliers are to have full access to every WTO member country's market and are to receive treatment 'no less favourable' than local suppliers.

GATS covers all existing services under the WTO's standard 12 sectoral and 155 sub-sectoral headings. OECD countries have agreed to completely liberalise (without caveats) market access and National Treatment in about a third of these sub-sectors and to partly liberalise (with caveats) in about half of them. Other countries have agreed to fully liberalise in only 8 per cent of the sub-sectors and partly liberalise in 15 per cent. The sectors most subject to liberalisation commitments include business services, computer-related services, telecommunications and construction, while extensive restrictions have been retained in areas such as finance, transport, agricultural services, health, education and recreation. Caveats in the schedules are mainly for the 'commercial presence' and 'presence of natural persons' modes of delivery (nos 3 and 4 above), including limitations for professional stays, limits on foreign equity and so forth (Hoekman 1995a: Table 4). Most countries' scheduled commitments are for 'bound standstills', meaning that ceilings have been placed on regulations and any future re-regulations may incur compensation claims by affected service suppliers.

Australia has scheduled liberalisation commitments in about 60 per cent of the 155 service sub-sectors, mainly in business services, insurance, banking and telecommunications, with no commitments made in a number of health, medical, postal, communications, media, audio-visual, education and transport services. All scheduled sectors have been subject to a few 'horizontal' caveats such as foreign investment review laws, certain limitations on personnel movements, subsidies for R and D and a requirement that at least two directors of a public company should ordinarily be resident in Australia. Individual scheduled sectors have also been subject to caveats such as insurance regulations, Reserve Bank authorisation requirements and a 15 per cent foreign equity limitation for banks.[4]

The WTO has a post-Round programme of ongoing negotiations in several sectors, with moderately liberalising, limited-term agreements having now been concluded for financial services and telecommunications, though signed only by a small number of countries, Australia being one of these. Attempts at a maritime services agreement have failed, mainly because of US refusal to make concessions until others, particularly the more reluctant Asian countries, do so more extensively.[5]

The trouble with services

The reluctance of many countries and commentators to embrace the notion of free trade in services stems in part from a perceived Western superiority in such sectors and aggressive tactics used by the USA to assert this, but also from what I believe is a flawed analogy between goods and services. Mainstream economists recognise some

differences between the two, particularly the intangible and differentiated nature of many (though not all) services which is said to
induce a heavily embedded protectionist culture, but this distinction
is usually only raised as a plea for more concerted liberalisation
efforts. If true, however, this 'embeddedness' might, alternatively, be
seen as being due to the crucial 'non-economic' role played by many
services. In my view there are also some more fundamental differences between goods and services, and these suggest limits to the
case for service trade liberalisation. Such differences relate in part
to the sensitive socio-cultural nature of services and in part to the
fact that many are extensively linked to other sectors and are based
on human skills which can be enhanced by practice, or 'learning-
by-doing', so are subject to learning curve economies, infant industry considerations and cumulative advantage mechanisms (see
Chapter 6). Although service liberalisation could likely bring some
efficiencies, a number of problems with the goods–services analogy
are noted below.

The numbers problem   Because services are often intermediates in
production processes, are embodied in goods, are not well recorded
in national accounts and are inadequately disaggregated in trade
accounts, many countries are by no means clear about the position
services hold in their economies or trade.[6] During the Uruguay
Round few Third World countries had much idea what impact
GATS would have when they signed it, as one Australian trade
official has admitted,[7] and they preferred more research be done, but
officials wanted GATS rushed through to complete the Round
(Raghavan 1990: ch. 5).

The development problem   Because of the linkage and 'learning by
doing' features of services, because most Third World countries have
large deficits in services trade and because just eight First World
nations account for two-thirds of world service exports (Nayyar
1988: 287), many countries argue that services should be treated as
'infant industries'. During the Uruguay Round many Third World
countries argued against extensive service liberalisation on the
grounds of a 'right to development' and ultimately only supported
GATS when such clauses (Preamble and Article IV) were included.
These clauses are vague in the extreme, however, and many commentators think that Third World nations are now too far behind
the cumulative advantage of First World service market leaders to

ever catch up under free trade conditions, and during the Round EC negotiators conceded that GATS would be of little benefit to Third World countries (Raghavan 1990: 108). It is claimed that with electronic delivery of services now possible—processing of First World insurance claims, for instance—Third World countries can readily generate cumulative advantage in such sectors. On the other hand, services of this sort are usually controlled by TNCs and whether taking people out of villages into computerised offices constitutes 'progress' needs to be debated.

The oligopolies problem Free Trade theory relies heavily on competitive processes for the benefits it claims can flow from trade liberalisation, but others are sceptical as to whether many countries would benefit from free trade in services owing to the increasingly oligopolistic markets for many services in which large TNCs have already extensively displaced small or individual providers (Clairmonte and Cavanagh 1985; *Vital Links* 1987: ch. 2). In tourism, for instance, 13 conglomerate TNCs dominate the industry, each having close links with hotel chains, airlines and related services in a way which gives them massive advantages over small local enterprises (Madeley 1992: 77ff.). Fast food chains gain advantages from advertising, finance and standardisation in a way which quickly drives out small local competitors, this being the experience in the USA itself and now internationally (Luxenberg 1985). In telecommunications, global oligopolies are able to establish themselves in local markets with technical systems which are well beyond the capacity of local networks to match.[8] Global retailing chains are gaining competitive advantages through expensive computerised centrally administered systems. GATS contains clauses allowing countries to take action against restrictive private business practices, but these are vague and the above-mentioned examples constitute structural advantages rather than illegal acts. Such structural factors may bring efficiencies to the importing countries but could also deprive them of cumulative advantage, along with a range of adverse social and cultural effects, such as the flood of US consumerist, fast-food culture into Mexico which is now being accelerated by NAFTA (Browne 1994).

The sovereignty problem Many of the above problems can adversely affect national sovereignty because, as one economist has put it, services and service investment go to the heart of a nation's identity in a way that goods cannot (Gray 1990: 68 and 85). This is particularly the case with finance, a crucial sector for national monetary policy, yet the WTO and many Free Traders are urging near-total de-regulation, except for mild prudential supervision, which would ultimately require nations to allow the world's private banks and financial institutions uncontrolled access to their markets (UNCTAD 1994b: 167). Service dependence can also render inexperienced countries vulnerable to unfair treatment, such as when one British business consultancy was found to be charging Kenya five times the normal fees (PIRG 1993: 9). Each country has its own traditions and culture of service provision or distribution, and these could be undermined by excessive liberalisation, especially sectors, where service imports come with extensive 'cultural baggage' (see below).

The community problem   Notwithstanding the Free Traders' contention that most services can, like goods, be discretely packaged and divorced from values, it is my view that many services are best offered in the context of a community, including communications, media, health, education and so forth. Private foreign suppliers are notorious for 'cream-skimming', or seeking the most packageable, profitable sectors of a service. Education, for instance, which should ideally play a wide ranging social and value-maintenance role, is increasingly being subject to privatisation, commercial sponsorship and a narrow industry-related focus. Australia has scheduled some educational services under GATS with a view to breaking into Asian markets, but this also potentially means opening our own education to foreign penetration. In many Third World countries government banks are used to favour community and co-operative ventures, with many beneficial and equity-enhancing developmental results, but such practices are invariably a target for cutting by privatised or overseas-owned banks in favour of the more profitable end of the market (Dunkley 1993; PIRG 1993).

In the case of the legal services, it has been suggested by some economists that law firms from a country with litigious values would have a competitive advantage and they imply that this would be legitimate (see Dunkley 1994a). Others, however, believe that the US litigious 'disease' could spread, especially if advertising is de-regulated at the same time, and that this could have disastrous social costs to an importing community, some fearing that the disease is already spreading in Australia as the legal profession is de-regulated and globalised. Australia has scheduled legal services under GATS, with only a few ownership and personnel caveats, which some observers believe will force Australian law firms into mergers with giant British or US groups.[9] Particular criticism has been directed at tourism, which has been known to take over whole communities, devastate coastlines, sequester valuable farm land for resorts or golf courses, exclusively employ specialised non-locals and demean local values and cultures, or else to encourage culture maintenance in a bastardised form.[10] Rectification of such problems would almost certainly require extensive domestic and trade regulation, investment controls and so forth, possibly to an extent that is now constrained by GATS.

The cultural problem Many services, notably education, media, entertainment, computer software and the food industry, directly embody cultural values and symbols, or so-called 'cultural baggage', although certain goods such as clothing, cars, toys and various consumer items do likewise to some extent. An oft-quoted example is that of McDonald's and their imitators who have duplicated worldwide the US fast-food culture, standardised popular tastes for low quality hamburgers, institutionalised exploitative US labour practices, destroyed regional or local cuisines, even within the USA itself, and blighted the landscape with their logos (Luxenberg 1985). Service TNCs usually claim that they respect host country values and can benefit from working within local cultures, but many management consultants are now telling them that homogenisation is cheapest. A spokesperson for Euro Disneyland once ruminated that theme parks are an American institution and so the company must work hard to sell Europeans the concept, which hardly demonstrates respect for national culture (see Dunkley 1994a; Barnet and Cavanagh 1994).

Classic cases of cultural embodiment in services are the media and audio-visuals sectors which are now so globalised that many countries are swamped by imports. In Canada, for instance, 67 per cent of books, 89 per cent of recorded music, 90 per cent of TV drama and 97 per cent of films are imported, mostly from the USA (*Vital Links* 1987: 11). In Australia 50 per cent of books (over 90 per cent of religious titles) and 93 per cent of films are imports, with imported TV programmes and advertising kept to 50 per cent and 20 per cent respectively by quota regulations. US films now account for 70 per cent of the market in Europe, over 90 per cent in the UK and Ireland and virtually 100 per cent in much of the Caribbean for both cinema and television, although the EU is now hitting back with a major media export promotion programme (GATT 1993: 9; Sussman and Lent 1991; Clarke 1995). Cultural embodiment can also become a Trojan horse for further import penetration through induced value changes, as revealed by one European TV export promoter who has said that 'the more European TV is watched and enjoyed, the greater the attractions will become of all things European, including European products and services' (Clarke 1995), a principle which US promoters discovered long ago. US film producer Francis Ford Coppola has said that US 'industrial cinema' makes films like Big Macs and now 'controls 80 per cent of the world's culture', while actor Dustin Hoffman believes that violent US films are likely to have influenced the actions of mass killers such as those in Scotland and Tasmania recently.[11]

Cultural embodiment in services such as audio-visuals reverses many traditional free trade assumptions. For instance, Free Traders always argue against governments attempting to rectify a trade deficit in any one sector because this will be countered by a surplus in another sector. In audio-visuals, however, this could mean constantly being subject to someone else's culture, and the idea that we should console ourselves with the thought of people in other countries wearing jumpers made of Aussie wool is a nonsense. The economists' notion of trade being a 'positive sum game' is a furphy in the case of audio-visuals because the more US culture we are forced to watch on prime time television the less of our own we see. Likewise, the 'market access' concept is fallacious because it is no cultural help to us if our films take 0.5 per cent of the US market when 80 per cent of our market is US material, and in fact it may be a cultural 'negative sum game' because films must contain Americanish style to sell in the USA. The popular theory that competitiveness begins with production for the home market, thus generating economies of scale, as in the US film, hotel or fast-food industries for instance (Porter 1990: 258ff.; Clarke, 1995), may be true economically, but could be a disaster culturally where importing cultures are swamped as a result. In a world where even culture and entertainment are commodified and mass marketed, free trade in these sectors is likely to mean that only countries possessing comparative advantage can have the privilege of retaining their national identities, which in my view is socially outrageous and should be resisted.

Audio-visuals were a major issue in the Uruguay Round with the USA and Japan pushing for an extensive liberalising agreement. Their chief targets were film and TV local content quotas used by many countries, including Australia, especially the European Broadcast Directive which at that time required all EU TV broadcasters to have a minimum of 51 per cent European content. Most countries resisted the US–Japanese push, some arguing for 'cultural exceptions' to be included in GATT. No agreement was reached and few countries have scheduled the media for market access liberalisation. US and Japanese motives in pressing for audio-visual de-regulation are not difficult to deduce, both being huge exporters of a wide range of audio-visual material, US films and TV programmes accounting for 40 per cent of the world market and audio-visuals being the second largest US export sector after aircraft (GATT 1993: 8), while in both countries imports account for barely 2 *per cent* of their domestic markets. Yet this obscene imbalance does not prevent US commentators from bombastically demanding ever more market access (e.g. Thurow 1996: 134). In the USA, media interests, especially Hollywood lobbyist Jack Valenti, pushed heavily for a global market access agreement through GATS, while many industry groups and Free Traders have described the lack of agreement as a *disappointing* aspect of the Uruguay Round (see Dunkley 1994a).

This issue also calls into question the simplistic 'Public Choice' view of interests (see Chapter 3) which would consider the USA and Japan to be morally correct because they do not use formal protection for audio-visuals. In reality these countries promote their exports through distribution cartels and even ownership of picture theatres, while keeping their domestic markets closed through language barriers (in Japan), public parochialism and tight distribution practices (UNCTAD 1994b: 162–3). Even if justifiable by Free Trade principles, from a cultural perspective the US–Japanese attitude is a staggering piece of hypocrisy, especially when contrasted with India and Egypt who are major film exporters but nevertheless, during the Uruguay Round, opposed audio-visual de-regulation on cultural–sovereignty grounds (Dunkley 1994a).

Some Free Traders claim that cultural protection is ineffective, but there is evidence to the contrary. French broadcasting regulations maintain 60 per cent European and 40 per cent French content, which is better than the European average and China maintains 70 per cent local content, while Canada has recently revived its music industry with local content quotas for radio air time. By contrast, complete de-regulation of the New Zealand media appears to have resulted in a collapse of local content and a ballooning of US material.[12] GATT has considered the 'cultural exceptions' concept but is in two minds on the issue, given the precedents of its own Article IV which allows some film protection, NAFTA's exception for Canadian culture industries and OECD provisions for some audio-visual protection on cultural and infant industry grounds (Dunkley 1994a). In many countries there is a demand for increased local media content, although Australian trade minister, Tim Fischer, has hinted at the option of dropping local content requirements and foreign investment controls in exchange for access to the US market in sectors such as high-tech ferries,[13] a policy which in my view would be cultural insanity. GATT allows local film quotas (Chapter 2) and in my view this should be extended to TV programmes. Further, given that a crucial cultural problem is US domination of media, MFN exemptions should be sought to enable countries to limit audio-visual imports from any *one* country–source.

In sum, GATS is a potentially far-reaching document although in its current form it is likely to have more limited effects than the equivalent provisions of NAFTA, owing to its 'softer' features such as 'positive listing', exemption of government services, omission of government procurement and less onerous compensation mechanisms (see Chapter 5), most of which were requested by Third World delegations. For this reason Free Traders are disappointed with GATS, preferring a 'negative listing' approach with full binding so as to 'lock-in' a de-regulatory impetus, ensure that new services are automatically covered and prevent governments from increasing regulations as a bargaining chip for the next round of negotiations (Hoekman 1995b: 26–7). However, the concepts of 'negative listing', 'locking-in' and automatic coverage of new services are, I suggest, unjustified because the issues are complex and disputed, because deregulatory proposals should be open to debate at all stages and because listing should be reversible, but these rights would be denied under a hard-edged full free trade regime. In my view there never will, nor ever should, be complete free trade in services.

How intellectual is property?

The TRIPs agreement, as briefly outlined in Chapter 4, is a highly controversial, some would say egregious, addition to GATT for it seeks to add rather than remove a form of protection. Some forms of IPR such as artistic copyright, trade marks, geographical marks and so forth are almost universally regarded as justifiable, but are probably adequately covered by existing agreements, while other IPR matters, such as the extension of patents to processes, seed patenting and so forth, are questionable.

The main pressure for the inclusion of IPRs in GATT came from US and European intellectual property-exporting TNCs on the grounds that they were losing up to $61b per annum through 'product piracy', especially by China, and that litigation was becoming expensive. Proposals made by groups of these TNCs during the 1980s became the basis of US submissions to Uruguay Round negotiations, which in turn became the basis of the TRIPs agreement.[14] The standard rationales offered by TRIPs proponents were that the lack of IPRs in some countries would distort trade against innovation-based goods or services, and that existing intellectual property conventions (see Chapter 4) were weak on definitions, coverage and enforceability. However, the prime goal was clearly to make IPRs enforceable through the GATT disputes-settlement system, the USA even adopting its own IPR enforcement through Special 301 (see Glossary and Chapter 3) and building a strong IPR regime into NAFTA. The term TRIPs was invented to make the issue look GATT-relevant, but many economists think it is meaningless because intellectual property cannot be trade-specific.

A few commentators want all IPRs abolished in the interests of a free flow of knowledge and some Free Traders tend to be suspicious of the protectionist interests behind the push for TRIPs, preferring that the issue be left to the various conventions. Most NGOs and Third World governments accept some forms of IPRs but are convinced that the *TRIPs Agreement* in its current form is massively slanted in favour of First World TNCs. The key to the debate lies in the nature of intellectual property itself, which has sometimes been defined as 'ideas with commercial value', or a composite of ideas, inventions and creative expression upon which governments are prepared to bestow the status of legal property (Braga 1995: 2). Without such a status most ideas would quickly become 'public goods' to which everyone would have access. The turning of ideas into formal property is, thus, a compromise between two competing principles—the right of access for all people to all knowledge versus the right of the creators of knowledge to treat their creations as private income-generating property for purposes of reward and incentive. Traditionally societies chose variously between these two principles, but when the industrial revolution brought an explosion of physical and intellectual property, Western countries adopted the property rights principle in the belief that this was the key to technological innovation and growth.

Mainstream economists are largely pragmatic in their views, accepting the incentive effect of IPRs as a key to economic 'progress', but believing that there is a trade-off between the adverse monopoly effects of patenting and its incentive effects for innovation and technology transfer. If the monopoly effect outweighs the incentive effect then local innovation could be discouraged and entrepreneurial income (or 'rents' in economics jargon) will be transferred to rich countries, courtesy of their TNCs, so world economic growth could be reduced by IPRs. But the nett outcome is indeterminate in theory, some economists believing that, for any one country, the result will depend on whether its comparative advantage derives from innovative or imitative activities, the former benefiting much more from IPRs than the latter (Trebilcock and Howse 1995: 252–3). The standard mainstream view is that current evidence suggests a positive association between IPRs on the one hand and technology transfer and DFI on the other, especially as TNCs increasingly demand an amenable IPR regime in host countries. If so, then it is likely that IPRs on balance enhance growth, except perhaps for those least developed countries which have difficulty absorbing innovations.[15]

Much hinges on whether the more valid development theory is that of market-based comparative advantage or those of cumulative advantage and unequal trade (see Chapter 6). Most Third World governments intuitively believe the latter two and fear that they will lose untold billions in rent transfers to rich countries under IPRs, especially as foreign TNCs control virtually, all Third World patents or potentially patentable products. Even in Australia the figure is around 90 per cent, although the government believes that Australian telecommunications, chemical, pharmaceutical, mining and agricultural technology exports will be boosted by the *TRIPs Agreement* (DFAT 1994d: 13). Some mainstream economists agree that there will be at least initial losses for Third World countries under TRIPs and that many poorer countries will gain little or nothing. One estimate suggests that India will have to transfer up to $800m per annum to TNCs under pharmaceutical patents alone and Brazil up to $1b, the exact figures depending on the market structures which would prevail before and after IPRs.[16] One African NGO claims, on the basis of World Bank data, that TRIPs royalties could amount to 5 per cent of world trade and may treble Third World debt servicing payments (Greijn 1991: 35), and it has been estimated that over 90 per cent of WTO members, possibly including Australia, will suffer trade balance deterioration due to IPR payments under the *TRIPs Agreement* (Braithwaite 1995: 116). The assertion by TRIPs advocates that stronger IPRs will stimulate more DFI and 'technology transfer' has been questioned on the grounds that such technologies often take an inappropriate form, that the consequent DFI flows may not be significant or beneficial and that some countries such as South Korea, which have already bowed to US pressure over IPRs, seem to be worse off as a result.[17]

Such losses would derive mainly from the fact that Third World countries currently offer few patents, and from the likelihood that once they begin extensive patenting their industries will be in a weak bargaining position relative to TNCs for determining royalties. Some commentators claim that TNCs are seeking IPRs, not for technology transfer purposes but to upstage potential Third World rivals, particularly in the case of the process patenting issue (PIRG 1993: 12). Hitherto many countries had granted patents only to products, not the processes for making those products, which enabled them to build local industries using slightly differing, or so-called 'reverse engineered', processes, particularly in the pharmaceutical sector. This strategy might not be quite cricket but its defenders say that it has enabled many countries to set up a local pharmaceutical industry and to provide low cost drugs for poorer sections of the population (PIRG 1993: 29). TNCs claim that they need high profits to develop new drugs and that these practices undermine their capacity to do so. Such claims are difficult to test, but there is some evidence of profiteering, over-charging and corruption by pharmaceutical TNCs.[18] In any case, drug companies vigorously sought the extension of patenting to processes and the negotiators of the TRIPs Agreement have duly complied, placing on imitators the onus to prove that their processes are different (Articles 27–1, 28 and 34). Already Canada has, under the IPR provisions of CUFTA/NAFTA and in anticipation of the TRIPs Agreement, abandoned earlier policies of 10-year patents, licensing and drug 'reverse engineering', which has resulted in higher priced drugs and adverse effects on the local industry. It has been suggested that some drug prices in Third World countries could rise by 400 per cent or more, especially as indicated by current world price differentials. Relative to Indian prices, for instance, some drugs cost 10 to 20 times as much in the UK and up to 50 times as much in the USA, which suggests that extended IPRs may gradually ratchet prices upward to First World levels.[19]

This issue is even more heated in the case of agriculture where the TRIPs Agreement requires plants and seeds to be either patented or subject to an effective 'sui generis' (national) control system, with a review of the situation required every four years (Article 26.3b). Third World farmers and NGOs claim that TRIPs will induce the displacement of local plant varieties by hybrids, prevent farmers from collecting their own seeds, reduce food security, make local agriculture dependent upon imported inputs, enable foreign biotechnology companies to control local species or germplasm and generally result in the patenting of traditional knowledge. In fact it is claimed that in some countries where IPRs have been granted under US or World Bank pressure, TNCs have already patented products developed entirely by indigenous farmers, one instance being the patenting of a West African cowpea by a British biotechnology firm (Greijn 1991: 36). Critics point out that, by declaring IPRs to be *private* rights and requiring patentable innovations to have industrial applications (Article 27.1), the *TRIPs Agreement* does not recognise the collective, accumulated knowledge of previous generations upon which Third World farmers and craftsmen still often draw but which TNCs, through so-called 'biopiracy', are beginning to buy up. There is now a world-wide NGO campaign to resist this trend, especially in relation to attempts by US biotechnology company, WRGrace, to patent products of the remarkably versatile Indian Neem tree.[20] In its present form the *TRIPs Agreement* might also misallocate resources by generating *too much* research or unduly biasing R and D towards commercial requirements rather than community needs.

Third World governments have expressed concern that the TRIPs system will be expensive to set up and is beyond their present capabilities, Bangladesh, for instance, having only three officers and a small support staff in its patent office at present (UNCTAD 1994b: 202). Many Third World countries opposed TRIPs throughout the Uruguay Round negotiations but, lacking expertise in most of the issues, ultimately found themselves out-argued by pro-TRIPs delegations, or sometimes, it is claimed, even excluded from drafting sessions by heavy-handed committee chairmen.[21] In short, very few countries really know how TRIPs will affect them, but for many there is good reason to doubt that the results will be beneficial.

Conclusion

Both the GATS and TRIPs agreements are extremely controversial additions to the GATT system, both were strongly resisted by Third World countries and their likely effects are barely understood by many countries at present. The theory behind GATS is that services are subject to the same 'gains from trade' benefits as goods, and the theory behind TRIPs is that the lack of IPRs can distort trade. There are good reasons to doubt both of these rationales. GATS also introduces into the GATT system, for the first time, extensive investment provisions through the 'right of establishment' concept and through limitations on DFI controls for scheduled sectors. Both agreements may bring some benefits to most countries but both entail a wide range of potential economic, social and cultural costs and the nett result may depend upon what sort of societies each country wishes to develop, a question which no country has adequately debated in relation to GATT in general or to GATS and TRIPs in particular. In my view the current 'soft' form of GATS is adequate and should not be hardened along the lines of NAFTA, but the whole concept of TRIPs should be reconsidered.

10

Greening the GATT or GATTing the Green?

Environment and standards in the Uruguay Round

GATT has never really concerned itself directly with environmental issues, preferring to stick narrowly, at times almost religiously, to trade matters, and so was largely ignored by environmentalists until the early 1990s when some apparently environmentally unfriendly disputes panel decisions and Uruguay Round proposals came to notice. Since then GATT has widely been depicted as the enemy of things green and labelled 'GATTzilla the Flipper Killer'. Conversely, strict Free Traders have spilled much ink fretting about the possibility of environmental provisions providing a Trojan Horse for dreaded protectionist interests. Most participants in the debate have sought a balancing act between the equally noble objects of trade liberalisation and environmental protection—should GATT be 'greened', the Greens GATTed or a bit of both? This chapter examines the environmental implications of GATT and the Uruguay Round and proposals for the global harmonisation of standards through the *TBT* and *SPS Agreements* (see Chapter 4). I conclude that GATT is certainly not green and that there is a real danger of standards being harmonised downwards in a 'race to the bottom'.

How green is our GATT?

GATT's green credentials have always been somewhat scanty but, such as they are, can be listed under four headings. First, of the Article XX exemptions noted in Chapter 2, those most commonly used for environmental purposes are XXb, which permits measures 'necessary to protect human, animal or plant life or health', and XXg, which approves of measures 'relating to the conservation of exhaustible natural resources if such measures are made effective in conjunction with restrictions on domestic production or consumption', so long as these do not involve 'arbitrary or unjustifiable discrimination between countries'. Second, in 1971 GATT formed a Group on Environmental Measures and International Trade, but which took twenty years to arrange its first meeting. This group has periodically considered matters such as the trade implications of environmental treaties, packaging and labelling requirements and the Agenda 21 world environmental programme, later being re-formed by the Uruguay Round as the Committee on Trade and Environment with the general remit of 'making international trade and environmental policies mutually supportive'.[1] Green NGOs have been critical of the earlier group's secrecy and lack of output (Charnovitz 1993: 478). Third, many GATT disputes panel decisions have had environmental implications (see below) and have influenced international law, as a result of which Green groups have unsuccessfully urged that people with environmental expertise be included on, or at least consulted by, disputes panels. Finally, the Uruguay Round nominally adopted the principle of 'sustainable development' (see p. 74 above), while the *TBT* and *SPS Agreements* allow environmental regulation, which was not previously mentioned in GATT, and some other agreements allow environmental exceptions.

These environmental provisions are skimpy indeed, reflecting GATT's traditional obsession with trade promotion above other goals. In particular GATT does not require countries to improve their environment, in contrast to NAFTA's mechanisms for upward harmonisation and the EU's clause which specifically encourages members to raise environmental standards (see Chapter 5), the latter having been invoked in several key environmental cases. In fact, some environmentalists are concerned that the Uruguay Round *Agreement on Agriculture* (7c, 8c, 11b etc. of Annex 2), which disallows assistance on the basis of *type* of production, may even *prevent* support for organic farming or other sustainable alternatives (Ritchie in Nader et al. 1993). In 1992 a group of thirty-five member countries unsuccessfully criticised GATT's lack of environmental leadership (Daly and Goodland 1993: 56).

Trading the environment

Trade and the environment intersect in a number of ways which are often classified as 'product', 'scale' and 'structural', each entailing both positive and negative potential effects (Stevens 1993; OECD 1994). *Products* can be positive in nature (e.g. anti-pollution equipment) or negative (toxic wastes). *Scale effects* refer to the growth-inducing tendency of trade which can be positive if it results in environment-improving innovation, but negative if pollution is exacerbated. *Structural effects* refer to economists' (disputed) notion of differential national pollution absorptive capacity, an extension of comparative advantage theory, which suggests that trade-induced structural change will be environmentally positive if resultant pollution increases occur mainly in high absorptive countries but negative in the obverse case. In addition, it is widely agreed that some environmental problems are now international, or 'cross-border', in scope, thus requiring international solutions, Free Traders and other economists accepting trade intervention for this purpose as legitimate and efficient (Stevens 1993). The crucial question is whether free trade should be interfered with for purposes such as environmental regulation, enforcement of international environmental treaties and so forth. Everyone wants the above-mentioned positive effects to outweigh the negative, and economists generally accept the need for environmental regulation, although they see the 'first best' solution to most environmental problems as being the use of appropriate domestic policies (see Chapter 6). However, Free Traders worry that 'trade-related environmental measures' (TREMs) will be misused for protectionist purposes, potentially undoing fifty years of progress towards a liberal world trading order, and thus they urge that trade and environmental or other 'non-economic' issues generally be kept separate (Anderson 1995: 19–20).

On the other hand, environmentalists, whilst accepting some virtue in trade liberalisation, worry that free trade and willy-nilly trade expansion may undermine international environmental agreements, aggravate growth-induced ecological damage and tempt growth-oriented governments to indulge in 'eco-dumping'; that is, the exploitation of low environmental standards to promote exports and attract investment. They therefore want GATT extended to formally encourage environmental improvement, to permit trade sanctions in environmental treaties, to allow 'green tariffs' against eco-dumping and to introduce the 'precautionary principle' in standard-setting, which would enable countries to set above-norm standards with a margin for uncertainty in areas where there are grounds for concern but not full 'scientific' information. The crucial philosophical difference between the two sides is that whilst Free Traders trace most environmental problems to inadequately defined property rights and under-pricing of resources or amenities (clean air etc.), environmentalists attribute such problems to a wide range of factors including under-pricing but extending to over-consumption, consumerist values, excessive population growth and industrialism in general. Nevertheless, the sarcastic political journal *The Economist* (1993), regularly rails against 'greenery' (i.e. environmentalism), its so-called 'viridian quirks' or its alleged ignorance of economics, and grumbles that greenies need a good GATTing.

Something's fishy in the state of GATT

GATT policy on the environment has grown like topsy particularly through environmentally-linked disputes panel cases, many of these involving fish. Two early panel decisions, a 1982 ruling against a US ban on Canadian tuna and a 1987 ruling against Canadian export embargoes on herring and salmon, were based on the inference that the respective actions were for protectionist rather than conservation purposes. In the latter case the panel also ruled that TREMs must be applied in the least trade-restrictive manner. Environmentalists have tended to accept these decisions, especially as alternative policies were later found and the original actions appear to have conferred no real environmental benefits (Arden-Clarke 1994).

More controversial was a 1987 decision against the US Superfund (an environmental restoration programme) which taxed imported petrochemicals to aid clean-ups. The panel deemed that the tax was discriminatory, a view which environmentalists accepted, but it also ruled that GATT does not recognise the key principle of 'polluter pays', despite this concept being strongly advocated by the OECD, and that panels have no authority to rule on environmental matters, only trade issues. So the case both presented some unfortunate precedents and gave rise to the dilemma that certain environmental measures might be unavoidably trade discriminatory or restrictive (Arden-Clarke 1994: 6). A 1994 disputes panel decision ruled as discriminatory against certain types of imports a US regulation which penalises low fuel-economy corporate car fleets, and a 1995 decision, the first under the new WTO framework, similarly ruled against a US law which compels the sale of less polluting, reformulated petrol in some parts of the country.[2]

In most of the above cases the 'offending' measures could possibly have been applied in a less trade discriminatory manner while still retaining environmental benefits, but many trade economists worry that measures such as deposit-based recycling, eco-labelling and product life-cycle systems are inherently discriminatory against imports because of the collection infrastructures and so forth which are required. This issue arose in the EC with the 1988 Danish bottle case in which the European Commission and British beverage exporters claimed that deposit requirements and bans on non-returnable bottles were trade discriminatory because of collection difficulties for non-resident or non-established suppliers. The European Court upheld the deposit system on the grounds that the EC required members to improve environmental quality, but struck down an official approval system aimed at encouraging reusable bottles on the grounds that this was disproportionate to the objects of the law (OTA 1992; McDonald 1993). The crucial implications of this case are that trade agreements tend to require a 'balance' between trade and environmental goals, and that a clearly effective environmental measure was probably only saved by the existence of the EC's environmental clause, a provision which GATT does not contain.

The most controversial GATT panel decision to date involved the 1991 so-called tuna–dolphin case in which the USA had, under domestic legislation, banned imports of tuna from Mexico, both directly and through third countries, because Mexican fleets were breaching permissible incidental dolphin kill rates of 1.25 times US kill rates. Mexico claimed that the US action contravened GATT Articles III (National Treatment), XI (restriction of import–export bans) and XIII (non-discriminatory quotas). The USA defended its action mainly under Article XX b and g (health and resource exceptions—see above). A number of countries, including Australia, formally supported Mexico. The panel upheld the main Mexican submissions and rejected the US defence on the following grounds: that Article XX does not apply 'extraterritorially' (outside the USA itself); that GATT rules and exceptions only apply to 'like products', not to processes of production; that the US legislation was discriminatory (dolphin kill quotas could only be determined after the US fishing season and administration was difficult for importers); and that methods other than bans, such as co-operative international monitoring, could have been found. The panel directed the USA to bring its legislation into line with GATT, but the USA negotiated (moderately) improved fishing methods with Mexico and the panel report was never formally adopted.[3]

The tuna–dolphin decision is probably GATT's most publicised act in its 50-year history. For environmentalists it was a bombshell because it seemed to undermine the right of individual countries to help protect the global commons, it potentially threatened the use of trade sanctions in international environmental agreements (through the 'no extraterritoriality' ruling) and it limited the possibility of import embargoes against ecologically damaging processes (the 'products only ruling'). Critics also pointed out that the three-person panel neither included any environmental experts nor accepted environmental submissions. The tuna–dolphin case has become a much-quoted landmark having already set precedents for later panel decisions, and its merits are still hotly debated, even some economists regarding the panel's interpretations as unduly narrowly based. In sum, rulings in various jurisdictions, especially GATT/ WTO panels, suggest that TREMs are acceptable for a limited range of environmental purposes so long as: they do not discriminate against exports, they are applied only within the country imposing them, they are implemented in the least trade restricting manner possible, they are used in relation to products but not processes of production, they are proportionate to their objects and less trade-interventionist measures have previously been sought. In other words, TREMs are meant to be limited, last-resort policies and GATT has tended to implicitly accord greatest priority to trade promotion.

GATT versus green or GATTing the green?

GATT's trade–environment policy has evolved through internal discussions, panel decisions and advice from mainstream trade economists (e.g. Anderson and Blackhurst 1992). The view which has emerged is that, as virtually all environmental problems purportedly originate with inadequate pricing or property rights, the solutions lie with optimal market-based domestic policies or, for trans-border and global commons problems, with international agreements enforced co-operatively rather than through trade sanctions. Trade between countries whose domestic prices adequately 'internalise' all externalities will reflect comparative advantage as adjusted for each nation's pollution absorptive capacity or environmental preferences. Trade-related environmental measures (TREMs), or even 'excessive' domestic environmental regulation, can distort both the economic and environmental benefits of trade, so should either be avoided or be conducted in the least trade-distorting manner possible. In the long term price-adjusted trade will bring economic growth and environmental improvement (GATT 1992). However, in my view and in the view of most environmentalists, there are some major flaws in this disarmingly simplistic picture and these will be briefly examined below.

'Greenery' begins at home No one disagrees that domestic environmental policies, which Free Traders want used in preference to trade intervention, are crucial, but trans-border spillovers and commons problems may be more complex than Free Traders acknowledge, so most domestic policies (or lack thereof) are likely to have trade implications and most TREMs will have domestic linkages. In the case of efforts to reduce the over-exploitation of rainforest timber, for instance, it is said that import-export bans would be sub-optimal because of trade distortion and circumvention, whereas in-country pricing to reflect externalities would be more effective, would provide governments with revenue and would be GATT-consistent (Repetto 1993: 6). This seems sensible enough and in my view there should be international 'carrots' to encourage such policies, but there are no schemes of this sort at present and bad, weak or corrupt governments continue to neglect such options. Some countries have tried log export bans but in Indonesia's case the

EU threatened action through GATT on grounds that the policy was aimed at protecting local 'value added' industries (plywood, furniture etc.) and so Indonesia desisted, apparently resulting in accelerated logging (Arden-Clarke 1994: 9). Yet a case could be made for trade intervention, on a combination of infant industry, environmental, community and cultural grounds, to shift export activities from raw forest products to value added industries, preferably by enhancing traditional timber-using craft skills which in many Third World countries are still village based.

The extraterritorial taboo   The view adopted by the tuna–dolphin panel that one country cannot and should not impose its ideology on other countries has been widely criticised. From the legal point of view it has been suggested that the history of environmental agreements and the drafting history of GATT indicate extraterritoriality is acceptable and was intended (Charnovitz 1991 and 1993). From the economic point of view it has been argued that measures such as the US tuna–dolphin legislation do not impose one nation's values on others as the panel claimed, but simply lay down conditions for market access through domestic rules which other countries can take or leave, and are primarily aimed at protecting the global commons, a motive approved of by most economists.[4] From the political point of view the assertion by many Free Traders (e.g. Anderson 1995: 9) that each country tends to have different environmental preferences and that developing countries do not share First World enthusiasm for 'greenery', is inaccurate. Green values tend to follow group rather than national lines so that, whilst Third World governments and elites favour development over the environment, countless individuals and NGOs favour the reverse and there is now a vast Third World green movement.[5] GATT (1992: 25) claims that there are 'always' viable non-trade methods for influencing other countries such as green labelling, consumer boycotts and NGO lobbying, but these methods might be too slow for emergencies and the suggestion arguably constitutes buck-passing to under-resourced groups.

Eco-dumping and all that   One of the environmentalists' main concerns with free trade is that it will encourage eco-dumping (the deliberate use of low environmental standards to foster trade competitiveness) or shifts of TNC production to 'pollution havens' (countries which use eco-dumping). Mainstream economists tend to admit this is theoretically possible but claim that it is unlikely in practice because the cost savings are insufficient, that there is no evidence of it occurring on a significant scale and that pollution-intensive production is common in the early stages of development (OTA 1992; Low 1992; Pearce and Warford 1993: 312–13; Stevens 1993). However, one study has found that some industries (e.g. chemicals) seek pollution havens, that some countries have fostered pollution-haven status and that eco-dumping by NICs may increase in future, others claiming that the latter trend is now occurring.[6] It was estimated in the early 1980s that low pollution standards saved NICs $14b in costs relative to industrial countries, a figure which would be much larger now, and TNCs have been known to threaten governments with re-location to pollution havens for cost-saving reasons (Shrybman 1993: 277–8). It has also been suggested that US chemical companies' environmental expenditure in their overseas plants is only half that in home plants (PIRG 1993: 37). So if eco-dumping is a possibility, albeit not used much at present, then there is a case for countries to have available, if required, a capacity for trade intervention through 'green tariffs' or 'green countervailing duties'. Despite this, however, one former GATT official, whilst accepting the need for such measures when eco-dumping is used for strategic trade purposes, has emphasised that 'green tariffs' would not be allowable under either GATT94 codes or the Uruguay Round Subsidies Agreement.[7] GATT itself (1992: 17) has hinted that such measures would not be allowable because of tariff bindings and MFN requirements.

The green Trojan horse   GATT (1992: 5) and many Free Traders (e.g. Oxley 1993; Anderson 1995) are inordinately petrified that environmental issues and green groups advocating them will be exploited by protectionist interests, and this 'danger' is used as a major argument against the routine employment of TREMs. *The Economist* (1993) has periodically made snide remarks about big bad greenies bullying poor Mexico and 'twanging the heartstrings of wealthy Westerners'. Greens variously reply that some links with anti-free trade groups are legitimate, that such links are arms' length and that misuse of TREMs for trade protectionist purposes is readily identifiable (Arden-Clarke 1994). In my view the issue has been greatly over-stated and the idea that well-organised greens can lord it over fragile trading interests (*Economist* 1993: 13) is ludicrous (also see Chapters 2 and 3). Disguised protectionism can occur, but the issues are seldom clear-cut. At present the USA has bans on prawn imports from about forty countries, including Australia, where netting methods are deemed to endanger turtles, and although the Australian industry denies prawning near turtle habitats, claiming the measure is protectionist, it is known that damage occurs in most countries concerned.[8] There is no evidence that protectionist motives predominate in such cases, so the solution would seem to lie with clearer guidelines and more systematic environmental advice for GATT panels.

The processes problem   As noted above, the tuna–dolphin panel ruled that GATT exceptions (Article XX) clauses only cover products, not production processes, the rationale seemingly being that these relate to a nation's legitimate comparative advantage and so an extension of exceptions to processes would open the floodgates of protectionism (e.g. *Economist* 1993). The Uruguay Round *TBT* and *SPS Agreements* reinforce this position. The result seems to be that, in the case of the Toronto greenhouse gas reduction agreement, for instance, TREMs could be used against CFC-using refrigerators so long as domestic 'like products' were treated identically, but not against processes such as computer chips manufactured with CFC solvents (OTA 1992: 6). However, there is a legal view (e.g. Charnovitz 1991: 53) that international law contains precedents for covering processes. Even some economists believe that differential treatment of products and processes does not make either environmental or economic sense because, in economics jargon, consumption and production externalities both have equal capacity to inflict damage and reduce welfare (Pearce and Warford 1993: 305–8). The political reality is that process-related TREMs, such as the EU ban on meat containing growth hormones, are increasingly being used and so the GATT exceptions should be extended to processes (Charnovitz 1995).

The treaty trauma   As noted above, environmentalists are concerned that the tuna–dolphin case may jeopardise the trade sanction provisions of international environmental treaties, while GATT and Free Traders worry about discrimination against non-signatories and the possible proliferation of TREMs, although in my view the 17 out of 127 such treaties which at present contain trade measures (GATT 1992: 10) does not seem excessive. Legal opinion generally suggests that trade sanctions are indeed GATT-incompatible and GATT does not recognise treaties which conflict with its own pro-visions (Charnovitz 1992; McDonald 1993). Already one treaty has eschewed trade sanctions because of uncertainties about their GATT-consistency (Charnovitz 1992: 216), and South Korea has contemplated challenging as GATT-incompatible the *Montreal Protocol on Substances that Deplete the Ozone Layer* (Hudson in Low 1992: 58). GATT's (1992: 10–12) stock answer to the problem is that any treaty with widespread support could seek a GATT waiver for the requisite TREMs, discriminatory requirements and so forth. However, there are a number of problems with this proposal (see Charnovitz 1992: 216–18). First, post-Uruguay waivers require a three-fourths majority, are annually reviewable and are granted only in 'exceptional circumstances', so they are not easy to obtain. Second, many treaties begin with only a few signatories, so waivers may not be attainable initially. Third, this process could be slow and non-treaty WTO members might demand compensation. Fourth, disagreements between the trade and environmental arms of govern-ment are not unknown, so the signing of a treaty might not auto-matically result in support for a waiver. Fifth, this waiver procedure would imply that the environment is subordinate to trade, a view which today would be highly questionable, especially given that most trade treaties, GATT included, allow sanctions for commercial disputes (Charnovitz 1995: 4). Many now believe that GATT should be amended to facilitate environmental treaties, but this may need unanimity, depending on which Articles are to be amended.

Green comparative advantage   One of GATT's (1992) key argu-ments is that 'countries are not clones of one another', differing in their resource bases, environmental absorptive capacities and degrees of preference for a clean environment, which thence deter-mine comparative advantage. The use of inappropriate TREMs or enforced harmonisation of environmental standards for Fair Trade purposes would, therefore, deprive low environmental-cost countries of a legitimate trade advantage. However, the notion of differing ab-sorptive capacities has been questioned scientifically on the grounds that ecological absorptive capacity can change (see below), that

ecosystems dilute rather than 'absorb' pollution, that there is no such
thing as a 'safe' threshold and that ecosystems are too integrally
linked to constitute a 'feature' of the economy in the way economists
see it (Buckley 1993: 32). The idea of national pollution preferences
is also questionable and leads to the absurd proposition that, as
former World Bank economist Lawrence Summers once put it,
African countries are 'under-polluted' so would be better off taking
more polluting industries.[9]

GATT (1992: 6) claims that suppression of these national differences through trade regulation would lead down a 'very slippery
slope' to protectionism, but that, so long as prices reflect environmentally adjusted comparative advantage and firms are willing
to 'internalise externalities', trade will enhance the environment.
However, even some mainstream economists (e.g. Anderson and
Blackhurst 1992; Hudson and Lopez in Low 1992) admit that if
prices do not reflect all externalities then trade might prove environmentally damaging, while many environmentalists fear that, due to
a range of market or administrative failures, prices may never adequately reflect all externalities. Moreover, as one study of European
corporate opinion has found that business accords the environment
a very low priority, firms probably cannot be relied upon voluntarily
to internalise externalities as required.[10] If this is so then much more
extensive interventions may be necessary to change environmentally damaging lifestyles or decision-making systems, and this would
probably include trade intervention.

Growth to the rescue?   A key argument used by GATT (1992) and
Free Traders for the compatibility of trade and the environment is
that trade leads to economic growth which leads to environmental
improvement. This sequence is counter-intuitive to most environmentalists who generally see growth as a villain. GATT's rationale is
based on what some call the 'bell-curve theory' which holds that per
capita pollution levels rise in the early stages of economic growth,
level out at a per capita GDP of about $5000 and thence decline as
increased efficiency of resource allocation reduces wastage, as more
research is devoted to environmental problems and as consumer
preferences shift from quantity of goods to quality of life. However,
in my view this theory, though not without some validity, is risky.
GATT largely relies on just one study for its thesis, that by Grossman

and Kreuger which uses UN data for only three pollutants (sulphur dioxide, smoke and particles) from forty-two cities world-wide. This study found a bell-curve for the first two and a gradual decline for particles, but an *increase* in per capita particle pollution when site factors are held constant (which GATT did not mention).[11] Other studies have found bell-curves for some pollutants, steady declines for others and increasing per capita levels for a few, most such studies finding that nitrous oxide emissions, municipal waste, traffic, noise levels and carbon dioxide all increase proportionately with growth.[12] In any case, absolute pollution levels often increase with growth even if per capita levels do not (Lopez in Low 1992), and for many pollutants it is the absolute level which does the damage.

In reality neither the data nor our knowledge of links between variables is sufficient to warrant definitive claims of the sort GATT makes. A recent study by Australia's national environmental body has said that current Australian data are inadequate, that a country's environmental absorbtive capacity may decline, that there are probably no technological 'magic bullets' to be invented (so increased research may not be the panacea GATT claims) and that Australian cities are likely to suffer increasing pollution due to growth. The equivalent Victorian body has said that Australian cities are losing the pollution battle because of continuing growth, particularly in vehicle numbers. The same is true of other cities around the world, such as Paris where proliferation of cars and business lobbying against traffic controls have taken their toll.[13]

It has been argued that agricultural trade liberalisation and market-oriented growth will improve the environment by shifting some output from intensively farmed locations, especially Europe, to areas of lower ecological-impact farming (Anderson and Blackhurst 1992: ch. 8). However, this assumes differential absorbtive capacities which, as suggested above, is questionable, and UN studies indicate that African cash cropping for food exports to Europe is now creating serious ecological problems.[14] A better solution may be to adopt more sustainable, self-reliant agricultural methods in all countries (see Chapter 8). Although some Free Traders manage to deny it (e.g. Oxley 1993), trade liberalisation and growth have historically been associated with increased transport and energy use, while the Uruguay Round is expected to enhance this trend.[15] As Europe becomes less self-reliant in food, a widening range of produce is being imported by air transport, which requires fifty times as much energy as shipping and up to 600 times as much energy as the calorific value of certain products.[16]

Some commentators anticipate that increased trade could induce more exports of unsustainably harvested rainforest timber, even though most of the current demand growth for forest products is domestic, as well as increase exports of other resources, toxic wastes and so forth,[17] while making it difficult for nations to resist biotechnology or protect biodiversity (see p. 171 above). Globalisation of production may also make more difficult the use of 'integrated life-cycle manufacturing', the type of production system required for extensive recycling, which is best done within national boundaries (Stevens 1993: 447). Overall, the hypothesis that trade liberalisation and any resultant acceleration of economic growth will significantly improve the environment must be considered dubious and risky, perhaps even nonsensical.

Trade first or green first?   Many commentators argue that GATT and its panels take an extremely narrow 'trade first' view on environmental questions of the sort discussed above, as well as on subsidiary issues such as proportionality, use of non-trade options, or the concept of 'least trade restrictive' measures (see above), and indeed the tuna–dolphin panel explicitly stated that it was adopting a narrow interpretation of Article XX. This is well illustrated by the 1990 *Thai Cigarettes* case in which the USA challenged a Thai government anti-smoking programme whose main feature had been a ban on cigarette imports and advertising, the rationale being that US products were more addictive and heavily promoted by TNC advertisers, especially amongst women and children, than were local (government-controlled) products. A GATT panel found against Thailand on the grounds that the import ban was illegal (under Article XI), that it breached National Treatment principles (Article III) and that other anti-smoking methods, such as publicity campaigns, should have been tried before restricting trade. Technically the panel decision was correct but was unduly narrow, as even some economists admit, because large-scale campaigns can be expensive for poor countries, and the World Health Organisation had approved the Thai government's policy. Moreover, the effects of cigarette promotion, which the policy was designed to counter, were well known, for smoking had resurged in Japan, South Korea and Taiwan after earlier cigarette import bans had, under US and corporate pressure, been lifted. The US government-backed tobacco market-opening push in Asia, which some health authorities are comparing with the nineteenth-century opium wars in China, has been a brilliant trading success story but a health disaster! In effect GATT has helped undermine a genuine public health programme in favour of the global tobacco trade![18]

In sum, Free Traders claim that trade and the environment are compatible so long as appropriate policies are used to 'internalise externalities', and that these should be domestic rather than trade interventionist, except for trans-border or 'global commons' problems. Many, including myself, disagree on the grounds that trade and the environment are not always compatible, and increasing numbers of RTAs contain environmental provisions (Charnovitz 1995). Proposed solutions are of three types—a broadening of panel interpretations; amendment of GATT rules to cover processes, trade sanctions, 'green tariffs', countervailing duties and so forth; and creation of a new body, either inside the WTO or independently, to assess the environmental aspects of trade and their implications. I favour the latter two, and these options will be further touched upon in Chapter 12.

Race to the top or bottom?

Whilst Free Traders dislike attempts to harmonise environmental standards between countries because ecological differences supposedly reflect 'natural' comparative advantage, they strongly favour harmonisation of product and process standards because these are thought to be discretionary and amenable to protectionist manipulation. Free Traders want a levelling of the playing field but not demolition of the whole stadium. Consequently, the *TBT* and *SPS Agreements* of the Uruguay Round (see Chapter 4) are seeking to harmonise technical standards and standard-setting systems while formally retaining national autonomy in such matters, the rationale being to reduce trading costs, to ensure transparency, to avoid 'unnecessary' barriers to trade and generally to promote globalisation. The standards harmonisation process can take several forms—'equivalence', or comparable but not identical standards, as used in CUFTA/NAFTA; 'mutual recognition', as used in the EU and ANZCERTA, which requires all member countries to admit goods produced by the standards of other countries; 'reference standards' as set by multilateral standard-setting bodies; 'ex-ante harmonisation', or formal standards and procedures agreed to by governments before goods enter markets; 'ex-post harmonisation', or the informal convergence of standards over the longer term through competition and arbitrage.[19] Of these options, the *TBT* and *SPS Agreements* appear to be aiming initially for reference standards and equivalence, but ultimately for ex-ante harmonisation.

The rationale for harmonisation is that, theoretically, uniform global standards, both domestically and internationally, will maximise trade, efficiency and economic welfare, so long as these are adequate for health, safety and environmental requirements, but not high enough to be protectionist (Hansson 1990). The problem, however, is that the borderline between virtue and vice is not always clear in practice, and the question being debated is whether the new agreements will tend to harmonise standards upwards ('race to the top') or downwards ('race to the bottom'); that is, whether quality standards and other such regulations will be strengthened or weakened. Most mainstream theorists believe the former on grounds such as a faith in corporate responsibility, the greening of consumerism and the global competitive advantages which green innovativeness can supposedly bring, while environmentalists, food NGOs and so forth fear a 'race to the bottom'. A few mainstream economists either take the latter possibility seriously or at least consider harmonisation politically difficult, US Managed Trader, Lester Thurow, observing that in globalised markets 'all of the pressures are to harmonise down'.[20] In theory there can be a number of benefits from fairly uniform world-wide standards and all international bodies *officially* encourage improved standards, but in practice there are various forces, outlined below, which may edge them downwards.

First, Codex Alimentarius, the WTO's designated food standards body, is a government–industry club, delegations from its 130 member countries consisting of government representatives with 73 per cent of all delegates, the food industry with 22 per cent but up to 50 per cent from some countries (only 11 per cent from Australia), and NGOs with a mere 0.4 per cent (Avery et al. 1993). There are virtually always business representatives on Australia's Codex delegation, whereas NGOs cannot afford to attend every meeting (Bún 1995). Some 140 delegates from the world's top food and agro-chemical companies, especially Nestlé and Coca Cola, have participated in Codex over the years (Avery et al. 1993). Strong industry representation need not discredit the organisation, but clearly some conflicts of interest are possible, and business delegates hold almost half the seats on some key committees. Like GATT, Codex places strong emphasis on the facilitation of trade, particularly global food trade, a goal of which many NGOs are critical (Avery et al. 1993; Webb 1994; Bún 1995).

Second, the central concepts of the *TBT* and *SPS Agreements*, 'least trade restrictive' measures and 'scientific justification' (see Chapter 4) are problematic as the former can entail political judgment, while in the latter case scientific opinion is seldom unanimous nor politically neutral. Concerns about drug safety which turn out to be warranted often emerge well before a scientific consensus is established. Some critics distinguish between 'risk assessment' which is scientific but not usually controversial, and 'risk management' which is political and administrative, often requiring national flexibility and sovereignty, features which may be undermined by the Uruguay Round (Webb 1994). Most countries maintain a 'precautionary gap' between their own 'maximum residue limits' and generally accepted safety standards, but with strict scientific criteria now being required this practice may be subject to challenge as protectionist, despite the fact that even some business opinion accepts the need for the precautionary principle in cases of serious or irreversible environmental threats (Schmidheiny 1992: 76). At times countries such as Germany or the USA have acted as 'standards leaders', as have individual states within some countries, but this role may now be rendered risky and under the Uruguay Round national governments must try to bring 'rebel' states into line (Daly and Goodland 1993: 72). Even where there *is* a scientific consensus, industry interests sometimes challenge agreed standards, such as with an early 1990s appeal by Canadian asbestos companies against US asbestos control laws (Charnovitz 1992: 212–13).

A third reason why downward harmonisation may be possible is that there can be powerful international competitive pressures for reduction of standards, and some commentators dispute the cosy claim that maintenance of high environmental or other such standards can bring competitive advantage for TNCs acting the 'good citizen'.[21] Under CUFTA and its 'equivalence' principle, for instance, Canada has gradually shifted from a 'full safety before approval' rule for pesticide registration to the weaker US rule of approval if the benefits outweigh the risks, clearly a case of harmonising downwards (Shrybman 1993: 282). One critic of harmonisation claims that the process has in practice almost never been upwards, and usually tends downwards (Lang 1993: 19). The ink was scarcely dry on the Uruguay Round when the EU announced there were dozens of US federal and state laws and standards it intended to challenge as unduly trade restrictive or scientifically unjustified, including various fuel economy, recycling and food safety laws, the tuna–dolphin legislation and even certain nuclear safety regulations.[22] The USA has done likewise through its 'watch list' (see Chapter 3) and Japan through a departmental monitoring committee (MITI 1996). Increasing global rivalry will exacerbate such pressures, one US commentator (Thurow 1996: 136) having complained, for instance, that the non-government International Standards Organisation, which co-ordinates the setting of many technical standards world-wide, is now European-dominated so that the USA can no longer *impose* its own standards on the world.

A fourth factor making downward harmonisation possible is that current Codex standards are modest or low compared with those of many OECD countries, particularly Europe. One sample survey found that 60 per cent of Australian standards were higher than those of Codex, but in almost all cases Australia's main food and health standard-setting body at the time recommended whichever was the lower standard (i.e. the *higher* permissible level of pesticide residue etc.), including over a thousand cases in which Australian authorities previously disallowed *any* chemical residues.[23] This would seem to be a clear case of harmonising down, although the government claims that Australia currently has wide safety margins, and standards reductions have not yet been implemented. In the EU the concept of 'mutual recognition' was adopted because attempts at ex-ante harmonisation (see above) were strongly resisted, but in the process many standards have been harmonised down, including, for instance, a doubling of allowable food additives.[24]

A final set of factors which may induce a 'race to the bottom' is world-wide domestic and international de-regulation. During the Reagan era many US health, safety and environmental standards were (sometimes corruptly) reduced, while during the Uruguay Round USTR, Clayton Yeutter, openly expressed the aim of using GATT to dilute state and local food safety regulations or to place downward international pressures on US and EU food standards.[25] USA–Canada border inspectors claim that, under CUFTA/NAFTA arrangements, food inspection has become minimal and sometimes corrupt, resulting in contaminated meat regularly crossing borders, yet Mexico has urged upon the USA further standards reductions for trade purposes.[26] In the EU a secret committee of industrialists and economists has advocated diluting or scrapping a range of health, safety and environmental regulations.[27]

In Australia regulatory systems for food and other standards are changing rapidly with moves afoot to de-regulate both process and product standards, as well as to harmonise most such standards with New Zealand, through ANZCERTA, by the end of the century. Government bodies are increasingly using voluntary industry codes, self-regulatory 'quality assurance' and cost-recovery systems (e.g. charging firms for inspections), although an attempt by the former Labor Government to reduce and privatise inspection services was successfully resisted by NGOs.[28] Government bodies routinely invoke the *TBT* and *SPS Agreements* and the concept of 'mutual market access' as justification for de-regulation, the National Food Authority (NFA) Act accordingly being amended in 1995 to remove a clause (10e) which required that Australian food standards not be lowered in the harmonisation process. The NFA has also greatly elevated trade expansion as a priority.[29]

As yet there is no clear evidence that Australian standards are being reduced, but periodic incidents illustrate the sorts of pressures which could arise. In recent years, for instance, Australian potato farmers in high-cadmium areas have tried to get permitted cadmium levels raised and the NFA was inclined to accede until NGOs objected, proposing instead a cadmium-reduction programme which has been adopted but has not been adequately implemented to date.[30] Reference to lower international standards can often aid industry pressure of this sort. Recently the NFA has allowed increased fortification of breakfast foods and higher vitamin additives to sugary cereals, a practice which consumer groups see as nutritionally misleading but which the Australian food industry had urged for reasons of choice and export advantages into Asia. The industry is now advocating similar changes in Codex standards on the basis of this precedent (Bún, 1995: 7). Australian quarantine standards for poultry and other products are now being changed from a 'minimum risk' to an 'acceptable risk' basis, both as part of our Uruguay Round obligations and in order to facilitate higher exports, a move which producers claim could lower quality and increase the risk of disease.[31] Likewise, NGOs and some industry bodies are concerned that standards could be jeopardised by recent APEC proposals for country-of-origin safety certification and by an Australian-sponsored move through Codex to abolish border inspection systems in favour of self-regulatory in-country certification by exporters.[32] Thus, a combination of commercial pressures, trade obsession and WTO- or RTA-induced de-regulation could hasten downward harmonisation.

In sum, advocates of standards harmonisation believe that this process can minimise bureaucratic processes, reduce handling costs, dispense with separate packaging for different countries, generally increase allocative efficiency and enhance trade based on genuine comparative advantage. Free Traders fear that the persistence of national standard-setting autonomy will perpetuate non-level playing fields and facilitate new forms of trade-restricting NTBs. Critics reply, however, that global harmonisation could ratchet standards downwards, bolster 'industrial' agriculture and food mass-marketing or enable TNCs to use promotional systems which inveigle consumers away from fresh foods to processed products (Lang 1993; Bún 1995). Australian authorities are convinced that level playing fields will enhance our export potential, but critics fear that, equally, these might reduce export quality, thus sparking rejection of our products in countries such as the USA, Japan and South Korea where recent health scares have made people nervous. Furthermore, our own industries could be weakened by lower-standard imports from burgeoning Asian food processors, a prospect which even the NFA has acknowledged.[33] Fair Traders and other such critics advocate continued national autonomy in standard-setting and risk management, the right of nations to the 'precautionary principle', some minimum-standard protection and policy mechanisms for upward harmonisation.

Conclusion

Although the environment is not formally covered by GATT it is rapidly becoming the most ticklish issue the new WTO faces. In its disputes panel decisions and formal pronouncements GATT has adopted a narrow view of its own rules in relation to the environment, a rather dogmatic position regarding the alleged complementarity between trade and the environment and a misplaced zeal for the international harmonisation of standards. A strong case can be mounted against GATT's position on these issues and commentators from a range of viewpoints believe that GATT must broaden its stance. Trade and the environment may conflict in a number of ways and harmonisation of standards, whilst not being without merit, may well result in greater costs than benefits. Ultimately, one's judgment on these issues depends on values or priorities and GATT has made its priority clear; that is, trade first! Greens have GATTed themselves a little but GATT is not showing many signs of being greened.

11

The Perils of Globalism

The WTO in the new world order

Images of the new GATT/WTO structure and how it will work range from a mild, consensus-based system of trading rules to a draconian global economic policeman and potential world government. This chapter briefly examines the proposed workings of the WTO in relation to the emerging global order and various issues arising therefrom. It concludes that for the moment the WTO is closer to the former image rather than the latter extreme, but that its proposed future agenda may move it in the latter direction, which in my view would be of highly questionable virtue.

The birth of a global bureaucracy

The new GATT system will differ from the old in a number of ways, notably: its decision-making structures will be tighter and more formal; its disputes-settlement mechanisms will be stricter and entail more automaticity; it will involve more continuous negotiations on a range of issues with a view to hastening liberalisation, possibly reducing the importance of the traditional 'rounds'; and there will be a good deal more surveillance, monitoring, notification and so forth.

As was outlined briefly in Chapter 4, the new GATT system is to be a three-legged stool with the WTO at the apex, its structure differing only slightly from the original model. The supreme decision-making body of the WTO is the Ministerial Conference, consisting of designated ministers from all member countries, which is to meet at least once every two years and which has the power to decide on all matters relating to Uruguay Round agreements and other WTO affairs. Subsidiary to the Conference is a General Council, also based on equal representation of Members, which meets between conferences 'as appropriate' and has the task of dealing with the regular functions of the GATT/WTO system. In particular the Council will itself convene when required as the Dispute Settlement Body and as the co-ordinating body of the Trade Policy Review Mechanism, two crucial functions of the WTO. Thus, the Council is sure to become the power centre of the GATT system. Subsidiary to these bodies is the Secretariat headed by the Director-General, three Agreement Councils for the WTO's three 'legs' (goods, services and IPRs), four Functional Committees and a number of Agreement Committees (my terms) covering the various sectors of the Uruguay Round (see Figure 11.1).

Voting procedures in the Ministerial Conference and General Council are similar to, but more complex than, those of GATT94. Article IX of the *WTO Agreement* expressly says that decision-making is to be by consensus, the practice evolved under GATT94, but by ballot when there is no consensus, with all Member countries having one vote, including each EU member country which belongs to the WTO. When voting occurs, decisions are based on a simple majority except in three crucial areas. In cases involving an interpretation of Uruguay Round agreements (except the plurilateral agreements) the Ministerial Conference or General Council makes the final decision on the basis of a recommendation from the Council covering the agreement concerned, and non-consensual decisions require a three-quarters majority. Waivers from the requirements of any agreement may be provided in 'exceptional circumstances', but require consensus or a three-quarters majority, must be reviewed annually, must terminate when the circumstances change and can only be granted by the Ministerial Conference. Waivers will thus be tougher to obtain than in the past.

In the case of amendments to agreements the procedure (Article X) is more complex. Amendment proposals can only be submitted by Member governments or by Agreement Councils, and the Ministerial Conference must decide within ninety days, either by consensus or by a two-thirds majority, whether to submit the proposal to

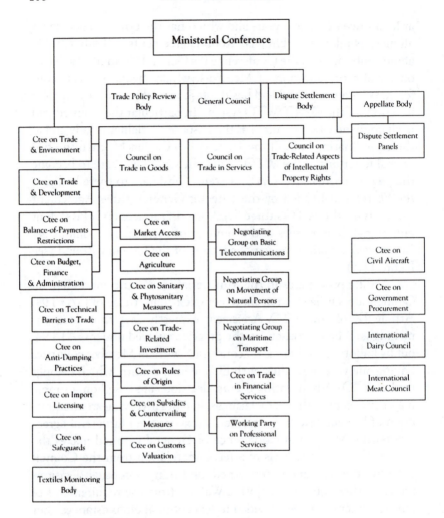

Figure 11.1: WTO structure
Source: *WTO Focus*, No. 1, January–February 1995: 5

Member governments. Amendments to WTO voting rules or to the MFN clauses of the various agreements must be by unanimous approval of Members. Amendments which would alter the rights or obligations of Members must be passed by a two-thirds majority of the Ministerial Conference, but will apply only to those countries which accept them unless the Conference decides by a three-quarters majority that a proposed amendment is important enough to be applied to all Members. A dissenting Member would thence have three choices—accept the amendment, apply for a waiver or withdraw from the WTO (Article X:3). Amendments which would not alter Members' rights or obligations must be passed by at least a two-thirds majority and will apply to all Members (Article X:4). Thus, changes to GATT rules, which previously required only a simple majority in non-consensual cases, now require majorities ranging from two-thirds to unanimity, so it will be very hard for individual countries or small groups of nations to obtain changes.

Little is said in any of the Final Act agreements about the structure of the various Agreement Councils and Committees. Article IV:5–8 of the *WTO Agreement* specifies that the Councils 'shall be open to representatives of members', their functions will be assigned to them by the General Council and they may appoint subsidiary bodies. The structures of Agreement Committees are outlined in the separate agreements, some specifying representation from all Members and meetings at least once or twice a year, but some providing no detail at all. So the likely shape and operations of these bodies remain vague, yet, as one commentator has pointed out (Evans 1994: 16), they are likely to become the working core of the WTO and may evolve considerable power, especially as the Councils can propose amendments to agreements. These bodies are theoretically open to all WTO Member countries, but it is hard to see smaller nations maintaining sufficiently large delegations to participate in the more than two dozen Agreement Councils and Committees, a fifth of GATT Members never having retained permanent delegations in Geneva.

The greatest controversy surrounds the new disputes-resolution mechanism, which is contained in the *Understanding on Rules and Procedures Governing the Settlement of Disputes* (hereinafter *Disputes Agreement*), although many of the other agreements also contain some dispute-settlement provisions. The new system centres around a Disputes Settlement Body (DSB), which is actually the General Council sitting in dispute-settlement mode, and is more uniform, centralised, time-bound and automatic than in the past. Dispute-settlement begins with an application to the DSB by a Member country aggrieved at some protective practice by another Member, whether by the national or a sub-national government or by a government enterprise, thence proceeding to negotiations under the auspices of the Director-General and to the other steps outlined in Figure 11.2. Unresolved disputes then go to a 3–5-person disputes panel convened by the DSB, the panel members being recommended by the Secretariat, and the disputing parties may only oppose the recommended panellists when there are 'compelling reasons'.

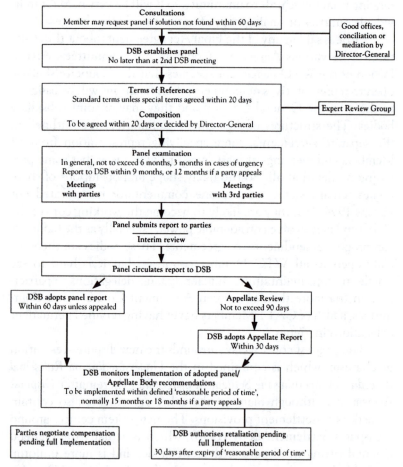

Figure 11.2: WTO Dispute-settlement flow chart

Source: 'The WTO Dispute Settlement Mechanism', *News of the Uruguay Round*, GATT, Geneva, April 1994: 7

Panellists are to be 'well-qualified governmental and/or non-governmental individuals' who have previous GATT experience, have 'taught or published on international trade law or policy' or have been a senior trade official in a Member country. Panellists must not be citizens of the disputant countries unless both sides agree otherwise. Appeals against panel decisions are made to a standing Appellate Body, which is appointed by the DSB and consists of seven persons, three of whom hear any one appeal. Appeals are 'limited to issues of law covered in the panel report and legal interpretations developed by the panel' (Article 17:6). Submissions to, advice sought by and deliberations of the panels and the Appellate Body are confidential, which has given rise to accusations of excessive secrecy. Panels may now seek individual experts' advice or commission an advisory report from an 'expert review group' (Article 13:2).

Once a panel report has been submitted to the DSB it proceeds through the system largely automatically and strict time limits (see Figure 11.2) prevent the delays which occurred under the old system. One of the most dramatic innovations of the Uruguay Round is the reversal of the GATT94 practice which required consensus for the adoption of, and action upon, a panel report. Under the new system a report will be adopted and acted upon unless there is unanimous agreement amongst Members' delegates on the DSB not to do so. If a panel finds against a particular country, appeal and arbitration can be resorted to, after which the 'guilty' country has fifteen months to rectify its offending practice, failing which the country will be requested to negotiate compensation for the 'aggrieved' country, and failing this the DSB may order retaliation unless there is a consensus against such action.

Retaliation would take the form of suspension of concessions by the aggrieved country against the offender, in the disputed product area if possible, otherwise in another product under the same agreement or in a product area under another agreement. The latter option is referred to as 'cross-retaliation' and is another dramatic innovation of the Uruguay Round, the old GATT permitting only retaliation in the same product area as that in dispute. For instance, in the case of a successful US TRIPs complaint against Uganda, which is not noted for its intellectual property exports, the USA may now choose to suspend previously negotiated tariff concessions on Ugandan peanuts. The value of the suspended concession is to be equivalent to the benefit allegedly gained through the practice which was found in breach of the agreement, as decided by the DSB. Appeal against the value of the suspended concession is possible but only to either the panel which found the country 'guilty' in the first place or to an arbitrator who can only rule on equivalence, not on underlying issues. The suspension is said to be only temporary until the offending practice is removed or some other solution is found, but no time limit is provided.

Overall, the new GATT/WTO system would appear to be a streamlined, perhaps more bureaucratised, version of the old, although various criticisms have been raised, some of which will be examined below, particularly those relating to coerciveness, impingement on national sovereignty, secretiveness and business influence.

An awakening giant?

For most Free Traders and mainstream trade commentators the new system represents a sensible tightening of a hitherto loose structure and a necessary addition of teeth, albeit leaving too many loopholes and discretionary mechanisms such as 'positive' rather than 'negative' listing systems and so forth. But for many critics the new system is a draconian global watchdog with fangs, this particularly being argued in relation to the new disputes-settlement system which allegedly is amenable to coercion and may be disproportionately advantageous to large countries. At first sight this critique seems overdrawn. GATT defenders point out that the old system worked mainly by consensus, amicable outcomes were usually reached, and retaliation was resorted to only once in fifty years, so a rash of sanctions under the new process seems unlikely. However, this misses the point that under the old 'consensus *for* action' system an accused country could veto sanctions, whereas the new 'consensus *against* action' system (see above) makes it impossible for one country voting alone to prevent hostile measures, and in theory an action could now proceed even if only the aggrieved country was in favour, so the incentive to seek retaliation is now strong. Use of the GATT/

WTO disputes system has been rapidly increasing in recent years, the USA now threatening action against the export enhancement components of Australia's car and textile policies, for instance (Dwyer 1996), Japan is challenging Indonesia's car policy, the EU is challenging many US regulations and Third World countries are challenging EU agricultural restrictions, so global litigiousness may be on the rise.

Under the new *Disputes Agreement*, compensation requirements are voluntary, sanctions (suspension of concessions, etc.) are temporary and least developed countries are to be treated leniently by panels (Article 24), while some other agreements, notably those on agriculture and TRIPs, disallow or postpone the right to suspend concessions. On the other hand, 'temporary' sanctions are open-ended, as noted above, and the CUFTA/NAFTA experience suggests that pressure for compensation under free trade agreements can be strong (see below). Moreover, the very geo-politics of sanctions and compensation claims makes these a much more feasible proposition for large than for small countries, as even Free Traders readily admit (e.g. Hoekman 1995a: 4). A mouse might roar but come the crunch its bite is small. This does not mean that the system will necessarily be coercive, and some point out that it is designed to avoid unilateralism (e.g. UNCTAD 1994b: 218) while a few cynics (e.g. Thurow 1996: 136) claim that the 'excessive' democracy of the 'one country/one vote' system will paralyse decision-making, but the possibility of coercion cannot be dismissed.

Historically much of GATT's work has been informal, including the negotiation of disputes and the surveillance of members' policies, the latter being aimed at 'shaming' countries into compliance with GATT rules (Trebilcock and Howse 1995: 386). The new system is to have more regular negotiations and monitoring (see below) so that such informal pressures may increase, and these may be especially unfair on poorer Third World countries which cannot fully participate in ongoing WTO politics (Shukla 1995). In fact, during recent years the GATT/WTO has issued rather directive-like requests to a number of Second and Third World countries for the removal of balance-of-payments safeguard measures, with which the Members concerned have duly complied (Ruggiero 1995: 6–7).

For many countries a major object of the Uruguay Round was to prevent the USA from using its economic gunboat diplomacy through Section 301, and Article 23 of the *Disputes Agreement* appears to do so by clearly indicating that action outside the WTO disputes-settlement system is not permitted. The EU believes this provision has killed further use of Section 301 by the USA, but US trade commentators claim that this and other unilateral measures could still be used for issues not covered by the Uruguay Round, for cases where there are gaps or inadequacies in the Uruguay Round agreements and so forth. Even more ominously, some US advisers have said that unilateral actions could be taken during the course of a disputes-panel hearing or on the basis that 'best endeavours' by the Administration could not get the Congress to change a law, and if necessary unilateral actions could even be taken in defiance of the WTO on the assumption that sanctions by a small country would not hurt the USA. The indications to date are that the US Government reserves the right to act inconsistently with its WTO obligations if the national interest so requires (GAO 1994: 41ff.), and a committee has been established to vet panel decisions with a view to withdrawing from the WTO if three cases in a row are deemed 'arbitrary, capricious or unfairly against US interests' (ICDA 17, 1994: 5–6). The Clinton Administration has intimated that the USA will use the WTO selectively, but that the latter cannot *force* the USA to do anything it does not wish (Dryden 1995: 390). The US attitude is understandable in relation to protecting national sovereignty, but, in my view, completely unjustifiable as a form of pressure on other countries to adopt policies tailored to US requirements.

Partly in response to this attitude and partly under business pressure, the EU has introduced its own version of Section 301, known as the 'illicit practices' regulation, under which other countries can be held to WTO rules or their markets, including those of non-WTO nations, may be prised open (ICDA 17, 1994: 5–6). Japan has a lower key version, a Sub-Committee on Unfair Trade Practices and Measures within MITI, and a list of concerns has been compiled (MITI 1996). In theory multilateralism through the WTO should guard small countries against such unilateralism, but in practice they could be caught between the new, tougher GATT rules against trade intervention and the defiant economic gunboat diplomacy of the two giants against which small nations may never be adequately indemnified.

Another area of concern to GATT critics is the possibility of the WTO impinging upon the national sovereignty of members. Former Director-General Peter Sutherland[1] has rejected this possibility (thereby implicitly accepting the undesirability of such impingement) on the grounds that Members are only bound to those amendments affecting their rights and obligations which they have ratified; that many other amendments now require three-fourths majorities or unanimity, thus precluding capriciousness; that each Member is free to decide whether or not to apply GATT rules to new WTO Members;[2] that the WTO cannot impose new trade policy obligations upon Members; and that the appellate review procedure provides added safeguards in disputes-panel cases. These points are valid but some are over-stated. The larger requisite voting majorities can cut both ways, for instance, probably making it harder to obtain favourable waivers, while the appellate procedures, as explained above, are rather limited and amendments *can* be forced upon all Members by a three-fourths majority.

The Uruguay Round has greatly increased the amount of reporting or notification required of Members and the degree of policy monitoring to be undertaken by the plethora of new Agreement Councils or Committees. Measures requiring notification include: all tariffs, quotas, NTBs, subsidies, TRIMs and taxes affecting trade; all safeguard, anti-dumping and countervailing actions; all procedures regarding customs valuation, import licensing, rules of origin, government procurement or SPS and TBT conformity assessment; any free trade zone systems, counter-trade arrangements or foreign exchange controls related to imports and exports; the existence of any state trading enterprises irrespective of whether or not these have engaged in imports or exports; all new regulations affecting trade in services and many other matters contained in specific agreements. In fact the list of compulsory notifications is so long that the WTO is to establish a 'central registry of notifications' which will inform all Members annually of the notifications required for the next year, and any Member who has forgotten what must be notified may request a reminder. Furthermore, some of the Uruguay Round agreements have 'dob-in' clauses which allow one Member to notify the WTO of another Member's suspected GATT-inconsistent practices, including NTBs not covered by any Uruguay Round Agreements.[3]

Such requirements need not in themselves constitute an encroachment upon national sovereignty, but they are to be accompanied by a wide range of regular monitoring by Agreement Committees and periodic scrutiny of policies by the Trade Policy Review Body. Each Member is to establish a network of 'enquiry points' for many of the agreements, set up appeals tribunals, and ensure that all laws, regulations or administrative procedures at all levels of government conform to GATT/WTO rules.[4] These processes are likely to tie Members into a spreading WTO web, albeit a loose one, and as a well-known Free Trader has pointed out, the purpose of this web is to submit to scrutiny and possible challenge all national policies, both internal and external, which might affect trade or market access (Hoekman 1995a: 3). A former Indian ambassador to GATT, S. P. Shukla (1995), has said that the WTO's purpose is 'continuous erosion of the authority and jurisdiction of the nation-states', and the Indian Government once claimed that limitation of export controls, subsidies and TRIMs by the Uruguay Round will jeopardise the use of economic planning for development (Watkins 1992: 41). US economists, Agosin and Tussie (1993: 2–3), have suggested that the new GATT/WTO system is designed to challenge national laws and institutions deemed impediments to 'market access', to tie the hands of governments with respect to traditional trade policies and to enforce 'new disciplines in an ever-widening number of areas'.

Even more fundamentally, certain key free trade concepts such as 'market-access' commitments and 'binding' (see Glossary) arguably entail adverse implications for national sovereignty and perhaps even democracy. Market-access concessions imply permanent admission to a country for foreign traders, with many of these concessions now to be bound. There are several channels, under GATT, for the re-negotiation of bound concessions, and although these officially require compensation payments, the 300 or so re-negotiations to date have resulted in only fourteen payments and four retaliations through withdrawal of equivalent concessions (Finger 1995). However, Member countries have increasingly been reserving the right to re-negotiate bindings (Hoekman, 1995a: 9–10), which suggests that the permanency of binding is not popular. GATT leaders and Free Trade commentators regularly speak of the supposed need to 'lock-in' liberalising reforms, to make marke-access commitments permanent, to bias policy systems towards exporter interests as against protectionists or to provide global agreements which timid de-regulators may invoke when endeavouring to resist protectionist demands. In New Zealand, even GATT's minimal investment provisions have been used to fend off public demands for more stringent DFI regulations (Kelsey 1995: 109). Australian trade theorist, Max Corden (1996: 152), has said that the issues have now largely been resolved (in favour of relatively free trade), and he hopes that 'the battles (will) not be fought over and over again'. This bears a touch of the 'end of history' thesis (see Chapter 1), of which harsher versions are now arising. A Canadian Conservative Minister has said, for instance, that the main reason for Canada entering NAFTA was 'to ensure that no future Canadian government could ever return to those bad old nationalist policies of the past' (Bienefeld 1994: 103-4). As noted in Chapter 2, some of the more militant Free Traders want their doctrine forced upon reluctant constituencies if necessary, so as to, in the words of US Free Trader Fred Bergsten (1996: 109), consign protectionist practices 'to the dustbin of history'. Such statements imply a permanent policy shift to be adopted irrespective of what future governments or public opinion might wish and this is perilously close to undemocratic.

Many 'Public Choice' theorists favour a constitutional amendment requiring legislative majorities of two-thirds or the like for trade policy decisions in order to stymie protectionist pressures, and one Free Trader proposes removing such decisions from the ambit of individual ministers or legislatures altogether (Hoekman 1995a: 77). On a number of occasions I have raised with Australian trade officials the possibility that the Uruguay Round might preclude options such as active, interventionist industry policies and the usual reply is that this is true but 'we wouldn't want to use such policies again'. When I point out that a future democratically elected government may wish to, the officials' reply is either that they had not thought of this, or that it is a constraint with which governments must live. The implication is that we have now entered an enlightened age in which intervention is a thing of the past, but in my view trade interventionist policies remain viable and legitimate (see Chapter 6) so that today's dogmatic constraints upon such options may potentially breach basic principles of national sovereignty and democracy by depriving future generations of certain options. Likewise, the notion of 'market access', a central leitmotif of the Uruguay Round, is arguably of dubious political morality because the lack of controls may preclude particular policy options (see next paragraph) and motives for market access might at times be questionable. Some research has, for instance, suggested that firms may seek entry to a national market primarily to forestall a potential global competitor (Yoffie 1993: 14). Former US Trade Representative, Carla Hills, once spoke of prying open other countries' markets with a crowbar 'so that our private sector can take advantage of them' (Dryden 1995: 355–6), while US tycoon, T. Boone Pickens, aggrieved at his lack of business success in Japan, once declared that 'external forces may be necessary to get rid of the *Keiretsu* system' (Ries 1990). Such attitudes clearly demonstrate a disregard for the principles of national sovereignty.

The potential for impingement upon national sovereignty in free trade agreements is strongly reinforced by compensation or penalty provisions, and although current GATT/WTO arrangements are soft-edged in this regard, the more hard-edged provisions of CUFTA/NAFTA (see Chapter 5) may presage some ominous implications. In various cases of threatened actions between the USA and Canada a Canadian reafforestation project was successfully challenged in the courts by US timber companies as a subsidy to local industry; the Canadian Government shelved a proposal for health warnings on cigarette packets after US tobacco companies threaened to challenge the measure as a breach of NAFTA's intellectual property clauses; the newly-elected Canadian Liberal Government was threatened with compensation claims by an aggrieved US airport company when that government sought to block a controversial (some say corrupt) decision by the previous Conservative Government to privatise Toronto airport; the Canadian provincial government of Ontario was forced to renege on an election promise to introduce a public car-insurance scheme when US insurance companies operating in the Canadian market threatened compensation claims under CUFTA on grounds that they stood to lose business if the scheme went ahead (Cohen 1994; Fuller 1994; Dunkley 1994b).

I have described such cases as ominous because they clearly involve breaches of national sovereignty in which domestic policy can be dictated by external private corporate interests acting upon the principles of liberalisation and market access. Arguably the most insidious aspect of this, as Canadian free trade critic Marjorie Griffin Cohen (1994) has pointed out, is that compensation threats may discourage governments from even considering controversial issues and the public will never have the chance to debate them.

Another area of criticism levelled against the GATT/WTO system, as well as against the Uruguay Round negotiations, is its alleged secrecy and domination by First World business-oriented agendas. Claims of secrecy relate to the exclusion of some governments and certain interests. The leading Columbian negotiator at the Uruguay Round, Luis Fernando Jaramillo, has said that proceedings were dominated by First World delegations with pre-emptive decisions often made in pre-arranged caucuses (Dunkley 1994b). A former Indian ambassador to GATT (Shukla 1995) has said that the much-vaunted conversion of Third World governments to the Geneva consensus is confined to the elite, with most interest groups having been excluded from the relevant decisions. Other criticisms relate to the alleged exclusion of NGOs from negotiations and from GATT bodies as well as to a lack of openness in general (e.g. IOCU 1994; Bach 1994). Such allegations are difficult to firmly substantiate, but in my view they are valid and GATT itself appears to have made only nominal attempts to deny them. As noted above, the *WTO Agreement* allows, albeit vaguely, for 'consultation and co-operation' with NGOs, many new committees have been formed and panels have now been nominally opened to external advice, but efforts to have formal NGO representation on panels, participation by environmental experts and greater public access were rebuffed, so panel deliberations are to remain confidential (GAO 1994: 168).

In response NGOs are urging more accountability and transparency in the new WTO, somewhat ironically given GATT's traditional emphasis on transparency of trade policies. Specific NGO proposals include: accreditation of relevant NGOs; regular consultations between the WTO and NGOs; financial assistance to facilitate participation by Third World NGOs; a detailed public file of potential panellists and this to include NGO representatives; regular input to panels and committees from NGOs; publication of all panel reports and proceedings, and of subsequent deliberations by the

DSB; consultation with relevant NGOs by governments involved in disputes. On the other hand, some NGOs are opposed to the WTO altogether and want it absorbed into the UN (see next chapter).[5]

Related accusations regarding business dominance in GATT and general free trade agendas are harder to assess. A wide range of commentators claim that business interests have been massively over-represented in GATT processes, in the Uruguay Round negotiations, in debates over NAFTA and so forth. Formally, most GATT officials and participants have customarily come from diplomatic and trade administrative backgrounds, with a good sprinkling of economists, lawyers and the like, but externally and more informally business groups appear to be the sector most commonly consulted, including during the Uruguay Round. This is also true of Australia, particularly regarding APEC negotiations (see Chapter 5), and towards the end of the Uruguay Round negotiations I could find few people outside government or business circles who knew much about the proceedings, let alone who had been consulted. This probably reflects both a pro-business bias and a myopic view of what issues are relevant for trade policy.

In the USA, business links with the free trade cause are clear-cut, even high profile. Many US delegation leaders at the Uruguay Round were business representatives or had strong business links, one being from the giant food TNC, Cargill, and another, one-time USTR, Carla Hills, being associated with the tobacco industry, even assisting in the above-mentioned case against Canadian health labelling (Cohen 1994; Fuller 1994). Former USTR, Clayton Yeutter, who played a key role in initiating the Uruguay Round, was given a directorship of the Caterpillar company for his role in negotiating the elimination of EU tariffs on construction equipment. US business groups were active in initiating the Round, were often formally consulted during the negotiations and were generally happy with the Round's outcomes.[6] Free Traders occasionally betray these deeper agendas, such as when former World Bank economist and Clinton Administration official, Lawrence Summers (in Garnaut and Drysdale 1994: 195) declared that global trade policy should be to 'lock-in' gains and 'ensure viable investment opportunities for OECD companies'.

There are also many claims that business interests are the crucial force behind NAFTA and the US Government's grandiose Enterprise of the Americas initiative to open up Central and South America to US trade and investment. It is easy to slip into conspiratorial mode when compiling the anecdotal evidence for such assertions. One group, for instance, claims to have a leaked Chase Manhattan Bank document which urged, in the supposed interests of Mexican political–economic stability, the suppression of the 1994 anti-NAFTA Chiapas peasant uprising and the rigging of forthcoming elections against opposition parties,[7] but the veracity of such claims is difficult to verify. There is also a good deal of scholarly evidence for such a view, however, and during the 1980s the Reagan and Bush administrations openly commissioned advice on how business interests and private enterprise could be advanced in the region and world-wide, one business report depicting a 'global struggle between free enterprise and statism'.[8]

In my view the Free Trade Adventure represents not so much a business-dominated agenda, though it is that to some extent, as a narrow 'trade first' view of economic policy-making and an addiction to free market, Economic Rationalist economics. A prominent GATT official observed at Marrakesh, that 'GATT is a sophisticated market economy agreement (which) limits the gains for those with a less developed market economy' (cited in Bach 1994: 2). Some claim that the Uruguay Round agreements display an anti-public sector philosophy and an institutional bias through, for instance, the requirement to notify the WTO of public enterprises (see above), which appears to implicitly assume that henceforth most Member countries will possess few of these. Formally GATT has never prejudged ownership structures, but now ex-Soviet bloc countries are having privatisation and marketisation criteria informally imposed as prerequisites for joining (Hoekman 1995a: 7). In my view the claim of an anti-public sector bias on the part of GATT is arguable but is much truer of NAFTA, as outlined in Chapter 5. The GATT text does not even recognise the role of firms, let alone the concept of TNCs or the distinction between their power and that of small arm's-length trading enterprises. Some commentators argue that GATT has totally accepted the world-wide corporate demand for minimal regulation (Korten 1995: ch. 13), or that the foray by the Uruguay Round into TRIPs and investment de-regulation is part of a world-wide campaign by business interests for new rules to secure private property rights (UNCTAD 1994b: 4–5).

A clearer picture of the GATT/WTO programme can be gleaned by examining its intended future agenda, and this appears to be what I would describe as private enterprise-led globalisation. Traditionally free trade did not require complete *laissez-faire* either domestically or externally, but today most champions of the Free Trade Adventure, especially within RTAs, vigorously advocate the new model free trade agreement (see earlier chapters) which is much more de-regulatory and 'deep integrationist' than previous, more limited models of free trade. Peter Sutherland (1994b) has declared that it was financial liberalisation which launched globalisation, and that the role of the Uruguay Round was to extend this process to goods, services and technology, a process which he insists must be completed.

Onward to globalism!

The WTO's likely agenda for the immediate future includes items such as the environment (see Chapter 10), labour standards (see Chapter 12), competition policy, possible extension of the *Agreement on Government Procurement* to all Members (see Chapter 4), a proposed agreement on investment de-regulation and continued negotiations for further liberalisation in services and other sectors, the ultimate aim being a highly globalised, 'deep integrated' world economy (e.g. Sutherland 1994b; Ruggiero 1995; Bergsten 1996). Other minor issues on the agenda are the effects of corruption on trade, and US attempts to sanction any companies dealing with countries it does not like, the most recent victim being Cuba, a fellow-member of the WTO.

Of these issues the most neglected is that of competition policy, which would seek international controls over restrictive business practices by TNCs and other traders. As noted in Chapter 2, the ill-fated ITO was to have competition policy as one of its tasks, including the job of co-ordinating national policies, hearing complaints and recommending remedies, but periodic attempts to include this function in GATT were fruitless, although a number of Uruguay Round agreements contain perfunctory competition provisions. The OECD and some RTAs have competition policies and several international bodies have issued (voluntary, and some say ineffective) codes of conduct for TNCs, but to date the USA has persistently opposed including such items in GATT. An international competition policy would not be easy to implement because many countries have no business regulations, the WTO officially deals only with governments and information on TNCs can be hard to obtain, but many economists, lawyers, NGOs and others believe the effort must be made, as globalisation proceeds, to ensure fairness and efficiency of trading relations.[9] I agree with this view, but suggest that the policy, which could be called 'business practice regulation', should extend well beyond competition enhancement to include worldwide monitoring and regulation of transnational business activities and related matters.

Potentially the hottest issue on the agenda is that of investment de-regulation, which has already been brought into the GATT/WTO system through GATS and the *TRIMs Agreement* (see Chapters 4 and 9). Traditionally economists have seen investment flows as linked to comparative advantage, but as a *substitute* for trade and being limited in volume. Today, however, with technological and deregulatory revolutions in full swing, Free Traders and WTO leaders insist that DFI and trade are integrally linked, that firms 'invest to trade and trade to invest', so that investment liberalisation is allegedly essential for economic efficiency (Ruggiero 1995; Bergsten 1996). The OECD is on the verge of adopting the world's first comprehensive investment agreement entailing the application of GATT-type rules to DFI, extensive opening of all OECD countries to TNCs, a 'negative listing' for exceptions, binding of all provisions and the use of 'peer pressure' among member countries to ensure its adoption. This is likely to set a crucial precedent for inclusion of a DFI in GATT as the WTO is an observer on the relevant OECD committee, and many countries, including Australia under the former Labor Government (McMullan 1995), have indicated a preparedness to de-regulate investment flows, primarily by relaxing or abolishing foreign ownership restrictions for domestic companies. Former WTO Director-General, Peter Sutherland (1994a: 3) has clearly stated the key post-Uruguay goal of the WTO to be the extension of liberalisation beyond just border measures to 'most aspects of domestic policy-making affecting international [trade and investment]'.

International bureaucrats are becoming increasingly militant about the notion of economic globalisation, one OECD group recently calling for the goal, by 2020, of a 'borderless' world and urging that protectionist opposition be resisted. However, any such move is likely to in turn evoke considerable world-wide resistance because investment liberalisation is opposed by a range of social groups, NGOs, Third World governments, even the Malaysian Prime Minister, Dr Mahathir, and arguably by public opinion. The rationale for opposition includes the right of every nation to economic sovereignty and the part that investment control can play in industrial development. I agree with these arguments, additional grounds being that liberalisation of DFI would incur even more non-economic costs than for trade (see Chapter 6) and I suggest that full de-regulation should not be contemplated.[10]

The ultimate goal of current WTO leaders and Free Trade activists is complete global free trade and free investment, with APEC-type target dates of 2010–20 being widely proposed (Sutherland 1994a; Bergsten 1996), the USA having even suggested, at the 1994 G7 Summit, the start of the new millennium as a target date, but this was rejected by the EU (Bergsten 1996: 112). The role envisaged for the WTO in the globalisation process is as the guardian of progress, the pace-setter for further liberalisation negotiations, the provider of sundry trade and dispute-resolution services, the co-ordinator of national economic policy-making for purposes of so-called 'global coherence' and the global curator of multilateral trade and investment rules. Director-General, Renato Ruggiero, claims that WTO-sponsored telecommunications liberalisation is helping to establish a 'global information society' which will revolutionise human life, bringing 'high quality education, health and business services to every village in the world'. Others have described the aim of WTO-sponsored liberalisation as being to 'dictate the terms of a single world-wide mode of economic policy-making'.[11]

As briefly outlined in Chapter 1, many theories of globalisation are complex, but not so the WTO's in-house hypothesis, which is delightfully simple. This postulates three forces influencing global integration—government policies, innovations in transport and communications and the 'evolving strategies of firms and individual investors'. The latter two factors are said to be providing a natural momentum for globalisation, impeded only by government interference, which is even capable of reversing the process if politicians were sufficiently misguided to try. Such a fate can be avoided by the use of trade treaties, these having an historically demonstrated capacity to place 'international constraints' on government policies which fail to 'nourish integration' (WTO 1995b: 21).

This characterisation is clearly over-simplified, the mechanisms of globalisation being complex, mutually intertwined and subject to a degree of debate which may never be resolved. Underlying forces of the process range from transport, communications and production technologies, corporate strategies, government policies, industrial development patterns and environmental problems to much vaster canvases such as the end of the Cold War, the rise of what has been called the 'trading state', universalist versus particularist ideologies and the rival historical imperatives of centralism versus localism. Today globalisation is proceeding via channels ranging from trade, investment mobility, financial integration and global production strategies of TNCs, through international treaties, national economic policy co-ordination and inter-governmental regulatory co-operation, to the growth of international organisations, proliferation of NGO networking, a rising tide of human migration and the interweaving of cultures.

The issues raised by globalisation are many and varied, the two most contentious being those of inevitability and desirability. On the spectrum from 'global fatalism' to 'autonomism' (see Chapter 1) the WTO and most Free Traders adopt the former view, believing a globally integrated economy to be, *à la* Fukuyama (see Chapter 1), the final and most beneficial possible destiny for the human race. In general the inevitability thesis holds that factors such as global production by TNCs, trans-boundary pollution, resource-management requirements, cross-border media and a range of other technological imperatives are creating a borderless world beyond the control of any one government, thus threatening to bring to an end the so-called Westphalian system of autonomous nation-states. The Free Trade economists' addendum to this thesis is that such factors lead, via the search for competitiveness, to global integration, during which process a 'critical point' (see Chapter 5) will be reached whence fuller or 'deeper' integration is required to avoid a global slide into inefficiency, instability and protectionist recidivism (Panic 1988; Lawrence and Litan 1990).

There is some ambivalence amongst economists as to how inevitable and how fully integrative this process may ultimately prove to be, but the global fatalists among them generally envisage a world of global consumers, outward-looking states and mobile companies united by multilateral economic rules, by macro-economic policy co-ordination, by a loose international administrative federation with minimal borders and by an electronic information 'super-highway', all happily juxtaposing their respective local identities with a dynamic, multi-faceted 'global culture'.

At present, however, the inevitability thesis is almost impossible to prove and there are several reasons for disbelieving it. First, as noted in Chapter 2, free trade-based globalism was experimented with in the nineteenth century and was sufficiently unsuccessful as to be widely rejected. Second, most nationally initiated globalisation policies are discretionary and readily reversible, notably those of floating exchange rates and financial de-regulation, a number of commentators now suggesting that government liberalisation decisions have been more central than technological forces in the explosion of global money markets and mobilisation of DFI.[12] Peter Sutherland (1994b) has depicted economic globalisation as beginning with 'spontaneous economic reform at the national level', and he fears that a revival of national protectionism could forestall this process. Third, nation-states will always be required for a range of regulatory functions even if supra-national authorities arise, including in the case of supposedly 'borderless' broadcasting because signals and programming decisions must begin somewhere. Fourth, although TNCs are often said to be rootless, some commentators believe that many firms need and prefer a national home-base, many now working through strategic alliances with national companies rather than via DFI, and that the bulk of TNC sales, assets and profits are still home-based (see Hirst and Thompson 1996). Fifth, there are feasible development models which rely less heavily on globalisation than does the Economic Rationalist, large-scale industrialisation model (see next chapter) and such options are likely to be always available. Finally, some believe that the nation-state is under siege internally as well as externally, perhaps as a reaction to excessive globalisation, so that, should national structures collapse, they will usually be replaced by smaller nations, witness the former Soviet Union or Yugoslavia, and there will always be a realm of the local as a counterweight to the global. If far-reaching globalisation is not inevitable, then it may be that governments of the present era, which are largely supportive of most globalising trends, are committing 'sovereignty suicide' rather than gracefully accepting ineluctable realities.[13]

There is even less resolution regarding the desirability of globalisation, both sides of the debate pointing to the sorts of costs and benefits discussed in Chapters 6–8. Additional factors will only be briefly touched on here. In the economic sphere, the costs of globalisation include: 1 instability arising from mechanisms such as floating exchange rates, mobile capital, speculative finance or 'hot' money, and a resultant loss of sovereignty; frequent references are now made to errant nations being 'punished' by financial markets; 2 loss of control over fiscal policies which, together with excessive reliance on tight monetary and interest rate policies, often results in a macro-contractionary bias, and thus higher unemployment (ILO 1995: ch. 5); 3 the ability of TNCs to manipulate exchange rates, taxes or other policies (Rupert Murdoch's global empire pays only 7 per cent), thus undermining national economic sovereignty, and one study has found that those South American countries with the most control over capital flows are the most economically stable;[14] 4 loss of export opportunities where TNC strategies favour other locations, at least two former cabinet ministers having admitted that TNCs are reluctant to export from Australia;[15] the capacity for organised crime to launder with relative impunity in global financial markets, currently investing some $85b per annum, more than the combined GDP of three-quarters of the world's nations.[16]

In other spheres, possible costs of globalisation relate to 'community–sovereignty' problems identified in Chapter 6, including loss of environmental amenities and community structures due to foreign-controlled investment priorities, promotion of consumerism, pressure on customary values, degradation of local cultures and so forth. Evidence on such issues is seldom clear-cut, but anecdotal confirmation is gradually emerging. In the case of consumer values, for instance, when Campbells (USA) took over Australia's Arnotts biscuit company, a top priority was not generating exports, as the government had hoped, but a campaign to promote impulse buying and increase biscuit consumption. Likewise, the US company which bought part of Victoria's privatised electricity industry pledged a campaign to raise power consumption because Victorians used 40 per cent less electricity than Texans! Such stories now abound. One UN report has attributed a wide range of social problems, including chronic unemployment, increasing poverty, rising crime, family breakdowns, loss of cultural identity and so forth, to a combination of globalisation and excessive free market policies, especially as enforced in the Third World by IMF/World Bank programmes (see next chapter).[17]

Some commentators claim that the homogenisation of national cultures is a necessary concomitant of global integration, while one international survey has found that 62 per cent of consumers see US films and TV as corrupting their cultures.[18] When an Indian politician once told Rupert Murdoch that foreign audio-visual material could have an adverse effect on his nation's culture, the media magnate agreed, explaining that MTV was considerably edited before being beamed into India and that he was not in favour of unrestricted cable TV for that country.[19] This incident confirms the capacity of media to impinge upon cultural sensitivies, but also raises the question of why a global network, let alone a single entrepreneur, should be the arbiter of those sensitivities. Such concerns do not mean that a degree of political, social, cultural and other humanitarian internationalism is undesirable, so long as it respects community sovereignty, and many groups now advocate the concept of 'globalisation from below', involving world-wide networks of NGOs, citizens' action groups or the like, although some groups also advocate active resistance to corporate-led globalisation.[20]

In my view the various global issues will ultimately have to be handled in differing ways. Many human rights and environmental issues will need to be covered by international treaties to which governments should be expected to surrender some national sovereignty, especially where these are literally matters of life or death. Other issues such as broadcasting, standard-setting and some macro-economic policies might be subject to a degree of co-operative supra-national regulatory governance of the sort which is already extensive,[21] but to be administered in a way which maximises national sovereignty and respects cultural sensitivities. Other issues again, such as industry policies, trade intervention, financial regulation and so forth should be largely national prerogatives, and subject to international rules no more de-regulatory than those of the Uruguay Round, perhaps with some gradual re-regulation. Certainly this sort of differential approach should be considered as an alternative to willy-nilly 'deep integration' proposed by many Free Traders and which is being hinted at by GATT/WTO leaders for future rounds. Ultimately, there are likely to be innumerable practical limits to globalism, particularly given that the globalisation of institutions is probably proceeding faster than people currently would like (see Introduction to Part Two) or may ever want. Indeed, some remain sceptical about a longer-term governmental commitment to free trade and globalisation, especially where there are no deeper goals than merely enhanced consumerism (e.g. Thurow 1996). In my view there is a firm commitment to the globalising Geneva consensus at present, but this may dissolve in time as the multifarious perils of globalism become increasingly apparent at more levels and in more societies.

Conclusion

If the WTO will be something less than a draconian global police force, then it may at least constitute, in conjunction with the IMF and World Bank, an embryonic economic world government, especially should its leaders choose to take it in that direction and should influential national governments accept such a trend. The new GATT/WTO system is likely to be tighter than its predecessor, especially regarding dispute-settlement procedures, to be more bureaucratic and to be more intrusive in minor ways, yet is unlikely to protect small nations against super-power economic gunboat diplomacy. The WTO's proposed future agenda appears to be to enhance private-sector-led globalisation, which could result in unwarranted incursions into national sovereignty and which could be inadvertently undemocratic by 'locking in' policy changes which preclude certain future options. In my view globalisation is not inevitable, current governments being intent upon 'sovereignty suicide', while its benefits are overstated and the costs greatly underestimated. World-wide resistance to globalisation is therefore increasing. In short, membership of the WTO is likely to be less a rope around a nation's neck than a belt around its waist, but the belt may be tightening.

12

Is There Life after GATT?

Alternatives to the Free Trade Adventure

The foregoing chapters of Part Two have argued that, although there can be real economic benefits from free trade, as measured by conventional criteria in relation to growth-oriented goals, there are also many hidden costs which have been inadequately canvassed in the debates of the present era. In my view Free Traders are correct that persistent, very high protection probably discourages industrial efficiency and dynamism, but are not correct in arguing that complete free trade or extensively levelled playing fields are best for structural adjustment purposes or for engendering cumulative advantage, let alone for achieving non-economic goals. In this chapter I will briefly examine evidence on these issues, especially in relation to the World Bank's 20-year-long SAP experiment, and discuss three alternative trade perspectives which are commonly advocated: Managed Trade, Fair Trade and Self-Reliant Trade, of which a number of variants are possible. These alternatives are not strict equivalents, Managed Trade being primarily a technique for trade policy-making, Fair Trade being a modification of trade procedures and Self-Reliant Trade being a partial negation of trade itself, the latter two usually entailing 'non-economic' goals alternative to those of both mainstream Free and Managed Trade schools. I will also propose some alternative structures for the world order which stem from such trade strategy options. The following outlines represent no more than brief, experimental sketches of the alternatives for purposes of debate and further development.

Managed Trade—a better master?

The philosophy of Managed Trade is often summarised in pithy observations such as that the market is better at disseminating innovations than making them, or is 'a good servant but a bad master' (Ozawa 1987). Managed Traders tend to each have their own rationales and the field is still developing, but most fit into one of two broad categories—pessimistic Free Traders or optimistic trade interventionists. The former tend to argue that Free Trade theory is valid in principle but cannot work adequately until all countries practice it, and thus they advocate protection in the meantime (e.g. Tyson 1993). Optimistic trade interventionists, by contrast, tend to reject Free Trade theory on some of the various grounds discussed in Chapter 6, especially in the light of imperfect markets, increasing returns and so forth, which are said to render 'free markets' a mythical beast, (e.g. Kuttner 1989 and 1991). Of course, Free Traders reject all such claims on the basis of 'unilateral benefit'.

Key instruments of managed trade include both domestic and trade intervention, both macro and micro. Macro measures include VERs, across-the-board trade restrictions and the like which, despite some claiming these were partly successful (e.g. Kuttner 1989 and 1991), are being eliminated under the Uruguay Round and the un-written Geneva consensus. Micro measures include sector-specific production or export assistance, industry policy systems and even Keiretsu-type arrangements which, being less conspicuous than macro measures, are likely to survive, as many Free Traders fear (Lawrence 1993; Sutherland 1994a). Managed Trade policy systems can take many forms, these varying with regard to goals, instruments and general levels of intervention adopted, but for simplicity I identify three gradations thereof, these being what I will call 'supportive adjustment' systems, 'indicative industry policy' systems and 'alternative development policy' systems.

The mildest form of 'supportive adjustment' system would entail little more than re-training programmes to minimise the costs of structural adjustment (see Kapstein 1996). Slightly more active versions, of which Australia's policy under the former Labor Government is arguably an example, may likewise barely qualify as managed trade, but nonetheless these tend to be more interventionist than Free Traders would wish. Australia's system, for instance, has used tariff and quota protection, export incentives, directed government procurement and (mildly) interventionist industry policy, despite eschewing the Managed Trade label, although the present Liberal Government is reducing the degree of domestic intervention. Labor's policy was a mix of Free Trade views and Porter-style 'strategic management' (see Chapter 6), being posited on the assumptions of inevitable globalisation and mild 'market failure', along with the alleged need to avoid the hazards of 'government failure' or major administrative mistakes (DIST 1994: 2–4). The goals of this policy were to enhance the 'competitive advantage' of Australian firms (rather than the 'comparative advantage' of local industries), to boost productivity through adoption of 'world best' industrial practices and the latest information technologies, to accelerate economic growth, to create a culture of 'export and innovation', to globalise the economy and generally to make Australia a 'clever country' (DIST 1994: 2–3; McMullan 1995).

The policy instruments used included: phased abolition or reduction of most tariffs, except in cars, textiles and clothing; general de-regulation and 'micro-economic reform'; enhancement of, rather than resistance to, structural change; minor supplementation of the market through assistance to innovative firms (in *any* sector), a 150 per cent tax concession for research and a number of co-operative R and D programmes, several tax-based export incentive schemes, subsidised computer production and some sectoral development programmes (e.g. cars, processed food, machinery); promotion of strategic alliances between complementary firms or industries; development of skills or 'human capital'; strategic government purchasing; the attraction of foreign capital and TNC corporate headquarters to Australia; implementation of tax, wage and other policies which were consistent with the above-mentioned goals, especially in order to increase the corporate profit share (DIST 1994).

On paper this policy looks quite interventionist, but most commentators have seen it as a largely free market, Free Trade agenda, especially given that protection has been declining for more than two decades now. The question of whether or not it has been successful is even more contentious. There is some evidence that Labor's policy has accelerated growth, stimulated some high-tech sub-sectors, created new 'info-tech' skills and generated some 'niche' exports for 'elaborately transformed manufactures' (ETMs), processed foods and so forth. On the other hand, few industries have greatly enhanced their export performance, mass export growth has been sluggish, only 13 per cent of Australian firms export at all and a negligible 1 per cent do so regularly, while our manufacturing trade deficit actually *increased* during the 1980s. There is anecdotal evidence that some potential export industries are languishing for want of 'infant industry' support; that Australian firms are increasingly shifting to cheaper government-supported overseas sites, especially in Asia; and that our hoped-for food export bonanza may be stymied by the understandable desire of Asians to produce their own food. Australia now exports A$1b of information technology per annum but imports some A$6b, with the latter figure heading for a staggering A$19b by 2003 (Davidson 1996). Similarly, in the motor vehicle industry, despite major productivity improvements, imports are rising rapidly, now accounting for over 50 per cent and almost 100 per cent of the car and commercial vehicle markets respectively, yet Asian targetting of our market is only just beginning.[1] From all this it is hard to see how trade liberalisation will rectify our external balance without some intervention to increase exports, reduce imports or both.

Free Traders tend to argue that most assisted sectors could survive on their own in some form, or else that Australia lacks comparative advantage in these sectors. However, increasing numbers of commentators disagree, various industry and research groups suggesting that many sectors could become well established, both domestically and internationally, with stronger, more reliable, targetted assistance in order to generate 'cumulative advantage'. For instance, Melbourne research economists, Peter Sheahan and his colleagues, have compiled evidence to suggest that interventionist industry policies and the encouragement of an 'export culture' under Labor, along with booming growth in Asia, have played major roles in Australia's gradual industrial recovery and export growth. They surmise that the creation of a 'knowledge economy' based on export of skill- or information-intensive goods and services could boost jobs and exports, raising economic growth by 0.7 per cent pa, but that this would need R and D assistance.[2] All this suggests that the unaided market is inadequate to the tasks of structural adjustment or other key developmental objectives, and that Australia's mildly interventionist 'supportive adjustment' policy of the last decade, which is now being scaled down, might not be much more adequate.

Such inadequacies have led many theorists and industrial practitioners to a more interventionist version of Managed Trade, which is usually advocated on the basis of various arguments outlined in Chapter 6, particularly the externalities, infant industry, cumulative advantage, strategic trade and industry balance cases. More generally, it is also argued: that markets cannot adequately create skills, generate innovations or contend with the transactions, bargaining and information costs of structural adjustment (Chang 1994); that institutional processes are just as important as markets for economic development in complex economies (Chang 1994); that private enterprise is too short-term in its perspective; that a firm's international competitiveness depends more on requisite technologies, appropriate pricing and quality of servicing than on costs (Fagerberg 1988), which suggests that Australia's current preoccupation with cost-cutting for competitiveness is not the answer; that establishment in the domestic market is a prerequisite for a firm to be able to compete globally (Ozawa 1987), and that government purchasing is often the main early stimulus to new industries (Davidson 1996), which suggests the need for some domestic industry support in the early stages of development; that innovation is 'endogenous' (generated within the economic process) rather than an 'exogenous' result of random inventions as neo-classical theory assumes, which suggests the need for some government assistance to 'externalise' the risks of R and D, promote skills, induce 'human development' and so forth (often called 'new growth' theory).[3]

Such arguments lead to more extensive intervention, an approach which I call 'indicative industry policy'. This view now emphasises targetted subsidies or other domestic assistance rather than high trade barriers, although structural instruments such as strategic government procurement, investment-inducing deals with TNCs and promotion of 'national champion' industries have also been popular. The most quoted examples are Japan and other Asian NICs, whose economic success Free Traders still attribute largely to the market, but whose rapid growth, especially in their early development phases, many others attribute to extensive direct and *indirect* state support to selected industries (Mutoh et al. 1986; Wade 1990;

Bello and Rosenfeld 1990; Amsden 1993; Chang 1994, Moreira 1995). Some European countries have also used such policies, along with extensive national planning, and the occasional Free Trader acknowledges that these have worked (e.g. EPAC 1995: 23; Jovanović 1992). Managed Traders variously argue that such policies are needed for 'cumulative advantage' in 'sophisticated' industries, to promote 'high' living standards or to counter the declining effectiveness of macro policies as a result of globalisation, and that governments, in consultation with industry practitioners, can pick 'winners'—cf. Chapter 6 (Hamilton 1991: ch. 15; Stewart 1994, Marsh 1994).

I partly agree with such arguments, but many Managed Traders are really only claiming that intervention can produce higher economic growth than can free trade, giving little consideration to the non-economic problems of trade or growth, while sometimes espousing what in my view are questionable values and goals. Prominent US Managed Trader, Lester Thurow (1992: 50; 1996: ch. 6 and 7), for instance, advocates strategic intervention, not only for growth purposes but also to restore US global economic dominance, to break the EU's media local content protection system, to seize the lead in global high-tech services and so forth. Another Managed Trader (Ozawa 1987: 51) deems that the USA has the 'advantage' of a 'tradition-free economic environment', a state which might in fact account for that country's appalling social problems. Competitiveness theorist, Michael Porter (1990: 703–4 and 715), almost obsessively preaches 'perpetual innovation', advising Sweden to abandon its egalitarian, welfarist values for greater competitiveness and berating Germany for sacrificing innovation to 'other dimensions of life', which indicates questionable priorities on his part. One Australian government report (DIST 1994: 2) has said that current policies commit us to the grim-sounding fate of 'an endless race to become, and remain, globally competitive', while some of the sectors being fostered in Australia, such as agribusiness, biotechnology and 'nanotechnologies' (atomic-level manipulation of substances), are in my view questionable on social and ethical grounds. Managed Traders tend to be enthusiastic about information technology, but this sector now accounts for a third of our trade deficit (Davidson 1996) and we are having trouble competing internationally even *with* subsidies to local computer production, so perhaps we should be questioning its true value and considering import reduction, especially given the wide range of adverse employment and social effects these technologies can have (Rifkin 1995; Keegan 1996). The Japanese-NIC model has been widely criticised for its neglect of non-economic problems (see below), and some Managed Trade sympathisers prefer a less growth-oriented, more environmental version (e.g. Daly and Goodland 1993: esp. 66). Managed Trade-sceptics like Krugman (1994) argue that competitiveness cannot be 'pedalled' or that macro adjustments such as increased savings are more likely to be effective than 'strategic' micro tinkering. I agree to some extent, but suggest that a degree of intervention is required to help shape 'cumulative advantage' and formulate appropriate national goals through an alternative version of trade management.

Such a version of Managed Trade, which I will call an 'alternative development policy', would retain domestic intervention, use a modest degree of long-term trade intervention where required, in the spirit of Keynes (1932), and most of its policy instruments (outlined below) would be acceptable to other advocates of Managed Trade, but it would encompass goals alternative to those of maximum growth, techno-obsession or the materialistically defined living standards which underlie present policies. This approach would aim to deal with the non-economic issues discussed in Chapter 6 and possibly seek a different sort of society in the longer term (see below). In Australia it should begin with a moratorium on further tariff reductions until these issues can be more fully debated.

Key elements of an 'alternative development policy' should include: a participatory planning system based on long-term consensus goals; much more critical public debate about current policy directions, especially globalisation, in order to formulate consensus goals; the use of alternative, broader social and economic indicators so as to avoid the 'tyranny of lists' (i.e. our obsession with our world rankings for per capita GDP, competitiveness etc.); encouragement of more ecologically oriented goals, backed by a system of 'green taxes'; an industry policy system with domestic and trade intervention measures (primarily tariffs and subsidies) targeted towards consensus goals, but with careful monitoring of the costs of protection; an industry restructuring programme which rationalises existing sectors where required (e.g. the car industry should be reduced to one locally owned firm); a process of technology assessment and a related system of research into more appropriate, less job-destroying alternative technologies (also see below); a re-training and skills development system linked to national plans for alternative technologies and consensus goals; a more expansionary macro-economic stance, co-ordinated internationally where possible, along with temporary import restrictions, import-replacing consumption (e.g. more public transport, fewer cars) and general contraction of demand for imports to reduce the trade deficit; a programme to increase national savings via employee saving schemes, incentives to save and promotion of less consumerist habits, so as to help reduce the trade deficit and DFI-dependence, ensuring, however, that the new savings are re-invested in a way which creates jobs (e.g. through the public sector and labour-using technologies); some re-regulation of the exchange rate and speculative capital flows, because 'over-shooting' by capital- rather than trade-driven exchange rates can seriously hamper exports (see Dunkley 1992: ch. 6 for more detail).

Two key questions arise in relation to this type of extensively interventionist model. The first is whether or not it would be permissible under the new GATT. In my view it would be so long as it did not rely too heavily on increased tariffs or macro NTBs (see above). However, if future WTO rounds were to further restrict TRIMs, subsidies, service regulation, investment controls and so forth, then it might not be permissible, and such an eventuality should be resisted because, as I argued in the previous chapter, every country should have the right to a Managed Trade option.

The second question is whether or not such a policy is workable in an era of global constraints, but this depends on whether globalisation is due to technological determinism or, as I argued in Chapter 11, to 'sovereignty suicide' by present-day governments. A combination of appropriate re-regulation and international co-ordination of macro, financial or other such policies would probably be effective, governments by no means being completely impotent in the face of globalisation (Maxfield 1990; Banuri 1991; Banuri and Schor 1992; Jovanović 1992; Helleiner 1994; UNCTAD 1994a: 146ff.; Hutton 1996: 312ff.). An 'alternative development policy' which confined itself to modest goals, avoided grand 'national ego' projects, used a wide range of policy instruments, both micro and macro (see above), and sought to change basic values, should be feasible. The supposed imperatives of export expansion and globalisation are posited heavily on continuing growth of present consumption patterns and materialistic living standards (see DIST 1994), which in Australia are highly import-intensive, whereas a lower-consumption, higher-savings, alternative technology 'economic culture' could be more self-reliant, as will be further outlined below. In short, an 'alternative development' model would be a Managed Trade approach, but with a planned focus on more socially and environmentally based goals than Australia has fostered to date.

In the Third World, Managed Trade issues centre on the renowned IMF/World Bank Structural Adjustment Programmes (SAPs), the alleged success of which Free Traders are claiming as the ultimate empirical justification for their doctrine. Begun in the late 1970s, SAPs entail borrowing countries agreeing to various 'conditionalities' designed to stabilise their internal economies and external balances, usually including exchange rate devaluation, trade liberalisation, domestic de-regulation, privatisation, public expenditure cuts and assorted country-specific obligations. In general SAPs require recipient countries to switch from an import-substitution industrialisation (ISI) policy, which has usually relied heavily on managed trade and domestic 'indicative industry policies', to a less interventionist export-oriented industrialisation (EOI) strategy. The World Bank regularly cites studies which purport to confirm the success of SAPs and to prove a positive association between trade liberalisation, export expansion and economic growth. There is doubtless some validity to the claims as innumerable Third World countries have long been plagued by corruption, inefficiency and mismanagement. ISI policies have generally failed, often generating more imports than they saved, and the highly publicised Third World debt crisis is as much due to the grandiose industrial or dam-building fantasies of undemocratic regimes as to greedy bankers, whereas EOI policies appear to have reduced debt, accelerated growth and alleviated poverty for some countries.[4]

On the other hand, there are grounds for arguing that SAPs have not been as successful, nor EOI as superior to ISI, as Free Traders claim. First, ISI strategies often have been successful for light industries, even if much less so for the more ambitious and arguably inappropriate 'heavy and chemical' (HCI) sectors. ISI was often mismanaged and badly applied, industries with inappropriate skill, technology or capital requirements often being fostered through a misconceived Western-style industrial and modernisation strategy. Agriculture was excessively taxed and frequently subjected to negative effective protection levels or over-valued exchange rates in a misplaced bias towards urban industry (Fontaine 1992; Edwards 1993; Auty 1994; Moreira 1995). Alternative ISI policies (see below) may therefore be more successful. Second, the two main methodologies used for gauging the efficacy of SAPs and EOI—case studies and cross-correlative econometric models—have been subject to many criticisms and have had difficulties in even defining liberalisation. For instance, most World Bank studies categorise Taiwan and South Korea as 'liberal' whereas critics disagree, one expert (Amsden 1993) estimating that the latter country maintained an ISI bias until about 1990, others suggesting that many policy regimes are a mix of ISI and EOI, with governments usually playing an active role even in EOI ventures (Moreira 1995). Some studies find little correlation between SAP/EOI strategies and growth, or even an inverse relationship.[5]

Third, where SAPs and EOI strategies have been successful in growth stimulation, these situations may not be widely replicable, especially as the number of exporting countries grows, the most successful EOI practitioners being the earlier industrialisers or those countries with favourable world market situations (Mutoh et al. 1986: 291; Edwards 1993). Fourth, SAPs may have been less important in stimulating growth than other factors such as active macro policies, exchange rate stabilisation or domestic demand expansions, as even the World Bank (e.g. 1989: 11) itself occasionally admits. In fact a few commentators argue the reverse causality—that domestically induced growth leads to export expansion (see Edwards 1993: 1388), one study finding only four out of thirty-seven countries where the direction of causality clearly ran from EOI to growth (Jung and Marshall 1985). Fifth, some evidence suggests that, for certain countries, SAPs have done more economic harm than good by excessively contracting the public sector and infrastructure development, by damaging existing industries before new ones could take root or by creating a climate of uncertainty for investment, as even the prestigious ILO has argued.[6]

Finally, there is research and anecdotal evidence, even from some World Bank studies (e.g. Zuckerman in Thomas 1991), that SAPs can have a wide range of adverse 'non-economic' effects on income distribution, the environment, social stability, community structures and sovereignty, many countries having experienced 'IMF riots' in reaction to SAP-inspired cuts in government expenditure, welfare, food aid or price controls. Papua New Guinea has gone as far as to expel World Bank representatives, the Prime Minister, Sir Julius Chan, declaring that Bank policies have 'destroyed many countries'.[7] Where SAPs and/or EOI do appear to have been successful, the new jobs are often in small, low-income, non-traditional micro-enterprises sub-contracted to TNCs, or sometimes in highly polluting 'factory farms' using short-term contract labour housed in patrolled shanties and cut off from the rest of the community.[8]

Even in the much admired, private-sector-driven, 'middle classing' EOI countries of East and South-East Asia (few of these have received SAPs) there is mounting criticism of the development models involved. Problems being experienced include: authoritarian politics, labour exploitation, environmental decay, uncontrolled urbanisation, destruction of traditional communities, excessive reliance on unsustainable agriculture, dependence on TNCs and so forth, while a quarter of Asia's city-dwellers still live in poverty. Although some NICs earlier redistributed wealth, inequalities now appear to be rising and a staggeringly opulent (often corrupt) elite is emerging, Asia now boasting five of the world's ten richest billionaires.[9] Curiously, Asian opinion polls have found, amidst rising general satisfaction with development, the poorest countries expressing least unhappiness and the richer (30 per cent in Japan) expressing the greatest, while in most Asian countries the environment is now seen as more important than economic growth.[10]

As alternatives to SAPs and EOI in the Third World, few are proposing a return to massive tariff walls or heavy-handed ISI of the past, but new mixes of domestic interventionism and managed trade are widely advocated, with two broad categories of models now emerging. The first, which I call an 'interventionist human development' stream, advocates a degree of domestic industry promotion, macro stabilisation and mild trade intervention on grounds such as various 'radical' arguments for protection (Chapter 6) and 'new growth' theory (p. 243 above), the key goals being skill formation, attraction of foreign capital and transfer of technology, usually with a preference for outward-looking trade policies.[11] The second stream, which I call the 'green villages' approach, is based on various 'non-economic' arguments against free trade (Chapter 6) and is commonly found amongst environmentalists, NGOs, grassroots activists and many 'ordinary' people in the Third World. This more holistic view of development advocates less focus on growth and 'modernisation'; more community-centred, ecologically sustainable development; organic or other sustainable forms of agriculture; appropriate or 'intermediate' technology (see below); avoidance of excessive dependence on trade or foreign capital; and maintenance of traditional cultures, usually with a preference for inward-looking trade policies or even self-reliance.[12]

In sum, there is a wide range of feasible theoretical arguments for Managed Trade, while the evidence for a direct link between economic growth and domestic/trade liberalisation is tenuous at best. Managed Trade strategies could take a number of forms, preferably using tariff-subsidy systems and employing more systematic targetting and general planning than hitherto. But these strategies should not include high tariff walls or rigid regulations of past models, should be fair, should be transparent and the costs of intervention should be regularly monitored. In my view every nation has the right, as Keynes once argued, to a permanent domestic and trade intervention policy system so as to ensure control of its own future in a planned way, with some possibility of insulation from the whims of markets and distantly controlled TNCs.

Fair Trade—for a more equitable world

The term Fair Trade is used in three distinct senses, which has given rise to some confusion. The first, originally used in Britain last century and in the USA since the early 1980s, refers to restrictive trade measures of other countries as being unfair to one's own nation, the only truly fair trade requiring completely level playing fields. As most Fair Traders of this sort do not believe that such a state will be achieved in the foreseeable future they constitute what I referred to above as pessimistic Free Traders and they effectively advocate Managed Trade, thus being seen by Free Traders as thinly disguised protectionists (see Bhagwati 1994). I will not use the term in this way.

The second sense of the term, used by many aid NGOs, refers to schemes which purchase goods or commodities from Third World producers at 'fair' prices rather than imposed market rates as do the TNCs, and retail these at modest mark-ups. There is evidence that such schemes greatly help Third World farmers and crafts people boost their incomes, enhance their autonomy and encourage environmentally-sound production methods.[13] The theory behind this notion of Fair Trade is that some international exchange is worthwhile, but that in an unequal world (arguments 8 and 9 in Chapter 6) the 'free market' is inherently unequalising, unfair and dominated by profit-motivated, exploitation-inclined TNCs. At present this type of trade represents a minuscule 0.03 per cent of Third World exports (Madeley 1992: 148), but in my view should be practised more widely, perhaps on a co-operative basis between nations, and could be used by governments as a substitute for many types of aid. I will call this a 'fair price' form of Fair Trade.

The third usage of the term refers to a policy of managing trade so as to avoid 'exploited labour' or 'social dumping' (see Chapters 6, 8 and 10), which are said to arise when firms or nations seek to obtain trading advantages or 'hidden subsidies' by withholding full human or labour rights, by paying unfairly low wages, by jeopardising the environment and so forth. In general Free Traders, whilst accepting that some exploitation and social dumping can occur, regard these as minor, temporary misdemeanours which disappear with economic development. They want trade and 'social' issues kept separate because they believe that many alleged unfair advantages are really legitimate manifestations of comparative advantage and that linkage of the two issues would open a Pandora's box of protectionism (World Bank 1991; Oxley 1993; Anderson 1995).

On the other hand, Fair Traders claim that there is ample evidence, some of which has been noted in previous chapters, that abuse of labour and human rights, including child labour, does occur, can persist for long periods, may undermine attempts to improve national and international standards and might confer some trading advantage on exploiting countries.[14] The ILO (1995: 10 and 72–5) has agreed that globalisation and capital mobility risk debasing labour standards, eroding the quality of employment and making more difficult the national enforcement of rights or conditions. Even the usually Economic Rationalist OECD, while denying that low labour standards or wage levels are particularly advantageous or persistent, has said that market forces will not automatically up-grade labour standards and has advocated incentives for improvement.[15]

Attempts to establish fair labour standards date back to early this century and Article 7 of the ill-fated ITO required members to eliminate unfair labour practices, but GATT47 provided only for a ban on the products of prison labour (Article XXe). The ILO, formed in 1919 and now part of the UN, has established comprehensive labour standards, or 'Conventions', and over 150 countries are members, many more than belong to the WTO at the moment, but these Conventions are often poorly enforced by member governments. The USA has periodically incorporated labour standards into certain of its international arrangements, notably its trade preferences for Third World countries, and has lobbied for the inclusion of such standards in GATT, ironically, without itself signing many ILO Conventions. Indeed, some observers believe that Clinton himself dislikes the notion of labour standards in trade agreements but is providing a political pay-off to trade unions.[16]

Broadly speaking, this version of fair trade could take three main forms. The first is a 'basic rights' system, which would require countries to grant a selected but limited set of labour rights, as advocated, for instance, by the politically moderate International Confederation of Free Trade Unions (ICFTU) and by some Asian trade unions.[17] The ICFTU proposes that all WTO members be required to ratify the key ILO Conventions relating to free association, bargaining rights, abolition of forced and child labour etc. A second option is a 'social clause' akin to that of the EU, which would require WTO members to grant a range of human, labour, social and welfare rights (see Cavanagh et al. 1988; Brecher and Costello 1994). A third, more radical, option would be a 'unit cost equalisation' system based on the specification of minimum wages and conditions, though not actual wage rates, the aim being to minimise international 'unit cost gaps' as calculated on the basis of relative productivity and real wage rates or the like (see Rothstein 1993; Stanford et al. 1993). This option is advocated by a few Managed Traders, usually on the, in my view questionable, grounds that Third World wages should be dragged upwards so as to generate markets for First World exports (Mead 1990; Rothstein 1993).

Fair Trade systems would be enforced by sanctions such as withdrawal of trade concessions, penalty imposts or 'red tariffs' ('green' for environmental versions) and anti-(social) dumping duties equivalent to the supposed hidden subsidy. These sanctions could be applied bilaterally, regionally or multilaterally, the latter presumably through an addendum to Article XXe of GATT, which at present relates only to prison labour.

Many Third World governments, NGOs and trade unions condemn such systems as discriminatory, protectionist and aimed at imposing Western middle-class values upon them, often arguing that poor families need the income of child workers. In many cases these groups fear unilateral enforcement by the USA. On the other hand, certain Third World NGOs and trade unions *do* support some form of labour rights or social charter as a likely fillip to their own rights struggles, usually also calling for compensation to poorer countries, fines against exploitative companies, involvement of the ILO and so forth (Brecher and Costello 1994: ch. 7).

WTO member governments are divided on the issue, the USA and France leading the charge for labour standards, while Malaysia and Singapore head the resistance. Renato Ruggiero has expressed doubts that the proposal will ever be adopted in even a mild form, let alone the social-clause version, although it is still on the WTO agenda and international bodies such as the ILO and the World Bank have begun to accept the idea.[18] Australia has generally sided with its APEC neighbours in rejecting the proposal, and at times has even opposed bans against goods made with prison or child labour on the grounds that such bans are ineffective, difficult to enforce and may jeopardise our access to Asian markets. The current Trade Minister, Tim Fischer, has pledged to pursue these matters through 'aggressive bilateralism' with APEC trading partners rather than multilaterally.[19]

Free Traders mostly reject Fair Trade systems on the grounds that differential labour standards reflect natural comparative advantage and that attempted harmonisation would reduce efficiency or impede trade (Hansson 1990). Some accept a mild version where there is a 'psychological' justification (e.g. to keep whingeing unions quiet) or a danger of a 'race to the bottom', which they think unlikely (e.g. Anderson 1995: 21–2). However, a few Free Traders sufficiently sympathise with the social aims of Fair Trade to approve of a mild 'basic rights' regime (e.g. Bhagwati 1994), but thenceforth suggest that a modest tariff-subsidy system of enforcement would be more efficient than a willy-nilly 'social clause', and they completely oppose a 'unit cost equalisation' process (Hansson 1990: ch. 5). Most non-economists believe that the social benefits of a 'labour standards' system of some sort would greatly outweigh the trade costs thereof, and many trade unions claim that such a system would forestall pressure for stronger protectionism. One commentator even claims that an earlier 'unit cost equalisation' scheme between Puerto Rico and the USA has succeeded in raising incomes of the former while preventing capital exports from the latter (Rothstein 1993: 14–15), although at the cost to Puerto Rico (in my view) of massive integration into the US economy.

In sum, whether Free Traders and authoritarian Third World regimes like it or not, demands for at least a degree of labour standards harmonisation will not go away and the evidence seems to warrant an experiment with such a system. In my view the best option would be to incorporate in GATT's Article XX a comprehensive 'social clause' requiring the signing and enforcement of key ILO Conventions and general adherence to basic human, labour and welfare rights, though the setting of precise minimum wages or conditions (let alone actual rates) should be avoided. The clause should be enforced through a system of 'red tariffs' for labour issues and 'green tariffs' for the environment which complainant countries could levy against others deemed by a WTO panel to be exploitative, with advice and monitoring being provided by the ILO and by an equivalent environmental body (see below). The system should include compensation packages for initial enforcement assistance to poorer countries and programmes to help such countries design appropriate technologies or other requisite social systems (also see below). This would entail a form of Managed Trade but with a limited range of alternative goals, so that Managed Trade policies of the sort discussed above would also be required, probably in conjunction with a more self-reliant approach to trading.

Self-Reliant Trade—a chance to be oneself

The central preachment of Free Trade doctrine is that any village, district or nation is economically better off trading freely with other such units on the basis of production specialisation rather than remaining autarchic. A few economists have noted circumstances where the reverse might apply (argument no. 6, Chapter 6) but Free Traders usually reject these as theoretical, pointing to the alleged horrors of Albania, Stalin's Russia or Mao's China. But contemporary Self-Reliant Traders do not admire such models and would not favour closure of borders to ideas or travel, although they defend any indigenous peoples who wish to remain autarchic. A distinction should be drawn between *autarchy* or isolationism, *self-sufficiency*, where some importation of necessities or exotics is allowed, and *self-reliance*, which seeks only to eschew heavy trade dependence for key capital, consumer, food, energy, cultural or social requirements. Self-reliance is usually advocated on non-economic grounds of the sort discussed in Chapter 6, traditionally on the basis of 'security' arguments (nos 13 to 15), but I would also emphasise the 'community–sovereignty' arguments (nos 17 to 20).

Although trade has an ancient lineage (see Chapter 2), most pre-industrial societies were largely self-reliant, many Third World countries were substantially so until recently and most of the world's 300 million indigenous peoples remain so. Development economists tend to concede that it is easy and practical enough for a society to be fairly self-reliant when its main requirements are food, handicrafts or light industry, and even in today's globalised economy the most commonly traded items are the more sophisticated, differentiated consumer and capital goods, high technology, luxuries and the like. Thus, for the society prepared to curb its consumerism, its sophistry and its growth-obsession, self-reliance is almost certainly quite feasible, although for most countries that would now require considerable restructuring. It must be remembered that economists *only* say free trade is best *if* a society wants the maximum possible consumption or income, an 'if' which may be much less desired or desirable than they believe.

Economics textbooks almost invariably scorn the general notion of self-reliance, but a few mainstream economists have shown flashes of sympathy for, as Keynes (1933) put it, '. . . those who would minimise . . . economic entanglement between nations'. Keynes' chief reasons for sympathy with 'self-sufficiency' (as he called it) were that the shift of demand towards non-traded services in industrially developed countries made it feasible, that it might stem the undesirable globalisation of finance and that it could create '. . . an environment in which other ideals can be safely and conveniently pursued'. Keynes warned that self-sufficiency came at a cost and that contemporary practitioners of the notion were mostly engaging in 'silliness' (Mussolini and Stalin) or undue haste (Ireland, where Keynes' lecture on the subject was given), whereas the ideal required 'slowly training a plant to grow in a different direction'. Among contemporary mainstream economists the doyen of trade theorists, Jagdish Bhagwati (1994: 574; Bhagwati and Srinivasan 1969), has hinted that trade restriction for purposes of increased self-reliance may be a legitimate non-economic goal. The enigmatic Paul Krugman (1991: ch. 9), though at most a mild Managed Trader, claims that the main effect of reduced trade would be marginally lower efficiency in resource allocation, and that a slashing of world trade by 50 per cent would only reduce world income by 2.5 per cent because, as noted in earlier chapters, a nation's living standards derive primarily from domestic productivity, not from trade *per se*. Others have pointed out that because so much trade now involves intra-industry exchange of only slightly differentiated items, substantial reductions in trade may not be a serious loss to consumers, except perhaps where there are extensive economies of scale (e.g. Streeten in Dunning and Usui 1987: 21).

A wide range of non-mainstream writers have presented quite an array of argument and evidence that, given appropriate economic structures and political will, not only is national self-reliance feasible,[20] but likewise so are the concepts of 'self-reliant cities' and 'local economies', or a reasonable level of regional self-reliance within nations.[21] Such concepts could not be implemented quickly in a 'modern', Western-style consumer economy, but would be more feasible with alternative technologies and structures such as renewable energy systems, organic agriculture, variegated public transport, manufacturing from recycled materials and so forth, or what I call a 'solar–organic economy', in contrast with our expensive, present-day machine–chemical systems. The underlying theory, as Schumacher first pointed out in *Small is Beautiful*, is that for many, perhaps most, sectors of an economy alternative technologies can be found which, while not competitive with conventional techniques for mass production, are adequately so at low output levels. Innumerable examples of alternative or intermediate technologies are now in operation world-wide, primarily but not exclusively in the Third World. Established alternative technologies in the First World include 'soft energy' systems, resource- and energy-saving innovations and steel mini-mills.[22]

Economists and business people have neglected such alternatives on the grounds that if these were worthwhile the market would select them automatically, and they usually dismiss claims of wider social benefits on the grounds that these are unmeasurable. However, small groups of economists have now devised a so-called 'social accounting matrix' which can measure a wider range of impacts than conventional input–output systems or GDP indicators, and these tell a different story. One ILO study of Indonesia, for instance, has found that traditional village-based technologies can produce more employment, greater social benefits and sometimes even higher income than imported, inappropriate Western systems.[23] But in a private-enterprise, market-dominated system decision-making tends to be biased against such alternatives because these are not amenable to high profits or growth, because many of their benefits are collective rather than private, because governments often favour big and supposedly growth-inducing projects over the small and because alternative frameworks for assessment have been ignored. If this is so then alternative development policies will require some domestic and trade intervention to plan new priorities, to encourage research on alternative technologies and to ensure their usage, i.e. to *create* alternative 'winners'.

A Self-Reliant Trade strategy would mean tailoring trade to our domestic requirements and social values rather than the reverse sequence which is rife today. This would probably be easier at present for Second and Third World countries with low trade ratios than for those of the First World with inordinately high ratios and heavily inter-dependent economies, but in the longer term almost any degree of dependency can be reduced. Self-Reliance need not mean return to a 'primitive' economy or to the unsuccessful ISI strategies of the 1970s and 1980s (see above) because alternative technologies and goals would be involved. In Australia this would only be a long-term aim, but planning could begin immediately for restructuring towards what I have elsewhere (Dunkley 1992) described as 'sustainably organised systems' (SOS), a state in which all our economic, social and ecological systems are established on a more sustainable basis at a micro level rather than merely on the basis of general macro, and sometimes cosmetic, environmental targets.

Self-reliance may require reduced material consumption, a redefinition of desired living standards and restructured social goals, thus contracting import requirements. Governments could aid this, initially by targetted fiscal and industry policies but ultimately by encouraging non-consumerist values and providing leadership towards alternative goals. New institutions would also be required to undertake research on alternative technologies and to foster public debate on long-term issues such as whether we really want the private enterprise-dominated, high-tech, high-stress competitive rat race that governments are determined to inflict upon us, whether we really need or want a highly computerised society and so forth. Some societies, notably in the Pacific, are now considering greater self-reliance and 'green village' development models (see above) in order to turn away from Westernisation which has brought materialistic lifestyles, TNC-induced fast-food habits, abandonment of rich, customary diets, destruction of traditions and dissolution of communities.[24] Even some mainstream economists obliquely admit that exposure to TNC advertising and 'aggrandizement' can adversely affect an importing society (e.g. Todaro 1994: 431).

A Self-Reliant Trade strategy may initially have some economic costs due to loss of specialisation, but longer-term advantages would include lower transport requirements and attendant environmental costs, less dependence on TNCs and less pressure, for reasons of trade or geo-politics, to appease countries such as China and Indonesia with appalling human rights records. The implementation of Self-Reliant Trade policies would initially require managed trade and industry policy, but if self-reliance were to be based on a solar–organic economy with extensive social consensus it might in time be compatible with relatively free trade (see Heierli, in Bassand 1986).

These three alternative trade strategies are not mutually exclusive, and a composite approach might even incorporate some concessions to Free Trade theory such as acknowledgement that very high protection can have economic costs, reduce efficiency, hamper export generation and so forth. A feasible general alternative to complete free trade might be a Managed Trade strategy which seeks, in the short term, balance of trade and macro stabilisation goals, in the medium term, development of 'cumulative advantage' in appropriate sectors, along with the 'social clause' and 'fair price' forms of Fair Trade, and in the longer term, a more self-reliant 'solar-organic' economy. It is important to understand that there is an integral link between trade strategy, the economic development model a country uses and the underlying values a society embraces, so that all societies must in future pay more attention to these links.

Another world order

Likewise, the international order is closely linked to strategies, models and values pursued by national or other units within that order, so the alternatives proposed above would imply alternative world structures. For purposes of constructing such an alternative I propose the following changes which would seek to deal with many of the problems identified in this book by bringing the Bretton Woods and UN systems closer together and by reconstructing the WTO in the spirit of the ill-fated ITO (see Chapter 2).

- The multilateral rules-making aspect of the GATT/WTO system should be retained and developed in preference to RTAs. However, disputes panels should be more flexible and more widely representative, while adoption of their rulings and action thereupon should require a simple or a two-thirds majority rather than, as at present, being automatically adopted unless there is unanimity to the contrary (see previous chapter).

- Alternative trade regimes such as the three discussed above should be recognised as legitimate and a country's right to trade interventionism should be accepted, with the proviso that these be primarily in a transparent tariff–subsidy form, not using hidden NTBs, and that the costs thereof be monitored and considered in policy-making. In my view GATT has had the wrong priorities over the years. Top billing should have gone to the elimination of the less justifiable NTBs such as VERs, leaving in place a system of both downwardly and upwardly flexible tariffs and subsidies, both still being legal under GATT but increasingly being frowned upon under the Geneva consensus.

- Article XX exemptions should be extended to allow trade intervention for a wider range of purposes, notably: sanctions for human rights violations; 'red tariffs' for the enforcement of labour rights and other 'social clause' matters (above); 'green tariffs' for the maintenance of environmental, food, health and other such standards; enforcement of ecological treaties; allowance for extraterritoriality of actions (see Chapter 10); cultural protection, primarily the allowance of discrimination in favour of local films, TV programmes and publications; community preservation, particularly to facilitate regional development, 'local economy' or other such schemes.

- In acknowledgement of Free Traders' concerns about such additional exemptions sparking rampant protectionism, a package system might be developed whereby exemptions are not granted willy-nilly but only where a well-researched rationale is presented. Thus, any country wishing to pursue alternative agriculture, an industry policy, a general Managed Trade approach or a long-term self-reliance programme, for instance, would be required to submit explanations of goals, detailed plans and so forth, then, once approved, would be granted waivers for all requisite interventions. Such deals would be unorthodox, but could provide a voluntary, more progressive version of IMF/ World Bank SAP packages.

- All this would greatly expand GATT's traditional role so the WTO may require additional sources of advice, the most feasible such sources being the ILO for labour standards (see above), the United Nations Environment Programme (UNEP) for environmental issues and other appropriate UN bodies for cultural and human rights issues. Greater participation by NGOs should be developed (see Chapter 11 and below).

- GATS should not be made any more liberalising of services trade than it is at present and the 'positive list' system should be retained so that services de-regulation remains optional (see Chapter 9), with de-listing of a sector even being allowable where adequate reason can be offered; this would mean some reversibility being built into the system as opposed to the current dogma of 'binding' and 'locking-in' (see Chapters 9 and 11).

- The TRIPs agreement should be abolished and its functions returned to the various pre-existing bodies (see Chapter 4), or at least its exemptions clause widened to include seeds, plants and drugs which are crucial for community health, the preservation of traditional agricultural systems and so forth (see Chapter 9).

- The WTO government procurement code should either remain voluntary or be abolished so that countries may retain the option of using public purchasing as part of a Managed Trade strategy.

- Proposals for investment de-regulation (see Chapter 11) should either be abandoned or else these should not restrict the right of governments to control DFI and short-term capital flows; GATT should also include a detailed international code of conduct for TNCs, should require member governments to take action against TNCs found to be in breach of the code and should contain an international system of general business practice regulations.

Such changes would be resisted by Free Traders and the current WTO leadership, but would broaden the GATT/WTO system, making it more like the model originally envisaged for the ITO, and ultimately these changes could result in a merger of the Bretton Woods system with that of the UN. In my view there will almost certainly be continuing political and social opposition to the GATT/WTO system unless such broadening reforms are effected. Some NGOs and commentators are advocating that the WTO be more closely linked to the UN, a proposal with which I agree. I suggest that the WTO be placed under the general supervision of the UN Economic and Social Council, as was originally proposed for the ITO, and be given a wider, more stabilising role, i.e. to fill the gap which many think the demise of the ITO has left. This might mean the WTO being, like the ILO, an independent body within the UN and receiving advice from various UN agencies (see above) rather than escaping UN social disciplines as the IMF and World Bank have done from the outset.[25] More direct NGO representation could be achieved through extension of the ILO model so that the WTO Ministerial Council, currently representing only governments, might consist of one delegate each from government, employers, unions and NGOs. This option would require large meetings, though the same size as those of the ILO, and may entail NGOs forming national bodies to select delegates.

This system should be supplemented by four other new institutions. The first would be an international central bank, in place of the IMF, which would function much as Keynes had proposed, by providing a world trading currency, partially re-regulating exchange rates, exercising mechanisms for reducing national trade surpluses and perhaps levying an international tax on speculative capital transactions as proposed by Nobel laureate James Tobin. The second would be a development body, in place of the World Bank, which would provide modest development programmes, encourage alternative 'green village' models (see above) where desired, conduct research on appropriate technologies and arrange commodity price stabilisation schemes as required, which was to be one of the ITO's functions (see Chapter 2).

The third body would be an environmental authority, perhaps an extended version of the present UN Environment Programme (UNEP), which would monitor environmental problems, formulate appropriate policies, supervise international treaties, arrange trade sanctions in conjunction with the WTO, advise governments and other international bodies and perhaps levy world-wide environmental taxes where feasible. The fourth body would be a cultural and media regulatory organisation which would supervise all telecomunications and broadcasting, seek to eliminate monopolies, endeavour to prevent direct global transmission to countries not desiring reception (though governments' motives should be scrutinised for undue censorial intent) and generally should encourage world-wide cultural diversity, preservation of languages and so forth.

Such a structure would not be a world government *per se* but a co-operative system based upon nation states (de-centralised internally where desired), these being linked by international negotiation, co-ordination and mutual aid rather than centralised bureaucratic administration. Such a system would not be one of free trade but would reflect more holistic values and should seek goals which are

alternative to growth and global consumerism. It would be internationalist rather than globalist. I suggest three broad alternative
goals for societies and the world system: 1 social justice: consisting
of adequacy and equitability in matters such as sustenance, health
care, civil liberties and gender rights; 2 sustainably organised
systems: entailing an economy which preserves eco-systems, biodiversity, landscapes and so forth (see Dunkley 1992: ch. 6); 3 cultural integrity: the evolution or maintenance of intellectual and
belief systems which are compatible with the other two goals, are
stimulating and are respectful of worthwhile traditions. A world-
wide shift to such goals is now occurring, along with increasing
numbers of proposals to reconstruct the world order from the
'bottom up'.[26]

Conclusion

There is a good deal of evidence, including the ambiguous results of
the world's greatest trade liberalisation experiment—the IMF/World
Bank SAPs—to suggest that free markets are not good at restructuring or that Free Trade is not as virtuous as is claimed, and there are
several valid alternatives to this doctrine. One of these, Managed
Trade, shares many Free Trade goals and world views but holds that
intervention rather than unrestricted markets is the best route to
high-tech prosperity, though in my view other goals are also possible
under a Managed Trade regime. The other two alternative schools,
Fair Trade and Self-Reliant Trade, believe that a free market world
would be economically, socially and culturally inequitable, the
former advocating social constraints on trade and the latter favouring greatly reduced levels of trade for the sake of national autonomy.
I propose a strategy of Managed Trade, but one which incorporates
international labour and social standards and which is directed at
longer-term self-reliance, along with other less growth-oriented,
'non-economic' goals. An alternative world order centred around
non-growth goals, less materialistic values and a reformed, UN-
linked WTO could produce a more equitable, sustainable world
without the need for 'deep integrated' globalism of the sort which
may risk the sovereignty and diversity of societies.

Conclusion

This book does not pretend to be any more than a sketchy, critical overview of a vast set of topics—the now legendary Uruguay Round, the 'Geneva consensus' regarding the supposed desirability of a new world-wide free trading order, the allegedly 'unstoppable' process of economic globalisation and how certain countries, particularly Australia, might fare in the new order. I have presented seven main themes and arguments.

The first is that the Uruguay Round is a genuine breakthrough for multilateralism but that, although governments are much more genuine in their desire for new multilateral trade rules than some cynics claim, this commitment is ambivalent. Most OECD governments are already committing 'sovereignty suicide' in areas such as financial regulation and are preparing to do so regarding DFI controls, but their preparedness to surrender autonomy may have limits. Former Australian trade minister, Bob McMullan, once hinted at this by suggesting that some measures, such as car industry protection, are likely to remain sacrosanct (Grennan 1996). The subtle art of double standards—free trade for our strong industries, tactful protection for the weak—is likely to long be with us, and some countries have used protection to establish core industries, later to 'discover' the supposed virtues of free trade—for everyone! This has been likened to climbing a ladder, then kicking it away so others cannot use it. In short, governments will continue with the

Free Trade Adventure for now, while retaining the option of early disembarkation.

The second argument is that the reincarnation of GATT and multilateralism has been due partly to the ongoing globalisation of finance, communications and the like, partly to the world-wide ideological ascendancy of Economic Rationalism, or the 'Geneva consensus', and partly to genuine conviction as to the virtues of free trade, but also to the crystallising in the 1980s of massive vested corporate interests in free global trade and investment. Although there can be vested interests in protectionism, I argue that there can also be vested interests in globalism and that many opponents thereof are sincerely motivated by some of the multifarious possible arguments against both free trade and excessive reliance on trade *per se*. Whether or not the pro-free trade forces hold the 'morally' superior position, as some Free Traders seem to believe, depends on how one weighs up the arguments for and against free trade, how much weight one places on the need for trade and the relative weights one places on economic as opposed to non-economic issues.

My third argument is that there is now a 'new model free trade agreement' which seeks to cover far more areas and to constrain national policy-making prerogatives more fundamentally than ever before. What I have called the Free Trade Adventure, the current push towards free trade and its concomitant long-term agenda of economic globalisation, seeks to encompass virtually all human economic activities including services, knowledge or intellectual property and investment. The Uruguay Round has embodied this model and the widely proposed future agenda of the WTO is to complete the task of full trade and investment liberalisation, or global 'deep integration', a process which is proceeding much faster within RTAs than multilaterally. My fourth argument is that the Uruguay Round and the longer term Free Trade Adventure will almost certainly bring some economic benefits, as conventionally measured, but that these have probably been overstated, their superficial, consumerist nature overlooked and their possible costs largely ignored. Econometric models have projected small economic gains from the Uruguay Round but losses for some countries, especially in the Third World. The technical reliability of these models depends

heavily on their in-built assumptions and they overlook a wide range
of possible socio-economic or non-economic costs and what I have
called community–sovereignty problems. Overall, my argument is
that the Free Trade Adventure may be economically beneficial, if
ambiguously and unevenly so, but could prove socially costly and
culturally *catastrophic*!

My fifth argument is that there are many possible cases against
free trade but that these have been neglected in the Uruguay Round
debate, which was conducted, throughout the world, almost entirely
amongst the pro-free trade elite. Most of these possible arguments
against free trade, even if not complete in themselves, contain some
validity and together constitute a strong case for maintenance of a
capacity for 'trade intervention'. My case against free trade is based
primarily on various 'non-economic' assertions, particularly what I
call 'community–sovereignty' arguments regarding the social, community, cultural and sovereignty costs of economic globalisation and
regarding the removal of some policy options for future generations.
My sixth argument is that world-wide there is a rising tide of popular opposition to free trade, and particularly to the 'deep integration'
which is occurring in many RTAs. This is indicated by the range of
social groups and NGOs which oppose the Free Trade Adventure
and the frequency of opinion polls which suggest considerable public
scepticism about its supposed virtues. Most of these movements
reflect sincere qualms about economic globalisation rather than
simply vested interests. At the end of the day free trade agreements,
with their concomitant structural changes, require substantial community support to be viable, but such support is not clearly in
evidence at present.

My final argument is that there are various possible alternative
theoretical and policy frameworks, as well as a number of proposed
alternative world order models, but that these have been neglected
in the debate, probably because the Geneva consensus and 'global
fatalism' have become the dominant world view. These alternatives
are: Managed Trade, which espouses some form of trade interventionism, though many sub-schools of this group share the Free
Traders' goals and are enthusiastic about globalism; Fair Trade, which
seeks a greatly broadened range of socially protective rules, one sub-
school endeavouring to construct a new form of co-operative 'fair-

price' trade; and Self-Reliant Trade, which seeks less dependence on trading or on TNC capital in the interests of more autonomous 'non-economic' goals. I have proposed a Managed Trade system centred around moderate planning, less growth-oriented goals and a carefully targetted tariff–subsidy system, which also could incorporate some Fair Trade and Self-Reliant Trade features in the longer term. Such a system would be compatible with maintenance of some multilateral rule-making, which I advocate should be retained in a broadened, loosened form. I propose that the GATT/WTO system be integrated into the UN system, as was the original intent, and that NGOs be granted a much more central role in the new structure. In formulating alternatives it needs to be recognised that there are crucial links between trade strategies, development models and social values, new models and values of the sort I have briefly proposed (Chapter 12) therefore implying alternative trade strategies.

There is no shortage of prognoses for the Uruguay Round and its likely fate, these ranging from adulatory hopes for 'deep integrated' globalism and the 'end of history', to anticipation of a satisfactory muddling through, cynicism about the decision-making capacity of the WTO and fear of serious encroachment upon national sovereignty (see Dunkley 1994b for more views). My expectation is that the new GATT/WTO system will function passably well, with increased usage being made of its dispute-settling procedures and so forth, although this success may lead to its undoing if a rash of global litigiousness begins to encroach too much upon national autonomy. I also expect continued pressure from Free Traders for further liberalisation, along with rising opposition thereto, culminating in greater friction than hitherto over economic versus 'non-economic' issues, particularly with regard to 'fair trade' matters and the environment.

The fact that the Uruguay Round was concluded at all is the first mark of its success, though a full assessment will not be possble until a least the end of its implementation period, and probably not until well into the new millennium. Some Free Traders hold that its extension of multilateral rule-making to most economic activities was its prime accomplishment. The Round was 'doomed to succeed' (see p. 45 above) because so many governments had accepted the

'Geneva consensus', under which the world's economic elites perceived a range of problems with interventionism and strove hard to find a new direction. It has undoubtedly opened up a new chapter in world history, but how the unwritten ending turns out will depend upon how people respond to the Free Trade Adventure, for it is unlikely to succeed without popular support. The central argument of this book is that the 'non-economic' costs of the Uruguay Round, free trade and associated globalisation, may eventually outweigh their (disputed) economic benefits, especially if the ultimate right of every society to control its own destiny is breached, as I believe it could be. The chief virtue claimed for free trade is that it can moderately increase (mostly private) consumption. However, if one of the world's great problems is Western over-consumption, as I (Dunkley 1992) and many others now believe to be the case, then this virtue is greatly discounted. In the near future all societies will have to decide whether they wish to lead the forces of trade, investment and technology or be *led by* them. This will be the *real* challenge of the age.

Postscript

In Pursuit of the Global Millennium

Economics has replaced ideology as the main driver of world politics. Technology and liberalisation are moving us towards a more integrated – even borderless – economy . . . [hence] the WTO system will have to interact with a whole array of non-trade policies and values which increasingly spill across national borders and transcend national solutions.
(Renato Ruggiero, outgoing Director General, WTO)[1]

The agenda for the conference had been decided in processes in Geneva to which many small developing countries were not privy. . . . Developing countries called, in vain, for detailed analysis of the impacts of the Agreements. But the inexorable process towards further liberalisation had already started and it wasn't going to be halted because certain countries were not managing to keep pace. . . . Another overwhelming impression from the Ministerial conference was the sheer enormity of the WTO . . . [which has] become more important than the United Nations – certainly more powerful.
(Beatrice Chaytor, Sierra Leone delegate to the WTO Singapore Ministerial Conference, 1996)[2]

In May 1998 WTO officials, trade enthusiasts and world dignitaries gathered in Geneva to celebrate the half century of the multilateral trading system and the foundation of GATT. The WTO has proudly reported that not a single speaker, including Bill Clinton, Nelson Mandela and Fidel Castro, questioned the validity of multilateral trade or the WTO itself.[3] The WTO's boast is slightly bizarre given that such fora are seldom used for uncharitableness and doubtless no known dissenters were invited, but the Geneva consensus on the virtues of free trade and globalisation is holding strong. The WTO can probably rely on a honeymoon of at least a decade, until the Uruguay Round is fully implemented, though the recent Asian Crisis has cast a shadow of doubt.

Founded on 1 January 1995 in place of the more limited GATT system, the WTO has, during its first half decade, steadily implemented the Uruguay Round agreements, expanded its membership and consolidated its role. The status and legitimacy of the WTO as centrepiece of the liberalising multilateral trade and economic system appears to have become widely, if not always happily, accepted.

On the other hand, chinks in the WTO's armour have appeared in the way I forecast in the first edition of this book. The system has become demanding, even onerous, for many countries; some members have backslid a little into protectionism; 'sacred' sectors have been further cossetted; trade disputes have greatly increased; 'liberalisation fatigue' (see below) has broken out; Beatrice Chaytor's exasperation (quoted above) is shared by many countries and non-economic considerations are being increasingly invoked.

The WTO had earlier claimed some credit for the 1994–5 trade boom, but this was looking tarnished by 1998–9. Although the volume of merchandise trade was sustained, the increase in value of both merchandise and commercial services trade had fallen sharply to around a modest 3 per cent per annum, due to many commodity price collapses and the Asian Crisis. The WTO's constant assertion of a close causal link between trade liberalisation and economic growth is now widely doubted, as will be discussed below.

This postscript will briefly review the Uruguay Round implementation process, the emerging character of the WTO, likely key issues for the mooted Millennium Round and some new critiques of globalisation.

The WTO—policeman or postman?

The WTO has already become an influential, respected and widely reported body, but also an over-worked and controversial one. To date it has set to implementing the Uruguay Round, monitoring progress, handling disputes, running worldwide information seminars, providing workshops or other assistance for poorer, supposedly marginalised Third World members, who are to be 'eased' into the new global order, and generally accumulating data on that order as much as policing it.

Major developments have included the growth of WTO membership to 134 (early 1999), the first biennial Ministerial Conference in Singapore in December 1996, the second in Geneva in May 1998 and the addition of several Protocols (sub-agreements) to the General Agreement on Trade in Services (GATS), notably in finance and telecommunications.

The acclaimed Singapore Ministerial Conference instituted work programmes on labour standards, investment and competition and adopted an initiative, begun separately through the Asia–Pacific Cooperation Forum (APEC), for free trade in information technology, known as the Information Technology Agreement (ITA) (see below). For the first time non-governmental organisations (NGOs) were invited, though many of those attending remained unimpressed. After meetings of Third World delegations to review the Conference Declaration, Beatrice Chaytor of Sierra Leone reflected that 'it was soon made clear to many of us that our views hardly mattered'.

The Geneva Ministerial Conference instituted an inquiry into the trade implications of electronic commerce and endorsed the (arguably questionable) practice amongst most members of not levying duties on electronic transactions. A third Ministerial in the US in late 1999 will decide whether there should be a full 'Millennium Round' of trade negotiations on a range of new issues or just a review of the Uruguay Round's 'built-in' agenda.

The WTO claims that Uruguay Round implementation is on target, the main shortcomings being some 'unsatisfactory' service negotiations (see below), tardy notifications and failure by some members to produce enabling legislation. But many waivers have been sought requesting extended implementation time and some observers are sceptical about the rate of progress, while many smaller countries would simply like to quantify the impact which the Uruguay Round and later agreements are having.

As regards trade in goods, there have been no formal complaints about members' failures to implement tariff reduction commitments, although the situation as regards non-tariff barriers (NTBs) and safe-guards is unclear because a third of members still have not notified these to the WTO as required (AP 1998: 87). Members have recently added some 400 pharmaceuticals to the tariff-free list, while the ITA (noted above) will phase out, by 2000, all duties on computers, semi-conductors, software, telecom equipment and scientific instruments. The ITA is voluntary but covers some forty members and over 90 per cent of world IT trade, with the schedules submitted electroni-cally—a WTO first.[4]

On the other hand, there has been some backsliding on goods trade commitments by various countries, or what the WTO calls 'backtracking' (AP 1998: 22), including sporadic tariff increases, some use of 'safeguards' (GATT-legal short-term protection) and many anti-dumping cases which critics claim are disguised protec-tionism (see below). The US has also used a number of, now GATT-illegal, voluntary export restraints (VERs), under which competitors are induced to withhold their own exports (see Glossary), especially against Russian and Japanese steel and South Korean memory chips. The WTO has gently hinted that many Third World members have been tardy with their tariff reduction commitments, and a few have even increased tariffs for revenue purposes. However, there has not been a flood of protectionism, mainly because the US economy has remained buoyant, the IMF has 'banned' protection increases by loan recipients and there is still a commitment to trade liberalisation amongst governments.

The WTO and Free Traders have also expressed concern at continuing practices such as: 'tariff peaks', involving remnant high tariff rates in a few sectors; 'tariff escalations', or progressively higher tariff rates on processed products to encourage local processing (see p. 57); the use of fixed sum duties rather than *ad valorem* (value-based) rates, the former tending to be heavier on lower-priced imports from developing countries; so-called 'nuisance tariffs' of around two per cent or less, maintained either through inertia or for residual minor protection; and 'high bindings', or binding (see Glossary) commitments at well above existing tariff rates, which provides the option of later rate increases if required.

In the textile and clothing sectors all members claim they are meeting their commitments, but some exporting countries have complained that First World importers are slacking on liberalisation commitments by manipulating the tariff reduction formulae (especially the early inclusion of low value-added items) and the excessive use of (short-term) safeguard provisions (see pp. 53–4). Exporters have queried the continued use of some import barriers and VERs, while a number of disputes in these sectors, including between competing Third World members, have been submitted to the WTO.

Agriculture has proved as much of a headache as anticipated, with many claims and counter-claims about members' conformity to commitments, as well as the referral of many disputes to the WTO. Specific complaints include disputed definitions of 'Green Box' exemptions from liberalisation requirements, calculation methods for Aggregate Measurement of Support (AMS) values, 'dirty tariffication' and the carrying forward of unused export subsidy commitments, made possible where rising commodity prices have precluded the need for the subsidies being phased out (see Ch. 4, pp. 54–5 on these issues).

Agricultural exporting countries do report some increased market access due to Uruguay Round implementation, although safeguard measures (such as a US decision against lamb imports) and high tariffication (conversion of quotas to tariffs) are having counteracting effects. The most blatant backsliding has been Japan's new rice tariffs of several hundred per cent which could see that country's 8 per cent market access commitment drastically cut, although some other agricultural sectors have been deregulated and had protection cuts. The total picture remains unclear, but the Australian Government's Bureau of Agricultural and Resource Economics (ABARE) has assessed that 'dirty tariffication' and the like has resulted in *higher* barriers in some agricultural sectors than before the Uruguay Round.[5]

In other goods-related areas, such as sanitary and phytosanitary (SPS) measures, technical barriers to trade (TBTs) and import licencing procedures, implementation has been confined to consultations, seminars and data consolidation. However, SPS measures have been the subject of many disputes, including in regard to Korean shelf-life and bottled-water standards, Japanese fruit and nut quarantine practices and EU bans on hormone-treated meat products, which was overturned (see below). Typical of emerging SPS issues was a Canadian case against Australian quarantine-based salmon import bans, in which a WTO panel ruled in favour of Canada on the grounds that Australian risk assessment studies did not adequately prove the vulnerability of salmon to a certain disease or justify confining the ban to salmon. Such cases seem set to become a battle of scientific reports, and it is by no means clear that WTO panels are capable of adequately adjudicating between them. The services area has seen the most active post-Uruguay negotiations, along with an ongoing information exchange programme (IEP) on current regulatory and market access practices, which Australia, for one, claims has been disappointing as not enough members have taken it seriously.[6] The sectoral negotiations have had mixed results, with success in telecommunications and finance and slow ongoing talks in professional services, but failure in maritime services due to inadequate commitments all round and US intransigence. In other areas, only 50 members have made market access commitments in general distribution services and just 14 in audiovisuals.

On 15 February 1997 a second round of post-Uruguay negotiations on telecommunications services was completed with a voluntary agreement between 69 members, with most favoured nation (MFN) status to non-signatories, covering 91 per cent of the global telecommunications market. Most signatories made commitments such as competitive voice telephony supply, though not all at each level, deregulation of data transmission, liberalised access to mobile phone markets and competition in leased circuits. The agreement also contains clauses which limit governments' regulatory powers, these—whether by oversight, caricature or hubris—being referred to as 'general obligations and disciplines' (GODs). The WTO proclaimed the deal as a great deregulatory advance, but there are many concerns about the degree of foreign access given to national markets and the issue remains a minefield.

Continuing financial sector negotiations resulted, on 12 December 1997, in a Financial Services Agreement (FSA) between more than 100 members for the deregulation of foreign access, right of establishment, admission of personnel and so forth in 95 per cent of the world's banking, finance and insurance markets. Hailed as a boon for prosperity, the FSA really only formalised previous unilateral deregulations by OECD countries, while accelerating deregulation in Latin America and Asia, the latter partly succumbing to IMF and US blandishments but, amid the Asian Crisis, resisting complete market access and full foreign ownership.[7]

As the Trade-Related Intellectual Property Rights (TRIPs)

Agreement is not yet fully implemented for Third World members, the WTO has confined itself to providing these countries with assistance to set up intellectual property rights (IPR) systems, conducting workshops and urging compliance with the contentious 'mailbox' provisions of the TRIPs Agreement (Article 70.8), which require members to grant *de facto* patents to pharmaceutical and agro-chemical companies pending full IPRs. More than a dozen TRIPs disputes have come before the WTO, these including a US victory over India on a long-rankling 'mail-box' issue. The US has also been threatening South Africa with action over its earlier (now diluted) legislation to allow cheap generic pharmaceuticals and to restrict tobacco products.[8] However, the whole area remains irksome to many Third World governments and NGOs, the latter wanting, at a minimum, the recognition of traditional community knowledge (see p. 190).

As anticipated in Chapter 11, there has been an upsurge in trade litigiousness, with some 50 disputes and a dozen panel cases arising annually, Third World members also becoming active on both sides of the dock. On several occasions the Appellate Body (see pp. 218–9 and below) has modified panel decisions or significantly reinterpreted a legal matter. A number of cases have arguably gone in favour of the trade dogmatist position as against the popular cause, notably: the overthrowing of the EU hormone-meat ban; the upholding of the case against a US ban on turtle-damaging shrimp imports; the overruling of Canada's restrictions on imported US magazines and the EU–US banana dispute (see below). The last-mentioned case brought the first significant instance of officially sanctioned retaliation in GATT/WTO history, with the US being permitted $200m in sanctions unless the EU changes its banana import preference system, which it has hinted it may. Both the US and EU maintain long lists of mutual complaints, and the surge of global litigiousness shows no sign of abating.

The WTO claims that its dispute resolution system is reducing trade tensions, but it is as likely to be highlighting or exacerbating issues which need not have become open disputes, and the system is not necessarily bringing justice, as the above-mentioned cases indicate. In the Canadian magazine case, for instance, the panel did not contest Canada's right to cultural protection, but effectively this right was overruled on technicalities relating to National Treatment and import restriction. In other cases, such as the banana and hormone-meat questions, there has arguably been a long-standing and generally accepted status quo in which certain moral issues were involved, until the new Uruguay Round dispute settlement system enabled priority to be given to trade technicalities.

In the banana case such technicalities also dominated. The EU's long-standing preferences to small African, Caribbean and Pacific (ACP) countries, effectively as a form of aid, has been legalised by a GATT waiver, but the resultant discriminatory quota system for both routine imports and so-called hurricane licences (emergency imports) are complex. The WTO dispute panel and Appellate Body ruled that, the waiver notwithstanding, the EU's banana import and distribution system still violated various provisions of GATT and GATS, as well as the Agreement on Import Licencing Procedures, a minor Uruguay Round agreement. It could well be argued that, technicalities aside, there is a moral case for the EU system, even if not in its current form. The US, which does not export bananas, was unabashedly acting on behalf of its banana-producing TNCs, especially Chiquita Bananas (formerly United Fruit Co.), a politically influential campaign donor. US-owned plantations in Latin America are known to minimise costs by being large, labour-exploiting, chemical-using industrial-type estates. By contrast, African and Caribbean producers tend to be small family or co-op groups and these countries are highly banana-dependent. Despite periodic attempts to restructure their economic bases, the global economy has proved unfriendly to their efforts.[9]

The hormone-meat case clearly illustrates the problems of the SPS Agreement's scientific standards requirement. In August 1997 a WTO panel ruled that the EU's decade-long ban on meat produced with growth hormones breached Article 5.1 of the Uruguay Round SPS Agreement, which requires that national SPS standards be subject to an internationally recognised form of risk assessment, the EU being deemed not to have done such an assessment. On appeal the Appellate Body broadened the decision somewhat by declaring that wider social risks could be considered and that higher-than-average standards could be used, so long as these were supported by scientific evidence, which the EU's ban was deemed not to be (AP 1998: 105–6). The EU was given further time to garner more scientific evidence and it claims to have, by mid-1999, made a strong argument, but the case was not finalised at the time of writing. Whatever the outcome the EU is pledged to retain the ban, even at the risk of yet more US sanctions.

The problem lies in assessment of scientific information. There is plenty of evidence for harmful effects of growth hormones, including the six in dispute, some of which are widely banned. Known effects include carcinogenicity, menstrual disruption, premature sexual development, illness or excessive weight in the treated animals and even the feminisation of species, including humans, which, by reducing male fertility, threatens their survival. The EU's panel of scientists has unanimously advised that hormone residues could have various carcinogenic, neurobiological and genotoxic effects. But such evidence is apparently not conclusive enough to convince trade-obsessed WTO panels.

Clearly there is a need here for the precautionary principle, along with the sovereign right of nations to apply this concept—i.e. to adjudge the evidence in a cautious way giving priority to environmental or health considerations, not trade. The same problem will arise in time with the issue of trade in genetically modified (GM) food or other organisms. The evidence for harm from GMOs is disputed, some research needing lead times of a decade or more, and the greatest ecological concern is on the process side, to which the GATT Article XX exceptions have been ruled inapplicable (see Chapter 10). Recent scientific evidence finds that transgenic or GM species cross-breed with wild plants at twenty times the rate of ordinary mutants, which gives rise to the danger of much more rapid spreading of GMOs than biotechnologists originally anticipated. In such circumstances, the precautionary principle is obviously called for.[10]

Yet WTO panels, often consisting of militant Free Traders, are showing signs of strict trade dogmatism and exclusion of 'extraneous' non-trade issues. The Appellate Body, consisting of legally trained personnel, is proving somewhat more broadminded, as noted above. Many highly technological Western countries, led by the USA, have intimated that they will press vigorously for free trade in GM products, officially on the (disputed) grounds that these are necessary to solve world food problems.

The WTO's Uruguay Round mandate to seek 'global coherence', or consistency and stability in trade, finance and macro-economic policies, is being implemented via co-operation agreements with the

IMF, World Bank, ILO, IPR bodies, SPS monitoring groups (see p. 66) and so forth. These and other bodies have observer status on certain WTO councils, especially the TRIPs Council (which boasts nine observers and further applicants), with some reciprocation. The WTO has also attended meetings of the G7 and the drafting committee for the OECD's abortive Multilateral Agreement on Investment (MAI) (see below).

The concept of global coherence is a vague and evolving one, some commentators suggesting that the WTO is not seriously compatible with the IMF and World Bank because the latter do research and give advice on policies and regulations while the former makes trade rules.[11] However, as Ruggiero has suggested, globalisation is making research advice, regulatory monitoring and in-country intervention increasingly requisite for all bodies. Moreover, WTO, IMF and World Bank officials meet regularly; all three are obsessively committed to the Washington–Geneva Consensus and each often does the other's job. The WTO, as noted above, is reinforcing financial deregulation while IMF/World Bank conditionalities enforce trade liberalisation, as was the case with the recent Asian Crisis packages. One IMF survey has found that three quarters of the World Bank's structural adjustment programme (SAP) recipients and all of the IMF's have liberalised their trade primarily or exclusively via SAPs, indicating that many Third World countries are being pushed into trade liberalisation without conviction.[12] In short, elite body collaboration may be moving towards a *de facto* system of world economic governance, backed by the WTO's sanctioning capacity and IMF/World Bank policy conditionalities, along with the extensive reportage now required by all these bodies, or what could be called 'global sticky-beaking'.

As regards NGOs, the WTO has been taking literally its new rule that it *may* consult them. One NGO survey has concluded that the WTO does not adequately consult civil society (NGOs or other social interest groups). Instead both the WTO and member governments mainly consult professional and industry groups. Moreover the WTO is excessively secretive, with no automatic document release mechanism, although recently the WTO has had broad (some say perfunctory) meetings with NGOs and has derestricted some documents. But NGO access to its committees and disputes panels is still not permitted and outgoing EU Trade Commissioner, Sir Leon

Brittain, has called on the WTO for more transparency, openness, NGO access, community consultation and an information ombudsman.[13] WTO staff and other commentators are concerned that the WTO Secretariat is grossly under-funded relative to the onerous requirements of the Uruguay Round. These now involve some 50 committee meetings each week, 400 meetings a year requiring interpreters, 175 matters for regular notification by members (see p. 223), countless policy issues which generate inquiries and 81 million pages of documentation to be processed annually. Senior WTO official Richard Blackhurst has said that the WTO's 1996 staffing of 513 made it only the 16th largest world body, smaller than many UN and regional agencies with much more modest briefs, so that the WTO clearly needs more resources to cope.[14] And certainly by no means all needs are covered; many Third World members want to know more about liberalisation impacts, as noted above, and, indeed, the WTO does virtually no research on the wider impacts of free trade. If the world's governments are so keen on globalisation, they may have to pay more for it.

WTO funds derive from compulsory, and some voluntary, member contributions, with extra resources from national delegations in Geneva and from ministerial staff in the capitals of member countries. This reliance on national delegations results in uneven participation, as about a quarter of poorer members have no permanent delegation, and the size of current national contingents in Geneva range from one to 22, averaging five.

So cliquism is already apparent in the WTO, as criticised by the Sierra Leone delegate quoted above. An inner directorial group of 18 was tried in the 1980s, a club of industrial-country members has been proposed, some initiatives now begin with a small group of interested members and it has been claimed that members with less than ten per cent of world trade in the relevant area are usually excluded from such circuits.[15] Some advocate an IMF-style contribution-weighted voting system, but whilst this may elicit more funds from power-minded rich countries, it would be disastrous for the present (moderately) democratic, member-driven nature of the WTO, whatever its current deficiencies.

In sum, the WTO's emerging role is part rule-maker, part judge, part policeman and even part postman as it demands increasing amounts of information and correspondence from liberalisation-fatigued, globalisation-weary members. But, being under-funded, making decisions through unequal peer pressure, its dispute panels regularly making socially questionable rulings and with many of its members forced to join, the WTO still lacks the authority and insight to induce wholehearted participation by members, to prevent some members backsliding on agreements or to attract the respect of world civil society.

Towards a Millennium Round?

Even the unromantic WTO has succumbed to the present craze for millennial allusions, so at the time of writing faces a choice between its limited built-in agenda requiring the review of many Uruguay Round agreements and a full Millennium Round open to new issues. The choice will probably have been made by the time this postscript goes to press, so I will confine the following comments to existing and new areas which various commentators claim are most in need of consideration. The existing areas I examine are goods, services and anti-dumping rules. The potential new areas include the environment, labour standards, competition policy and investment.

• *Goods:* as goods tariffs are on the verge of extinction, Free Traders are now seeking mainly to wear down the tariff peaks and other persistent forms of protection mentioned above, to widen the range of goods sectors subject to nil tariffs and to dislodge remaining NTBs. In textiles and clothing, whose agreement is slated for full implementation in 2004, the aim would be to enforce and tighten the Uruguay Round rules so as to ensure continuing liberalisation and to fend off any persisting VERs and the like. In agriculture a similar ambition seeks to eliminate export subsidies, scale down other assistance and trim high tariffication rates. For the SPS, TBT, subsidies, safeguards and trade-related investment measures (TRIMs) areas, no major changes are anticipated at the time of writing, although Free Traders want accelerated liberalisation. Many governments and NGOs will, however, resist further liberalisation of these, especially TRIMs and subsidies, while environmentalists want more acknowledgement of the precautionary principle in the SPS Agreement. In any Millennium Round, some tariff cuts would probably be made for various goods sectors, but in a more subdued manner than during the Uruguay Round.

- *Services*: the built-in services agenda requires a review of GATS in 2000, including with regard to coverage, market access, safeguards, subsidies and government procurement. The WTO and Free Traders want to see more countries making more liberalisation commitments by broadening their coverage schedules and reducing exceptions, along with tighter safeguards, less discriminatory government procurement, fewer exclusive regulatory measures, the elimination of subsidies and perhaps a switch to 'negative listing', a system which requires liberalisation of all sectors except any specifically exempted (see Glossary and Chapter 9). Some members want a full renegotiation of GATS with updated sectoral classifications. The US has indicated that it will press for further transparency and liberalisation in government service procurement and audiovisuals. For reasons outlined in Chapter 9, I expect resistance to further substantial service liberalisation especially in socially sensitive areas such as education or audiovisuals, a stance with which I sympathise.

- *Anti-dumping*: many believe that anti-dumping and countervailing duties are being widely used for surreptitious protection, with a surge of cases apparently occurring during recessions. Hard-line Free Traders claim that the Uruguay Round Anti-Dumping Agreement is too lax to prevent this, so they want it tightened or else abolished in favour of a global competition policy (see below), as has been done in the EU. Current theory suggests that damage from dumping depends on how competitive domestic markets were in the first place, whether or not foreign and domestic firms collude to raise post-anti-dumping duty prices and whether normal (justifiable) below-cost pricing is being used by importers (that is, for temporary or start-up purposes in the legitimate way a local firm might). Hard-liners want national anti-dumping measures abolished, but moderate theorists want WTO provisions modified merely to prevent collusion, to allow for pre-dumping monopoly by locals and to facilitate normal price reductions.[16]

These proposals are reasonable, but in my view caution should be exercised before weakening or eliminating anti-dumping instruments, as there can be a genuine need for them. Australian economist Donald Feaver has found that a large number of allegedly protectionist Australian anti-dumping cases are *bona fide*, and that the recession link is not so much protectionism as, in many instances, a response to foreign predatory practices or to cyclical dumping which arises because Australia is a convenient dumping ground due to proximity and seasonal appropriateness. US historian and former International Trade Commission (ITC) member Alfred Eckes claims that the reverse of protectionism often occurs—that is, legitimate anti-dumping or safeguard cases are overruled for various political, diplomatic or pro-free-trade reasons. Eckes also suggests that the resurgence of anti-dumping cases since the early 1980s has been mainly due to better enforcement of anti-trust law, along with a surge in dumping as global competitive pressures have grown, rather than due to egregious protectionism.[17]

Given that unfair or aggressive pricing behaviour is likely to increase as a result of globalisation, and that a uniform global competition agreement is improbable due to the complex variety of national competition regimes, substantial national sovereignty to regulate anti-dumping should be maintained, albeit perhaps with some international coordination of new national competition policies over time.

- *Trade and Environment:* the environment–trade link has become such a major issue that it is likely to be on any Millennium Round agenda, even though Free Traders do not welcome the idea (see Chapter 10). The WTO's Committee on Trade and the Environment (CTE), widely criticised for its trade bias and exclusion of NGOs, has been investigating the trade implications of trade sanctions in Multilateral Environmental Agreements (MEAs), eco-labelling, recycling schemes, life-cycle production systems and trade-related environmental measures (TREMs) in general. But no definite policies have been formulated and the issues at stake remain unclear. The Geneva Consensus still insists that playing fields should be levelled only for products, not for the inputs (labour, resources, etc.) that make up comparative advantage, and that trade liberalisation is unambiguously good for the environment. In this vein several panels have made pro-trade decisions that some say are bad for the environment, notably in the shrimp–

turtle, hormone-meat (and perhaps banana) cases discussed above.
There is mounting evidence against this consensus, as I argued in Chapter 10, even if 'pollution havens' do not abound as such. Recent studies by the OECD and various scholars suggest that trade or trade-driven growth benefits the environment in only some countries and industries, notably where trade favours cleaner technologies and low pollution-intensive activities, but that such benefits are policy-dependent, not automatic, especially where governments are heavily indebted and the trade gains go to private industrial interests. In contrast, transportation, adverse social impacts around airports, carbon dioxide emissions, traffic congestion, solid waste, chemical-intensive commercial agriculture and so forth appear to rise directly with increases in trade and economic growth. The British House of Commons Environment Committee has concurred, additionally suggesting that the TRIPs Agreement may conflict with the 1992 UN Convention on Biological Diversity, that some business interests are undermining environmental policies and that British trade negotiators often underplay the Government's environmental concerns in the supposed interests of trade diplomacy.[18]

There is a multitude of policy proposals. The WTO broadly concurs with most Free Traders in wanting to retain the status quo, perhaps with advisory links to the UN Environment Programme (UNEP) and waivers for trade penalties in MEAs. Environmentalists want GATT revised to allow green protection, to cover processes and production methods (PPMs), to permit MEA sanctions and to incorporate the precautionary principle, some even wanting animal rights and the like added. The EU has proposed amending Article XX to specify the environment (in XXb) and to allow MEAs as grounds for trade restrictions. Some commentators advocate handing the issue over to an international panel of experts or to a whole new specialist organisation. The outcome, however, is likely to be near the standard Free Traders' position noted above, with possibly a select panel of environmental advisers.

- *Labour standards:* strong pressure from the US, France and Norway is likely to place this on the Millennium agenda. The WTO is formally committed to supporting core labour standards and promoting these through collaboration with the ILO, while still insisting that, in the interests of Third World labour-intensive industries, labour playing fields should not be levelled (see Chapter 12).

The WTO, the OECD and other Geneva Consensus bodies still argue that 'exploited labour' (my term, see pp. 120–1) can exist but cannot persist, although the latter has admitted that textile industry direct foreign investment (DFI) does seek lowest cost sites. US economists Dani Rodrik and Robert Feenstra have recently shown that low labour standards can undermine First World wage levels via trade, although transnational companies (TNCs) prefer somewhat higher standards so as to induce better labour quality. Rodrik uses information on adherence to ILO Conventions and Feenstra data on global out-sourcing which previous studies have neglected. However, some commentators claim that, as a result of NGO criticisms, codes of conduct, voluntary labelling schemes, consumer boycotts and the like, controversial TNCs such as Nike are mending their ways and Third World governments gradually upgrading standards.[19]

The most likely outcome is a mild social clause specifying basic labour standards (see p. 252), perhaps as sanctionable exceptions in Article XX. Many Third World governments are resisting and others urge reliance on voluntary mechanisms of the sort noted above, so the issue will be contentious. Trade guru Jagdish Bhagwati says labour standards and human rights are important, but should be left to NGOs for implementation on the ground,[20] an incongruous proposal when the WTO deals with these bodies only minimally. Rodrik suggests that trade has a similar structural effect to technological change, which all governments regulate, and that the adverse social effects of labour exploitation could be worse than the alleged costs of standard-setting. I concur, arguing for moderate labour standards and human rights requirements (e.g. fair trial, no torture, etc.) on the part of WTO members, for monitoring in conjunction with the ILO and NGOs, and for priority to social justice over trade.

- *Global Competition Policy:* from its inception GATT has sought to control only government regulation of business, not the behaviour of private firms, and indeed it does not even require members to have a national competition policy—only two thirds have— apart from occasional consultations on the issue and some anti- restrictive provisions in GATS. This is due partly to the complexity of the issues, partly to US protectiveness of its own anti-trust standards and partly to business opposition on the issue, stretching back to ITO days.

Today the globalisation of business is changing the nature of the links between trade and competition, such as when the US allowed Boeing and McDonnell Douglas to merge and the EU objected, in defence of its own aircraft industry. But developments have moved so quickly that nobody understands the full picture. The main general concerns are that restrictive business practices may counteract gains from trade liberalisation and that, in theory, markets need to be reasonably competitive, or 'contestable', for free trade to work. Many NGOs agree, hoping that the more dis- reputable TNC practices such as aggressive takeovers or transfer pricing might be targeted as well. However, this is not quite what the supporters of global competition policy have in mind. Their specific concerns are: routine business malpractices such as price fixing and resale price maintenance; vertical and horizontal mergers; cartels, especially for exports; import restricting practices by public enterprises; and government use of competition laws or other regulations in a way which disadvantages foreign firms.

There are several problems with the idea of a global competi- tion policy. First, national policies, administrative systems and ideologies regarding competition differ so much that harmonisa- tion looks almost impossible. Second, for individual countries, would harmonisation mean stronger laws, weaker laws or a 'race to the bottom'? Third, commentators differ as to goals—e.g. dif- fering national laws on mergers make TNC takeovers difficult, but some want them made easier and some harder. Fourth, a legally enforceable global competition system would create an unprecedented inroad into the heart of national policy-making. For example, US TNCs would love to destroy the Japanese *kieretsu* system (see Glossary) and global retail giants want to tackle laws in certain countries which protect small shops or other businesses. Would a global competition system allow such challenges, or should nations be able to retain sovereignty over these matters? The options are not clear-cut; the WTO has not got a strong opinion on the matter and mainstream economists disagree. Many free marketeers want total free trade and no interventionist pro-competition policy, while gurus like Bhagwati oppose compulsory harmonisation. The main options proposed are: general co-operation and co-ordination among WTO members on competition policy; harmonisation around some basic principles; a strong compulsory code; a separate global competition body; and a competition code designed to replace anti-dumping provisions (see above).[21] The most likely outcome is co-operation and moderate steps towards harmonisation, as is already occurring bilaterally. I oppose any global competition policy system until an enforceable code of conduct for TNCs can be developed. The UN and OECD have designed such codes of ethics for TNCs, but these have never been taken seriously, let alone enforced.

- *Investment:* this would be the hottest topic of the Millennium Round, should it make the agenda. A 'GATT for Investment' has long been proposed and the current rationale for this is the supposed extensive integration of trade and investment today—TNCs 'trade to invest and invest to trade'—so that efficient globalisation purportedly requires harmonised investment deregulation for maximum market access. GATS and the TRIPs Agreement entail some DFI deregulation but GATT is silent on the matter.

    Perhaps the most dramatic development since the Uruguay Round has been the OECD's proposed Multilateral Agreement on Investment (MAI) which was drafted in great secrecy (denials notwithstanding). The MAI was to: increase the security of DFI; greatly reduce government restrictions thereof (barring listed exceptions); abolish most TRIMs; create international dispute settlement panels, with the possibility of aggrieved TNCs suing governments over unfriendly decisions; build in long-term liberalisation commitments; and tie countries into the system for up to twenty years. At present the MAI is on hold (probably indefinitely) due variously to rejection by France and Canada over cultural issues, cynicism by the US over proliferating exemption listings, hesitation by Australia because of domestic dissent and a worldwide resistance campaign by NGOs.

    If the WTO tried to adopt a similar model, the same resistance would arise and many Third World countries have already strongly rejected the MAI proposal. It is likely that the WTO will either leave the issue alone or seek a mild code providing for co-ordination and transparency. If investment is to be included in GATT, there certainly should be some reciprocal obligations placed upon TNCs. However, I argue that DFI policy should be left entirely to national governments and that DFI is not as beneficial as is usually claimed. Trade and DFI may be linked, but this is because of TNC integration and dominance, which is not necessarily good. Moreover outward DFI played a destructive role in the recent Asian Crisis. It should also be noted that in recent years the top 100 global TNCs have increased turnover by 30 per cent but employment by only four per cent. Scholars have identified situations where DFI may not be beneficial and some suggest that it might *follow* rather than *cause* growth.[22]

My hunch is that a Millennium Round would stick primarily to the 'built-in' agenda, along with a bit more tariff-cutting in goods and coverage-widening in services, as well as some transparency improvement and discipline-strengthening in other areas, especially anti-dumping. New topics broached may include the environment and labour standards but with unadventurous outcomes, while competition and investment will be left largely alone. The US has also hinted at raising the issues of extensions to the Government Procurement Agreement (pp. 72–3), corruption as a trade barrier and formal NGO participation in the WTO. The EU has vaguely suggested the notion of consumer rights as grounds for trade inter-vention, a concept which would allow protection against items of consumer concern, such as hormone-bred meat or genetically mod-ified food (discussed above), irrespective of WTO rulings. A number of countries, as anticipated in this book, are now using cultural or other non-economic justifications for various measures, including protection of agriculture, which the EU describes as multifunctional. Whether or not cultural issues, perhaps in the form of a cultural exceptions clause, are raised in the Millennium Round, they will not go away, the EU having stated that it will not sacrifice its rural her-itage on the altar of free trade.

Free Traders are near-apoplectic at the prospect of such issues, but if the WTO wants wider acceptance in the world it will have to confront them eventually. To many the most urgent need is for studies of the impact of WTO agreements on Third World countries, women and society in general, but, unsurprisingly, this is *not* on the agenda, both because the WTO is under-resourced and because it is in the business of *promoting* free trade, not critically analysing it.

Free trade and globalisation—an end to history?

Already some commentators are posing the question of whether or not Ruggiero's global free trade millennium is achievable. Will there be a utopian 'end of history', will WTO members call a halt at some point or will it all end in catastrophe? There are adherents of each viewpoint, the WTO, IMF, OECD and the like still pursuing the free-trade millennium through liberalisation of everything, despite recent economic crises. The WTO has even revived the old utopian claim that free trade and globalisation will bring world peace (AP 1998: 37). Others are more sceptical, even a few mainstream pundits surmising that the world is still not ready for full-blast free trade and globalisation, or at least seeing limits to the potential of free trade. Catastrophe scenarios can be found variously amongst some greens (due to environmental impacts), some left theorists (due to capitalist/TNC triumphalism) and many right-wingers (due to the undermining of national sovereignty and national industrial power).[23] My view is that there are limits to how far nations wish to move towards free trade, that there is a mild 'between rounds' backlash going on at present and that there are many uncounted costs of free trade and globalisation which will always undermine their desirability.

Indications of a backlash include the backsliding towards some protectionism noted above; hesitation about the globalisation project among leading globalisers at the February 1999 World Economic Forum; warnings about global financial instability by famed speculator George Soros; and the worldwide campaign against the MAI.[24] Public opinion remains divided and sceptical. An opinion survey of 22 countries by *The Economist*, using a fairly neutral question, found overall protectionist views slightly outnumbering free trade opinions (47 per cent to 42 per cent), but with an increasing vote for protection in most countries. The margin favouring capital controls was even greater (49 per cent to 37 per cent). Anti-free trade views are strong in most of the countries hit by the Asian Crisis, and are stronger still on specific issues. In quarantine-conscious Australia, for instance, a private poll found 82 per cent of respondents opposing poultry imports, 95 per cent doing so when disease risks were mentioned in the question.[25]

Likely causes of this backlash include: persistent recession and high unemployment in many countries; enduring trade imbalances in the US (protectionism is not, of course, an automatic solution to these problems); chronic and worsening inequality and (relative) poverty everywhere; structural change and declining regions; financial crises in many countries; and widespread criticisms of IMF/World Bank policies. Regarding free trade specifically, as I anticipated above (pp. 264–5), there has emerged what could be called liberalisation fatigue, not just temporary negotiation fatigue as many expected. This means that societies are becoming exhausted by the gradual but remorseless structural changes resulting from two decades of unilateral and multilateral economic and trade deregulation, so that people are anxious about the increasingly apparent costs of globalisation.

A range of anecdotes, evidence and trends indicate these costs, both economic and non-economic, suggesting limits to the virtues of trade liberalisation. In Australia during a 1997 public debate about car tariff reductions to 5 per cent by 2010, as proposed under APEC, econometric modeller Chris Murphy estimated that this would bring national benefits of $A50m, much less than Free Traders claimed, and that these would be outweighed in the (almost certain) event that one fifth of the displaced car workers could not find new jobs, with additional regional and non-economic costs likely.[26] Despite Free Traders' proclamations, structural change has not brought enough new jobs. ABS data show that between 1974 and 1996, a period of persistent tariff reductions, the Australian manufacturing sector shrank from 20 to 14 per cent of GDP, at a cost of 400,000 jobs, while aggregate unemployment more than quadrupled. Clearly other sectors have not made up the difference, even in 22 years!

An increasing number of studies contradict habitual WTO, IMF and World Bank claims of SAP and trade liberalisation successes, suggesting variously that: Sub-Saharan African will be worse off due to the Uruguay Round (see pp. 145–6 for reasons); that there are no clear links between liberalisation and growth; that many liberalising countries actually suffer deindustrialisation; that where exports do respond positively, this is not due to improved productive capacity, which often requires initial government assistance; that trade liberalisation can bring a flood of destabilising imports and stagnant investment, especially where very unequal incomes induce luxury imports rather than saving; and that import floods can inhibit cumulative advantage (pp. 121–2) or what some are calling dynamic comparative advantage.[27]

A study of Zimbabwean trade liberalisation concurs with the above, a flood of luxury and other imports devastating production and employment levels, leading to deindustrialisation and social unrest. An analysis of the EU/Tunisia–Morocco free trade agreement suggests that any benefits to the latter will be dependent upon induced capital inflows and an (unlikely?) absence of market distortions. Some Mexican commentators blame NAFTA and other economic deregulation, rightly or wrongly, for the social unrest and crime waves which currently grip that country.[28] Clearly trade liberalisation is not as uniformly or unambiguously beneficial for all countries, all circumstances or all stages of development as the WTO unabashedly preaches, and there is an urgent need for it to do more objective impact analysis.

Even some mainstream economists are reconsidering at least certain aspects of free trade and globalisation. Bhagwati, for instance, whilst still a zealous Free Trader, concedes that freer trade can bring volatility, insecurity, 'thinner' margins of comparative advantage (hence sectoral instability) and loss of jobs for older workers and others. He recommends domestic policy solutions, a position I consider unrealistic in an age of chronic deregulation and public sector slashing. Bhagwati also rejects, due to resultant instability and speculation, the case for free capital movement, a case which he says has hijacked Free-Trade ideas and is pushed by a 'Wall Street–Treasury complex'. Lord Eatwell agrees, arguing that global financial deregulation and exchange-rate instability undermine confidence, leading to the sluggish investment and deficient demand which he believes to be the main causes of global unemployment.[29]

Harvard economist Dani Rodrik cautiously suggests that globalisation may have gone too far, especially as regards its effects on unskilled workers and a reduced ability of nations to fund their customary quality of governance. He warns that globalisation gives international markets greater say over national policies and income distribution, arguing, as I have throughout this book, that economics is an excessively narrow discipline which neglects such considerations.[30] There is even internal dissent within the IMF/World Bank system, World Bank chief economist, Joseph Stigler, ruminating of the Asian Crisis, that 'government has done too little, not too much' and that the famed Asian Model is not as much at fault as the 'dogmatic Washington Consensus' holds.[31] Indeed, the Asian Crisis has thrown up a heated 'over-governance and cronyism' versus 'excessive deregulation' debate which remains unresolved. According to the latter position, extensive financial deregulation, trade liberalisation and general economic decontrol have greatly undermined the successful state-centred Asian Model and closely preceded the Crisis.[32]

Undeterred by criticism and contrary evidence, the international institutions are pushing ahead with their globalisation project, the IMF even seeking to make totally deregulated capital accounts a compulsory condition of membership, which could mean the outlawing of all capital controls, this being in the interests of Western financiers according to some critics. On the other hand, certain IMF and World Bank officials, including IMF head, Michel Camdessus, now concede that financial markets are subject to volatility, 'herd' behaviour or 'contagion', that some countries' financial liberalisation was premature and that there may thus be some role for (temporary) capital controls.[33]

The WTO acknowledges growing discontent with globalisation, but persistently reasserts the alleged greater benefits, once declaring that globalism is 'not a policy to be judged right or wrong but a process driven by a much deeper current of technological and economic change' (AP 1998: 6). Such techno-globo determinism is partly belied by the WTO's regular assertion that globalisation is also the product of policy liberalisation, surely a discretionary rather than inevitable force. The backdown by many governments over MAI clearly shows that deregulation is discretionary. Rather than the supposed bicycle effect (see Glossary) I argue that there is a worldwide bulldozer effect whereby major governments and global institutions are pushing globalisation, against the preferences of many smaller countries and the citizens of most nations. The WTO has attempted to answer critics of globalisation, unconvincingly in my view, particularly claiming that national sovereignty is not an issue because global agreements are voluntary (AP 1998: 32ff.). But this misses the points made in this book that nations can be pressured and gradually locked into these agreements (see Chapter 11), that many governments are committing sovereignty suicide and that nowhere have citizens been consulted about all this.

Various current theories of globalisation hold that globalism will bring world peace and understanding through a universalisation of values; is necessary for continued prosperity; strengthens *both* international *and* local foci (or so-called glocalisation); generates beneficial hybrid systems and so forth. Such theories are questionable and often overlook the variegated general effects of globalisation, of which three are notable. One is a referential effect whereby environmental, human rights or other such standards are generalised through demonstration or pressure. Another is an integrative effect whereby national economic or other systems become increasingly integrated, both structurally and functionally. A third is a displacement effect whereby global or hegemonic national cultures or other systems displace local, traditional ones in particular localities. An example of the third is the little-noticed displacement of Australian English by US language and culture, especially amongst young people whose ideas, according to one recent values survey, are dominated by American images and consumer items, although they do not wish to live in the USA.[34]

Of these effects, arguably the first is generally beneficial, the second is of mixed virtue, as suggested throughout this book, and the third largely detrimental. Yet it would appear that the WTO is not encouraging referential effects as much as it might, is obsessively fostering integrative effects without adequate consideration of possible costs and is probably inadvertently inducing displacement effects, especially in the area of services, without any real consciousness of the processes involved or their long-term implications.

In addition to possibly adverse integrative and displacement effects, the WTO needs to scrutinise some broader concerns such as: what Soros calls market fundamentalism; what I call over-technification of society—that is, increasing reliance on controversial technologies such as super-information systems or biotechnology; and the likely questioning by future generations of sovereignty-reducing global agreements entered into on their behalf by present-day politicians and bureaucrats. Also in need of questioning is the WTO's millenarian desire, as expressed by Ruggiero, to change the entire structure of the planet in accordance with a theory, that of free-market economics, whose validity is so widely questioned outside the globalising elite and whose projected material benefits are so meagre (see Chapter 7). If, as Ruggiero claims, economics is now driving world politics, this should perhaps be seen not as a development to be celebrated but as a disease to be cured.

As I have suggested in this book, globalisation is not inevitable and there are alternatives, but we may need new clauses in national constitutions limiting the extent to which governments can bargain away national democratic rights through global agreements. Ultimately all these issues are about development, and to deal with the problems discussed here we will need to investigate an alternative development paradigm of the sort briefly outlined in Chapter 12. An interesting enunciation of what I call the self-reliant trade alternative (Chapter 12) has been made, since the Thai financial crisis, by the King of Thailand, who said that community and national self-sufficiency are more important than 'tiger' status, while other Thais have warned against further seduction by Western-style consumerism.[35] Currently our main ailment is the lack of political will to seek such alternatives, but this is not incurable. The internationalisation of peace and understanding, which so many seek, is surely achievable through appropriate education and should not be unduly juxtaposed with full-force integrative economic globalisation, which is demonstrably undesirable and avoidable.

Glossary

autarchy the complete absence of trade, or virtually total economic self-sufficiency of a society.

bicycle theory the claim that trade negotiations must be continuous or they will regress.

bilateral arrangements between two countries.

binding an undertaking to fix maximum tariffs or other measures at the agreed level; actual tariffs can be below this level, but at higher levels compensation may be claimed or retaliatory actions taken by countries adversely affected.

deep integration economic and administrative integration between countries in the way that has occurred internally over time.

de-regulation reduction in the number or scope of specific or general regulations.

dirty tariffication a reference to the possibility that governments might convert quotas to tariffs, as required by the Round, in a way which maintains protection, because the quota-equivalent size of tariffs is not clear-cut.

econometric models mathematical systems of equations representing economic relationships and used for economic forecasting or other forms of analysis—notably the CGE form.

Economic Rationalism the term used in Australia (usually 'neo-liberalism' elsewhere) for doctrines and policies based on neo-classical (q.v.) economic principles plus market-oriented agendas such as de-regulation (q.v.) and privatisation.

economies of scale   factors which result in unit production costs declining as output level rises.

economies of scope   factors which result in unit production costs declining as additional complementary product lines are combined in the one plant or enterprise.

externalities   factors external to the market which result in collective benefits being greater than private benefits (e.g. education) or collective costs being greater than private costs (e.g. pollution).

free trade   trading across national boundaries unimpeded by tariff duties, quotas, regulations or other barriers to the movement of goods and services.

G5 or 7   group of major Western industrial powers—USA, Japan, Germany, UK and France (five) plus Italy and Canada (seven).

GDP/GNP   GDP is the total production of a country; GNP is this figure adjusted for ownership of assets.

harmonisation   the process of bringing technical processes (e.g. product testing) or standards (e.g. food quality requirements, pollution residues etc.) into uniformity or close consistency between countries.

imperfect competition   breaches of multi-firm, price-competitive conditions through monopoly, limited numbers of firms, collusive activities or the like.

increasing returns (to scale)   a more-than-proportionate rise in output for any given increase in all inputs, as opposed to 'constant returns' which entail only proportionate rises; natural or engineering factors determine the relative proportions involved, and the degree of returns assumed can greatly influence the results of econometric modelling (q.v.).

intra-industry trade   trading between countries within product categories (e.g. manufactures for manufactures, cars for cars, etc.) rather than the traditional inter-industry trade (e.g. cars for pineapples).

Keiretsu   a Japanese term and concept for a cartel-like system of closely linked companies, sometimes also referring to links with government.

learning-by-doing   the 'learning curve' effect of gradual improvements in knowledge and familiarity with production processes, which results in unit costs declining with cumulative national output over time, not just with plant production levels as in the case of economies of scale (q.v.).

level playing field   the Free Traders' ideal state in which there are no policy impediments to international trade, including no taxes or other domestic measures which would discriminate against foreigners or between countries, nor any differences in technical standards which are not justified by 'externalities' (q.v.).

liberalisation   the act of altering policies so that market forces, in any sectors, can operate freely, including tariff or quota cuts, de-regulation (q.v.), changes in administrative practices and so forth.

market access   the ability of firms to enter or sell to a country unimpeded by trade, regulatory or other barriers.

market failure   any deficiency in the market mechanism which results in an economy failing to reach optimal economic or social efficiency; this may arise from a range of factors including unequal income or wealth distribution, externalities (q.v.), imperfect competition (q.v.) and so forth.

most favoured nation   the principle that concessions within a trade agreement must be granted equally to all members.

multilateralism   relations and agreements between, or rules pertaining to, all or many countries jointly.

National Treatment   the principle that a country must treat foreign firms in the same way as domestic firms with regard to all trade, investment or regulatory matters so as to ensure equal market access (q.v.).

negative listing   a system used for structuring liberalisation commitments —tariff cuts or market access concessions for instance—entailing application of commitments to all sectors unless specifically scheduled for exemption, and automatically covering new products or services.

neo-classical economies   the predominant present-day framework of economic theory which asserts that the principle of 'marginality' operating through free markets can (with a few exceptional cases such as market failure, q.v.) produce 'optimal' economic states—i.e. maximise individual welfare.

non-governmental organisations   independent social organisations, usually referring to oppositional, activist groups ranging from 'grassroots' local welfare lobbyists to Greenpeace or Oxfam.

non-tariff barriers (NTBs)   impediments to trade deriving from a range of indirect, often invisible, technical, administrative or organisational processes other than conventional tariffs, quotas or subsidies (see Chapter 3).

positive listing   the obverse of negative listing (q.v.) which entails liberalisation commitments only for those sectors specifically scheduled for the purpose; Free Traders prefer negative listing as more likely to 'lock-in' widely-applicable liberalisation.

protection   the use of policy devices to shelter domestic industries from the full effects of international competition; usually applied to directly protective measures such as tariffs, quotas, subsidies or NTBs, but some now use the term for any measures which affect trade.

rules of origin   provisions within RTAs or other preferential systems as to what percentage of product content must originate within the system, e.g. to qualify for NAFTA concessions most products require 50 per cent North American-made content.

safeguards   escape clauses usually included in trade agreements for temporary exemption from certain provisions, most commonly allowing temporary tariff increases for purposes of trade balance or industry relief.

Section 301   the section of the United States 1974 Trade Act which permits investigation of, or retaliation against, countries whose practices are deemed to be against US commercial interests or otherwise 'unfair'; for convenience the term will also encompass Special 301 and Super 301 (q.v.).

social dumping   the concept that some countries may export goods at prices which do not fully reflect social costs or 'externalities' (q.v.) such as labour exploitation, environmental damage, deprivation of human rights or the like.

Special 301   the section of the United States 1988 Omnibus Trade and Competitiveness Act which operates similarly to Section 301 of the Trade Act (q.v.), but in relation to alleged breaches of intellectual property rights by other countries. **Super 301** is that section of the same Act which permits action against countries for a wide range of practices which allegedly impede US exports.

terms of trade   the ratio of a country's export prices to its import prices and is, thus, a crucial influence on its trade balance.

Third World   the group of less industrially developed nations which constitute most of the world's states. Less often used, but employed in this book, the term First World applies to industrially developed nations, most of whom belong to the OECD, and Second World refers to ex-Soviet bloc countries, though some now belong to the OECD. The Uruguay Round uses a distinction between developed, 'less developed' and 'least developed' countries based on various UN criteria of development, and 'transitional economies' for the Second World.

trade intervention   a term I use roughly synonymously with 'protection' (q.v.) but covering a wider range of measures than the latter term traditionally entails. When I advocate trade intervention my preference is for a planned, systematic network of policies, including domestic measures with trade implications such as industry policy, rather than just *ad hoc* protective devices.

trade-related environmental measures (TREMs)   domestic environmental policies with trade implications.

trade-related intellectual property rights (TRIPs)   private rights to the benefits of intellectual property such as copyrights, patents and so forth (Chapter 9); 'trade-related' appears to designate no more than operation of these rights at the international level.

trade-related investment measures (TRIMs)   policy measures used by a country to control or place conditions upon the activities of foreign investors within that country.

unilateral   action by one country alone.

unilateral benefit   my term for the notion, integral to orthodox Free Trade theory, that a country can obtain gains from trade by reducing or eliminating its own protection irrespective of other countries' protection levels.

unit cost gaps   a term I use for differences in costs per unit of output which arise between countries for institutional reasons, and which may persist even where technological and productivity levels of those countries are similar.

voluntary export restraints (VERs)   a form of protection (q.v.) in which the protecting country inveigles an exporting country to 'voluntarily' limit its exports of a particular item, usually backed by implied threats of formal protection. The best-known case was that of the multi-fibre arrangements (MFA) in textiles (see Chapter 3).

Notes

Part One: Introduction
1 *GATT Focus*, 107, May 1994.

1   The Spirit of the Age?
1 See Bhagwati (1989 and 1994); also Chapter 12.
2 *News of the Uruguay Round*, GATT, Geneva, 31 August and 6 September 1993.
3 J. Nieuwenhuysen (ed.), *Towards Freer Trade Between Nations*, Oxford University Press, Melbourne, 1989.
4 M. Anderson and R. Blandy, 'Academic Economics on Trial', *Australian Quarterly*, Autumn, 1993: Tables 1 and 2.
5 The literature on globalisation is extensive and complex, but for some introductory general and sociological overviews see: A. Giddens, *The Consequences of Modernity*, Polity, Cambridge, 1990; R. Robertson, *Globalization*, Sage, London, 1992; P. Beyer, *Religion and Globalization*, Sage, London, 1994; B. Axford, *The Global System*, Polity, Cambridge, 1995; M. Waters, *Globalization*, Routledge, London, 1995; T. Spyby, *Globalization and World Society*, Polity, Cambridge, 1996; Hirst and Thompson (1996). More economically-related material is cited throughout the book and further general references are provided in Chapter 11.
6 For a much-quoted, though rather meagre, encapsulation of this view, see Paul Kelly, *The End of Certainty*, Allen and Unwin, Sydney, 1992: Introduction.

2   How We Got GATT
1 On such issues, see B. M. Fagan, *People of the Earth*, Scott Foresman, Illinois, 1989, esp. pp. 383ff. and p. 408; Norberg-Hodge (1992).
2 G. Meier, *Problems of World Trade Policy*, Oxford University Press, New York, 1973: 3. D. Lal, *Poverty of Development Economics*, London, 1983: 33.

3   The above account is based variously on Wilcox (1949): esp. chs 2 and 3; Kuttner (1991); Ferguson and Rogers (1986); Schor in Epstein et al. (1993) and other general histories.

4   'Havana Charter for an International Trade Organization' in *United Nations Conference on Trade and Employment: Final Act and Related Documents*, UN, Havana, March 1948. The conference began on 21 November 1947 and concluded with the signing of the Charter on 24 March 1948. Australia's signatory was H. C. Coombs. On pre-conference politics and related issues see Wilcox (1949); J. Spero, *The Politics of International Economic Relations*, Allen and Unwin, 1985; Dryden (1995): ch. 1. For a brief outline of these and following issues, see Hans Singer in Griesgraber and Gunter (1996).

5   The following draws on GATT, *What it is, What it Does*, GATT, Geneva, 1991 and other GATT publications; also see Trebilcock and Howse (1995): ch. 2. Textual references are to *The General Agreement on Trade and Tariffs*, Geneva, 1986.

6   The 'grandfather' clause was Article 1b of the *Protocol of Provisional Application*, an appendix to GATT47. This clause was abolished by the *Agreement Establishing the World Trade Organization*, Annex 1A 1(b)ii. Article 3(a) of the same Annex effectively reprieves the US Jones Act, which confines coastal shipping to national lines, so long as that measure is not made more protective.

7   *Understanding in Respect of Waivers of Obligations Under the General Agreement on Tariffs and Trade 1994*, which is contained in Annex 1A of the *WTO Agreement*.

8   *WTO Focus*, 1, January–February 1995: 4–5 and 11, June–July 1996, 16.

3   The Fall and Rise of GATT

1   These and some following cases are mainly from J. Woronoff, *World Trade War*, Lotus, Tokyo, 1983; Waldman (1986); C. Prestowitz, *Trading Places*, Basic Books, New York, 1988; Christelow in King (1990); Oppenheim (1992).

2   S. Maswood, *Japan and Protection*, Routledge, London, 1989; Ries (1990); Kuttner (1991): ch. 5; Oppenheim (1992); Miyashita and Russell (1994).

3   Industry Commission, *Annual Report*, various years; *Trade Policy Review: Australia*, GATT, Geneva, various years; A. Woodland, 'Trade Policy in Australia' in D. Salvatore (ed.), *National Trade Policies*, Greenwood Press, New York, 1992; Bell (1993). Also see Chapter 12.

4   N. Fieleke, *The International Economy Under Stress*, Ballinger, Cambridge Mass, 1988: ch. 2; Grilli (1991); Choate and Linder in Prestowitz (1991).

5   Leutwiler Report (1987); C. Prestowitz et al., 'The Last Gasp of GATTism', *Harvard Business Review*, March/April 1991; Destler (1992); V. Curzon Price, 'The Decay of GATT', in R. Morgan et al. (eds), *New Diplomacy in the Post-Cold War World*, St Martin's Press, New York, 1993.

6   See Hudec in Bhagwati (1990) and Dornbusch in Lawrence and Schultze (1990). On this issue generally, see Bhagwati (1990), especially Helen Milner's article; J. Bhagwati, *The World Trading System at Risk*, Harvester Wheatsheaf, New York, 1991, esp. Appendix IV; USTR, various years.

⁷ Lake (1988); Destler (1992): 174ff.; D. Verdier, *Democracy and International Trade*, Princeton University Press, Princeton, 1994; C. Doran and G. Marchildon, *The NAFTA Puzzle*, Westview Press Boulder (1994).

⁸ Ferguson and Rogers (1986); Mishel and Teixeira (1993).

⁹ The Cairns Group was named after the Queensland town where it first met in 1986. Its members are Argentina, Australia, Brazil, Canada, Chile, Colombo, Fiji, Hungary, Indonesia, Malaysia, the Philippines, New Zealand, Thailand and Uruguay—see DFAT (1994a): 10–11.

¹⁰ For an outline of the events and procedures, see Oxley (1990), Leutwiler Report (1987) and the WTO's official history of the Round—Croome (1995). On Sutherland: Dryden (1995): 389; Croome (1995): ch. 9; *The European*, 8–14 February, 1996: 22.

¹¹ On such issues see C. Hamilton and J. Whalley, 'Coalitions in the Uruguay Round', *Weltwirtschaftliches Archiv* 125, No. 3, 1989. On Blair House: EC *Background*, various issues; Croome (1995): 340ff. G7 Summit: *The Age*, 8 July 1993; Croome (1995): 347ff.

¹² On ratification world-wide, *ICDA* No. 17, November 1994–February 1995; *WTO Focus*, 1, January–February 1995.

4 Towards a GATT-fearing World

¹ The official title of the Uruguay Round Agreement is: *Final Act Embodying the Results of the Uruguay Round of Multilateral Trade Negotiations*, GATT Secretariat, Geneva, 30 March 1994. I will hereinafter refer to the document as *Final Act* and citations will be from this edition unless otherwise specified. The following account of the Round also draws on DFAT (1994 a–d); GAO (1994); UNCTAD (1994b), Croome (1995), Trebilcock and Howse (1995), Cline (1995) and various GATT documents.

² The time limits contained in Article 31 apply to actionable subsidies which 'seriously prejudice' competitors (Article 6.1) and to all non-actionable or 'green light' subsidies (Articles 8 and 9).

³ D. Feaver and K. Wilson, *Material Injury Determination Under Australia's Countervailing and Anti-Dumping Law*, Working Paper No. 6, Department of Applied Economics, Victoria University of Technology, Melbourne, June 1995; 'An Evaluation of Australia's Anti-Dumping and Countervailing Law and Policy', *Journal of World Trade*, 29/5, October 1995.

⁴ G. Horlick, 'How the GATT Became Protectionist', *Journal of World Trade*, 27/5, October 1993; UNCTAD (1994b): ch. 3; M. Leidy, 'Antidumping: Unfair Trade or Unfair Remedy?', *Finance and Development*, March 1995: 27–9; Cline (1995): 8–9; Finger (1995).

⁵ See Trebilcock and Howse (1995): ch. 7; Cline (1995): 9–11; GAO (1994): 68ff.; G. Holliday, 'The Uruguay Round's Agreement on Safeguards', *Journal of World Trade*, 29/3, June 1995.

⁶ This account has drawn on D. Greenaway, 'Trade Related Investment Measures: Political Economy Aspects and Issues for GATT', *The World Economy*, 13, 1990;

McCulloch (1990); GAO (1994): 119ff.; Evans (1994); UNCTAD (1994b); Croome (1995): 138ff. and 256ff.
7 Miscellaneous Provisions Nos 3 and 4, *Final Act*: 18.
8 Atlas Air Australia Pty Ltd vs. Anti-Dumping Authority, (1990–91) 99 ALR 29. Minister for Immigration and Ethnic Affairs vs. Teoh (1995) 128 ALR 353. For a discussion of these issues, see Alston and Chiam (1995).
9 See, for example, P. P. McGuinness, 'Out to Curb the Monster Makers', *The Age*, 4 May 1996: A25.
10 Quoted by Tim Colebatch in *The Age*, 13 October 1994.

5   There Goes the Neighbourhood!

1 GATT Council, *Overview of Developments in International Trade and the Trading System*, GATT, Geneva, 5 December 1994; Sutherland (1994a, 1994b): 3; WTO (1995a): Appendix, Table 1. On the new committee: *WTO Focus*, no. 8, January–February 1996: 4.
2 On such issues see Jovanović (1992); Anderson (1993), R. Snape et al. *Regional Trade Arrangements*, AGPS, Canberra, 1993; EPAC (1995), Garnaut and Drysdale (1994); Panic (1995); C. Shiells, 'Regional Blocs: Trade Creating or Diverting?', *Finance and Development*, March 1995.
3 T. Georgakopoulos et al. (eds), *Economic Integration Between Unequal Partners*, Edward Elgar, Aldershot, 1994; Helleiner in Grinspun and Cameron (1993).
4 For background and details of ANZCERTA, see I. McLean, 'Trans-Tasman Trade Relations: Decline and Rise' in R. Pomfret (ed.), *Australia's Trade Policies*, Oxford University Press, Melbourne, 1995; P. J. Lloyd, 'The Future of the CER Agreement' in Garnaut and Drysdale (1994). The official documents are entitled *Australia–New Zealand Closer Economic Relations Trade Agreement (CER) and Amending Documents*, Department of Foreign Affairs and Trade, Canberra, March 1992.
5 The BIE's 1989 welfare estimates were A$649m for Australia and A$1117m for New Zealand over an unspecified period based on 1983–84 data. I have estimated the percentages based on 1983–84 current price GDP for both countries and the mid-1984 exchange rate. The two BIE studies are: *Trade Liberalisation and Australian Manufacturing*, AGPS, Canberra, 1989 and *Impact of the CER Agreement*, AGPS, Canberra, September 1995 (esp. Table 5.8 for a summary of impacts). On intra-industry trade and related matters, see J. Menon, 'Trade Liberalisation, Closer Economic Relations and Intra-Industry Specialisation', *Australian Economic Review*, 2, 1994 and J. Menon and P. Dixon, *How Important is Intra-Industry Trade in Trade Growth*, Centre of Policy Studies, Monash University, Melbourne, 1994.
6 See references in n. 4; AFR, 28 September 1995: 36.
7 Pacific Business Forum, *A Business Blueprint for APEC: Strategies for Growth and Common Prosperity*, APEC, Singapore, October 1994; Eminent Persons Group, *Achieving the APEC Vision*, APEC, Singapore, August 1994. Australia's delegates

to the Forum are Imelda Roche from Nutri-Metics and Philip Brass from Pacific Dunlop, while our delegate to the EPG is former NSW Premier Neville Wran.

8 *APEC Economic Leaders' Declaration of Common Resolve*, Bogor, Indonesia, 15 November 1994; *Asia–Pacific Economic Co-operation Briefing Notes*, DFAT, Canberra, December 1994.

9 Eg. various statements by Hawke and Keating—*The Age*, 6 July 1994: 1 and 11 October 1994: 6. On US views: *The Australian*, 7 May 1993: 8; *The Age*, 7 July 1994: 9 and 3 April 1995: 8.

10 J. Maggs in *The Australian*, 28 October 1994: 7; D. Sanger in *The New York Times*, 2 May 1994.

11 Grennan (1996); Colebatch in *The Age*, 7 August 1996: C3; Skelton in *The Age*, 10 and 15 August 1996: B1.

12 *The Australian*, 15 November 1994; M. Daly and M. Logan, *The Brittle Rim*, Penguin, Melbourne, 1989; R. Manning and P. Stern, 'The Myth of the Pacific Community', *Foreign Affairs*, November/December 1994; V. Clad, *Behind the Myth*, Grafton Books, London, 1991; Thurow (1996): 124–5. Hughes, *The Age*, 30 August 1994: 8.

13 Bello and Rosenfeld (1990); J. Atkinson, *APEC—Winners and Losers*, ACFOA and CAA, Melbourne, 1995; *The New Internationalist*, No. 263, January 1995; also see Chapter 12.

14 ABC Radio National, *PM*, 11 April 1996.

15 The following account draws extensively on the official document, *The NAFTA*, US Government Printing Office, Washington DC, 1993, esp. vol. 1; GAO (1993); J. Holbein and D. Musch, *NAFTA*, Oceana Publications, New York, 1994.

16 P. Clark, 'US Trade Strategy Favours Latin America', *Age*, 7 July 1994: 9; GAO (1993): ch. 1.

17 On Free Trader views, see G. Hufbauer and J. Schott, *NAFTA: An Assessment*, Institute for International Economics, Washington DC, 1992. Critiques: D. Cameron (ed.), *The Free Trade Deal*, Lorimer, Toronto, 1988; Grinspun and Cameron (1993); Browne (1994); Cohen (1994); B. Coote, *NAFTA, Poverty and Free Trade in Mexico*, Oxfam, London, 1995.

18 *The European*, 22–28 February 1996: 2.

19 *The European*, 28 March–3 April 1996: 20; B. Eichengreen, 'European Monetary Union', *Journal of Economic Literature*, September 1993. The requirements for joining the single currency are an inflation rate no more than 2 per cent above the average of the three lowest-inflation members, a budget deficit not exceeding 3 per cent of GDP and a public debt not exceeding 60 per cent of GDP. In general, see Hama (1996).

20 *The European*, 22–28 February 1996: 1 and 14–20 March 1996: 2.

21 Horsman and Marshall (1994): ch. 4; *The European*, 2–8 November 1995: 1; 15–21 August 1996: 9.

22 See, for example, Brok in *The European*, 19–25 October 1995: 9; McAlpine in *The European*, 21–27 March 1996: 11 and V. Smart, 'European Union Loses its Appeal', *The European*, 3–9 August 1995.

[23] For examples and analysis, see DFAT, *Growth Triangles of South East Asia*, AGPS, Canberra, 1995.

[24] On such issues see: Trebilcock and Howse (1995): ch. 4; Panic (1995); Cooper (1994); Oxley (1994); articles by Bhagwati and others in Garnaut and Drysdale (1994), Part 3.

Part Two: Introduction

[1] For a brief account see Brecher and Costello (1994): Chapter 5.

[2] *Alternative Treaty on Trade and Sustainable Development*, NGOs International Forum, Rio de Janeiro, 9 June 1992. An early NGO statement on the Uruguay Round followed a June 1990 meeting at The Hague—see 'The Uruguay Round: Third World Sovereignty, Environmental Concerns and Intellectual Property', *Third World Economics*, 16 December–15 January 1991: 26–30.

[3] For an overview of concerns amongst such groups and individuals, see Nader et al. (1993) and Cavanagh et al. (1992). Early Canadian critiques of free trade include Cameron (1988) and E. Finn et al. (eds), *The Facts on Free Trade*, James Lorimer, Toronto, 1988. Action Canada issues a series called *ACN Dossier*, The Canadian Environmental Law Association issues *NAFTA Facts* and the Ecumenical Coalition for Economic Justice issues *Economic Justice Report* which covers many trade and NAFTA questions.

[4] Lang and Hines (1993); M. Khor in *Third World Resurgence*, No. 39, November 1993; Browne (1994); NGO Forum (1994); Shukla (1995); V. Shiva, 'The Effects of WTO on Women's Rights', *Third World Resurgence*, No. 61/2, 1995. India: PIRG 1993; New Zealand: Kelsey 1995: 104.

[5] For an early Canadian report in this vein, see Bob Davis, 'US Grassroots Coalition Unites Against NAFTA', *Globe and Mail* (Toronto), 26 December 1992.

[6] A Gallup Poll of 11 May 1992, cited in B. Campbell, *We Need Free Trade Abrogation to Rebuild the Nation*, Canadian Centre for Policy Alternatives, Ottawa, June 1992.

[7] Unless otherwise indicated, the following results are from *Eurobarometer* (1994).

[8] *The European*, 7–13 July, 31 August–6 September 1995; 2–8 May and 18–24 July 1996.

6   Doctrine and Heresy

[1] P. Sutherland, 'GATT Equals Growth', *News of the Uruguay Round*, GATT, Geneva, 31 August 1993.

[2] On mercantilism generally see W. Allen, 'Mercantilism' in J. Eatwell et al. (eds) *The New Palgrave*, Macmillan, London, 1987: vol. 3; Rima (1993); Hudson (1992).

[3] I. Kravis, 'Trade as a Handmaiden of Growth', *Economic Journal*, December 1970; E. J. Hobsbawn, *The Age of Capital*, Abacus, London, 1977: 53; Jung and Marshall (1985).

[4] R. Brecher, 'Minimum Wage Rents and the Pure Theory of International Trade', *Quarterly Journal of Economics*, 88, 1974.

[5] J. Eaton and G. Grossman, 'Tariffs as Insurance', *Canadian Journal of Economics*, 18, 1985.

[6] J. Markusen and J. Melvin, 'Trade, Factor Prices, and the Gains from Trade with Increasing Returns', *Canadian Journal of Economics*, August 1981.

[7] For various versions of this sort of argument, see: E. Hagen, 'An Economic Justification of Protectionism', *Quarterly Journal of Economics*, November 1958; S. Matusz, 'International Trade Policy in a Model of Unemployment and Wage Differentials', *Canadian Journal of Economics*, XXVII, 4, November 1994; J. Bulow and L. Summers, 'A Theory of Dual Labor Markets', *Journal of Labour Economics*, 4/3, 1986.

[8] Keynes put this position in his 1931 *Essays in Persuasion*, in Keynes (1932), in his addendum to the Report of the Macmillan Committee of 1935 and sketchily in the *General Theory*. Kaldor's views are contained in Kaldor (1964, 1980 and 1983); 'The Nemesis of Free Trade', *The Spectator*, 27 August 1977. Also see Robinson (1960); Kindleberger (1987): 126–7; Dunkley (1995).

[9] M. Kitson and S. Solomou, *Protectionism and Economic Revival*, Cambridge University Press, Cambridge, 1990 and sources cited there; K. Kennedy et al., *The Economic Development of Ireland in the Twentieth Century*, Routledge, London, 1988: ch. 2; studies by Eichengreen and Foreman-Peck cited in Ford and Sen (1985): 220; T. Rooth, *British Protectionism and the International Economy*, Cambridge University Press, Cambridge, 1993.

[10] Kaldor (1964, 1980 and 1983: ch. 18); Culbertson (1984, 1986).

[11] Culbertson (1984 and 1986); Michalet (1987); Daly and Cobb (1989): ch. 11; Daly and Goodland (1993); Toohey (1994): 184.

[12] Edwards (1985); Madeley (1992). For evidence on the severe decline in terms of trade for commodity exporters since see Spraos (1983); A. Maizels, 'The Continuing Commodity Crisis of Developing Countries', *World Development*, 22/11, 1994.

[13] P. Krugman, *Rethinking International Trade*, MIT Press, Cambridge Mass, 1990: ch. 6; R. Lucas, 'On the Mechanics of Economic Development', *Journal of Monetary Economics*, 22, 1988; R. Solow 'Growth Theory', in D. Greenaway et al. (eds), *Companion to Contemporary Economic Thought*, Routledge, London, 1991; J. Eaton and H. Kierzkowski, 'Oligopolistic Competition, Product Variety and International Trade', in Kierzkowski (1984); Griffin and Kahn (1992). In general see Ropke (1994); T. Georgokopoulos et al. (eds), *Economic Integration Between Unequal Partners*, Edward Elgar, Aldershot, 1994. Non-mainstream versions: Spraos (1983); Edwards (1985); Thirlwall, Gibson in P. Arestis and M. Sawyer (eds), *The Elgar Companion to Radical Political Economy*, Edward Elgar, Aldershot, 1994.

[14] B. Elbaum and W. Lazonick (eds), *The Decline of the British Economy*, Clarendon Press, Oxford, 1982; B. Elbaum, 'Cumulative or Comparative Advantage? British Competitiveness in the Early 20th Century', *World Development*, 18/9, 1990; W. Lazonick, *Business Organization and the Myth of the Market Economy*, Cambridge University Press, Cambridge, 1991.

[15] For general or slightly sympathetic studies: Kierzkowski (1984); A. Venables and A. Smith, 'Trade and Industry Policy under Imperfect Competition', *Economic Policy*, 3, October 1986; Fagerberg (1988); Krugman (1986 and 1990); D. Laussel and C. Montet, 'Strategic Trade Policies', D. Greenaway and L. Winters (eds), *Surveys in International Trade*, Blackwell Oxford, 1994; Krugman and Obstfeld (1994: ch. 12).
For advocacy of 'new international', strategic or related policies: Pearce and Sutton (1985); some contributors to Krugman (1986); Kuttner (1989 and 1991); Scott in King (1990); Prestowitz (1991); Hamilton (1991): ch. 15; Thurow (1992); R. Scott, 'Flat Earth Economics', *Challenge*, September–October 1993; Dore (1993)—also see Chapter 12. Critiques: Waldman (1986); Bhagwati (1989); R. Pomfret, 'The New Trade Theorics', *The World Economy*, 14/3, September 1991; M. Corden, *Strategic Trade and Industrial Policy*, Centre for Economic Policy Research, ANU, Canberra, January 1996.

[16] Porter (1990); M. Porter and C. van der Linde, 'Toward a New Conception of the Environment-Competitiveness Relationship', *Journal of Economic Perspectives*, Fall, 1995.

[17] E. Jones in *AFR*, 1 August 1990; S. Turnbull, Letter to *AFR*, 1 August 1990; Yetton et al. in Marsh (1994). Also see Chapter 12.

[18] Krugman (1987, 1990, 1991: 111 and 1994) and 'Does the New Trade Theory Require a New Trade Policy?', *The World Economy* 15/4, July 1992; Krugman and Obstfeld (1994): chs 9–12.

[19] See J. Bhagwati, *Trade Tariffs and Growth*, Weidenfeld and Nicholson, London, 1969: ch. 5; Bhagwati and Srinivasan (1969); Corden (1974).

[20] Daly and Cobb (1989): Appendix, Table A.1, Column Y, pp. 418–19; Dunkley (1992): 46–51 and sources cited there.

[21] UNDP (1996) cited in Keegan (1996).

7   The Best Thing since Sliced Bread?

[1] Address to the Summit Conference for the Middle East and North Africa, Casablanca, 1994; *GATT/WTO News*, Geneva, 31 October 1994; *WTO Press Release*, 31 March 1995; Sutherland (1994a).

[2] Discussions with the author, November 1993; *The Uruguay Round: Outcomes for Australia*, DFAT, Canberra, 15 December 1993. Global figures: GATT (1994).

[3] G. Ohlin, 'Trade in a Non-Laissez-Faire World', in P. Samuelson (ed.) *International Economic Relations*, Macmillan, New York, 1969.

[4] E.g. by *IC* (1994): 238; Nguyen (1993); Murtough (1994a and b); Abayasiri-Silva and Horridge (1996).

[5] *IC* (1994): 238. The IC's definition of national income is nett factor income plus indirect taxes plus nett overseas interest income, so is a large negative figure because of our huge overseas debt, see *The SALTER Model of the World Economy*, IC, Canberra, April 1994: Box 1–8, p. 26.

[6] Deardorff (1994); Thurow 1996: 132; J. Francois et al., *Assessing the Uruguay Round*, World Bank Conference Paper, 26–27 January 1995: Table 9.

[7] T. Hertel et al., *Liberalising Manufactures Trade in a Changing World Economy*, World Bank Conference Paper, 26–27 January 1995; AFR, 7 April 1995; Nguyen (1993).

[8] *Benefits from GATT's Uruguay Round for the American Economy*, US Treasury, Washington DC, 24 September 1994; Ralph Nader, *How Treasury Created $200 billion in GATT GDP Gains*, GATT Project, 1994.

[9] The projection assumes removal of all tariffs and NTBs in all sectors other than services (Goldin et al., 1993: 83–5).

[10] *The Dynamic Effects of Trade Liberalisation: A Survey*, US International Trade Commission, Washington DC, February 1993; USITC (1994). Baldwin's estimates are explained and some sceptical views put forward in Baldwin (1989).

[11] M. Emerson et al., *The Economics of 1992*, Oxford University Press, Oxford, 1988; Baldwin (1989); D. Neven, 'EEC Integration Towards 1992', *Economic Policy*, 10, April 1990; Jovanović (1992), ch. 5.

[12] Dee and Welsh (1994) and summarised in BIE (1995): 63ff. Also see Chapter 8.

[13] Sources: as for Table 2; also, Wilkinson in Panic (1995).

[14] See Lau Kin Chi, 'Reform and Resistance in China', *Asian Exchange*, 10/1, 1994 and sources cited there.

[15] Richardson (1989): 14; Stanford (1993); Thea Lea, 'Comment', in Collins and Bosworth, (1994): 30; Abayasiri-Silva and Horridge (1996).

[16] Quiggin (1993); Toohey (1994): ch. 9; Abayasiri-Silva and Horridge (1996). I am indebted to Jay Menon for helpful discussions on these matters. The global adaptation of the ORANI model known as the SALTER model is now used as the basis of much trade modelling (IC, 1994).

[17] S. Page et al., *The GATT Uruguay Round: Effects on Developing Countries*, Overseas Development Institute, London, 1992; ICDA Update, No. 18, 1995: 6; *Impact of the Uruguay Round on Agriculture*, FAO, Rome, 1995.

[18] Koechlin and Larudee (1992) and more generally, Faux (1993).

[19] R. Blecker, T. Lee and R. Scott, *Trade Protection and Industrial Revitalisation: American Steel in the 1980s*, Economic Policy Institute, Washington, 1993.

[20] See, for instance, J. Menon and P. Dixon, *How Important is Intra-Industry Trade in Trade Growth?*, COPS, Monash University, Melbourne, 1994, and *ANZCERTA and Intra-Industry Trade*, COPS, Monash University, Melbourne, August 1994.

[21] Dunkley (1992): 41ff. and sources cited there; C. Paepke, *The Evolution of Progress*, Random House, New York, 1993; ILO (1995): 167; J. Gimpel, *The End of the Future*, Adamantine Press, London, 1995.

[22] B. Head, 'IT Chiefs Don Their Hair Shirts', AFR, 7 August 1995: 33; G. Phillips, 'When Software is not Tough Enough', *The Sunday Age*, 7 January 1996: 3; S. Collins, 'Do Deadly Errors Lurk in Unproven Software?', *The European*, 25–31 January 1996: 19.

[23] See Krugman and Obstfeld (1994): 54; B. Södersten, *International Economies*, Macmillan, London, 2nd edn, 1980: 21–2.

[24] R. Myer, 'Why the Top Few Earn Big Dollars', *The Sunday Age*, 26 March 1995.

[25] F. Bourguignon et al., 'Poverty and Income Distribution During Adjustment', *World Development*, 19, 1991; also see Chapter 8.

8   Structural Change for Whom?

[1] I am grateful to Brian Brogan for this choice report.

[2] R. Baldwin and J. Mutti, 'Policy Issues in Adjustment Assistance: The United States' in H. Hughes (ed.), *Prospects for Partnership*, Johns Hopkins, Baltimore, 1973; M. Bale, 'Estimates of Trade-Displacement Costs for US Workers', *Journal of International Economics*, 6, 1976.

[3] Naudin in *The European*, 11–17 November 1994; Tagliabue in *The Age*, 21 June 1996: B1; Maiden (1996). Other general data are from OECD, *Employment Outlook* (various issues).

[4] Arlene Cullen, in *The Sunday Age*, 6 November 1994: 16; *Australian*, 6 April 1994: 5; Spindler Report (1993): esp. 15 and 25.

[5] L. Rodwin and H. Sazarami (eds), *Reindustrialization and Regional Economic Transformation*, Unwin Hyman, Boston, 1989; P. Kresl, *The Urban Economy and Regional Trade Liberalisation*, Praeger, New York, 1992. On Australian regional issues, Spindler Report (1993): 15–16 and 39–42.

[6] E. Garnsey and L. Paukert, *Industrial Change and Women's Employment*, Institute for Labour Studies, Geneva, 1987; Ward (1990); K. Ram, *Contending Discourses, Conflicting Methodologies: Choices for NGO Groups*, Australian Council for Overseas Aid, Canberra, 5 November 1993; C. Otto, 'Does Free Trade Free Women?', *ICDA Journal*, 2/1, 1995; G. Moon, *Free Trade: What's in it for Women?*, CAA, Melbourne, 1995; *Women in a Changing Global Economy*, UN, New York, 1995.

[7] M. Cohen, *Free Trade and the Future of Women's Work*, Garamond, Toronto, 1987. *The North American Free Trade Agreement: Implications for Women*, Ontario Women's Directorate, Toronto, 1993; 'Women Bear the Brunt of Economic Restructuring', *Economic Justice Report*, Ecumenical Coalition for Economic Justice, Toronto, 111/4, December 1992; IPS (1996): 6–7. Australia: Fagan and Webber (1994): 84–5.

[8] *Women: Looking Beyond 2000* and *World's Women 1995: Trends and Statistics*, UN, New York, 1995.

[9] Richardson (1989): 15; Ocampo in Agosin and Tussie (1993: 128). On Australia: P. Brain, 'Employment, Trade and an Export-Oriented Manufacturing Sector', in *Trade: To Whose Advantage?*, ANU, Canberra, 1980; K. Davidson, 'Toss-up of Models in the Tariff Protection Policy', *The Age*, 14 November 1992: 29; J. Quiggin, 'Tariff Misunderstandings', AFR, 22 June 1994: 19.

[10] *Age*, 15 May 1991: 16; AFR, 28 September 1995: 10.

[11] United Electrical, Radio and Machine Workers of America (UE), *NAFTA Workers Rights*, Pittsburgh, 1994 and *Testimony Before the US National Administrative Office*, 12 September 1994; UE-FAT Strategic Organising Alliance, *Chronology of Worker Rights Violations*, 1994; Cavanagh et al. (1992); *Guardian Weekly*, 15 October 1995: 4; Browne (1994).

[12] Stanford et al. (1993): 11–13 and Table 3.4, p. 17. Social spending relative to GDP (late 1980s)—US 7.7 per cent, Brazil 6.9 per cent, Korea 6.7 per cent, Mexico 3 per cent, Indonesia 0.3 per cent (Mead, 1990: Table 15, p. 23). Capital shifts and related: Campbell (1993); Stanford et al. (1993): 26; Anderson (1993).

[13] C. Pierson, *Beyond the Welfare State*, Polity, Cambridge, 1991; A. Pfaller et al., *Can the Welfare State Compete?*, Macmillan, London, 1991; Clark et al. (1991); UNCTAD (1994a); G. Garrett and D. Mitchell, *Globalization and the Welfare State*, Centre for Economic Policy Research, Australian National University, Discussion Paper No. 330, July 1995. Canada: CLC (1993): 19; ACN (1994): 4.

[14] M. Beenstock, *The World Economy in Transition*, Allen and Unwin, London, 1983; Culbertson (1984, 1986); Gray (1985); T. Burchill, 'Global Pressure Will End Wage Fixing: Banker', *Sunday Age*, 14 November 1993.

[15] On mainstream views see J. Bhagwati and M. Kosters (eds), *Trade and Wages: Levelling Wages Down?* AEI Press, Washington, 1994: J. Bergstrand et al. (eds), *The Changing Distribution of Income in an Open US Economy*, North-Holland, Amsterdam, 1994; J. D. Richardson, 'Income Inequality and Trade', *Journal of Economic Perspectives*, 9/3, Summer 1995; R. Freeman, 'Are Your Wages Set in Beijing', *Journal of Economic Perspectives*, 9/3, Summer 1995; *The Employment Crisis in Industrial Countries*, World Bank, Washington, August 1995. Advocates of the 'Third World competition' view include: A. Wood, *North-South Trade, Employment and Inequality*, Clarendon Press, Oxford, 1994 and 'How Trade Hurt Unskilled Workers', *Journal of Economic Perspectives*, 9/3, Summer 1995; E. Leamer, 'Wage Effects of a US-Mexican Free Trade Agreement' in P. Garber (ed.), *The Mexico-US Free Trade Agreement*, MIT Press, Cambridge Mass. 1993; G. Borjas and V. Ramey in Bergstrand op. cit.; L. Karoly and J. Klerman in Bergstrand, op. cit.; Hutton (1994); Thurow (1996): 66ff.; Hirst and Thompson (1996): 117–18. For an excellent overview: G. Burtless, 'International Trade and the Rise in Earnings Inequality', *Journal of Economic Literature*, June 1995.

[16] S. Cohen and J. Zysman, *Manufacturing Matters*, Basic Books, New York 1987; Kuttner (1991); Sassen (1991); Tyson (1993). Stewart (1994) on Australia.

[17] Goldin et al. (1993): 78–9; *The Age*, 16 December 1992; DFAT (1994a). On agricultural protection issues in general, D. Blandford, 'The Costs of Agricultural Protection and the Difference Free Trade Would Make' in F. Sanderson (ed.), *Agricultural Protection*, Resources for the Future, Washington, 1990.

[18] W. Berry, 'Conserving Communities', *Resurgence*, No. 170, May/June 1995: 6; Rifkin (1995): ch. 8. Australia: *The Age*, 4 July 1996: B3. New Zealand: Kelsey (1995): 95ff.

[19] Moore Lappé and Collins (1982): esp. 186–7; S. Sargent, *The Foodmakers*, Penguin, Melbourne, 1985. M. Ritchie (1992) and *Disappearance of Family Farm Agriculture in the US*, State of Minnesota, Department of Agriculture, November 1984; Thaman (1982); Bassand et al. (1986): 21; Daly and Cobb (1989): ch. 4; Winson (1993); D. Francis, *Family Agriculture*, Earthscan, London, 1994.

[20] W. Goldschmidt, *As You Sow*, Harcourt Brace, New York, 1947. Goldschmidt's research was terminated by an embarrassed Department of Agriculture, but his conclusion was confirmed by other investigations in the 1970s—W. Goldschmidt, 'Large-Scale Farming and the Rural Social Structure', *Rural Sociology*, 43, 3, 1978; Moore Lappé and Collins (1982): 187. On Canada: Winson (1993): ch. 6. On New Zealand: Kelsey (1995): 95ff.

[21] I am indebted to Pat Ranald for information on this point and to Hiro Take for information in relation to Japan.

[22] *Kairos*, 25 December–1 January 1995: 9.

[23] A survey by the research group Mintel, cited in D. Nicholson-Lord, 'No Room to Breathe', *Resurgence*, No. 167, November/December 1994.

[24] Ritchie in Nader (1993); A. Lipietz, *Towards a New Economic Order*, Polity, Cambridge, 1992: 137; N. Dudley, *The Soil Association Handbook*, Optima, London, 1991; NGO Forum (1994); H. Norberg-Hodge, 'From Catastrophe to Community', *Resurgence*, July–August 1995.

[25] E.g., see G. Andrae and B. Beckman, *The Wheat Trap*, Zed, London, 1985 (on Nigeria); S. de Vylder, *Agriculture in Chains*, Zed, London, 1982 (on Bangladesh); Moore Lappé and Collins (1982): Chapters 19 and 20; Thaman (1992). Biotechnology: *The Age*, 2 October 1996, p. A3; *Greenweek*, 22 March 1996.

[26] Dunkley (1993); *The Ecologist*, Special Issue, March–April, May–June 1995; B. Helgadottir in *The European*, 9–15 June 1995: 11.

9   At Whose Service?

[1] T. Noyelle and A. Dutka, *International Trade in Business Services*, Ballinger, Cambridge Mass, 1988; Sassen (1991); Porter (1990): ch. 6. Australia: A. Stoeckel and D. Quirke, *Services: Setting the Agenda for Reform*, Dept. of Industry Technology and Regional Development, January 1992.

[2] Article I; the titles of the modes are from the schedules and are not used in the GATS text.

[3] *Annex on Article II Exemptions*, paragraph 6; *Australia: Final List of Article II (MFN) Exemptions*, GATT, Geneva, 15 April 1994; Hoekman (1995b): 6–7.

[4] *Australia: Schedule of Specific Commitments*, GATT, Geneva, April 1994; for an outline—DFAT (1994c); sectors not listed: IC *Annual Report 1994–5*, Table G11: 231–2.

[5] AFR, 29 March, 11 April and 26 April 1996; *WTO Focus*, various issues.

[6] On some of the technical issues see Nayyar (1988); K. Tucker and M. Sundberg, *International Trade in Services*, Routledge, London, 1988; A. Sapir and C. Winter, 'Services Trade' in D. Greenaway and A. Winters (eds), *Surveys in International Trade*, Blackwell, Oxford, 1994.

[7] Justin Brown, Director of the Americas and European Division, DFAT, at the 21st International Trade Law Conference, Sydney, 17 October 1994. Also see Raghavan (1990): 108ff.

[8] J. Hills, *Deregulating Telecoms*, Quorum, Westport, 1986; Sussman and Lent (1991).

[9] D. Flint in AFR, 12 May 1994: 24; *The Law Report*, ABC Radio, 3RN, 22 August 1995.

[10] Madeley (1992): Chapter 5; T. Ewing, 'Bali High', *The Age*, 25 August 1995: 13; J. McCarthy, *Are Sweet Dreams Made of This?*, Indonesia Resources and Information Program, Melbourne, 1994.

[11] *The Age*, 12 and 13 May 1996.

¹² GATT (1993): 9; Clarke (1995); N. Jennings, 'Canadian Rock Explodes', *Macleans*, 27 March 1995: 40–2; more generally, *Vital Links* (1987). New Zealand: Kelsey (1995): 113 and 329ff.

¹³ *The European*, 15–21 and 22–28 February 1996. *The Age*, 16 February 1996: A11.

¹⁴ One group was the US-based International Intellectual Property Alliance which included computer hardware and software, film, publishing and recording companies—see their report: *Trade Losses Due to Piracy and Other Market Access Restrictions Affecting the US Copyright Industries*, Washington, April 1989. Another US group, the Intellectual Property Committee (IPC), consisted of 13 computer, communications, pharmaceutical and other TNCs such as IBM, Rockwell, Warner, Du Pont, General Motors and General Electric. A 1988 report by this group, in conjunction with EC and Japanese employer associations, was a crucial influence on the structure of the TRIPs Agreement—'Basic Framework of GATT Provisions on Intellectual Property', June 1988, reprinted in F. Beier and G. Schricker (eds), *GATT or WIPO*, Max Planck Institute, Munich, 1988.

¹⁵ A. Deardorff, 'Should Patent Protection be Extended to all Developing Countries?', *The World Economy*, 13, 1990; J. Beath, 'Innovation, Intellectual Property Rights and the Uruguay Round', *The World Economy*, 13, 1990; Braga (1995).

¹⁶ Markus and Konan quoted in Braga (1995): Table 2; more generally, K. Markus, 'Normative Concerns in the International Protection of Intellectual Property Rights', *The World Economy*, 13, 1990; UNCTAD (1994b): 196–7.

¹⁷ PIRG (1993): 29; US IPR specialist S. La Croix quoted in R. Umoren, 'Will TRIPs Benefit Developing Countries?', *Third World Network Features*, No. 1379, 1995.

¹⁸ J. Braithwaite, *Corporate Crime in the Pharmaceutical Industry*, Routledge and Kegan Paul, London, 1984.

¹⁹ R. Snider, *New Internationalist*, August 1993: 220–1; Braithwaite (1995): 116. Price differentials: B. Keayla, *Uruguay Round Final Act 1994—TRIPs Agreement*, Centre for Study of GATT Issues, New Delhi, 1994.

²⁰ V. Shiva in *Economic and Political Weekly*, 3 April 1993; V. Shiva and R. Holla-Bhar, 'Intellectual Piracy and the Neem Tree', *The Ecologist*, November–December 1993; M. Khor in *Third World Resurgence*, No. 39, November 1993; T. Hormeku-Ajei, 'Copyrighting Knowledge', *Panoscope*, 172, January 1994; F. Ringo, 'The Trade Related Aspects of Intellectual Property Rights', *Journal of World Trade*, 28(8), December 1994. Campaigns: *Third World Resurgence*, No. 63, 1995; *IFOAM Press Releases*, International Federation of Organic Agriculture Movements, Tholey-Theley, Germany, 1996.

²¹ C. Correa, 'Uruguay Round Talks on Patenting Lopsided against South', *Third World Network Features*, No. 1127, 1993.

10   Greening the GATT or GATTing the Green?

¹ *Trade and the Environment*, GATT, Geneva, 1 April 1993; *GATT Activities*, GATT, Geneva, various issues.

² *GATT Focus*, 12, November 1994; *WTO Focus*, 8, January–February 1996. Other cases: Trebilcock and Howse (1995): ch. 6.

[3] *United States—Restrictions on Imports of Tuna: Report of the Panel*, DS 21/R, GATT, Geneva, 3 September 1991. For commentaries: OTA (1992), Charnovitz (1993); McDonald (1993); Arden-Clarke (1994); Trebilcock and Howse (1995): 344ff. The panel used the term 'extrajurisdictional' but 'extraterritorial' is more standard in the literature.

[4] Daly and Goodland (1993): 70; H. Daly, 'The Perils of Free Trade', *Scientific American*, November 1993: 26; Shrybman (1993): 279–80; Trebilcock and Howse (1995): 346ff.

[5] See, for example, *Third World Economics* and other publications by the Third World Network, Penang, Malaysia; Khor (1994); Dunkley (1992): 7–8, 53 and 73; Dunkley (1993).

[6] H. J. Leonard, *Pollution and the Struggle for the World Product*, Cambridge University Press, Cambridge, 1988; Browne (1994); IPS (1996).

[7] V. Rege, 'GATT Law and Environment-Related Issues Affecting the Trade of Developing Countries', *Journal of World Trade*, 28(3), June 1994: 156–7.

[8] M. Jones, 'Ban has Prawns off US Barbies', *The Age*, 27 April 1996: A7.

[9] *The Economist*, 8 February 1992: 62; Summers later claimed that he was hyperbolising to promote discussion, *The Economist*, 15 February 1992: 4.

[10] Daly and Cobb (1989); Dunkley (1992); Daly and Goodland (1993); Buckley (1993); Ropke (1994); OECD (1994). Business views: *The European*, 21–27 March, 1996: 24.

[11] G. Grossman and A. Krueger, 'Environmental Impacts of a North American Free Trade Agreement' in P. Garber (ed.), *The Mexico-US Free Trade Agreement*, MIT Press, Cambridge Mass, 1993. GATT views: GATT (1992); GATT *Activities*, GATT, Geneva, August 1994: 93ff.

[12] N. Shafik, 'Economic Development and Environmental Quality', *Oxford Economic Papers*, 46, 1994; World Bank, *World Development Report*, Oxford University Press, New York, 1992: 9ff.

[13] *Australia's Urban Air Quality Management: A Discussion Paper*, Commonwealth Environment Protection Authority, Canberra, 1995; *The Age*, 1 November 1995: 7; *The European*, 26 October–1 November 1995: 3.

[14] J. Schofield, 'Trade Policy Blamed for Loss of Land', *The Age*, 31 May 1993.

[15] *The State of the Environment*, OECD, Paris, 1991: ch. 12; Gabel in OECD (1994).

[16] H. Girardet, 'From Mobilization to Civilization', *Resurgence*, 167, November/December 1994; Lang and Hines (1993): ch. 6.

[17] Hudson in Low (1992); Barbier in OECD (1994); N. Dudley et al., *Bad Harvest?*, Earthscan, London, 1995.

[18] Charnovitz (1991, 1992 and 1993); McDonald (1993); Repetto (1993). Thai case: Trebilcock and Howse (1995): ch. 13; P. Simmons, 'Free Trade and Ill Health', *The Ecologist*, 20/6, November/December 1990; AFR, 19 May 1994: 13; Korten (1995): 175–6.

[19] Hansson (1990); C. Stevens, 'Harmonization, Trade and the Environment', *International Environmental Affairs* 5, 1, Winter 1993; P. Lloyd in Garnaut and Drysdale (1994): 335ff.

[20] Mainstream: Schmidheiny (1992); Porter (1990): 648–9; G. Clark, 'Global Competition and Environmental Regulation: Is the "Race to the Bottom"

Inevitable?', in R. Eckersley (ed.), *Markets, the State and the Environment*, Macmillan, Melbourne, 1995; Trebilcock and Howse (1995): 332; Hansson (1990). Critics: Lang and Hines (1993); Lang (1993); Nader et al. (1993); Webb (1994); Thurow (1996): esp. 130.

[21] F. Lazar, *Environmental Regulation as a Tool of Industrial Policy*, paper presented to the Economic Society of Australia, Gold Coast, Queensland, September 1992. More generally, Korten (1995).

[22] Services of the European Commission, *Report on US Barriers to Trade and Investment*, Brussels, April 1994. Also, Sierra Club, GATT *Double Jeopardy*, Washington, February 1994 and *European Union Targets US Environmental Laws*, Washington, 31 May 1994.

[23] Australian Consumers' Association, *How Safe is our Food?*, Random House, Sydney, 1991: 279; *The Future of Australian Food Standards*, Food Policy Alliance, Sydney, 1992. The Department of Health has confirmed the results of the latter study in a letter to the author from Mr Michael O'Connor, Chemicals Safety Unit, Canberra, 25 November 1994.

[24] Buckley (1993): 42–3. T. Lang, *Codex Alimentarius Commission: The Consumer Challenge*, Paper presented to IOCU Seminar, New Delhi, February 1994: 5.

[25] J. Claybrook, *Retreat from Safety*, Pantheon, New York, 1984; Ritchie in Nader et al. (1993): 184; Korten (1995): 179.

[26] *Nutrition Week*, Community Nutrition Institute, Washington DC, 31 January 1992; J. Castaneda and C. Heredia, 'Another NAFTA' in Nader et al. (1993).

[27] A. Stern, 'Alarm at Secret Plan to Scrap EU's Green Laws', *The European*, 9–15 June 1995.

[28] GATT *Alert*, Food Policy Alliance, Sydney, August 1993; *Codex at the Crossroads*, Community Nutrition Institute, Washington DC, 15 March 1995.

[29] National Food Authority, *Annual Report*, various years; Minister for Human Services and Health, *National Food Authority Amendment Bill 1995; Explanatory Memorandum*, Commonwealth Parliament, Canberra, 1995; Bún (1995): 7.

[30] *Eco-Consumer Newsletter*, August 1995; T. Webb, *Potatoes, Power and Politics*, Food and Power Symposium, Sydney, April 1996. I am grateful to Max Ogden, Dick Copeman, Tony Webb and Sally Nathan for information on this and other matters discussed here.

[31] *The Age*, 23 May 1996: A4; M. Dwyer, 'Food Imports Raise Disease Fear', *AFR*, 30 May 1996.

[32] E.g. *The Age*, 3 June 1996: A4; I am grateful to Tony Webb for information on these matters.

[33] National Food Authority, *Final Report of the Policy Review*, AGPS, Canberra, May 1993: Chapter 8.

11   The Perils of Globalism

[1] P. Sutherland, 'The World Trade Organization and the Future of the Multilateral Trading System', *GATT Press Communiqué*, Geneva, 30 May 1994.

² Article XIII of the *WTO Agreement* permits an existing Member who has not approved of a new Member to withhold application of standard GATT obligations to the latter.

³ General notification requirements are outlined in the *Decision on Notification Procedures* and the Annex thereto, as well as in individual agreements. Also see Hoekman (1995a): 57ff.; Ruggiero (1995): 9.

⁴ Article XXIV: 12 of GATT94 requires that national governments take 'such reasonable measures as may be available' to ensure that 'regional and local governments and authorities' observe GATT rules. A Uruguay Round *Understanding on the Interpretation of Article XXIV* reiterated this clause, emphasising that WTO Members are 'fully responsible' for actions of sub-national entities and that national governments may be liable to compensation claims or suspension of concessions if such entities breach GATT rules (Articles 13 and 14).

⁵ On such proposals: NGO Statement (1992); Watkins (1992); IOCU (1994); NGO Forum (1994). For more general criticisms: K. P. Khor, 'GATT Talks may Assault Third World Economic Autonomy and Environment', *Third World Network Features*, No. 620, 1990; P. Madden, *The Uruguay Round and the Issue of Poverty Reduction: What Role Should the WTO Have?*, Mimeo, Christian Aid, London, 17 October 1994.

⁶ *Wall Street Journal*, 16 December 1993: A13; Watkins (1992): 37–8 and Chapter 3 above. In general, Korten (1995): ch. 13.

⁷ K. Silverstein and A. Cockburn, 'Who Broke Mexico?', *The Ecologist*, January/February 1995.

⁸ The President's Task Force on International Private Enterprise, *Report to the President*, US Government Printing Office, Washington DC, December 1984; R. Cox, *Power and Profits: US Policy Central America*, University of Kentucky Press, Lexington, 1994.

⁹ UNCTAD (1994a: Annex 3); Evans (1994): 96; *ICDA* No. 18, March–May 1995: 25–6; *OECD Letter*, 4/9, November 1995: 4. On general items periodically being mooted for the WTO agenda see *WTO Focus* (various issues) and Fred Brenchley's weekly column in *AFR*.

¹⁰ OECD policies: A *Multilateral Agreement on Investment: Report by the Committee on International Investment and Multinational Enterprises*, OECD, Paris, 1995; *OECD Letter*, August/September 1996. Critiques: NGO Forum (1994); *ICDA* 18, March–May 1995: 24–5; S. Das, 'WTO Should not Take up Investment Issue, say NGOs', *Third World Network Feature*, No. 1384, 1995; C. Raghavan, 'UNCTAD Caution on New Trade Issues' and M. Khor, 'Malaysian Premier Opposes Investment Treaty in WTO' in *Third World Network Features*, 6 February 1996.

¹¹ Ruggiero in *WTO Focus*, 5, 1995; Agosin and Tussie (1993): 2.

¹² L. Pauly, *Opening Financial Markets*, Cornell University Press, Ithaca, 1988; Banuri and Schor (1992); M. Bienefeld, 'Financial Deregulation: Disarming the Nation', *Studies in Political Economy*, 37, Spring 1992; Helleiner (1994) and sources cited in each.

[13] On such issues see the articles by P. Hirst and G. Thompson, in *Economy and Society*, November 1992 and August 1995; J. Camilleri and J. Falk, *The End of Sovereignty?*, Edward Elgar, Aldershot, 1992; Horsman and Marshall (1994); COGG (1995); Panic (1995); Hirst and Thompson (1996).

[14] S. Holland, *The Global Economy*, Weidenfeld and Nicholson, London, 1987; Maxfield (1990); Korten (1995): esp. Part IV; UNCTAD (1994a): ch. 3 esp. 151ff. Murdoch: News Ltd minimises its tax liabilities through investment tax concessions, use of tax havens, creative accounting, inter-subsidiary loans and so forth—see R. Crowe and L. Buckingham, 'Murdoch and his Small Tax Secret', *Guardian Weekly*, 28 July 1996: 14.

[15] John Kerin, *The Age*, 5 January 1991; John Button PM, ABC Radio 3 RN, 14 July 1995; Fagan and Webber (1994): ch. 3.

[16] UN Secretary General, Boutros-Ghali, quoted in *The Age*, 6 June 1996: B1.

[17] Australia: *The Age*, 31 July 1993: 7 and 8 November 1995: 38. UN Report: *States of Disarray*, UN Research Institute for Social Development, Geneva, 1995. General: Barnet and Cavanagh (1994); Korten (1995).

[18] Panic (1988): 7; Fukuyama (1992): xiv and 235. Survey by Roper Starch (International), *The Age*, 23 June 1995: 9.

[19] *The Times of India*, 11 February 1994: 11.

[20] Brecher and Costello (1994); Cavanagh et al. (1994). For general critiques see M. Castells, *The Informational City*, Blackwell, Oxford, 1989; Epstein et al. (1993); Barnet and Cavanagh (1994); Korten (1995).

[21] *Regulatory Co-operation for an Interdependent World*, OECD, Paris, 1994.

12   Is There Life after GATT?

[1] P. Daniels, 'International Trade Competitiveness, Protection and Australian Manufactures', *Economic Analysis and Policy*, 23/2, September 1993; Bell (1993): ch. 8. Stories and anecdote: E. Jones, 'Policy Links to the Foreign Debt', *Frontline*, No. 25, June 1995; S. Neales, 'Why Your Job Could be Heading Overseas', The *Age*, 8 June 1992; M. Walsh, ' "Starving Millions" Myth Meets Reality', *The Age*, 23 June 1995: 22; L. Kearns, 'Manufacturers Ignore Export Push', *The Age*, 6 November 1995: 35; S. Schaetzel, 'Shot Down in Flames', *The Bulletin*, 10 October 1995 (aircraft industry); Grennan, 1996 (vehicles); Davidson, 1996 (info-tech).

[2] P. Sheehan et al., *The Rebirth of Australian Industry* and *Australia and the Knowledge Economy*, Centre for Strategic Economic Studies, Victoria University of Technology, Melbourne, 1994 and 1995. Also see B. Pinkstone, *Global Connections*, AGPS, Canberra, 1992; Spindler Report (1993); Bell (1993). Business advocates of intervention include The Society for Balanced Trade, industrialist John Siddons and businessman Ernest Roedek, among others. Also see BIS Shrapnel, *Economic Outlook*, August 1996.

[3] On the theory of 'new growth': P. Romer, 'Endogenous Technological Change', *Journal of Political Economy*, 98/5, 1990. On industry policies in practice: Pearce and Sutton (1985); Ozawa (1987); P. Blackburn and R. Sharpe (eds), *Britain's Industrial Renaissance?*, Routledge, London, 1988; J. Stanford (ed.), *Industrial*

Policy in Australia and Europe, AGPS, Canberra, 1992; Jovanović 1992, 182ff.; Tyson (1993).

4 The World Bank's views and SAP case studies are contained in: World Bank (various years); M. Michaely et al. (eds), *Liberalizing Foreign Trade* (7 vols), Blackwell, Oxford, 1991; Thomas et al. (1991).

5 Streeten (1982); Jung and Marshall (1985); Heierli in Bassand et al. (1986); L. Taylor, 'Trade and Growth', *The Review of Black Political Economy*, Spring 1986, *Varieties of Stabilisation Experience*, Clarendon Press, Oxford, 1988 and 'Economic Openness: Problems to the Century's End' in Banuri (1991); Edwards (1993); ILO (1995): 70.

6 R. Faini et al., 'Growth Oriented Adjustment Programs: A Statistical Analysis', *World Development*, 8, 1991; J. Harrigan and P. Mosley, 'Evaluating the Impact of World Bank Structural Adjustment Lending: 1980–87', *Journal of Development Studies*, 27, 1991; Banuri (1991); Fontaine (1992); M. Bleaney and D. Greenaway, 'Adjustment to External Imbalance and Investment Slumps in Developing Countries', *European Economic Review*, 37, 1993; G. Helleiner (ed.), *Trade Policy and Industrialisation in Turbulent Times*, Routledge, London, 1994; ILO (1995): Part 2.

7 *Structural Adjustment: Who Really Pays?*, Public Interest Research Group, New Delhi, 1992; Bello (1993); J. Dohnal, 'Structural Adjustment Programs: A Violation of Rights', *Australian Journal of Human Rights*, 1, 1, 1994. Papua New Guinea: AFR, 7 March 1996.

8 F. Levia, 'Chile—The Other Face of the Economic Miracle', *Free Trade or Fair* (London), 1/2, September 1992; C. Schneider, 'Chile: The Underside of the Miracle', *Report on the Americas*, February 1993; Barry (1995): esp. 83–4.

9 Bello and Rosenfeld (1990); Bello (1993); Jayasuriya and Lee (1994); *State of Urbanisation in Asia and the Pacific*, UN, New York, 1993; M. Bunting, 'Taiwan's Scramble for Wealth Breeds a Green Nightmare', *The Age*, 16 January 1995: 8. Billionaires: Keegan (1996). Also see the journals *Third World Resurgence* and *Third World Economics*.

10 SRG Happiness Index, *Press Release from the Survey Research Group*, Hong Kong 1993; *SRG News*, various issues.

11 Mild interventionist: Mutoh, 1986: ch. 15; Fontaine (1992); Agosin and Tussie (1993); Auty (1994); Moreira (1995). More radical: Streeten (1982); Edwards (1985); Banuri (1991); Tavara in Epstein et al. (1993); Chang (1994). Human development approach: UNDP (various years); Griffin and Kahn (1992).

12 Daly and Cobb (1989); T. Trainer, *Development to Death*, Green Print, London, 1989; W. Pereira and J. Seabrook, *Asking the Earth*, Earthscan, London, 1990; Norberg-Hodge (1992); Ekins (1992); Douthwaite (1992); Dunkley (1993); Korten (1995); Tato and Smith, Henderson and others in Griesgraber and Gunter (1996).

13 M. Barratt Brown, *Fair Trade*, Zed, London, 1993; Madeley (1992): ch. 10; B. Coote, *The Trade Trap*, Oxfam, Oxford, 1992; International Federation of Organic Agriculture Movements, *Trade in Organic Products*, the 4th International IFOAM Conference, Frankfurt, 1995.

[14] Cavanagh (1988); Rothstein (1993); Brecher and Costello (1994); Browne (1994); Jayasuriya and Lee (1994).

[15] *OECD Letter*, July 1996: 6–7.

[16] This and following material draws on S. Charnovitz, 'The Influence of International Labour Standards on the World Trading Regime', *International Labour Review*, 126/5, September–October 1987 and 'Environmental and Labour Standards in Trade', *The World Economy*, 15/3, May 1992; Cavanagh (1988). Clinton: Chong in *The Australian*, 18 May 1994.

[17] Cavanagh (1988); *International Workers' Rights and Trade: The Need for Dialogue*, ICFTU, Brussels, September 1994; *Free Labour World*, No. 11, November 1994: 3; Lambert in Jayasuriya and Lee (1994).

[18] *The European*, 8–14 April 1994; *ICDA Update*, No. 18, March–May 1995; Hutton (1994).

[19] AFR, 26 May 1995 and 22 February 1996.

[20] J. Galtung et al. (eds) *Self-Reliance*, Bogle-L'Ouverture, London, 1980; D. Senghaas 'The Case for Autarchy' and P. Streeten 'Self-Reliant Industrialisation' in C. Wilbur (ed.), *The Political Economy of Development and Underdevelopment*, Random House, New York, Third Edition, 1984; Bassand (1986); P. Ekins (ed.), *The Living Economy*, Routledge, London, 1986 and 'Trade and Self-Reliance', *The Ecologist*, September/October 1989; Lang and Hines (1993); S. Amin, 'Moving Beyond Structural Adjustment', *Third World Network Features*, No. 1077, 1993; Cruttwell (1995), ch. 10.

[21] D. Morris, *Self-Reliant Cities*, Sierra Club, San Francisco, 1982; H. Thomas et al. (eds), *Small Scale Production*, IT Publications, London, 1991; R. Diwan and M. Lutz (eds), *Essays in Gandhian Economics*, Gandhi Peace Foundation, New Delhi, 1985; Bassand (1986); Douthwaite (1992); J. Pearce, *At the Heart of the Community Economy*, Gulbenkian Foundation, London, 1993. Also see the work of the Intermediate Technology Group, London and the Institute for Local Self-Reliance, Washington DC.

[22] D. Evans and L. Adler (eds), *Appropriate Technology for Development*, Westview, Boulder, 1979; G. McRobie, *Small is Possible*, Abacus, London, 1982; M. Carr (ed.), *The AT Reader*, IT Publications, London, 1985.

[23] H. Khan and E. Thorbecke, *Macroeconomic Effects and Diffusion of Alternative Technologies Within a Social Accounting Matrix Framework*, Gower, London, 1988.

[24] Thaman (1992); A. Robillard (ed.), *Social Change in the Pacific Islands*, Kegan Paul, London, 1992.

[25] For a range of alternative structural proposals, see Streeten in Dunning and Usui (1987); E. Childers and B. Urquhart, 'Renewing the UN System', *Development Dialogue*, 1994: 1; J. Cavanagh et al. (eds), *Beyond Bretton Woods*, Pluto, London, 1994. COGG (1995); Griesgraber and Gunter (1996).

[26] Daly and Cobb (1989); Ekins (1992); Douthwaite (1992); Brecher and Costello (1994); J. Brecher et al. (eds), *Global Visions*, South End Press, Boston,

Postscript: In Pursuit of the Global Millenium

¹ R. Ruggiero, 'Whither the Trade System Next?' in J. Bhagwati and M. Hirsch (eds), *The Uruguay Round and Beyond*, Springer, Heidelberg, 1998: 123.

² B. Chaytor, 'Participation in the First Ministerial Conference at the World Trade Organisation—A Southern Perspective', in E. Haxton and C. Olsson (eds), *Gender and Sustainability in International Trade*, Global Publications Foundation, Uppsala, 1997.

³ WTO *Annual Report* 1998: 2. In this Postscript information on the WTO and Uruguay Round implementation is from WTO Annual Reports unless otherwise indicated. These will be cited in both text and notes as (AP 1996 etc).

⁴ *WTO Focus*, 17 March 1997; the ITA was ratified on 27 March 1997.

⁵ *WTO Agricultural Negotiations: Important Market Access Issues*, ABARE, Canberra, 1999; Commonwealth of Australia, *Trade Outcomes and Objectives Statement*, DFAT, Canberra, 1999.

⁶ WTO, Communication from Australia, *Preparations for the 2000 Services Negotiations*, 20 November 1998.

⁷ W. Dobson and P. Jacquet, *Financial Services Liberalization in the WTO*, Institute for International Economics, Washington, 1998; *The Age*, 15 December 1997: B13; AP 1998: 99ff.

⁸ On South Africa: 'A Fight to the Death', *Managing Intellectual Property*, 84, November 1998: 18–19.

⁹ AP 1998: 106–7; International Coalition for Development Action (ICDA), *An Alternative Report on Trade*, Brussels, 1995: 23ff; B. Welch, 'Banana Dependency: Albatross or Liferaft for the Windwards', *Social and Economic Studies*, 43: 1, 1994.

¹⁰ J. Bergelson et al., 'Promiscuity in Transgenic Plants', *Nature*, 3 September 1998: 25 and D. Cadbury, *The Feminization of Nature*, Hamish Hamilton, London, 1997. On all the above issues, E. Goldsmith and N. Hildyard (eds), *The Earth Report*, Mitchell Beazley, London, various editions.

¹¹ G. Sampson in A. Krueger (ed.), *The WTO as an International Organization*, University of Chicago Press, Chicago, 1998; D. Vines in ibid.

¹² R. Sharer et al., *Trade Liberalization in IMF-Supported Programs*, IMF, Washington, 1998.

¹³ C. Bellmann and R. Gerster, 'Accountability in the World Trade Organization', *Journal of World Trade*, December 1996; AP 1998: 3–4; *European Union News* (Australia), November–December 1998.

¹⁴ R. Blackhurst, 'The Capacity of the WTO to Fulfill its Mandate' in Krueger, op. cit.

¹⁵ See R. Ricupero in Bhagwati and Hirsch, op. cit.; House of Commons Environment Committee, *World Trade and the Environment*, HMSO, Vol. 1, 17 June 1996: xxii (hereinafter HCEC).

¹⁶ *The Economist*, 7 November 1998: 20; Baldwin in Krueger, op. cit.

¹⁷ D. Feaver, 'Unlocking Australia's Contingent Protection Black Box', *Economic Record*, March 1998 and *The Political Economy of Australian Anti-Dumping and Countervailing Law and Policy*, PhD, Victoria University of Technology, Melbourne, 1998; also, see Chapter 4, Note 3. A. Eckes, *Opening America's*

Markets, University of North Carolina Press, Chapel Hill, 1995: Chapters 7 and 8.

[18] Globalisation and Environment, OECD, Paris, 1997; P. Kageson, Growth Versus the Environment: Is there a Trade-Off?, Kluwer, Dordrecht, 1998; M. Rauscher, International Trade, Factor Movements and the Environment, Clarendon Press, Oxford, 1997; G. Monbiot in The Guardian (reprinted, The Age, 26 May 1998: 7); HCEC, op. cit.

[19] OECD, Trade, Employment and Labour Standards, Paris, 1996 and Open Markets Matter, 1998 (textiles p.31). D. Rodrik in R. Lawrence et al., Emerging Agenda for Global Trade, Overseas Development Council, Washington, 1996; R. Feenstra, 'Integration of Trade and Disintegration of Production in the Global Economy', Journal of Economic Perspectives, Fall 1998; The Economist, 27 February 1999: 68–9.

[20] Bhagwati in Bhagwati and Hirsch, op. cit.

[21] For a non-committal WTO study, AP 1997: 30ff. Also: OECD, Market Access After the Uruguay Round, Paris, 1996, especially Janow article; Lawrence in Lawrence et al, op. cit. and The Economist, 4 July 1998: 97–8.

[22] For a non-committal analysis of trade and DFI by the WTO, see AP 1996: 44ff. In general, see: UNCTAD, World Investment Report 1997 (employment: 28ff); G. Dunkley, 'The MAI: A Critical Analysis', Arena, 11, 1998; A. Rodriguez-Clare, 'Multinationals, Linkages and Economic Development', American Economic Review, September 1996; L. De Mello, 'Foreign Direct Investment in Developing Countries and Growth', Journal of Development Studies, October 1997.

[23] See, for example, De Clercq in Bhagwati and Hirsch, op. cit.; C. Carlisle, 'Is the World Ready for Free Trade?', Foreign Affairs, November–December 1996. Green and some Left views: J. Mander and E. Goldsmith (eds), The Case Against the Global Economy, Sierra Club, San Francisco, 1996. Right views: J. Cregan (ed), America Asleep, US Industrial Council, Washington, 1991; P. Buchanan, The Great Betrayal, Little, Brown and Co., Boston, 1998.

[24] The Economist, 20 January 1999: 71ff; The Age, 1 February 1999; AFR, 4 February 1999; G. Soros, The Crisis of Global Capitalism, Little, Brown and Co., London, 1998.

[25] The Economist, 2 January 1999: 53ff; The Age, 4 December 1996: A7.

[26] C. Murphy, Tariffs: How Low Should We Go?, Information and Research Services, Parliament of Australia, 1997.

[27] L. Taylor (ed), The Rocky Road to Reform, MIT, Cambridge Mass, 1993; D. Ghai (ed), The IMF and the South, Zed, London, 1991; M. Shafaeddin, 'The Impact of Trade Liberalisation on Export and GDP Growth in Least Developed Countries', UNCTAD Review, 1995; P. Skott and M. Larudee, 'Uneven Development and the Liberalisation of Trade and Capital Flows: The Case of Mexico', Cambridge Journal of Economics, 22, 1998; S. Redding, 'Dynamic Comparative Advantage and the Welfare Effects of Trade', Oxford Economic Papers, 51, 1999.

[28] J. Rattso and R. Torvik, 'Zimbabwean Trade Liberalisation: Ex Post Evaluation', Cambridge Journal of Economics, 22, 1998; M. Boughzala, 'Impact on Workers of Reduced Trade Barriers: The Case of Tunisia and Morocco', International Labour Review, Autumn, 1997; J. Ward, 'Fear of Crime Haunts Mexico', Guardian Weekly, 11 April 1999: 17.

[29] J. Bhagwati, *The Feuds Over Free Trade*, Institute of Southeast Asian Studies, Singapore, 1997; 'The Capital Myth', *Foreign Affairs*, May–June 1998; J. Eatwell, 'Disguised Unemployment: The G7 Experience', *UNCTAD Review*, 1995.

[30] D. Rodrik, *Has Globalisation Gone Too Far?*, Institute for International Economics, Washington, 1997; 'Symposium on Globalisation in Perspective: An Introduction', *Journal of Economic Perspectives*, Fall 1998.

[31] Quoted in UNCTAD, *Trade and Development Report 1998*, New York, 1998: 75–6.

[32] Mainstream view—M. Goldstein, *The Asian Financial Crisis*, Institute for International Economics, Washington, 1998. Critics—Jomo K.S. (ed), *Tigers in Trouble*, Zed, London, 1998; *Cambridge Journal of Economics*, 22, 1998; UNCTAD, op. cit., Chapter 3.

[33] R. Wade, 'The Gathering World Slump and the Battle over Capital Controls', *New Left Review*, 231, 1998; M. Guitian in *Finance and Development* (IMF), March 1999; Jomo, op. cit; *The Age*, 18 May 1999: 5 (Camdessus).

[34] This observation is based on my own research, which I hope to publish, and an unpublished values survey by sociologists Beryl Langer and Estelle Farrar of La Trobe University, Melbourne. I am grateful to Estelle Farrar for relevant information. Also, *The Sunday Age*, 27 December 1998: 3.

[35] W. Bello et al., *A Siamese Tragedy*, Zed, London, 1998: 8–9.

Bibliography

Abayasiri-Silva, K. and M. Horridge, 1996, *Economies of Scale and Imperfect Competition in an Applied General Equilibrium Model of the Australian Economy*, Centre for Policy Studies, Monash University, Melbourne, Working Paper No. OP-84, March.

ACN, 1994, *Living With FTA/NAFTA*, Action Canada Network, Ottawa, December.

Agosin, M. and D. Tussie (eds), 1993, *Trade and Growth*, St Martin's Press, New York.

Alston, P. and M. Chiam (eds), 1995, *Treaty-Making and Australia*, Federation Press, Sydney.

Amsden, A., 1993, 'Trade Policy and Economic Performance in South Korea', in Agosin and Tussie (1993).

Anderson, J., 1993, *Trade, Technology and Unions*, Ontario Federation of Labour, Ottawa, June.

Anderson, K., 1993, 'NAFTA, Excluded Pacific Rim Countries, and the Multilateral Trading System', in R. Cushing et al. (eds), *The Challenge of NAFTA*, CEDA, Melbourne.

—— 1995, *The Entwining of Trade Policy with Environmental and Labour Standards*, Paper to World Bank Conference on The Uruguay Round and Developing Countries, Washington DC.

Anderson, K. and R. Blackhurst (eds), 1992, *The Greening of World Trade Issues*, University of Michigan Press, Ann Arbor.

Arden-Clarke, C., 1994, *Green Protectionism*, World-Wide Fund for Nature, Gland.

Auty, R., 1994, *Economic Development and Industry Policy*, Mansell, London.

Avery, N. et al., 1993, *Cracking the Codex*, National Food Alliance, London.

Bach, C., 1994, *Report from the Marrakesh Conference: GATT*, Danish North/South Coalition, Copenhagen, May.

Baldwin, R., 1989, 'The Growth Effects of 1992', *Economic Policy*, 9, October.

Banuri, T. (ed.), 1991, *Economic Liberalisation: No Panacea*, Clarendon Press, Oxford.

Banuri, T. and J. Schor (eds), 1992, *Financial Openness and National Autonomy*, Clarendon Press, Oxford.

Barnet, R. and J. Cavanagh, 1994, *Global Dreams*, Simon and Shuster, New York.

Barry, T., 1995, *Zapata's Revenge*, South End Press, Boston.

Bassand, M. et al. (eds), 1986, *Self-Reliant Development in Europe*, Gower, London.

Bell, S., 1993, *Australian Manufacturing and the State*, Cambridge University Press, Melbourne.

Bello, W., 1993, *Dark Victory*, Pluto, New York.

Bello, W. and S. Rosenfeld, 1990, *Dragons in Distress*, Food First, San Francisco.

Bergsten, F., 1996, 'Globalizing Free Trade', *Foreign Affairs*, May/June.

Bhagwati, J., 1989, 'Is Free Trade *Passé* After All?', *Weltwirtschaftliches Archiv*, 125.

—— 1990, *Aggressive Unilateralism*, University of Michigan Press, Ann Arbor.

—— 1994, 'Fair Trade, Reciprocity and Harmonization', in A. Deardorff and R. Stern (eds), *Analytical and Negotiating Issues in the Global Trading System*, University of Michigan Press, Ann Arbor.

Bhagwati, J. and T. Srinivasan, 1969, 'Optimal Intervention to Achieve Non-Economic Objectives', *The Review of Economic Studies*, 36.

BIE (Bureau of Industry Economics), 1995, *Potential Gains to Australia from APEC*, AGPS, Canberra.

Bienefeld, M., 1994, 'Capitalism and the Nation State in the Dog Days of the Twentieth Century', in R. Miliband and L. Panitch (eds), *The Socialist Register*, Merlin, London.

Braga, C., 1995, *Trade-Related Intellectual Property Issues*, World Bank Conference on The Uruguay Round and Developing Countries, Washington DC, January.

Braithwaite, J., 1995, 'Sovereignty and Globalisation of Business Regulation', in Alston and Chiam (1995).

Brecher, J. and T. Costello, 1994, *Global Village or Global Pillage*, South End Press, Boston.

Brenchley, F., (1996), 'Britain Winning the EU Game Hands Down', *AFR*, 18 July: 15.

Browne, H., 1994, *For Richer, For Poorer: Shaping US-Mexican Integration*, Resource Center Press, Albuquerque.

Buckley, R., 1993, *International Trade, Investment and Environment*, Griffith University, Gold Coast.

Bún, M., 1995, *Safe and Sustainable Consumption in an APEC Environment*, Paper to Fair Trade Forum, Canberra, 18 October.

Campbell, B., 1993, *Free Trade: Destroyer of Jobs*, Canadian Centre for Policy Alternatives, Ottawa.

Capie, F., 1983, 'Tariff Protection and Economic Performance in the Nineteenth Century', in J. Black and A. Winters (eds), *Policy and Performance in International Trade*, Macmillan, London.

Cavanagh, J. et al., 1988, *Trade's Hidden Costs*, International Labor Rights Education and Research Fund, Washington DC.

—— et al. (eds), 1992, *Trading Freedom*, Food First, San Francisco.

—— et al. (eds), 1994, *Beyond Bretton Woods*, Pluto, London.

Chang, H., 1994, *The Political Economy of Industrial Policy*, Macmillan, London.

Charnovitz, S., 1991, 'Exploring the Environmental Exceptions in GATT Article XX', *Journal of World Trade*, 25/5.

—— 1992, 'GATT and the Environment', *International Environmental Affairs*, 4/3, Summer.

—— 1993, 'The Environment vs. Trade Rules: Defogging the Debate', *Environmental Law*, 23/2.

—— 1995, 'Regional Trade Agreements and the Environment', *Environment*, July/August.

Cheng, L., 1987, 'Uncertainty and Economic Self-Sufficiency', *Journal of International Economics*, 23.

Clairmonte, F. and J. Cavanagh, 1985, 'Transnational Corporations and Services: The Final Frontier', *Economic and Political Weekly*, 23 February and 2 March.

Clark, G. et al., 1991, *Objections to Restructuring and the Strategies of Coercion*, Development Studies Centre, Monash University, Melbourne.

Clarke, H., 1995, 'Programme Makers Tune into Global TV Market', *The European*, 30 November – 6 December: 21.

CLC, 1993, *Submission on NAFTA to the Sub-Committee on International Trade (Parliament of Canada)*, Canadian Labour Congress, Ottawa, January.

Cline, W., 1995, 'Evaluating the Uruguay Round', *The World Economy*, 18/1, January.

COGG (Commission on Global Governance), 1995, *Our Global Neighbourhood*, Oxford University Press, Oxford.

Cohen, M., 1994, *Negotiation in the New Economic Environment: The Dangers in International Trade Agreements*, Mimeo, Simon Fraser University, Burnaby, Canada.

Collins, S. and B. Bosworth (eds), 1994, *The New GATT*, Brookings, Washington DC.

Cooper, R., 1994, 'World-wide Regional Integration: Is There an Optimal Size of the Integrated Area?', in Garnaut and Drysdale (eds), 1994.

Corden, M., 1974, *Trade Policy and Economic Welfare*, Clarendon, Oxford.

—— 1996, 'Protection and Liberalisation in Australia and Abroad', *Australian Economic Review*, 2, 1996.

Crawford, J.G., 1968, *Australian Trade Policy 1942–1966*, ANU Press, Canberra.

Croome, J., 1995, *Reshaping the World Trading System*, WTO, Geneva.

Cruttwell, P., 1995, *History Out of Control*, Resurgence Books, Dartington.

Culbertson, J., 1984, *International Trade and the Future of the West*, 21st Century Press, Madison.

—— 1986, 'A Realist View of International Trade and National Trade Policy', *International Law and Politics*, 18.

Daly, H. and J. Cobb, 1989, *For the Common Good*, Beacon Press, Boston.

Daly, H. and R. Goodland, 1993, 'An Ecological-Economic Assessment of Deregulation of International Commerce', *International Journal of Sustainable Development*, 1/4.

Davidson, K., 1996, 'Narrow Vision Will see IT's Future Unplugged', *The Age*, 3 August: B2.

Deardorff, A., 1994, 'Economic Effects of Quota and Tariff Reductions', in Collins and Bosworth (1994).

Deardorff, A. and R. Stern, 1983, 'The Economic Effects of Complete Elimination of Post-Tokyo Round Tariffs', in W. Cline (ed.), *Trade Policy in the 1980s*, Institute for International Economics, Washington DC.

Dee, P. and A. Welsh, 1994, 'Implications for Australia of Regional Trading Arrangements in Asia', in EPAC, *Regional Trading Arrangements*, AGPS, Canberra.

Destler, I. M., 1992, *American Trade Politics*, Institute for International Economics, Washington DC, 2nd edn.

DFAT, 1994, *Uruguay Round Outcomes*, Department of Foreign Affairs and Trade, Canberra: a. Agriculture; b. Industrials; c. Services; d. Intellectual Property.

Dillon, P. et al., 1990, 'Assessing the Usefulness of International Trade Theory for Policy Analysis', in J. Odell and T. Willett, *International Trade Policies*, University of Michigan Press, Ann Arbor.

DIST, 1994, *Industry Policy in Australia*, Department of Industry, Science and Technology, Canberra, October.

Dore, R., 1993, 'Rethinking Free Trade', in R. Morgan et al. (eds), *New Diplomacy in the Post-Cold War World*, St Martin's Press, New York.

Douthwaite, R., 1992, *The Growth Illusion*, Resurgence, Harland.

Drake, W. and K. Nicolaidis, 1992, 'Ideas, Interests and Institutionalization: Trade in Services in the Uruguay Round, *International Organization*, 46/1, Winter.

Dryden, S., 1995, *Trade Warriors*, Oxford University Press, New York.

Dunkley, G., 1992, *The Greening of the Red*, Pluto, Sydney.

—— 1993, *People for Change: Four CAA Projects in India*, Victoria University of Technology and Community Aid Abroad, Melbourne.

—— 1994a, 'GATS: A Critical View', *Twenty-First International Trade Law Conference*, Attorney-General's Department and Australian Law Council, Canberra.

—— 1994b, *The Uruguay Round of GATT: Benefits and Hidden Costs*, Paper to Political Economy Conference, Sydney, October.

—— 1995, 'Is There a Case for Import Controls?', *Journal of Economic and Social Policy*, 1/1, Summer.

Dunning, J. and M. Usui (eds), 1987, *Structural Change, Economic Interdependence and World Development*, St Martin's Press, New York.

Dwyer, M., 1996, 'US Threat to Car, TCF Industries', *AFR*, 20 June: 1/8.

Economist, The, 1993, 'Don't Green GATT', *The Economist*, 26 December 1992–8 January 1993: 13–14.

Edwards, C., 1985, *The Fragmented World*, Methuen, London.

Edwards, S., 1993, 'Openness, Trade Liberalization and Growth in Developing Countries', *Journal of Economic Literature*, September.

Ekins, P., 1992, *A New World Order*, Routledge, London.

EPAC (Economic Planning Advisory Commission), 1995, *Tariff Reform and Economic Growth*, AGPS, Canberra.

Epstein, G. et al. (eds), 1993, *Creating a New World Economy*, Temple University

Press, Philadelphia.

Eurobarometer: Public Opinion in the EU, Trends 1974–1993, European Commission, Brussels, May, 1994.

Evans, P., 1994, *Unpacking the GATT*, International Organisation of Consumer Unions, London.

Fagan, R. and M. Webber, 1994, *Global Restructuring: The Australian Experience*, Oxford University Press, Melbourne.

Fagerberg, J., 1988, 'International Competitiveness', *Economic Journal*, 98, June.

Faux, J., 1993, *The Failed Case for NAFTA*, Economic Policy Institute, Washington DC.

Ferguson, T. and J. Rogers, 1986, *Right Turn: the Decline of the Democrats and the Future of American Politics*, Hill and Wang, New York.

Finger, J. M., 1995, *Legalized Backsliding: Safeguard Provisions in the GATT*, Paper to Conference on the Uruguay Round and Developing Countries, World Bank, Washington DC, January.

Fontaine, J-M (ed.), 1992, *Foreign Trade Reforms and Development Strategy*, Routledge, London.

Ford, J. and S. Sen, 1985, *Protectionism, Exchange Rates and the Macroeconomy*, Blackwell, Oxford.

Fukuyama, F., 1992, *The End of History and the Last Man*, Penguin Harmondsworth.

Fuller, C., 1994, *Free Trade and Canadian Health*, Canadian Health Services Association, British Columbia.

GAO, 1993, *North American Free Trade Agreement*, United States General Accounting Office, Report to Congress, Washington DC, September, vol. 2.

—— 1994, *The General Agreement on Tariffs and Trade*, United States General Accounting Office, Report to Congress, Washington DC, July, vol. 2.

Garnaut, R. and P. Drysdale (eds), 1994, *Asia Pacific Regionalism*, Harper Educational, Sydney.

GATT, 1992, *Trade and the Environment*, GATT, Geneva.

—— 1993, 'Background Note on the Audiovisual Sector', *News of the Uruguay Round*, GATT, Geneva, 14 October.

—— 1994, *Results of the Uruguay Round of Multilateral Trade Negotiations*, GATT, Geneva, November.

Goldin, I. et al., 1993, *Trade Liberalisation: Global Economic Implications*, OECD and World Bank, Paris.

Goldsmith, J., 1994, *The Trap*, Macmillan, London.

Gray, H.P., 1985, *Free Trade or Protection: A Pragmatic Analysis*, Macmillan, London.

—— 1990, 'The Role of Services in Global Structural Change', in A. Webster and J. Dunning (eds), *Structural Change in the World Economy*, Routledge, London.

Greijn, H., 1991, *GATT, Environment and Development*, Environment Liaison Centre International, Nairobi.

Grennan, H., 1996, 'Strife in the Fast Lane', *The Bulletin*, 23–30 January.

Griesgraber, J. and B. Gunter (eds), 1996, *Rethinking Bretton Woods*, Pluto, London, 2 vols.

Griffin, K. and A. Kahn, 1992, *Globalisation in the Developing World*, UN Research

Institute for Social Development, Geneva.

Grilli, E., 1991, 'Contemporary Protectionism in an Unstable World Economy', in G. Fels and G. Sutija (eds), *Protection and International Banking*, Macmillan, London.

Grinspun, R. and M. Cameron (eds), 1993, *The Political Economy of North American Free Trade*, McGill-Queens University Press, Montreal and Kingston.

Hama, N., 1996, *Disintegrating Europe*, Adamantine, London.

Hamilton, C. (ed.), 1991, *The Economic Dynamics of Australian Industry*, Allen and Unwin, Sydney.

Hansson, G., 1990, *Harmonization and International Trade*, Routledge, London.

Helleiner, E., 1994, *States and the Reemergence of Global Finance*, Cornell University Press, Ithaca.

Hirst, P. and G. Thompson, 1996, *Globalization in Question*, Polity, Cambridge.

Hoekman, B., 1995a, *Trade Laws and Institutions*, Paper to Conference on the Uruguay Round and Developing Economies, World Bank, Washington DC, January.

—— 1995b, *Tentative First Steps: An Assessment of the Uruguay Round Agreement on Services*, Paper to Conference on the Uruguay Round and Developing Economies, World Bank, Washington DC, January.

Horsman, M. and A. Marshall, 1994, *After the Nation-State*, Harper Collins, London.

Hudson, M., 1992, *Trade, Development and Foreign Debt*, Pluto, London.

Husted, S., and M. Melvin, 1995, *International Economics*, Harper Collins, New York, 3rd edn.

Hutton, W., 1994, 'Job Worries Flow from Freer Trade', *The Guardian Weekly*, 20 November.

—— 1996, *The State We're In*, Vintage, London.

IC (Industry Commission), *Annual Report*, various years.

IC, 1994, *The SALTER Model of the World Economy*, Industry Commission, Canberra, April.

ICDA, Bi-annual. *ICDA Update on Trade Related Issues*, International Coalition for Development Action, Brussels.

ILO, 1995, *World Employment 1995*, International Labour Office, Geneva.

IOCU, 1994, *The Case for Openness*, International Organisation of Consumer Unions, London, November.

IPS, 1996, *No Laughter in NAFTA*, Institute for Policy Studies, Washington DC.

Jayasuriya, L. and M. Lee (eds), 1994, *Social Dimensions of Development*, Paradigm Books, Perth.

Jovanović, M., 1992, *International Economic Integration*, Routledge, London.

Jung, W. and P. Marshall, 1985, 'Exports, Growth and Causality in Developing Countries', *Journal of Development Economics*, 18.

Kakabadse, M., 1987, *International Trade in Services*, Croom Helm, London.

Kaldor, N., 1964, 'Foreign Trade and the Balance of Payments' in *Essays on Economic Policy*, Duckworth, London, vol. 1.

—— 1980, 'The Foundations of Free Trade Theory', in E. Malinvaud and J-P.

Fitoussi (eds), *Unemployment in Western Countries*, Macmillan, London.

—— 1983, *The Economic Consequences of Mrs Thatcher*, Duckworth, London.

Kapstein, E., 1996, 'Workers and the World Economy', *Foreign Affairs*, May/June.

Keegan, V., 1996, 'Highway Robbery by the Super-Rich', *The Guardian Weekly*, 28 July: 13.

Kelsey, J., 1995, *Economic Fundamentalism*, Pluto, London, 1995.

Keynes, J. M., 1932, 'Pros and Cons of Tariffs', *The Listener*, 30 November. Reprinted, *The Collective Writings of John Maynard Keynes*, (ed. D. Moggridge), Macmillan, London, 1982, vol. 21: 204–10.

—— 1933, 'National Self-Sufficiency', *The Yale Review*, Summer; Reprinted in ibid: 233–46.

Khor, M., 1994, 'Operationalising Sustainable Development in Trade', *Third World Economics*, 1–15 September.

Kierzkowski, H. (ed.), 1984, *Monopolistic Competition and International Trade*, Oxford University Press, Oxford.

Kindleberger, C. P., 1987, *The World in Depression 1929–1939*, Penguin, Harmondsworth.

King, P. (ed.), 1990, *International Economics and International Economic Policy*, McGraw Hill, New York.

Koechlin, T. and M. Larudee, 1992, 'The High Cost of NAFTA', *Challenge*, September/October.

Korten, D., 1995, *When Corporations Rule the World*, Kumarian Press, West Hartford.

Krugman, P. (ed.), 1986, *Strategic Trade Policy and the New International Economics*, MIT Press, Cambridge Mass.

—— 1987, 'Is Free Trade Passé?', *Journal of Economic Perspectives*, 1.

—— 1990, *Rethinking International Trade*, MIT Press, Cambridge Mass.

—— 1991, *The Age of Diminished Expectations*, MIT Press, Cambridge Mass.

—— 1994, *Pedalling Prosperity*, Norton, New York.

—— 1995, 'Dutch Tulips and Emerging Markets', *Foreign Affairs*, July/August 1995.

Krugman, P. and M. Obstfeld, 1994, *International Economics*, Harper Collins, New York, 3rd edn.

Kuttner, R., 1989, *Managed Trade and Economic Sovereignty*, Economic Policy Institute, Washington DC.

—— 1991, *The End of Laissez Faire*, Knopf, New York.

Lake, D., 1988, *Power, Protection and Free Trade*, Cornell University Press, Ithaca.

Lang, T., 1993, *Food Fit for the World*, SAFE Alliance, London.

Lang, T. and C. Hines, 1993, *The New Protectionism*, Earthscan, London.

Lawrence, R., 1993, 'Futures for the World Trading System' in Agosin and Tussie (1993).

Lawrence, R. and R. Litan, 1990, 'The World Trading System After the Uruguay Round', *Boston University International Law Journal*, 8.

Lawrence, R. and C. Schulze, 1990, *An American Trade Strategy*, Brookings, Washington DC.

Leutwiler Report, 1987, *Trade Policies for a Better Future*, Martinus Nijhoff, Dordrecht.

Low, P. (ed.), 1992, *International Trade and the Environment*, World Bank, Washington DC.

Luxenberg, S., 1985, *Roadside Empires*, Viking, New York.

Madeley, J., 1992, *Trade and the Poor*, Intermediate Technology, London.

Maiden, M., 1996, 'Downsizing', *The Age*, 17 June: C1–2.

Marsh, I. (ed.), 1994, *Australian Business in the Asia Pacific Region*, Longman, Melbourne.

Maxfield, S., 1990, *Governing Capital*, Cornell University Press, Ithaca.

McCulloch, R., 1990, 'Investment Policies in GATT', *The World Economy*, 13.

McDonald, J., 1993, 'Greening the GATT', *Environmental Law* 23.

McKibbin, W. and D. Salvatore, 1995, 'The Global Economic Consequences of the Uruguay Round', *Asia-Pacific Economic Review*, 1/3, December.

McMullan, R., 1995, *Winning Markets*, DFAT, Canberra, June.

Mead, W. R., 1990, *The Low-Wage Challenge to Global Growth*, Economic Policy Institute, Washington DC.

Michalet, C-A, 1987, 'Strategies of Multinational Companies in the Economic Crisis', in Dunning and Usui (1987).

Mill, J. S., 1848, *Principles of Political Economy*, Penguin, Harmondsworth, 1970.

Milner, H., 1988, *Resisting Protectionism*, Princeton University Press, Princeton.

Mishel, L. and R. Teixeira, 1993, *The Political Arithmetic of the NAFTA Vote*, Economic Policy Institute, Washington DC.

MITI, 1996, *Report on the WTO Consistency of Trade Policies by Major Trading Partners*, MITI, Tokyo.

Miyashita, K. and D. Russell, 1994, *Keiretsu*, McGraw Hill, New York.

Moore Lappé, F. and J. Collins, 1982, *Food First*, Abacus, London.

Moreira, M., 1995, *Industrialization, Trade and Market Failures*, Macmillan, London.

Murtough, G. et al. (1994a), *APEC Trade Liberalisation Post-Uruguay Round*, ABARE, Canberra, September.

—— (1994b), *Gains to Australia from Trade Liberalisation: APEC and GATT*, ABARE, Canberra, October.

Mutoh, H. et al. (eds), 1986, *Industrial Policies for Pacific Economic Growth*, Allen and Unwin, Sydney.

Nader, R. et al., 1993, *The Case Against 'Free Trade'*, Earth Island, San Francisco.

Nayyar, D., 1988, 'Some Reflections on the Uruguay Round and Trade in Services', *Journal of World Trade*, 35, October.

NGO Forum, 1994, *The Marrakesh Proposals for Sustainable Trade*, Institute for Agriculture and Trade Policy, Minneapolis.

NGO Statement on the Proposed MTO of the Uruguay Round Negotiations of the GATT, A Statement by International NGOs, Hamburg, 1992.

Nguyen, T. et al., 1993, 'An Evaluation of the Draft Final Act of the Uruguay Round', *Economic Journal*, 103, November.

Norberg-Hodge, H., 1992, *Ancient Futures*, Rider, London.

OECD, 1994, *The Environmental Impact of Trade*, OECD, Paris.

Oppenheim, P., 1992, *Trade Wars: Japan Versus the West*, Weidenfeld and Nicholson, London.

Ormerod, P., 1994, *The Death of Economics*, Faber, London.

OTA, 1992, *Trade and Environment: Conflicts and Opportunities*, Office of Technological Assessment, Congress of the USA, Washington, May.

Oxley, A., 1990, *The Challenge of Free Trade*, Harvester Wheatsheaf, Hempel Hempstead.

—— 1993, *The Looming Issue of Trade and the Environment*, International Trade Strategies, Melbourne.

—— 1994, *Liberalisation in Asia Pacific—Why A Free Trade Area Would Benefit Australia*, Paper to Economics in Business and Government Conference, Gold Coast, 29 September.

Ozawa, T. 1987, 'Can the Market Alone Manage Structural Upgrading?', in Dunning and Usui (1987).

Panic, M., 1988, *National Management of the International Economy*, Macmillan, London.

—— (ed.) 1995, *Economic Integration in Europe and North America*, UN Commission for Europe, New York and Geneva.

Pearce, D. and J. Warford, 1993, *World Without End*, World Bank/Oxford University Press, New York.

Pearce, J. and J. Sutton, 1985, *Protection and Industry Policy in Europe*, Routledge and Kegan Paul, London.

PIRG, 1993, *GATTastrophe*, Public Interest Research Group, Delhi.

Polanyi, K., 1944, *The Great Transformation*, Reprinted Beacon Press, Boston, 1957.

Porter, M., 1990, *The Competitive Advantage of Nations*, Macmillan, London.

Prestowitz, C., 1991, *Powernomics*, Madison Books, Washington DC.

Quiggin, J., 1993, 'The Industry Commission Approach to Public Sector Reform', *Evatt Papers*, 1/1.

—— 1996, *Great Expectations*, Allen and Unwin, Sydney.

Raghavan, C., 1990, *Recolonization: GATT, the Uruguay Round and the Third World*, Third World Network, Penang.

Repetto, R., 1993, 'Trade and Environmental Policies', *WRI Issues and Ideas*, World Resources Institute, Washington, July.

Ricardo, D., 1817, *Principles of Political Economy and Taxation*, Penguin, Harmondsworth, 1971.

Richardson, J.D., 1989, 'Empirical Research on Trade Liberalisation with Imperfect Competition: A Survey', *OECD Economic Studies*, 12, Spring.

Ries, I, 1990, 'Club Japan in Corporate Command', *AFR*, 1–2 August.

Rifkin, J., 1995, *The End of Work*, Tarcher/Putnam, New York.

Rima, I. (ed.), 1993, *The Political Economy of Global Restructuring*, Edward Elgar, Aldershot.

Ritchie, M., 1992, 'Free Trade Versus Sustainable Agriculture', *The Ecologist*, September/October.

Robinson, J., 1960, 'The Pure Theory of International Trade', in *Collected Economic Papers*, Blackwell, Oxford, vol. 1.

Ropke, I., 1994, 'Trade, Development and Sustainability: A Critical Assessment of the "Free Trade Dogma" ', *Ecological Economics*, 9.

Rothstein, R., 1993, *Setting the Standard*, Economic Policy Institute, Washington DC.

Ruggiero, R., 1995, 'Overview of the WTO's First Year', *WTO Focus*, 7, December.

Samuelson, P., 1969, 'The Gains from International Trade Once Again' in J. Bhagwati (ed.), *International Trade*, Penguin, Harmondsworth.

Sapir, A., 1993, 'Regionalism and the New Theory of International Trade', *The World Economy*, 16/4, July.

Sassen, S., 1991, *The Global City*, Princeton University Press, Princeton NJ.

Scott, R. and T. Lee, 1991, *Reconsidering the Benefits and Costs of Trade Protection*, Economic Policy Institute, Washington, April.

Schmidheiny, S., 1992, *Changing Course*, MIT Press, Cambridge Mass.

Shrybman, S., 1993, 'Trading Away the Environment', in Grinspun and Cameron (1993).

Shukla, S., 1995, 'The WTO and the Nation State', *Third World Resurgence*, 60, August.

Sloman, J., 1991, *Economics*, Harvester Wheatsheaf, Hempel Hempstead.

Smith, A., 1776, *The Wealth of Nations*, (ed. E. Cannan), Unwin, London, 1961, vol. 1.

Snape, R. et al., 1993, *Regional Trade Agreements*, AGPS, Canberra.

Spindler Report, 1993, *Independent Parliamentary Inquiry into Tariffs and Industry Development*, Senator S. Spindler, Melbourne, April.

Spraos, J., 1983, *Inequalising Trade*, Clarendon, Oxford.

Stanford, J., 1993, *Estimating the Effects of North American Free Trade*, Canadian Centre for Policy Alternatives, Ottawa, September.

—— et al., 1993, *Social Dumping Under North American Free Trade*, Canadian Centre for Policy Alternatives, Ottawa.

Stevens, C., 1993, 'The Environmental Effects of Trade', *The World Economy*, 16/4, July.

Stewart, J., 1994, *The Lie of the Level Playing Field*, Text, Melbourne.

Stoeckel, A. et al., 1990, *Western Trade Blocs*, Centre for International Economics, Canberra.

Streeten, P., 1982, 'A Cool Look at "Outward-Looking" Strategies for Development', *The World Economy*, 5/1.

Sussens-Messerer, V. and B. Smit, 1996, 'Jobs Become Precious Commodity as Industry Restructures to Survive', *The European*, 8–14 February.

Sussman, G. and J. Lent (eds) 1991, *Transnational Communications*, Sage, London.

Sutherland, P., 1994a, 'Global Trade: The Next Challenge', *News of the Uruguay Round*, GATT, Geneva, 28 January.

—— 1994b, 'Consolidating Economic Globalization', *News of the Uruguay Round*, GATT, Geneva, 22 March.

Thaman, R., 1992, 'Deterioration of Traditional Food Systems, Increasing Malnutrition and Food Dependency in the Pacific Islands, *Journal of Food and Nutrition*, 39/3.

Thomas, V. et al. (eds), 1991, *Restructuring Economies in Distress*, Oxford University Press and World Bank, New York.

Thurow, L., 1992, *Head to Head*, Allen and Unwin, Sydney.

—— 1996, *The Future of Capitalism*, Allen and Unwin, Sydney.

Todaro, M., 1994, *Economic Development*, Longman, New York, 5th edn.

Toohey, B., 1994, *Tumbling Dice*, Heinemann, Melbourne.

Trebilcock, M. and R. Howse, 1995, *The Regulation of International Trade*, Routledge, London.

Tyson, L., 1993, *Who's Bashing Whom*, Institute for International Economics, Washington DC.

UNCTAD, 1994a, *World Investment Report 1994*, UN, New York.

—— 1994b, *The Outcome of the Uruguay Round: An Initial Assessment*, UN, New York.

Underhill, G., 1993, 'Negotiating Financial Openness: The Uruguay Round and Trade in Financial Services' in P. Cerny (ed.), *Finance and World Politics*, Edward Elgar, Aldershot.

United Nations Development Program (UNDP), *Human Development Report*, UN, New York (annual).

USITC, (United States International Trade Commission) 1993, *Potential Impact on the US Economy and Selected Industries of the North American Free-Trade Agreement*, No. 2596, Washington DC, January.

—— 1994, *Potential Impact on the US Economy and Industries of the GATT Uruguay Round Agreements*, No. 2790, Washington DC, June.

USTR, *Foreign Trade Barriers*, Office of United States Trade Representative, Washington DC, various years.

Vernon, R. and D. Spar, 1989, *Beyond Globalism*, Free Press, New York.

Vital Links, 1987, Canadian Ministry of Supply and Services, Ottawa.

Wade, R., 1990, *Governing the Market*, Princeton University Press, Princeton.

Waldman, R., 1986, *Managed Trade*, Ballinger, Cambridge Mass.

Ward, K., (ed.), 1990, *Women Workers and Global Restructuring*, ILR Press, Ithaca.

Watkins, K., 1992, *Fixing the Rules*, Catholic Institute for International Relations, London.

Webb, T., 1994, *Report on OECD Informal Meeting on Trade and the Environment*, Food Policy Alliance, Sydney, July.

Wilcox, C., 1949, *A Charter for World Trade*, Macmillan, New York.

Winson, A., 1993, *The Intimate Commodity*, Garamond, Toronto.

World Bank, *World Development Report*, Oxford University Press, New York, various years.

WTO (World Trade Organization) 1995a, *Regionalism and the World Trading System*, World Trade Organization, Geneva.

—— 1995b, *International Trade: Trends and Statistics*, World Trade Organization, Geneva.

Yoffie, D. (ed.), 1993, *Beyond Free Trade*, Harvard Business School Boston.

Index